Hard Right Turn

Brooke Jeffrey

Hard Right Turn

THE NEW FACE OF NEO-CONSERVATISM IN CANADA

A Phyllis Bruce Book
HarperCollins*Publishers*Ltd

For Chris

First edition

Canadian Cataloguing in Publication Data

Jeffrey, Brooke
Hard right turn:
the new face of neo-conservatism in Canada

"A Phyllis Bruce Book"
ISBN 0-00-255762-2

1.Conservatism – Canada.
2. Canada – Politics and government – 1993– .*
I. Title.

JC573.2.C3J43 1999   320.52'0971   C98-932573-3

99 00 01 02 03 04 TC 6 5 4 3 2 1
Printed and bound in Canada

It is largely up to the politicians which social forces they choose to liberate and which they choose to suppress, whether they rely on the good in each citizen or the bad.

— Vaclav Havel, *Summer Meditations*

Contents

Acknowledgements

I am deeply indebted to a number of individuals for their assistance in the preparation of this book. In addition to the many friends and colleagues in Ottawa and Montreal who offered helpful comments at various stages during its gestation, I was fortunate to receive assistance from Gordon Laxer and Mark Lisac on specific issues relating to Alberta, and from Mark Leiren-Young and Murray Dobbin on matters concerning Reform.

Several individuals provided me with invaluable information and insights on the inner workings of the Reform Party and the Harris government, on the understanding that their contributions would remain confidential. They all know who they are, and how much I appreciate their assistance.

My thanks also to my superb editor, Phyllis Bruce, and the staff at HarperCollins, especially Nicole Langlois and Doré Potter, and my copyeditor, Beverley Endersby.

A book of this length does not happen overnight. I would be remiss if I did not also thank my family, and especially my long-suffering spouse, for their patience and understanding through a year which included domestic chaos and many cancelled tennis games, skiing and canoe trips. Their support was invaluable.

Introduction

As the taxi mounted the curb and made a hair-raising U-turn in the middle of University Avenue, my driver muttered something about the "fools" who were causing the rapidly spreading traffic jam around Queen's Park. Assuming he meant the thousands of protesters effectively blocking our path, I decided not to comment even if I survived the next few seconds. We had already spent more than ten minutes trying to go four blocks, and his annoyance was growing exponentially. I had no intention of adding to his aggravation, at least not until we reached our destination.

His next remark led me to believe he was on the side of the marchers, not the government. After we successfully negotiated a tricky manoeuvre that brought us within striking distance of my goal, I risked a question: Who did he think was at fault in the dispute, and why? "Mike Harris," he replied without hesitation. Not "the premier." Not "the government." Not "the Conservatives." Just "Mike Harris." "Who wouldn't be upset with this guy?" he added. Then he launched into a lengthy tirade about the premier and his "ridiculous" plans to cut government spending on health care, education and social services. It was these plans, of course, that were galvanizing thousands of public servants and ordinary citizens to protest in front of the provincial legislature in downtown Toronto despite the sub-zero temperatures, causing our traffic woes that morning.

To my surprise he volunteered that he had voted for Mike Harris and his "Common Sense Revolution" the year before. "But I didn't expect them to do this. I thought they'd be different, I figured they'd get tough on crime and welfare cheaters for a change — but I didn't know they were *stupid*." What did he mean by that? "Well, you know, I didn't expect them to pick on blind people and little old ladies. And I sure didn't think they were going to start World War Three. Who do they think they are? Can you believe this is the third time we've had riots at Queen's Park since they got elected? What kind of way to run a government is that?" I asked if he really thought this was all the premier's fault, and he nodded his head vigorously while negotiating around a stalled delivery truck. "I guess we should have known better," he added. "I mean, what can you expect from a golf pro? These guys don't know anything." Recalling some of the more outrageous comments of the many colourful ministers in the Harris cabinet, I certainly had to agree with his last point. Mike Harris was not just a golf pro, but he was a long way from Bill Davis, and his cabinet seemed to be even worse.

A few months later I found myself in Edmonton and the sense of *déjà vu* was overwhelming. For days the local newspapers were full of little else but the protests taking place, or being planned, by teachers, nurses, municipal workers and various other groups of concerned citizens. All of them were furious with the Klein government's cutbacks. The premier and his controversial treasurer, Stockwell Day, were adamant the cuts would go forward as planned.

The striking thing about Klein's comments was his choice of language. It was almost identical in tone and content to arguments Mike Harris had used to defend his actions in Ontario a few months earlier. Klein's refusal to consult in any meaningful way with the affected groups was equally firm. This came as quite a surprise since I, like most people, thought Klein's reputation as a folksy populist was well established. Mike Harris admitted his "Common Sense Revolution" took its inspiration from the Klein government's neo-conservative agenda, but he failed to mention an authoritarian attitude was also part-and-parcel of the package.

The success of Ralph Klein in Alberta in 1993 was dismissed by many as a regional fluke, but the election of Mike Harris in 1995 in Ontario raised serious concerns about the direction the country seemed to be taking. Neo-conservative politicians — whatever their party labels — were now in power in two of Canada's richest and most important provinces.

Concern turned to disbelief when the upstart Reform Party of Preston Manning became the Official Opposition after the 1997 federal election. This development came as a bolt from the blue for political insiders in central Canada, almost all of whom believed that Reform was a one-term wonder, taking fifty-two seats in the 1993 election primarily because the Mulroney Conservatives collapsed. Conventional wisdom said the party was really just another Western protest movement. Founded in white-hot anger, it would soon fizzle and collapse now that Mulroney had retreated from the national stage to the comfort of corporate boardrooms.

As a Westerner with first-hand experience of Reform in the 1993 election, when I ran in Okanagan-Shuswap, I was less convinced. Certainly I was less surprised than most observers at the turn of events in 1997, but probably more distressed. My in-depth knowledge of Reform's extreme positions and unprecedented rejection of basic liberal values made me more inclined to take them seriously than most mainstream politicians, and I worried about the potential damage they could inflict on the fabric of Canadian society if they succeeded in becoming a force to be reckoned with.

Despite their new-found status as the Official Opposition, however, they were still an Opposition party, not the Government. Their performance in Parliament was not helpful. Whatever influence they might have had was diminished by the irrelevance of much of their platform and the inexperience of their MPs. After four years in Ottawa they were still unable to command respect, and little serious attention was paid to their views by the government or the national media.

The same could not be said for the "Common Sense Revolution" of Mike Harris and the Klein Revolution in Alberta. Having taken over the reins of power, both men were zealously implementing their new, hard-line version of neo-conservatism in societies which — judging from the levels of social unrest — were deeply divided over the direction their governments were taking.

The initial questions raised by their electoral victories were obvious. Were we on a slippery slope, with even more right-wing governments about to take office in other parts of the country? Had there actually been a massive shift in public opinion from the traditionally centre–left majority? Were many Canadians abandoning their well-known compassion and tolerance for the politics of self-interest, anger and resentment, and if so, why?

Critics of the two governments were often dismissed in the early days as alarmists or rigid traditionalists, unwilling to recognize the pressing need for a major overhaul of government policies and structures. Like Preston Manning, Klein and Harris portrayed themselves as the wave of the future, with a vision of the state that was more appropriate to the changing nature of the global economy and the troubled tenor of the times. Like neo-conservatives everywhere, their belief in the need for less government was deeply rooted. They denied that their many cuts were either heartless or irresponsible. Instead, they argued they were simply bringing the system back into balance, restoring a level of individual responsibility and private-sector freedom that had too long been curtailed by liberal governments eager to intervene and manipulate. In the New Right's view, the voters, or at least the responsible ones — taxpayers, parents and middle-class workers — would thank them one day for this revolutionary program.

As for the undeniable resistance to their agenda by some of their citizens, it was clear to Harris and Klein that most if not all of this opposition was motivated by self-interest, especially on the part of the bureaucrats and special-interest groups who had benefited the most from big government. Both premiers believed the protests and civil unrest were inevitable. The visceral opposition to their plans had nothing to do with the draconian measures they adopted to implement their radical agenda, or their steadfast refusal to consult with stakeholders.

This combination of haste and ruthlessness in implementing their agenda is actually typical of the approach followed by neo-conservatives elsewhere, including Margaret Thatcher and Ronald Reagan. Yet in Canada, a country where compromise and civility have been hallmarks of the political culture, their authoritarian style of government — and the resulting polarization of society — have been almost as much of a shock as the neo-conservative values they promote.

Another unexpected element of the neo-conservative approach to politics in Canada has been their willingness to cross partisan lines and ignore traditional regional interests. Their degree of political integration is remarkable, as is their affinity for the American political system and its politicians of the New Right. Ignoring the long-standing Canadian aversion to American influence, they openly acknowledge their linkages with well-known Republican radicals and stress their intention to follow similar agendas.

Unlike the Reagan Republicans, however, Canada's neo-conservatives have not succeeded in taking power at the national level. The limitations of their impact on Canada's political culture have, in that sense, been both real and frustrating. On the other hand, their majority governments have allowed them to influence the course of events in Alberta and Ontario unhampered by serious legislative opposition.

As both Mike Harris and Ralph Klein delight in repeating, they have already accomplished much of what they set out to do. They have kept their election promises and, in some cases, gone beyond them. Yet they remain extremely controversial, and the impact of their actions is still unclear to most voters. With Ralph Klein securely in power for a second term, and Mike Harris rapidly approaching the end of his first, a comprehensive assessment of their efforts is overdue.

Enough time has passed to allow for a serious evaluation of their record — their successes and failures, and their impact on their respective societies. Such an assessment must also address a number of broader questions if it is to provide a meaningful perspective. For example, it is important to understand what factors have united the New Right's political leadership in Canada across the traditionally important partisan and regional cleavages. Why do these new-style politicians appear more at home with the views of Margaret Thatcher, Ronald Reagan or Newt Gingrich than with the long-standing values of any of the three mainstream political parties? Why do most of the New Right's leaders seem to be political outsiders, lacking the usual education and experience of their traditional counterparts? And, given these obstacles, how have they achieved power, and with whose support?

The arrival of the neo-conservatives on the political scene in Canada some fourteen years after Margaret Thatcher first became prime minister in Britain raises other interesting questions. Why have they emerged in

Canada so late in the day, long after their role models elsewhere have been replaced and largely discredited? More important still, does their electoral success really represent a major shift to the right in the political culture of Canada — a hard right turn — or are the reasons for their sudden rise to prominence more complex and problematic? And what, if anything, can be done to ensure their views do not become entrenched in the mainstream of Canadian politics?

This book begins by examining the roots of the current neo-conservative movement in Margaret Thatcher's Britain, and its progress in the United States under Ronald Reagan, George Bush and the politicians of the New Right, such as Newt Gingrich, before turning to the individual Canadian "success" stories of Ralph Klein, Mike Harris and Preston Manning.

It reveals a surprising commonality of backgrounds, life experience and career patterns of the New Right's leadership, as well as a number of striking similarities in the way they and their parties achieved power. It highlights the important role played by the corporate elite, right-wing lobbyists, think-tanks and special-interest groups in helping the neo-conservatives gain legitimacy. Along the way it also catalogues the failure of liberal politicians to defend the values and beliefs that have formed the cornerstone of Western democracies since the Second World War.

With the reins of power in two of Canada's most important provinces now held by neo-conservative politicians, and the Reform Party having grasped the brass ring of the Official Opposition in Ottawa, their right-wing views can no longer be dismissed as insignificant or even temporary phenomena. On the contrary, their efforts have already had serious consequences for the political culture, consequences that would have been inconceivable only a decade ago.

If Canada is to avoid the fate of Britain and the United States, now struggling to repair the damage caused by their decade of right-wing excesses, the very real and disturbing consequences of the neo-conservative agenda must be clearly understood by all Canadians.

1

Breaking The Liberal Consensus: Thatcher, Reagan and Mulroney

There is no such thing as society.

— Margaret Thatcher

America isn't finished — her best days have just begun.

— Ronald Reagan

Those of you who are nostalgic for the good old days will be reassured since we seem to be headed back there quite rapidly under the new Republican leadership.

— Molly Ivans, political correspondent for the *Dallas Times*

I know that the enemies of Canada will not be happy. And they're going to be out in full force.

— Brian Mulroney, describing opponents of the Charlottetown Accord

In 1943, a young woman left her father's modest home in the provincial English town of Grantham and headed for the fabled spires of Oxford. Her acceptance as a student at that venerable institution, the training ground for Britain's academic and social elite, was a remarkable feat. Her gender was only the first of several strikes against her. Her social status was another. Her father was a small trader re-establishing his business after the wild uncertainties of the Depression. As a result she lacked both the financial resources and the social standing normally required for such an education. Her success against the odds is a tribute to her determination, which even then was iron-willed. But some of the credit must go to the political system in which she lived. Although she had her father's encouragement and some savings, Margaret Thatcher went to Oxford primarily because she received scholarships.

As someone whose "unwavering commitment" to conservatism was "the only thing her college principal found interesting about her," the lessons the young Margaret learned from her early experiences were not typical of those facing English youth in the postwar era. Just as she refused to blame her father's financial struggles on the vagaries of the unregulated marketplace, she failed to acknowledge the role of the state in achieving her goals. Instead, she concluded that the most important reasons for her eventual success were hard work, individual merit and self-sacrifice.

Yet the sacrifice was not only hers, but her father's, a man she greatly admired. As a result, she also emerged from her formative years with "a deep feeling for small businessmen and people who are staking their livelihoods on their activities." Apparently she was unable to break out of this limited world view, despite her subsequent education and wide-ranging travels on the world stage. Years later, one of her own supporters described her as having "a certain impatience with subtlety of feeling, a lack of sympathy with people unlike her, and a definitely limited range of experience." Of course, it was chemistry that Thatcher studied at Oxford, not law or political philosophy, a fact which might help to explain her surprisingly parochial viewpoint and ignorance of certain issues.

The England of Margaret Thatcher's youth was dominated by Labour governments. Yet Clement Attlee's initiatives — including the nationalization of nearly one-fifth of the British economy — were not unique. Motivated by the same concerns that led to Franklin Roosevelt's New Deal and Mackenzie King's Family Allowance Act, Attlee was intent on ensuring that the economic and social horrors of the worldwide Depression never recurred. When Britain moved quickly after 1945 to put in place the fundamentals of the welfare state, the liberal democracies of Europe and North America were engaged in similar exercises. Their common goal was to establish a "social safety net" through the creation of state-sponsored welfare, unemployment, pension and health-care programs.

There was also widespread consensus that governments had a positive role to play in the economy. The Keynesian model — in which full employment was viewed as the priority, rather than low inflation or interest rates — was enthusiastically adopted as the best way to provide stability. In recessionary times, spending by governments would increase to support the extra demands on the social safety net. In good times, governments could eliminate the resulting deficit. Both regulation and a certain amount of judicious intervention in the economy through public enterprise were also widely accepted as legitimate tools of the state, in order to discourage monopolies and restrain the unbridled market forces that led to the Crash of 1929.

For nearly forty years, this consensus on government intervention held. In most countries, political debate centred on the proper *degree* of state intervention — the right mix of state and private enterprise, the best way to redistribute wealth, the ideal level of regulation, and so on.

Even Conservative political parties, whatever their actual name, accepted the welfare state and the Keynesian model as the norm, and simply disagreed with their liberal counterparts on the details.

In Britain, the liberal consensus produced one of the most advanced versions of the welfare state in Europe. However, by the mid-1970s, as Thatcher started her climb to power, the country's economy, like those of other Western capitalist nations, was being subjected to a variety of destabilizing forces. Foremost among these was the oil crisis. Other crucial problems were the state of Britain's manufacturing sector, which was far more outdated and uncompetitive than those of its trading partners, and its labour unions, which were aggressive and hugely powerful. Failure to remedy these problems in a timely fashion meant that successive Labour and Conservative governments were forced to run up growing deficits to maintain the welfare state, but the economic recoveries were weaker and slower in coming, and the deficits were becoming unmanageable.

By 1974, Thatcher had progressed from the ranks of the Young Conservatives to become Minister of Education in the government of

Edward Heath. As many observers have since noted, her radical right-wing tendencies were well concealed for the four years she held that post. During this time, Heath continued to support the interventionist role of the state. His Education minister oversaw major government spending on programs and services, apparently without raising any serious concerns about her party's platform. However, with the fall of the Heath government in 1974, Thatcher began to re-examine her commitment to traditional conservatism. She talked openly of a new approach, but few of her caucus colleagues were actually listening.

When she won the party's highly controversial leadership battle in February of the following year, emerging as the victor over Heath and William Whitelaw, her win was attributable to her strong personality and political skills, as well as the lack of acceptable alternatives — not to her increasingly radical views. Most of the party's old guard saw her as "very much an intruder" who prevailed "principally because she was not Edward Heath." One of her colleagues at the time, Christopher Patten (later the last governor of Hong Kong), described her victory as "more of a peasants' uprising than a religious war." In fact, her triumph was seen by the broader party membership as "the overthrow of a tyrant king rather than as a great ideological shift."

Of course, the party membership was wrong. Margaret Thatcher was about to propose a revolution. As they later learned to their regret, many of them had bought into more than they had bargained for by choosing the girl from Grantham.

"Right Thinking" and Thatcherism

The "crisis" of the welfare state provided Margaret Thatcher with her opportunity to seize control of the political agenda and take the Conservative party sharply to the right. In so doing she altered the course of British politics for decades and influenced political developments in many other Western democracies.

After her leadership victory, the first woman in Britain to head a political party did not rest on her laurels. A tireless worker, in public she was active in Parliament and attended countless party events across the country. Privately, she was crystallizing her thinking, largely through intensive reading of the works of Friedrich von Hayek, the Austrian economist and doyen of New Right philosophers. By 1976, with high unemployment and inflation fuelling the anxiety of Britain's middle class, Thatcher was ready to present her ideas for public consumption in a Conservative party policy document entitled *Right Thinking*.

This was not a manifesto for the faint of heart. As Labour party leader James Callaghan declared, "It broke the consensus." It was a revolutionary tract that rejected almost all of the traditional liberal social and economic doctrine of the previous thirty years, and proposed in its place a new, minimalist approach to government. "Conservatives are not egalitarians," the document proudly proclaimed. This alone was heresy of the highest order in liberal democracies, where the state's role in ensuring inclusiveness and equality of opportunity had long been taken for granted. For Margaret Thatcher, however, individual rights — and, more important, individual responsibilities — replaced the collectivity, the public good and the "paternalistic" role of the state as guiding principles. "There is no such thing as society," Thatcher declared, meaning there are only individual citizens or, as she would call them, "voters, property owners, entrepreneurs and taxpayers." The basic integrative role of the state was rejected. The social deintegration of Thatcherism was launched.

As political commentator Rudolph Klein put it, "What really mattered [to Thatcher] was not what the state did for people, but what people did for themselves." Thatcher's vision in *Right Thinking* included a commitment to "personal responsibility, self-reliance and initiative ... to maintain the traditional structure and role of the family, and to recognize the demands of duty as well as the allure of 'entitlements'." To do this, there must be a significant "reduction in the powers of the state," whose intervention "must be strictly limited to defined purposes, and justified by particular circumstances rather than doctrinaire theories." Her objectives were not for the faint of heart either. In her own words, "Economics [are] the method; the object is to change the heart and soul" of English political culture.

What Thatcher was proposing was nothing less than the dismantling of much of the infrastructure of the modern liberal-democratic state. Government was the enemy and it needed to be cut back as much as possible. The woman who later would be described by former Labour cabinet minister Denis Healey as "La Passionaria of middle-class privilege" wanted to privatize, deregulate and otherwise reduce state intervention in the economy, along with total government spending. At the same time, she was determined to eliminate the "privileges" of various interest groups for whom the government provided services and programs. Most of all, she wanted to break the power of the unions, whom she loathed. All of this would reduce inflation, create a climate for investment and eventually produce a new British "entrepreneurial culture."

If it had been the nineteenth century, Thatcher's views would have been described as liberal, and her propositions in 1976 would have been more properly described as "neo-liberal." But words change their meaning over time, and her vision of government and politics has now been indelibly etched on the public consciousness as "neo-conservative." In Britain, of course, it also came to be known as "Thatcherism," and a whole new vocabulary flowed from it. Her disdain for the "weak-willed" moderates in the party led her to define such people, including ministers in her own cabinet, as "wets." Her aggressive tactics and ruthlessness, as well as her demonstrated personal courage in the face of physical danger (notably in the Bristol hotel bombing), led to her nickname of "The Iron Lady." When Conservative MP Julian Critchley wrote, "She cannot see an institution without hitting it with her handbag," a new verb was born to describe the fate of her many victims.

Thatcher had the chance to put her beliefs into practice when the Labour government was toppled in 1979. Nevertheless, many people argue she "handbagged" both her own party and the country. Certainly no one but Thatcher believed the election represented a national endorsement of her radical program. The Conservatives' victory resulted from voter dissatisfaction with the status quo; the desire for new leadership; and a course correction, not a ninety-degree, hard right turn.

The traditional Nuffield College election study confirmed that the election was lost by Labour, not won by the Conservatives. Not only had the governing Labourites failed to address a number of emerging problems adequately, but they had fallen into the trap of complacency. Worse still, they had failed to rein in the unions, whom the general public increasingly viewed as out of control. Their unsuccessful efforts to do so had, nevertheless, cost them dearly, and they lost the backing of many of their core union supporters. Adding insult to injury, the Labour party failed to ensure a strong successor to Harold Wilson and a convincing platform. As a result of these classic political mistakes, Nuffield authors Butler and Kavanaugh concluded that the Conservatives, with their detailed plan of action and decisive-looking leader, "were well-placed to catch the plum that fell into their laps. But it was the Labour movement that shook it off the tree."

The rest is history. Thatcher wasted no time in implementing her agenda, and she did so with a commitment and determination that impressed even her most ardent opponents. As one observer put it, Thatcher "has a messianic side" which accounted for her willingness to pursue objectives whatever the cost. In a Thatcher retrospective presented by the BBC, Julian Critchley declared that the prime minister "is a fundamentalist ... Margaret is a crusader leaping upon horses the whole time [and] she has by sheer force of will elevated the simplicities into the verities ..."

Certainly her pursuit of the verities resulted in a contempt for the legislative process, and an authoritarian streak, that made her a legend in her own time in parliamentary circles. One old Westminster hand declared that, while the prime minister had "not yet 'handbagged' traditional cabinet government beyond recognition," there was overwhelming evidence from cabinet colleagues and others that "she has nonetheless flouted much of its spirit and given its conventions their greatest hammering since the epoch of Lloyd George." A close confidant tactfully agreed: "She is not averse to the exercise of prime-ministerial power right up to its legitimate constitutional limits." Cabinet critics such as Michael Heseltine argued that she often went *beyond* the limits in pursuit of her objectives. Labour MP David Owen once decried "her total contempt for the democratic basis of cabinet." Long-time Tory Francis Pym went so far as to claim that Thatcher used her electoral victory and public support like a club, and "all other views which exist in the Conservative Party tend to be pushed to one side or ignored or turned down." Cabinet ministers disagreed with her at their peril. Over time many of the "wets" found themselves demoted to the backbenches, looking on. Members of her own caucus variously described her as "The

Great She-Elephant," "She-Who-Must-Be-Obeyed" and "Catherine the Great of Finchley."

In the beginning, however, she had the public on her side, hoping for improvements in their economic situation. Most important, she had the support of small-business people, entrepreneurs and the middle class. Detractors argued that Margaret Thatcher represented the "suburbanization of the Conservative party," in which middle-class business interests were the top priority of her economic agenda. Although it is difficult to consider her a populist in the North American sense — and in fact most Britons would describe her as a member of the elite or upper class — she did claim her appeal to the voters was based on an understanding of "what the people, the majority, who care about the country" want.

In addition to the middle class, luck was on her side, at least in the beginning. Many of her most drastic measures were implemented during an economic recovery, minimizing their impact in the short term. When she got into difficulties with the electorate and her party during her first term of office, it was as much for her imperious leadership style as for her draconian policies. There were many direct and violent confrontations with labour, and various groups whom the prime minister dismissed as "special interests." Society became visibly more polarized as the winners and losers of Thatcherism emerged. Many argue she was saved from the voters' wrath and electoral defeat in 1983 only by the Falklands War, although this would seem to be an exaggeration. For one thing, the results of her handiwork were not yet evident for all to see.

Her second victory allowed her to carry on with her program. In fact, Margaret Thatcher went on to become the longest continuously serving prime minister since the Second World War. She took full advantage of her unprecedented time in office, selling off public enterprises and dismantling key elements of the welfare state that had taken forty years to create.

Her favoured method of deconstruction was privatization. By 1986, some forty-eight major publicly owned services — ranging from water and gas to telephones, buses and rail transport — had been sold off to private-sector monopolies, bringing in more than $130 billion in revenue for the state. As for her "popular capitalism" project, there can be little doubt she succeeded in increasing the number of small businesses and independent entrepreneurs, and the percentage of shareholders and homeowners. Inflation had also been reduced considerably, and the British pound was doing well. For some 55 per cent of the population, the Thatcher years were boom times.

These were not insignificant achievements. The woman who had explained in a 1983 BBC interview that "what I am desperately trying to do is create one nation, with everyone being a man of property, or having the opportunity to be a man of property" could certainly claim to have made major progress in implementing her neo-conservative economic agenda. Of course, her comments also revealed that her agenda was almost *exclusively* an economic one. Margaret Thatcher may have demonstrated some inclination towards conservatism on social issues, but she was forced to recognize those views were "significantly at odds with the bulk of public opinion." The political culture of Britain continued to rule out fundamental changes to social-welfare and health-care services, or a major shift in attitude towards the administration of justice, even with the promise of tax cuts.

Over time, however, even her economic achievements began to appear less impressive. It was found that shareholdings and business starts had increased primarily because of her wholesale privatization of public enterprise. Similarly, private home ownership had increased only through the selling-off of the "council houses," the subsidized housing that constituted a basic building block of the social-welfare system.

Other aspects of her record proved less than convincing with the passage of time. By 1996 there was little doubt privatization had resulted in increased costs and decreased customer service, without the promised increase in competition. Horror stories abounded. As Canadian journalist Madeline Drohan reported in a May 1996 article for the *Globe and Mail*'s *Report on Business Magazine*, "the British experience with privatization can claim few successes." Drohan chronicled a litany of service and safety problems resulting from the switch to private-sector telephone, gas, electricity, water, rail and bus companies. She also pointed out the indirect costs — some 32,000 jobs lost in the electricity sector alone — and highlighted the fact that, even as problems were coming to light, the new owners of these enterprises were raking in major profits and providing themselves with inflated salaries. For many Britons, British

Gas executive Cedric Brown's 75 per cent pay raise while his company's workers were being laid off came to symbolize everything that was wrong with privatization. The popular consensus, according to Drohan, was that "it allowed the select few to enrich themselves at the expense of the many."

The transportation sector was a case in point. The government had parcelled out sections of local bus service and national rail lines to different companies, none of whom had any incentive to coordinate either fares or timetables. Profit, not passenger convenience, was their priority. Travellers were now faced with a dizzying array of schedules, often doubling the time it took to get from one part of the country to another, or even across town. As Drohan pointed out, would-be bus passengers left stranded in the rain by too few buses saw no reason to believe Thatcher's program was the upbeat "Way of the Future" hailed in Conservative ads. In fact, most viewed the scheme as a return to the not-so-good old days. Many complained they had had better service during the Second World War.

Worse still, since all of the new companies enjoyed monopoly status, the public had no option to switch to a competitor. Needless to say, consumers did not suffer in silence for long. By the time Thatcher's successor, John Major, attempted to impose order on the chaos, it was too late, at least politically. A severe water shortage in Yorkshire in the summer of 1995, power outages during a winter cold snap the following January, and chronic problems with slow and uncoordinated regional bus and rail service pushed cranky consumers to the edge of their tolerance less than a year before the next election was expected.

Ironically, for all her determination and ruthlessness Margaret Thatcher failed to accomplish a fundamental objective of neo-conservatism. Not only did she not achieve a significant reduction in overall government spending, but it actually rose. Then, just as the social consequences of her draconian cutbacks were emerging, the economy began to slow and inflation increased. Unemployment was already high and mounting. Meanwhile public disapproval was growing, largely because the implications of her drastic measures were becoming increasingly visible.

Nor had she succeeded in creating the "one Britain" of which she had spoken in 1983. Resentful of the elites and the upper classes in general,

Thatcher had in mind a "classless" society in which individual merit, hard work and enterprise determined the individual's material worth and fate. But her efforts to achieve this vision actually resulted in a polarized society in which 45 per cent of the citizens were significantly worse off than before.

Not only was the gap between rich and poor growing, but it was unfolding along regional lines. As London and the south were enjoying an economic boom, the north and the manufacturing areas were rapidly becoming ghettos for the unemployed and the disadvantaged. Youth unemployment soared, making a mockery of her efforts to change the nation's "heart and soul" through the next generation.

James Prior, a prominent Conservative "wet," publicly declared that Margaret Thatcher's goal of "one Britain" was becoming less likely every day. "I think the country is more divided now than it was," he said, "and I think that there is a penalty to be paid for all that." While acknowledging her accomplishments, Prior stressed that Thatcher was no Benjamin Disraeli. "She isn't a One-Nation Conservative," Prior concluded, to the nods of many of her colleagues.

In the end, despite an unprecedented third electoral victory in 1987, she was ousted by her own caucus, a humiliating event which resembled her own treatment of Edward Heath. Her replacement was the ineffectual John Major, a pale imitation of "The Iron Lady." A bitter Thatcher — now a member of the ruling elite as the newly elevated Baroness Kesteven — did not hesitate to criticize her successor scathingly and often from her seat in the Lords when he threatened to stray from the straight and narrow.

No doubt she realized her legacy was in danger, but she targeted the wrong source. John Major was only a symptom of the Conservatives' problems. The "wets" in the party had never been convinced of the merits of Thatcher's neo-conservatism, and she did little to bring them on board. As dissident Peter Shore put it earlier, "She wins arguments, she defeats opponents, but she doesn't convince them." The problem was fundamental. Her opponents in the party continued to believe in a more progressive form of conservatism which balanced social and economic interests and integrated the various elements of society. Put bluntly by the party's elder statesman Norman St. John Stevas, he and many of his colleagues "had never expected to see the day when economic materialism could deck itself out in Tory colours and claim to be not only the authentic voice of conservatism but its only legitimate manifestation."

Major survived the first test at the hands of the voters largely because the Labour Opposition self-destructed. With no viable alternative, and the economy at least not deteriorating further, voters reluctantly gave the Conservatives another chance. Their confidence soon faded, however, as more of the Thatcher chickens came home to roost and the economy worsened.

Major then tried to do something Thatcher had not. With the neo-conservative economic agenda in difficulty, he began to embrace more of the elements of social and moral conservatism in a vain effort to salvage the situation. His trial balloon on the merits of "family values" policies soon exploded in his face, however, as one after another of his cabinet ministers were forced to resign in disgrace for flagrant violations of their own rigid moral code.

By now the public, already disenchanted with the consequences of Thatcherism, had had enough. Neither a softer stand on the economic front nor a renewed effort to take the initiative on the social front — through anti-immigration and crime control measures and determined resistance to the perils of the European Union — could save the Conservative government. After the 1997 election, Labour under Tony Blair was back in power.

The damage to the fabric of British society was nevertheless done, and it is unclear how much of it can or will be reversed. Meanwhile, in North America, Margaret Thatcher's reputation preceded her. Before the results of her economic and social experiment were clear, her views had an enormous influence on a man who had just become the president of "the greatest nation on earth."

The Teflon President

Long before it became known he was suffering from Alzheimer's disease, there were those who wondered about a president who had trouble distinguishing between his film roles and reality. If Ronald Reagan surprised the liberals in the United States with his election win in 1980, he probably surprised a good number of traditional Republicans as well. The man who would become famous as "The Great Communicator" was not someone most people had expected to rise from his lowly place on Hollywood's B-movie treadmill to become the country's chief executive.

Margaret Thatcher may have been an outsider as far as the British elites and the traditional Conservative party hierarchy were concerned, but at least she had a long association with the party and had risen through the ranks. Ronald Reagan, on the other hand, was an unemployed millionaire movie actor with time on his hands. His stint as head of the Screen Actors Guild was not a typical qualification for public office, and his one-time role as governor of California had been a lark. As a result, his seemingly sudden emergence on the national scene, capturing first the Republican nomination and then the White House, was a much greater shock than Thatcher's victory had been.

Reagan's success in 1980 was even more surprising in light of the disastrous showing of Republican presidential candidate Barry Goldwater nearly twenty years earlier. Despite his impressive credentials, Arizona's native son with the impeccable elite pedigree, intellectual bent and years of Senate service had gone down in flames in 1964 trying to sell a right-wing agenda to the American people. His campaign slogan "Deep in your hearts you know he's right" led one Democrat to quip: "Deep in your hearts you know he's crazy." Most Americans agreed.

How, then, did Ronald Reagan manage to sell a similar package to the electorate in 1980? The explanation lies partly with Reagan himself. He packaged the right-wing agenda quite differently, and he was a much better salesman. But it was also true that America in 1980 was not the same as it had been in the glorious 1960s, and neither were the voters.

As many people have remarked, Reagan was the perfect man for the times, a media star for the the emerging phenomenon of the media-based election. Things had come a long way from the famous televised debate between a youthful Kennedy, and a haggard-looking Richard Nixon devoid of make-up. Reagan's stint in Hollywood seemed more relevant by the minute as The Great Communicator demonstrated how to reach millions of viewers and manipulate the broadcast media to suit his purposes during the 1980 election campaign. Holding up his dollar bill in front of the cameras and looking straight into the eyes of each and every potential voter, Reagan kept his message simple and his look sincere. His homey style and genuine conviction touched a chord with the viewing public, so much so that, for some, the message hardly mattered.

Reagan's populism was almost as important as his communications skills. Egalitarianism has always been an important part of the American myth. In the land of the American Dream, pollsters had long ago switched to asking questions about income levels, rather than social standing, to obtain meaningful results, since 90 per cent of their respondents would otherwise choose to describe themselves as "middle class." Of course, there is a *de facto* political and social elite in the United States, but they have tried hard not to show it, at least since the advent of liberalism. Much was made by their press agents of the fact that Ethel Kennedy drove a Mustang, and the whole Kennedy clan liked hot dogs. Americans might buy a *liberal* message from a Roosevelt or a Kennedy, but a right-wing message could not be sold by a member of the American upper class, even if he came from Arizona.

Ronald Reagan, on the other hand, was seen as a party outsider whose tentative advances had been rebuffed by the Republican hierarchy in 1976. As a result, he was able to position himself as not only folksy, but anti-politician. Joel Krieger's brilliant analysis of Reagan's 1980 campaign and subsequent political career concludes: "This representation of Reagan ... as a citizen leader reluctantly performing his civic duty and not a professional politician pursuing personal ambition ... has been the fundamental stock line for more than twenty years."

Nevertheless, Reagan's success was not achieved without help. In fact, he had a great deal of help for many years before his arrival on centre stage. Some of this help came from developments outside the country, like the oil crisis which had also affected Britain so dramatically. Some of it came from the Democrats — liberal politicians who, like the Labour party in Britain, failed to deal effectively with crucial issues. Jimmy Carter alone was a godsend. And some of his help came from inside the Republican party. Wounded and deeply divided after so many years in Opposition, the party had decidedly limited leadership options.

As with Margaret Thatcher, timing again would prove to be the key to the success of a neo-conservative politician. In Reagan's case, the timing could hardly have been better. The Vietnam War, Watergate and the botched Iran rescue mission had shaken Americans' confidence and raised doubts about their status as the "greatest nation on earth" at precisely the same time as a series of economic shocks — including the oil crisis, Japan's technological wizardry and the emerging Asian tigers' cheap labour — had called into question American dominance of the global economy. As in Britain, this challenge to Americans' sense of manifest destiny sent the markets, the capitalist elites and the middle class reeling, ready to embrace strong medicine and a strong leader.

When it came to intellect, however, Ronald Reagan was no Margaret Thatcher. His version of neo-conservative philosophy in 1980 was both simple and simplistic — hardly the coherent set of values and principles Mrs. Thatcher was able to outline for her followers and then act upon with such consistency. But Reagan's views, though limited, happened to coincide nicely with the major concerns of three different groups of Americans, all of whom were looking for a leader in troubled times.

Reagan's economic conservatism — like Thatcher's, although more primitively expressed as the "trickle-down theory" — appealed, first and foremost, to the hard-pressed middle class. But it also enchanted the capitalist elites, who would actually be the chief beneficiaries of his lower taxes, regardless of what the middle class thought or wanted to believe. For both groups, Reagan's blatant appeal to self-interest over the public good was apparently irresistible.

Meanwhile, his anti-statist, anti-welfare message resonated with the populist right-wing groups that had been operating at the margins of American politics until then — as taxpayers' associations, public-transit foes or opponents of equal-opportunity legislation, for example — concentrating their efforts at the local or state level. Reagan's emphasis on social issues, in addition to the neo-conservative economic agenda Thatcher had pioneered, appealed to this disaffected group of largely middle-aged, working-class voters, many of whom were also evangelical Christians. Anxious about the pace of change and fearful for their jobs and lifestyle, they worried about family values, growing crime and immigration, and Reagan reassured them with his social conservatism. Similarly his stance as a proud nationalist, with his pro-military, anti-communist rhetoric about the "Evil Empire," gave new credibility to their belief that America could and should be restored to greatness.

The combination of economic and military themes was unbeatable with a third category of Americans. As economists Ferguson and Rogers put it, the corporate elite actually suffered a sort of "collective nervous breakdown" after the Iran affair. With America's apparent inability to influence events and maintain control in Iran, or elsewhere in the third world, the minds of many CEOs with heavy investments there were "driven almost to distraction by the awful thought that something similar could happen in, say, Saudi Arabia ... The chorus of voices demanding rearmament swelled to an insistent roar."

The 1980 election was a watershed in more ways than one. Not only did it put a right-wing Republican in the White House, but it did so by dividing the nation in a way previously unheard of since the New Deal. Just as Reagan's views broke the liberal-democratic consensus about the role of the state, so his campaign platform and electoral strategy broke the Democrats' traditional electoral coalition. Jimmy Carter was lucky to hold on to blacks and the working poor. Even the unions split almost evenly in their support for the two parties.

Reagan had captured much of the white middle class with his economic conservatism, and much of the South and rural America with his social conservatism. His campaign had deliberately targeted these voters, just as it had deliberately ignored others. With Reagan's outspoken opposition to the Civil Rights Act in 1964, Republican strategists knew, for example, that they would have to write off the black vote. But although 90 per cent of black voters cast their ballots for the Democrats, only some 30 per cent of eligible black Americans voted. As the percentage of Americans who voted in federal elections continued to decline to dangerously low levels in the 1970s, it was possible for the Republican strategists to separate voters into categories, and then target those whom they believed would not only buy their message, but go to the polling booth and support them.

One of the New Right's professional technocrats, Paul Weyrich — director of the Committee for the Survival of a Free Congress — spelled out this reality very clearly. "I don't want everyone to vote," he said flatly. Speaking at a rally for campaign workers in Dallas during the election, he continued, "Our leverage in the election quite candidly goes up as the voting populace goes down. We have no moral responsibility to turn out our opposition." Weyrich was right. Reagan took 28 per cent of the eligible vote, compared with Carter's 22.6 per cent, but fully 49.9 per cent of potential American voters did not bother to cast a ballot.

This was also why Reagan scored a major victory along gender lines, as his advisers were quick to point out. Although women traditionally supported the Democrats, they came to Reagan in 1980 in large numbers. Of course, it was "large numbers" only in terms of the votes cast, not in terms of the real number of American women voters. And this was precisely the point. The issue for the Republicans was not "the female vote," but the "female voter." Focusing on the economic and moral-conservative issues with women audiences, the Republicans were able to overcome the traditional female bias in favour of the Democrats as the party of peace. According to one analysis, "by appealing to married women, and especially those between the ages of 45 and 65, on a 'pro family' platform, Reagan maximized the electoral value of gender politics."

Reagan's sweep of the South and the Southwest, including many traditional Democrat strongholds, was due almost entirely to the phenomenon of regional alienation, similar in many respects to the pattern of the Canadian West. Not only were Southerners predisposed to his conservatism, but they were very supportive of his championship of local and states' rights. This was particularly true of the many evangelicals in the region, anxious to reinsert religion and "family values" into the public education system. In addition, Reagan's arrival on the national political scene corresponded with the economic boom of the Sunbelt, which had followed the rapid collapse of the eastern and Midwest manufacturing economies of the so-called Rust Belt. The new technocratic middle class of the region was as receptive to his commitment to lower taxes and less government intervention as was the middle class elsewhere. With one-third of the U.S. population residing in the South by 1990, and the state of Texas poised to surpass New York as the second-largest state (California having taken over first place nearly a decade earlier), the Southern vote was critically important in Reagan's victory.

Reagan's election provoked widespread disbelief in the country, and around the world. As one journalist put it, Americans had elected a "two-dimensional" cartoon character just when they needed a real heavyweight to deal with some fundamental economic and social problems. *The New*

Republic's TRB column of December 6, 1980, less than a month after Reagan's surprise win, concluded that "the country elects an affable Hollywood actor whose whole skill is communicating ... How he will boost defence spending, cut taxes, end inflation, and balance the budget all at once nobody knows."

The article unerringly put its finger on the problem with Ronald Reagan's platform. It was patently unrealistic. It offered a simple, apparently painless solution to a complex problem. As the next eight years would show, the trickle-down theory did not work. Nor could Reagan deliver on his twin promises of low inflation and a balanced budget. Instead, he drove the deficit and the debt to soaring new heights in order to make good on his promises of tax cuts and increased defence spending, both of which were much higher priorities for the new president. By the end of his second term, the word "Reaganomics" had lost its lustre and was most often used disparagingly to refer to someone talking nonsense.

The Reagan Record

In the end, Reagan suffered the same fate as Margaret Thatcher on his major commitments. Despite his aversion to "big government," the size of government under the Reagan administration actually grew. And although he tried to eliminate outright a large number of institutions from the liberal legacy, such as the Environmental Protection Agency, the Legal Services Corporation and the Consumer Protection Agency, he largely failed to do so. Even more ironic, the man who came to power campaigning against the "Evil Empire" of communism — and actually ordered the mining of the main harbour in Nicaragua during the height of the left-wing Sandinista struggles shortly after he took office — is credited by many with having furthered the Cold War thaw through diplomacy, rather than force, to the point where the Iron Curtain fell, and America emerged as the only true world power.

Many ardent American neo-conservatives were dismayed by the record of the Reagan years. Republican strategist Paul Weyrich declared, "If you look at the domestic context the 'Reagan effect' is negligible." Acknowledging the foreign-policy and defence successes, Weyrich nevertheless insisted, "He didn't veto [liberal] legislation to speak of. He didn't veto budgets ... It is very hard to say what he accomplished that has had any permanent effect except that the debt grew by such an enormous proportion that the liberals today are unable to impose the kind of new spending programs that they would like." Conservative Caucus spokesman Howard Phillips was even less charitable: "I don't think there has been any president in American history who was less engaged in the conduct of affairs than Ronald Reagan since Woodrow Wilson was confined to quarters after a stroke." While veteran conservative journalist Irving Kristol agreed that "there was no Reagan revolution," he argued that "there was at least a shift of emphasis."

This is not to suggest that Reagan did nothing. Even legendary Democratic House Speaker Tip O'Neill, who once referred to Reagan as the worst president since Harry Truman, recognized that his first two years in office were a period of significant change. O'Neill simply didn't like the changes. As he himself noted, in Reagan's "rookie" year he "pushed through the greatest increase in Defence spending in American history, together with the greatest cutbacks in domestic programs and the largest tax cuts the country has ever seen."

As president, Reagan also had direct access to a number of powerful tools that could undermine the liberal establishment. His most important legacy in that regard was his replacement of judges on the Supreme Court. By the end of his eight years in office, Reagan had managed to replace four of the nine justices with individuals whose views were much farther to the right. This included the position of Chief Justice. When noted liberal Warren Berger stepped down, Reagan chose William Rehnquist, a man whose extreme right-wing tendencies were well known, to lead the Court. Even his lone female appointment, Sandra Day O'Connor, was a conservative opponent of affirmative action whose nomination caused considerable controversy. With the justices appointed for life, Reagan's presence in the Oval Office at a time when so many liberals were departing was a stroke of luck, of which he took full advantage.

Like Margaret Thatcher's privatization and regulation policies, Reagan's aggressive pursuit of deregulation caused considerable chaos in the transportation and communications industries. Harrison and Bluestone chronicled the drastic decline in service in the airline industry in their book *The Great U Turn*, noting that "the combination of delayed and cancelled flights, lost baggage, and an increase in the number of 'near misses' resulted in a soaring number of complaints to the Department of Transportation ..." They also concluded that there was "a good deal of evidence that deregulation actually produced less true competition." Another critic noted that, "during the four years following deregulation in 1978, weekly departures from large cities had risen 5%. Weekly departures from small towns, by contrast, had dropped 12%. By 1988 approximately 140 small cities and towns had lost all their air service, and in 190 other large airlines had handed over responsibility to smaller commuter carriers lacking comparable comfort, convenience and safety."

Another obvious legacy of the Reagan years was the deintegration of American society, similar to what Thatcher had caused in Britain. The gap between rich and poor grew dramatically over the eight years Reagan was in power, and not by accident. "What I want to see above all," he said, "is that this remains a country where someone can always get rich." In fact, it became a country in which the comfortably rich became fabulously wealthy, and the middle class shrank, largely as a result of his government's policies of deregulation, loosening of anti-trust provisions and major tax breaks for the well-to-do. Between 1980 and 1988, the Congressional Budget Office reported that the wealth of the top 1 per cent of the population rose a stunning 3 per cent, from 9 to 12 per cent of the total pie. In the same period, the net worth of the Forbes 400 richest Americans *tripled*.

The amazing accumulation of wealth and the shifting patterns of wealth accumulation in the Reagan era were chronicled in detail in a scathing account by Kevin Phillips, a well-known former Republican adviser and national business editor. Phillips's best-selling book, *The Politics of Rich and Poor*, became a liberal must-read. As Phillips notes, the Reagan administration produced not only billionaires, but homeless Americans, in unprecedented numbers. It was an era of shameless indulgence and excess, in which many Americans gave themselves permission to be rich, and then blamed the victims of Reaganomics — the poor and the disadvantaged — for their lot.

As was true of Thatcher's policies, Reagan's, too, had regional consequences. In Britain, the southern half of the country had benefited at the expense of the north. In America, the two coastal areas — East and West — enjoyed huge growth, while the interior heartland suffered badly. Even more striking was the phenomenon of "suburbanization." As the middle class left large urban centres for new suburban and ex-urban developments, taking their high incomes and tax dollars with them, urban centres began to decay at alarming rates, leading to the "hollow core" problem. Urban municipalities simply could not afford to maintain services for those "losers" of the Reagan era who remained trapped there. Phillips notes that "the new suburbs created by these developments became staunch cheering sections for the policies that nurtured them, and one side-bar of the 1984 and 1988 elections was the huge margins turned in by a little-known group of counties for Reagan and then Bush ..."

The gap between winners and losers in Ronald Reagan's America was also based on race and gender. Several studies showed that "overall a disproportionate number of women, young people, blacks and Hispanics were among the decade's casualties." Joel Krieger argues this was a deliberate strategy on Reagan's part. Given the Great Communicator's limited grasp of policy, it seems more likely this result was an unplanned, if inevitable, consequence of his efforts to benefit the corporate elite, although these secondary results were no doubt ones with which he would have been unconcerned, and possibly pleased.

Certainly Reagan's vigorous opposition to affirmative action, unions and other integrative liberal projects lent credence to the argument that he was essentially anti-feminist, anti-black and anti-worker. Critic Robert Leachmen bluntly described the Reagan administration as "the most racist in recent history," and concluded that "the president and his co-conspirators have been conducting undeclared war against blacks and Hispanics, welfare clients, women and children, and blue collar workers."

Leading American activist Hayward Burns points out that, in addition to his direct influence on the Supreme Court through appointments, Reagan was also responsible for a Justice Department that "unashamedly seeks to turn back the civil rights clock." During Reagan's tenure, Justice officials refused to pursue discrimination cases, resisted affirmative action in hiring policy and argued *against* previously established rights protection before the courts. For Burns, this was a president "who invokes the racist code words 'states' rights' to defeat federally legislated integration measures" implemented by liberal administrations more than twenty years earlier.

How much of this outcome was intentional on Reagan's part is difficult to know, as he was unquestionably one of the least prepared and least equipped American presidents of the century. He was neither well informed nor diligent at his job, arguably the most demanding in the world. He spent so much time horseback riding, travelling and socializing with the movie set at his home in California that a "Western White House" had to be set up to accommodate him.

He was basically ignorant of most policy issues on his arrival at the Oval Office, and his intellectual capacity to master them on the job was modest, to say the least. His own supporters, while tactful, admitted as much many times. Former Budget Office director David Stockman told one interviewer that Reagan's "body of knowledge is primarily impressionistic. He registers anecdotes rather than concepts." Stockman also recalled Reagan's campaign debates in 1980 as "miserable. His answers just weren't long enough, and what time he could fill he filled with wooly platitudes."

In an interview with journalist Godfrey Hodgson, Reagan actually confused the Reagan Doctrine (on America's third-world policy) with Reaganomics (his economic policies), a blunder Hodgson attributes to the fact Reagan was simply "mouthing" the foreign-policy arguments of writers in *The New Republic* when he first articulated the Reagan Doctrine, and did not really understand them. This is enough to give anyone pause, considering the power at the discretion of the President of the United States. Many Reagan intimates have suggested he was influenced by his wife on foreign policy, and indirectly by her astrologer. Over time, Reagan and Margaret Thatcher became close friends, and Reagan's foreign policy was widely believed to have been heavily influenced by her as well. Shortly after Thatcher described Mikhail Gorbachev as "a man we can do business with," for example, Reagan dropped the "Evil Empire" line and soon developed a close relationship with the Russian leader.

Support for Hodgson's thesis can also be found in the comments of General Colin Powell that Reagan "may not have commanded every detail of policy but he had others to do that." Reagan himself once said he had "plenty of smart people working for me who could take care of the details." Or, as Robert McFarlane, a national security adviser under Reagan, declared in sheer amazement, "He knows so little and accomplishes so much."

Like Thatcher, Reagan benefited from a "defining incident" that shaped the electorate's favourable image of him and allowed him to proceed without penalty. In Reagan's case, it was not a bomb in a Bristol hotel but a deranged would-be assassin at the Washington Hilton, who shot and wounded the president when he was leaving a meeting. His famous comment to wife Nancy when she arrived at the hospital — "Honey, I forgot to duck" — was one that led millions of Americans to conclude their president had "the right stuff." His image as a man of action was reinforced by his authoritarian handling of bureaucrats in Washington, and his brash (if not reckless) decision to fire all 11,400 members of the air traffic controllers' union in 1983, both moves the public supported at the time.

Apparently the voters also interpreted Reagan's decisiveness to mean he knew what he was doing, which was another matter entirely. Although it always takes longer for the effects of dismantling to be felt than the reverse, evidence of cracks in the Reagan scheme to save the economy through the trickle-down theory was mounting before the end of his first term. Reagan did have some trouble with the electorate in his first term, as his economic policies clearly failed to help the suffering Midwest farmers, auto workers and Rust Belt manufacturers who had been counting on him to produce a miracle. Nevertheless, he was rewarded for his courage, sincerity and showmanship with a stunning majority in the 1984 election. The Democrats, shell-shocked by the first term and rudderless under the solid but uninspiring Walter Mondale, had never really been in the race.

By the midpoint in his second term, however, it was patently obvious the country's economy was in deep trouble. The debt and the trade deficit had ballooned, and inflation and unemployment were up. By 1986, the United States had become a net debtor nation, a dubious distinction it had not achieved since 1919. The 1986 congressional elections showed that the writing was on the wall for Reagan's brand of neo-conservatism.

Despite his administration's efforts to stave off growing opposition by imposing more authoritarian measures from the executive branch, Reagan's second term was characterized not only by ideological intransigence, but by what Joel Krieger describes as "errors of judgement, wild reversals of policy, last-minute compromises and opportunistic maneuvers." It was also marred by the ongoing Iran–Contra fiasco, several political funding and corruption scandals, and his failure to secure congressional approval for Robert Bork, his most prominent nominee for the Supreme Court. These developments alienated many of his original supporters as well as the moderate core of the Republican Congress. Spared a humiliating departure *à la* Thatcher by the fact he was limited to two terms in office, Reagan's record may have been tarnished, but he left the Oval Office with his popular support largely intact, the original "Teflon Man."

Kinder, Gentler Republicans?

It was Reagan's replacement, George Bush, who was forced to live with the results and attempt to clean up the mess, and he failed badly. On the one hand, his efforts to present a kinder, gentler face to neo-conservatism were dismissed by the electorate — now seeing the effects of all the cuts — as too little, too late. On the other hand, Bush's moderation appalled the true believers on the far right, already upset that Reagan had not done more with his full eight years.

Part of the problem was Bush himself. The former vice-president was actually not a neo-conservative. He was a traditional Republican conservative, moderate and reasonably cosmopolitan, and he was never comfortable with the neo-conservative agenda. After all, this was the man who had once termed Reaganomics "voodoo economics." Before he realized he was going to have to deal with them, he also commented that Republicans didn't need "the crazies" to win.

Another problem with Bush was that he was not a populist, but a blue-blooded member of the elites. A Yale graduate from Connecticut, he vacationed in Maine, not Texas, and dressed like the preppie he was. Even worse, the man following in the footsteps of the Great Communicator was barely able to communicate in any medium. Asked to explain what Americans were looking for in a president, the "vision thing" was the best Bush could do, despite having far superior intelligence and education than his predecessor, proving that words as well as looks can be deceiving.

Bush had trouble inside the Republican party from the start. The New Right had become far more radical and aggressive within the party ranks as the Reagan era slipped away. Led by extremists such as Pat Buchanan, they viewed Bush with disdain bordering on disgust. Buchanan once accused Bush — whom he ran against in the 1988 primaries — of being a closet "Eastern Establishment liberal" who "has sold us down the river again and again." If this evangelical faction felt betrayed by Reagan's lack of action on moral issues, they were horrified by Bush.

The evangelical contingent of the New Right distrusted anything that smacked of intellectualism, since they apparently equated this with a tendency towards moral decay and/or untrustworthiness. By the early 1990s, their fears led them to attack even long-standing members of the traditional neo-conservative movement such as William F. Buckley, Jr. The new journalistic hero of the New Right was the outrageous Rush Limbaugh. Former Republican aide and journalist Alan Crawford's conclusion that the New Right had "turned their guns on genuine conservatives who, by their cultural styles, appear to the New Right primitives as enemies" was backed up by one well-known conservative newspaper publisher's comment that Buckley "spends too much time skiing with that [John Kenneth] Galbraith."

No one had ever accused Reagan of being an intellectual, of course, but it was now obvious to many evangelicals that ignorance was not enough. They needed a true believer who would not be influenced by crass political considerations. Some prominent members of the New Right began to consider their best hope for making a difference was outside the two mainstream parties, running independent campaigns for the presidency. (Hence, Ross Perot, whose 19 per cent of the popular vote actually allowed Bill Clinton to seize control of the White House for the Democrats.) Others were less adventurous, and tried to concentrate on ideologically pure candidates from within, such as former Tennessee governor Lamar Alexander.

Neither strategy worked. George Bush won the primary despite their efforts. He was soon out of a job, however, as Bill Clinton regained the White House for the Democrats. For many on the Far Right in the United States, the 1992 election was a sharp lesson in the importance of focus and timing. The Republicans licked their wounds after their loss of the Oval Office and then started to regroup. They did not give up, but they changed their plan of attack. Having lost the Executive, they decided to counteract the Democrats by taking control of the agenda in the legislative branch. To do that, they would need someone with experience in Washington.

The man they chose seemed to be everything they were looking for: a populist, a true-believer neo-conservative and, if not an evangelical, at least a moral conservative who could talk a good line about family values. He was also a long-serving member of Congress who presumably knew the ropes and could be counted upon to cause the Democrats as much procedural trouble as possible, thwarting their agenda at every turn. And so the New Right resurrected itself by turning to a rotund congressman from the Deep South, Representative Newt Gingrich of Georgia.

Born-Again Republicans

Newt Gingrich was no Ronald Reagan. A career politician, he was first elected to the House of Representatives in 1978, at the age of thirty-five, and became the Republican Whip in 1989. Despite this measure of success, however, he was never part of the traditional Republican inner circle, largely because of his extreme views and independent, if not maverick, tendencies. With a Ph.D. in European History from Tulane University, in New Orleans, he had spent seven years teaching at a small religious college in west Georgia before embarking on a political career. Clearly this was a man with potential for the Moral Majority, having also been a member of both the Georgia Conservative Society and the Conservative Opportunity Society. A polished public speaker with a folksy, down-home air about him, Newt Gingrich looked like a promising find.

Nevertheless, things did not look too promising for the Republicans as they assembled for Bill Clinton's swearing-in ceremony in Washington in blustery January weather. With the popular new president committed to an aggressively liberal agenda, including the introduction of a publicly funded medicare program along the lines of the Canadian model, things actually looked very bleak indeed for the neo-conservatives who wanted to see less, not more, government spending and far fewer government programs.

Their dismay turned to cautious optimism fairly quickly, however, as Bill Clinton and the Democrats experienced a number of public-relations disasters just months after their promising start. Hillary Rodham Clinton's handling of the medicare file was widely criticized and eventually had to be shelved. The president's efforts to normalize the status of gays in the military produced a huge outcry from the military brass as well as the Moral Majority. The Somalia mission was a failure, and feelings against the U.N. were running high. Most important, the country was in a foul mood over the economy. Voters were now feeling the full effects of Reagan's reckless spending spree at the same time as the pain of downsizing and deindustrialization — the effects of economic globalization, aided and abetted by the North American Free Trade Agreement (NAFTA) Clinton had supported — worked their way through the economy.

Americans were certainly in no mood to put up with the material extravagances of the 1980s. They were first outraged and then cynical, as a series of financial scandals unfolded "inside the beltway" of Washington, D.C., involving politicians from both parties. But Republican senator Bob Packwood's sexual-harassment problems paled in comparison with the corruption charges levelled at several Democrats, including the House Whip, Tony Coelho of California. Among the most important of these was the issue of party funding. The Political Action Committees (PACs) of individual congressmen came in for detailed scrutiny after Ways and Means Committee chair Dan Rostenkowski, a veteran Illinois Democrat, was convicted of embezzlement, mail fraud and conspiracy charges relating to the use of his office funds. A debate ensued over Clinton's decision to change the PAC rules, effective after the 1994 congressional elections, and many veterans from both parties decided not to run rather than lose the funds they had accumulated.

These scandals caused Americans to become even more cynical about their government, and politicians in general. They also had an important impact on both parties' strategies for the mid-term elections. The resignation of so many veterans opened up many districts to real competition for the first time in many years, since, unlike in Canada, in the United States incumbents are almost always re-elected. For the Democrats this was a problem. Many of their big guns were lost. The Republicans, meanwhile, saw this as an opportunity. They could recruit new, right-wing candidates in those seats where more traditional Republicans had stepped down. These newcomers could distance themselves from the "goings-on" in Washington and present themselves as part of a new broom that would sweep the place clean.

By February 1994, many Republicans in the Grand Old Party (GOP) were upbeat about their chances of doing well in the mid-term elections scheduled for November, despite the fact the Democrats had maintained a vise-like grip on Congress, and especially the Senate, for over forty years. An optimistic group of members of the House of Representatives met in Salisbury, Maryland, to discuss their platform in February. Overwhelmingly male, middle-aged and white, with a large contingent from rural and southern states, they could hardly have claimed to be representative of the American people, but they were certainly indicative of the constituency that had elected them. Over the course of several days, this Republican caucus hammered out five "principles" they modestly called their "basic philosophy of American civilization."

Contract with America

The so-called Salisbury principles were classic neo-conservative fare: limited government, individual liberty, personal responsibility, economic opportunity, and security of the individual and the state. In the next few months, the five principles were massaged by various groups of Republican members into a campaign platform document called *Contract with America*.

By September, their manifesto was unveiled at a massive rally of all the Republican candidates, held in Washington, D.C. Under the political leadership of Newt Gingrich, now Minority House Leader, some 367 candidates staged a major media event, publicly signing the "contract" and declaring: "If we break this contract, throw us out." Republican candidates for state and local office would eventually engage in similar public-relations exercises, a classic bit of populist manipulation that had considerable impact on a jaded electorate.

The content of the *Contract* was cleverly designed to play on the public's concerns. Rather than referring to their proposals as a conservative doctrine, the Republicans presented their ideas in the form of ten major pieces of legislation to "make America great again." First and foremost, they took advantage of the recent scandals and pledged to "clean up Congress" by making many changes to financing and electoral legislation, including limiting the term of office of members. Other social conservative measures focused on *reforming* welfare, *stopping* crime, *reinforcing* families, *enhancing* fairness for seniors and *reforming* the legal and immigration systems. On the economic agenda were such familiar Reaganesque items as balancing the budget, cutting government regulations, reducing taxes and, despite past experience, a renewed promise to strengthen national defence.

The language used in the *Contract* was masterful. A chapter titled "Strengthen our families and protect our kids" — objectives with which very few Americans would disagree — was actually the platform for major proposals to weaken public education, undermine child-care programs and reduce the separation of church and state. "Increase personal responsibility" was the New Right's way of saying they would eliminate welfare. One proposal was prominently trumpeted as "an important new piece of legislation," ignoring the fact it represented a major reversal of existing practice. "It is through the family that we learn values like responsibility, morality, commitment and faith," the document declared. The solution was "Our Family Reinforcement Act ... [which] will strengthen the rights of parents to protect their children against education programs that undermine the values taught in the home." Every neo-conservative and every liberal politician knew what the code words meant. Yet the proposals were persuasive for large numbers of ordinary middle-class Americans who believed their economic and physical security were threatened, and particularly for the growing number of moral conservatives and religious fundamentalists who were becoming politically active.

Even before the ink had dried on the *Contract*, there were problems with several of its measures. Its proposals on immigration, for example, were not only patently racist, but unworkable, catering to the fears of the electorate rather than offering constructive suggestions. Some, such as a commitment to withdraw access to public education or welfare for landed immigrants, were simply unconstitutional. When legal experts pointed this out, Gingrich proposed modifying the Constitution rather than changing his position. Despite pledges to reduce spending and balance the budget, the *Contract* also proposed massive increases in funding for prisons, law enforcement and immigration officials. Cuts to welfare and contentious measures relating to drug use vied for media coverage with radical proposals concerning teenage pregnancies, "truth in sentencing" and the "effective" use of the death penalty.

By releasing their document in September, the Republicans astutely ensured maximum publicity yet minimized the opportunity for informed criticism of their platform before the mid-term elections. Their landslide victory in November 1994 looked like a reward for their efforts and the beginning of a new era in American politics. Republicans captured both the House and the Senate after more than forty years of Democratic domination. The true measure of their victory was also to be found in the individual details. For the first time ever, an incumbent Speaker of the House was defeated when Democrat Tom Foley of Washington lost his seat. From his viewpoint as the new Speaker of the House of Representatives, a smug Newt Gingrich surveyed the battlefield and declared that the election was "the most shatteringly one-sided Republican victory since 1946."

No one disagreed with him. Certainly not Canada's Preston Manning, the leader of the like-minded Reform Party which a year earlier had taken fifty-odd seats in the federal election. Not only had Manning visited Gingrich for a photo opportunity, but Gingrich now attributed part of *his* electoral success to techniques he had learned from Manning and his Reformers.

Among these, organized religion was clearly uppermost in Gingrich's mind. The role of the evangelicals in assuring Gingrich's victory was far greater than it had been for Reagan. As Rosalind Petchesky points out in an article on anti-feminism and the New Right, this heightened emphasis on moral conservatism in the American neo-conservative movement was unprecedented. It was also producing a situation in which the party's platform was being increasingly designed to meet the requirements of these supporters. "What has given the New Right both ideological legitimacy and organizational coherence," she wrote, "has been its focus on reproductive and sexual issues. If there is anything new about the current right wing in the United States, it is its tendency to locate sexual, reproductive and family issues at the centre of its political program." This was an unusual development in Canada as well, but Gingrich could not have been expected to know that.

As the Republicans quickly learned, the problem with the evangelicals' support was that they expected their political representatives to "walk the walk" as well as "talk the talk." With Newt Gingrich as their principal spokesperson, this would prove a major challenge. Unlike Manning, Gingrich was no role model for the Moral Majority.

Georgia's Good Old Boy

With increased fame and publicity also came more intensive examination of Gingrich's private life, and the evangelicals were not amused by what soon became widespread public knowledge. It transpired that Gingrich had divorced his dying wife, failed to make alimony payments, and engaged in other questionable activities of which the Moral Majority did not approve.

Even more unsettling was the new Speaker's quick lapse of memory on key issues of interest to his fundamentalist supporters. The opportunistic congressman from Georgia — who in the 1994 campaign had called for an end to the PACs and new legislation to strictly limit fundraising — began raising large sums of money for the GOP the moment his party took control of the legislature. In May 1995 Gingrich declared that "there is zero grassroots pressure for campaign reform." In the first six months of 1995, the National Republican Congressional Committee alone raised $18.7 million, or four times the amount given to the Democrats.

Both Democrats and many Republican moderates were shocked by the amounts raised and the techniques used to bring in the funds. Among the most offensive were the *Contract with America* "coalitions" Gingrich created, lobby vehicles for special interest groups who wanted to ensure passage of one or more of the *Contract*'s legislative proposals. So many of these were set up that even the participants began to question the strategy. "You have coalition creep," complained Mark Isakowitz of the Coalition for America's Future, a group pushing for tax cuts. "You could spend most of your time going from one coalition meeting to another."

To solve this problem a Gingrich lieutenant, congressman John Boehner, began holding weekly Thursday meetings of the leadership of all the various coalitions, in order to coordinate activities and, more important, to organize financial contributions. During the Republican campaign to introduce a legislated end to budget deficits, for example, the Coalition for a Balanced Budget was "allowed" to provide some $80,000 for Republican radio advertisements and another $250,000 to sponsor a phone-in campaign to congressional offices immediately before crucial House votes.

This was not what either the evangelicals or the independents like Ross Perot had in mind when they urged Gingrich and his Republican Revolution to clean up in Washington, and they soon let him know it. So did the American people, who were also not amused by Gingrich's authoritarian attitude to House business, the White House and the media. Nor were they impressed by his peevish complaint that he had been badly treated on an overseas trip with the president and other dignitaries aboard *Air Force One*. His widely reported remarks blaming the murder of an Illinois family on "the welfare state" were the last straw. By December 1995 — barely a year after the Republicans' smashing victory — even Gingrich had concluded he should "keep his head down" for a while, as his personal popularity slipped below 34 per cent.

It was not long before Newt Gingrich was also in trouble personally, with seven charges laid against him before the House of Representatives' Ethics Committee. These included allegations concerning his acceptance of a $4.5-million book advance from publisher Rupert Murdoch, whose corporate empire was involved in several issues before Congress, as well as questionable accounting practices in his office expenses and the illegal use of GOPAC money to bankroll Gingrich's 1990 election campaign, which he won by barely nine hundred votes. Gingrich returned the book advance and, in December 1995, the committee dismissed three of the charges, "slapped his wrist" but imposed no penalty for three others, and referred the seventh to an independent counsel.

Unfortunately for Gingrich, this was not the end of the matter. Enraged Democrats argued that the committee, run by Republicans, was biased. They promptly laid more charges, and it became apparent the trials of the Speaker would continue for some time. After the counsel tabled his report in June 1996, the committee appeared to be on the brink of dismissing further allegations concerning tax matters related to Gingrich's GOPAC activities and to college courses taught at several Georgia universities. Then a sudden request for further information concerning office expenses led the committee to consider new charges of violating House rules and providing misleading information to the committee. In the end, after months of tension and serious concerns among Republicans as to whether Gingrich should be re-elected Speaker in January 1997, the matter was settled by Gingrich's admitting he "gave inaccurate, incomplete and unreliable statements" to the committee, but had not intended to mislead them. (It was all his lawyers' fault, Gingrich implied, as his long-time legal adviser resigned in a snit and many Republicans winced.)

A formal apology to the House and a severe fine were part of the price Gingrich had to pay, but they were hardly the extent of the damage. At one point it appeared Gingrich's post as Speaker was in jeopardy, as prominent conservatives such as William Safire and Robert Bork called for him to step aside, and several key congressmen deserted him. But the feisty Georgian managed to hang on by rallying his troops in time for his re-election on January 7.

The matter did not end there. In July 1997, in the middle of the Republicans' battle with Bill Clinton over the budget-reconciliation process, several of Gingrich's top deputies and supporters attempted a "coup" which became embarrassingly public. It was aborted after less than a week. However, the fallout from this public-relations disaster was considerable. Not only did it demonstrate that Republicans themselves were still worried about the Speaker's crediblity, but it derailed their policy agenda at the very moment it was making considerable headway.

As one commentator put it, up until then "the Democrats were [reduced to] attacking the Republicans for balancing the budget on the backs of the poor, the elderly and children, charging that the GOP was financing tax cuts for people who did not need them by cutting Medicare benefits for people who did." In fact, "the Republicans had so utterly changed the political discourse that what just a year ago would have been a debate over *whether* to balance the budget at all was transformed into a debate about how to do it."

The Democrats could hardly believe their good fortune. With Congress distracted by internecine warfare, the Democrats went on the offensive and secured major concessions from the Republicans. By then Newt Gingrich's *disapproval* rating had soared to 66 per cent, far higher than Bill Clinton's on his worst days.

The result was predictable. By mid-1996 the president, whose wild ratings swings had stabilized in recent months, was looking more and more like a man who might win a second term. Before the campaign even began, the Republican's presidential hopeful, none other than Senate Majority Leader Bob Dole, was looking like a lame duck. His party's primaries had featured serious infighting, sharp personal attacks and heated debates over former Klansman David Duke of Louisiana, who had actually run against Bush in the 1992 Republican primaries and was now trying for a Senate seat.

The Liberal Comeback

Bob Dole's 1996 campaign slogan "Mainstream, not extreme!" demonstrated how far from grace the neo-conservatives had fallen. At the party's convention in San Diego, Newt Gingrich was not allowed to appear on stage during prime time. Instead, he was reduced to introducing a gold-medallist in volleyball from the Atlanta Olympics. Evidently trying to make the best of his situation, Gingrich breathlessly announced that volleyball was now played in thirty countries. Linking this fact to some neo-conservative language about reducing the size of government with a logic only his closest admirers could appreciate, he then declared: "There's a whole world of opportunity opening up that didn't exist thirty years ago and no bureaucrat would have invented it. And that's what freedom is all about." As one observer commented, "In front of the cameras the Republicans were happy and ignorant."

They were not happy for much longer. The bottom fell out of Dole's approval ratings and the candidate himself fell off the podium during a televised appearance. As the campaign progressed, Dole spent considerable time criticizing Gingrich rather than the Democrats, trying hard to distance himself from the "extremists." To no one's surprise, Bill Clinton returned to the White House in November 1996. But the economic legacy of the Reagan years, and the significant impact of Gingrich and the New Right in shaping the public debate for the prior two years, meant Clinton was still obliged to proceed carefully and slowly with any attempts to restore the liberal agenda in his second term. On some issues he was forced to compromise far more than he wanted, although less than Gingrich had demanded. Nevertheless, he did make progress.

A former Rhodes scholar with many years as governor of the have-not state of Arkansas behind him, Clinton had much relevant knowledge and experience on his side. He pursued the liberal social-policy agenda above all else, and he increasingly did so by outmanoeuvring the Republicans. The president launched a series of brilliant tactical sorties, and even managed to turn some of their code words to his advantage. The grimaces on the faces of Gingrich and his New Right colleagues were plainly visible during his State of the Nation address as Clinton used their "tough on crime" and "family values" terminology to sell his liberal initiatives to improve access to education and reduce disadvantages for the growing inner-city underclass of blacks and Hispanics.

In exchange for his concessions to the Republicans on the law-and-order front — such as his successful effort to have the United Nations assist in the "war on drugs" despite overwhelming evidence this approach would not work — Clinton was also able to secure a commitment from Congress for the country's $1.5 billion in U.N. arrears that had been accumulating for several years due to Republican opposition. (The appropriation was held up at the eleventh hour, however, as right-wing Republicans added an unrelated anti-abortion clause to the bill, forcing the president to reject it.) With several other successful foreign-policy initiatives to his credit, including personal missions to the Middle East and Ireland, and the domestic economy continuing to soar, his popularity remained high despite a number of personal debacles, including the emerging Monica Lewinsky affair.

The Republicans initially feared they would attack Clinton's personal behaviour at their peril in the court of public opinion. In fact, the New Right were fast becoming the object of public ridicule. At a conference sponsored by *The Nation* on potential implications of the end of the Cold War for government policies — the so-called peace dividend — political columnist Molly Ivans of the *Dallas Times* brought the house down with her acerbic critique of the Gingrich Republicans. She began by suggesting they had wasted valuable time trying to focus debate in America on "whether or not we should *have* government," rather than examining what could be done "to bring about justice and prosperity for all." Next she addressed the Republicans' fascination with "the good old days," which she viewed as an unwelcome hold-over from the Reagan era. Referring to Gingrich's vow to "root out every single last vestige of the Great Society, root and branch," and his subsequent threats to "repeal the New Deal" and "restore Victorian values," Ivans concluded: "These people are doing their best to replicate Victorian social conditions. Of course they would want Victorian values to go along with them. At the rate they're going, we're soon going to be discussing Cave Man values."

By now Newt Gingrich was also considered a pariah by many of his own party's leadership. His popularity ratings had plummeted to the low 'teens. The man who only a few years earlier had been touted as a potential presidential candidate in 2000 was clinging to his post and barely tolerated by the moderates in his party, who were again in the ascendancy.

In a desperate attempt to salvage the situation, Gingrich published an autobiographical account of his time in office, entitled *Lessons Learned the Hard Way*. In it, the "acid-tongued, overweight, suit-and-tie conservative" of 1994 was now talking about consensus politics and vowing he "would not allow President Clinton to outflank him on the *left*" on the issue of damages from the tobacco industry. This remark prompted a swift rebuke from the old-guard conservatives that Newt and his boys had disdained only a few years earlier. "It's a fifth dimension where you locate Newt Gingrich's politics these days," scoffed veteran pundit George Will.

Gingrich's position on the political spectrum may have been in doubt, but the fate of the neo-conservatives was not. The Republican Revolution of 1994 that was to have changed the face of the nation had sputtered to a standstill much sooner than anyone expected, least of all the opportunistic good old boy from Georgia.

Drastic measures were called for, Gingrich believed. Despite overwhelming evidence the American people did not consider the president's admittedly reprehensible behaviour in the Monica Lewinsky affair a "hanging offence," Gingrich personally stage-managed a blatantly partisan campaign to attack Bill Clinton through the extraordinary use of a special prosecutor and grand jury. Republican-appointed family-values zealot Ken Starr and a background cast of Moral Majority financial supporters kept the president's sexual peccadilloes on the front pages for months.

This was all to no avail. The more Gingrich took a hard line, the more people viewed the affair as a partisan issue. By insisting on wringing every last drop of sensationalism out of the case — including their unprecedented decision to release Clinton's grand-jury testimony — the Republicans gave up any claim to the moral high ground. As Gingrich and his allies forged ahead, most Americans tuned out in disgust. Meanwhile, the rest of the world watched the self-destructive frenzy with horrified fascination.

As the November mid-term elections neared, the Republicans once again went on the attack, issuing a flurry of negative ads about Clinton's integrity in the last weeks of the campaign. Having rashly predicted a Democratic disaster, the Gingrich team was beginning to panic. Poll after poll indicated the American people simply did not share their righteous wrath. On November 4, it was clear the polls, not the Republican ad men, had been right. The Democrats held their own, and even scored some surprise gains, including the defeat of hardline Republican senator Alphonse D'Amato of New York. Black voters in particular had turned out in substantial numbers to shore up the Clinton presidency, apparently determined to avoid a replay of Ronald Reagan's 1980 victory by default.

Given the traditional pattern of mid-term reversals for the party in charge of the White House, the results could only be seen as a stunning rebuke for the Republicans, and for Newt Gingrich personally. He resigned as Speaker a few days later, in high dudgeon, before his colleagues could organize a mutiny.

Yet the new Republican hierarchy, including Majority Whip Tom DeLay, were still intent on pursuing an impeachment trial. With nearly 70 per cent of Americans opposing this strategy, DeLay bluntly declared he was unconcerned with the wishes of the majority of voters. His only concern was for the wishes of those social-conservative Republicans who had elected him and his colleagues. These voters, he assured the press, wanted moral retribution. Democrats, meanwhile, argued that what the Republicans really wanted was political revenge for Nixon and Gingrich. Whatever their motives, the Republican-dominated House of Representatives easily impeached Clinton in the dying days of the Congress, forcing a Senate trial and ensuring further political gridlock. Then, after an ambitious State of the Union address in January 1999, in which an unapologetically liberal Clinton declared that "government is a progressive instrument of the common good, rooted in our oldest values of opportunity, responsibility and community," the president's approval rating soared to an unprecedented 70 per cent.

Deep down, the Senate's Republican leadership knew that evangelist Pat Robertson was right when he declared that the President had won and they should call off their inquisition. Unfortunately, they had no choice but to move ahead. Although Republican Majority Leader Trent Lott tried hard to minimize the damage, the trial dragged on for nearly five weeks as Henry Hyde, the unrepentant House prosecutor, insisted on hearing testimony from several witnesses, in what Washington insiders termed the "Hail Monica" strategy. When no new evidence emerged, even Hyde was forced to admit defeat. In the end, the Republicans could not even field a simple majority of votes on either of the charges, and Bill Clinton was left with two years in which to repair the political damage and try to rehabilitate his image.

The Canadian Connection

All of these developments were still to come, however, when the neo-conservative agenda finally reached the shores — or, more accurately, the prairies — of Canada in late 1993. Coming to Canada some fourteen years after Maggie Thatcher first seized power in Great Britain, radical right-wing politics in Canada is seen by some analysts as a "second wave" rather than a continuation of the original neo-conservative trend she began. There is some truth to this argument, since it took far more to sell neo-conservatism in Canada than it did in Britain or the United

States. In the end, both the message and the medium would have to be modified for Canadian consumption in order for neo-conservative politicians like Preston Manning to achieve a breakthrough.

In popular terminology, Canada's political culture has always been more "left wing" than that of the United States. What seems moderate or middle-of-the-road to Canadians is often viewed by Americans as a socialist plot. Our publicly funded health-care system is a perfect example. Many mainstream Americans describe it as evidence of a near-communist system. Former prime minister Pierre Trudeau's position on issues such as nuclear disarmament and foreign aid — views considered mainstream in Canada — led American politicians like Jesse Helms and Richard Nixon to describe Trudeau as a "socialist" and a "pinko." Meanwhile, prominent Democrats such as Senator Edward Kennedy, a staunch advocate of a national health-care plan, are considered borderline extremists in the United States but fit easily within the Red Tory or Liberal party labels in Canada.

At the same time, Canadians have always demonstrated a greater respect for authority and deference to elites than have Americans. The most common explanation for this difference is that it flows from the influence of the different groups of settlers who emigrated to the New World. In Canada's case, the British influence was greater, since immigrants from England and Scotland continued to arrive from abroad as well as from the American colonies, as Loyalists, long after the United States had ceased to be a welcoming place for them. Much has also been made of the fact that immigrants to Canada were most likely to be traditional Anglicans or Catholics, rather than the Calvinists and other fundamentalists who settled in the United States.

Another explanation has centred on the "revolution versus evolution" theory, in which Americans early on learned to distrust government and favour individual rights above all else, while Canadians continued to demonstrate considerable deference for state authority and a preference for collective action.

In his classic study of the two cultures, *Continental Divide*, Seymour Martin Lipset emphasizes the dominant role of the Canadian government in the country's expansion westward. The planned settlement of immigrants and the ever-present authority of the Royal Canadian

Mounted Police are in stark contrast to the *ad hoc* American approach. As Lipset points out, with its anti-government settlers and vigilante justice the American "wild west" could hardly have been more different from the staid, law-abiding Canadian experience. (With the recent anti-government paramilitary activities in Montana and several other western states, it would appear Lipset's distinctions are equally valid today.)

The combination of these different factors produced a political culture that is more left-wing but less aggressive than that of the United States. The liberal consensus of the postwar era was also more deeply ingrained in the fabric of Canadian society. With a much smaller population and far less capital for private-sector investment, state intervention in the economy and the provision of government-sponsored social programs through the welfare state came to be not only strongly supported, but expected. Many Canadians considered it a right of citizenship. Risk-taking and entrepreneurship, by contrast, never figured prominently in the Canadian identity.

Thus, in crisis situations, where Americans would typically turn to individuals or charitable organizations for assistance, Canadians would expect government to look after them. While Americans distrusted government, and sought through their constitution to limit its powers over the individual citizen, Canadians saw government as a positive force for good with an important role to play in society.

The consequences for the neo-conservative agenda are obvious. Since the goal posts of political discourse in the United States are farther to the right than in Canada, even the views of moderate Republicans appear extreme to Canadians. The populism of Reagan and Gingrich would normally have failed to excite much interest in Canada as well, because of the deeply entrenched respect for political elites. With the exception of regional protest movements originating in the West, there has been no real populist tradition in Canada. Moreover, the limited attempts at populism that did emerge were most successful as a left-wing, socialist movement rather than a radical right-wing force. In fact, the major regional protest movement — the Co-operative Commonwealth Federation (CCF) of Saskatchewan — later evolved into the national New Democratic Party (NDP) and eventually became a mainstream element of Canadian political culture. Only in Alberta did a right-wing strain of populism make any significant headway, in the form of the provincial Social Credit Party.

Efforts to convert this provincial phenomenon into a Western protest party at the national level were conspicuously unsuccessful.

Neo-conservatism had another hurdle to clear in Canada. Although Margaret Thatcher was the first politician to implement the neo-conservative agenda in a Western liberal democracy, Canadians were more likely to identify it as an American phenomenon due to their greater familiarity with American politics. Since most Canadians define their national identity as one that is emphatically not American, they have been very unwilling to import American political baggage. As Allan Gregg and Michael Posner note in their 1990 compendium of Canadian attitudes, *The Big Picture*, "What made us distinct was that we weren't Americans, and we were proud of it." Among these distinctions was the Canadian tradition of compromise and consensus, so clearly at odds with the Americans' more adversarial and combative approach.

Despite these fundamental differences between the two countries, neo-conservatism has made significant inroads in Canadian politics in the past few years. Two of the most important provinces are now in the hands of neo-conservative governments and the Official Opposition in Ottawa is expressing views unthinkable for a federal party only a decade ago. Not surprisingly, the success of these radical right-wing politicians has come hard on the heels of several major assaults on our political culture over the past decade.

The Mulroney Legacy

The discontent that allowed neo-conservatism to take hold in certain parts of Canada was the result of three separate developments. The first of these was economic upheaval. Like Britain and the United States, Canada experienced the severe economic dislocation of globalization. But the Canadian economy — and the Canadian middle class — were hit with the additional problems of a free-trade agreement with the United States, and the introduction of a new sales tax (the GST), at the same time as the negative effects of the economic restructuring were working their way through the system. (Some authors, such as Linda McQuaig, have argued the Bank of Canada's monetary policy of high interest rates was another significant factor.)

As several studies have demonstrated, the decision by the Mulroney government to proceed with these two initiatives at the same time as international forces were causing fundamental restructuring was unwise, to say the least. The impact of this triple whammy was naturally a far more severe economic downturn than elsewhere. In many cases these developments spelled disaster for middle-class professionals and middle managers in corporate Canada, the backbone of the liberal consensus. For the first time since the Second World War, the children of the middle class began to suspect they might not do as well as their parents.

Canadians in large numbers began to question their traditional reliance on the state. The federal government seemed helpless to protect them from the negative effects of international forces, and unwilling to help them weather the storm. Cuts to the social safety net and the national infrastructure further damaged the state's credibility at a crucial moment. Support for the liberal consensus of the past forty years was weakened, and liberal politicians — unwilling or unable to recognize the seriousness of the threat — made no concerted effort to stem the tide by defending that consensus.

While this loss of faith affected Canadians in every part of the country, the political implications were more important in certain regions. Atlantic Canada, with its long-standing economic difficulties and heavy reliance on federal transfer payments, was hardly likely to be moved by neo-conservative arguments that the answer was to *cut* government spending and eliminate a number of government services and programs. By contrast, Ontario, with its huge manufacturing and industrial base and disproportionate number of professionals and middle managers, was among the hardest hit by the economic dislocations. Its citizens were also among the most susceptible to the argument that spending cuts might reduce the tax burden on the middle class and increase employment. Meanwhile, in Western Canada, the perception that governments were no longer able to handle crises was heightened in Alberta and British Columbia, where the resource-based economy was threatened more than ever by international events beyond the government's control.

Severe as the economic difficulties were, they likely would have been insufficient to entice large numbers of Canadians away from their commitment to compassion and the collective well-being. Unfortunately the Mulroney government further weakened the state's positive image in two important ways.

The first was to destroy Canadians' respect for politicians, already sorely tried as a result of the Meech Lake fiasco several years earlier. Undeterred by the warning signals sent out with this first failure, the Mulroney government decided to launch a second round of constitutional negotiations. They resulted in the disastrous Charlottetown Accord and subsequent nationwide referendum in which the prime minister accused opponents of the deal of being "enemies of Canada." Those "three little words," as journalist Graham Fraser noted, just wouldn't go away. Although Mulroney later tried to tone the rhetoric down somewhat, contenting himself with the idea that opponents were merely "not proud Canadians," the damage was done.

By the time the dust had settled in late 1992, the referendum had killed the accord and the careers of several politicians. Not only politicians, but the leaders of many of the traditional interest groups, had been thoroughly discredited. Worse still, having used apocryphal language to sell the accord, the prime minister had also opened the door to apocryphal solutions. If the nation was in crisis as a result of the accord's failure, as he had threatened, then desperate measures might be required to save the nation. If the old-line parties were not up to the job, it might be time to try something new. This loss of faith in government paved the way for a populist, anti-elite, anti-government protest movement.

Canadians' traditional respect for authority was further undermined by a second negative development — the series of scandals plaguing the Mulroney government and several provincial governments during the 1980s. After a record number of federal cabinet ministers (notably Sinclair Stevens) had been forced to resign in disgrace and several backbench Conservative MPs were charged with criminal offences relating to misuse of public office, Canadians began to re-examine their implicit faith in the good intentions of those seeking elected office. Similar scandals in Saskatchewan under the Devine Conservatives, and in British Columbia, where the premier, Bill Vander Zalm, was essentially found guilty of profiting from public office in his personal business ventures, only worsened the poisonous atmosphere of traditional Canadian politics.

Even these blows to traditional liberal values and beliefs might not have been sufficient to overcome most Canadians' resistance to a radically different right-wing agenda. What finally tipped the balance and made the agenda palatable for many voters were the significant modifications made by its Canadian advocates.

First, in a move more reminiscent of Thatcher than of Reagan, those advancing neo-conservative values in Canada emphasized, first and foremost, the *economic* agenda rather than the social and moral aspects. Not only did they focus on the deficit and the debt, but Canadian neo-conservatives placed their proposals in the context of a *politically acceptable* Canadian objective. Rather than emphasizing the potential for individual gain and wealth creation, as Thatcher and Reagan had done, Canadian neo-conservatives promoted their economic agenda as unpleasant but necessary medicine to ensure the common good and the well-being of future generations. Implicit in this approach was the promise that, once the economic crisis was rectified, Canadian governments could return to some measure of their former activist role. For many voters — especially those who supported the federal Reform Party and the Harris Conservatives in Ontario — this was the only message they heard.

Similarly, Canadian neo-conservatives were even more careful than their counterparts elsewhere to use deceptive code words on the few social issues they *did* decide to tackle. In Canada, liberal terms such as "fairness," "equality" and "democratic" were used to promote ideas which would achieve the opposite effect. Nevertheless, there were certain subjects — such as medicare — the New Right elite understood were sacrosanct and could not be broached if they hoped to win converts.

As for the American emphasis on moral conservatism, this has been the least important part of the Canadian neo-conservatives' message. The political culture simply is not receptive. As subsequent chapters demonstrate, the "family values/moral majority" dimension of the American New Right has been virtually ignored by the Klein and Harris governments, although there are many supporters within their caucuses. More to the point, the federal Reform Party's decision to highlight its commitment to moral conservativism has been a significant factor in its inability to expand from its Western base in Alberta and the Bible Belt of British Columbia.

A second and equally important element of the Canadian neo-conservative equation has been its proponents' ability to marry their right-wing views with the tradition of Western protest movements. They did this by focusing on long-standing Western alienation. This alienation was exacerbated by the economic turmoil of the past decade, but also by the disenchantment of Westerners, who had heavily supported the Mulroney government in two elections. For many Western voters — and especially those in Alberta — it seemed that politicians, and mainstream political parties, and specifically the Conservative party, were either unwilling or unable to recognize their concerns.

Nowhere was the phenomenon of Western alienation more prevalent than in Alberta. Voters in a province with overwhelming dependency on one commodity — energy — increasingly believed they had been hard hit by federal policies over the years, culminating in the much-reviled National Energy Program of Pierre Trudeau. Unlike Saskatchewan, where a heavy reliance on federal transportation and agricultural policies to support the grain industry led most residents to look favourably on the federal government, Alberta saw its most important commodity as being hurt, not helped, by restrictive federal policies. Always more likely to support a free-market, American-style approach to economic matters, Albertans viewed federal energy policy as an unwelcome intrusion into their jurisdiction.

Coincidentally, Alberta was also home to the only remotely successful right-wing populist movement, Social Credit. Like the United States, it was the one province that had been settled by a number of groups with fundamentalist religious ties, making the moral aspect of American neo-conservatism more appealing there than elsewhere.

Given these circumstances, it is hardly surprising that Alberta should have been the birthplace of both the first neo-conservative provincial government and the first "national" party to espouse neo-conservative values — the federal Reform Party. Yet when Ralph Klein took over the Conservative party in 1992, no one expected his government to make such a hard right turn in such a short space of time. In fact, no one expected him to be the premier for more than a few months. The history of Canada's neo-conservative "success" story begins with a man whom no one actually expected to amount to much of anything, let alone become premier of Alberta.

2

Klein's Cowboys

> We spent a lot of time trying to predict where a student would
> end up, . . . to help them get there. Boys like Ralph are proof
> that we didn't do a very good job of it.
> He was completely unpredictable.
> — Ran White, former teacher

> His candour is a terrific political weapon
> and the most insincere thing about him.
> — Kenneth Whyte, *Saturday Night*, May 1994

> Bums, creeps and ... unskilled workers are not welcome.
> We will use cowboy techniques [to deal] with people who rob
> our banks, add to our welfare rolls, add to our
> unemployment lines and create rising crime rates ...
> — Ralph Klein

Looks can be deceiving. With his beefy face, jug ears and ski-slope nose
and his short, pudgy body, Ralph Klein looks every bit the son of an
amateur wrestler and grandson of sturdy German immigrants. No one
would mistake him for the patrician Peter Lougheed or his lanky college

football chum Don Getty. The first word that comes to mind in describing Ralph Klein is "ordinary." In fact, most people would say Klein looks very ordinary indeed. However, those people would be making a mistake. People who know him, and especially those who have crossed swords with him, are only too well aware that nothing could be further from the truth.

Something about his eyes gives Ralph Klein away. Small, but bright and intense, they shift focus almost all the time, looking at everything and nothing, checking the angles or just watching. They make it clear there are deep waters behind the easygoing, folksy exterior. A high-school dropout with a fondness for drinking and partying, an outdoorsman who spent years driving around Calgary with a canoe strapped to the roof of a Volkswagen, and a devotee of many of the practices of Blackfoot spiritualism who speaks the language fluently, Klein is obviously a bit of an oddball. He is also an enigma. Nothing in his past suggested he would one day become, in quick succession, a popular mayor of Calgary, an Environment minister in the Getty cabinet and, finally, one of the most successful premiers of Alberta.

His reign is far from over, unless he chooses to end it himself, something his past behaviour proves is not out of the question. Having taken over a party in deep electoral trouble and won two majorities, single-handedly wiping out the Alberta deficit, providing the role model for Mike Harris and his "Common Sense Revolution" and receiving awards from virtually every right-wing think-tank in the country, the poster boy for neo-conservatism in Canada may be getting bored. On the other hand, he may not. Ralph Klein is nothing if not unpredictable.

Klein's success is certainly due in large measure to his personal attributes, but it is also due to his perfect timing. For one thing, his brand of populist conservatism works best when Alberta's economy is in a nose-dive — the "bust" factor in the roller-coaster boom–bust cycles its residents have come to know only too well. For another, his leadership style owes much to several of his predecessors, and to the history of Alberta's political party system. All of these factors meant that, unlike Harris in Ontario or Manning federally, Klein was not obliged to explain anything to his electorate. He did not have to convince them they needed his "tough love" remedies, because many of his voters were already asking for them.

In a province with the most conservative viewpoint in the country, Ralph Klein would have been a sure thing in his first election if it hadn't been for the highly unpopular legacy of his predecessor, Don Getty, and the stain on his party's good name left by Brian Mulroney. In light of these drawbacks, Klein's most amazing accomplishment was to convince voters that he and his party were reborn. His Conservatives could do the job that needed to be done, and there was no need for the electorate to look around for another alternative. Certainly not the already-salivating provincial Liberals under Laurence Decore, who thought they smelled a kill. In 1993, Ralph Klein managed to break the "third man" jinx, a feat only students of Alberta politics can appreciate.

The Social Credit Dynasty

Klein's takeover of the Conservative party was made easier by the fact that Albertans were accustomed to one-party rule and lengthy dynasties, a tradition which had begun long before the Conservatives emerged victorious under Peter Lougheed in 1971. In fact, Albertans were accustomed to an almost non-partisan type of electoral system, in which anti-politicians were the norm. Nowhere was this more evident than under the Social Credit dynasty that ruled Alberta for more than thirty years prior to the Conservative breakthrough. For premiers Aberhart and Manning, the religious fundamentalism which motivated them to enter politics was the key to their success. Not only were the Depression-era voters ready for the moral conservatism they preached, but they were eager to reject traditional politicians.

Aberhart and Manning were the original anti-politicians. They viewed their role more as "ministering" to people than as governing citizens. "Bible Bill" Aberhart, a high-school principal and hugely successful radio evangelist, persisted in claiming he was not a politician even after he was elected premier in 1935. His successor, Ernest Manning, followed suit. "I wasn't looking for this at all," he said after being sworn in. "I'd just as soon be busy with my Bible work. We're not politicians. We've [Social Credit] always opened our meetings with our hymn, and there has been an atmosphere wholly different from that of a political campaign."

For voters, the reason for Social Credit's success in Alberta was not just religion, but its attack on the elites (Aberhart's "Fifty Big Shots"), its charismatic leadership, and, most important, its offer of a pipe dream. Social Credit appeared on the scene during another "bust" period in Alberta's economic cycle, but this one was the worst yet. The Depression bred desperation. While Saskatchewan turned to socialism, Albertans turned to the monetary theories of a delusional Scottish engineer, Major Douglas, who concluded that the root cause of the worldwide recession was simply a lack of money. Print more money and give it to consumers to spend, and all would be well. In Alberta, this meant voters were promised a $25-a-month "social credit dividend." Many believed the promise.

Outside of Alberta, however, Douglas's monetary theory did not catch on. (Although the eccentric W.A.C. [Wacky] Bennett and flamboyant ministers like "Flying Phil" Gagliardi used the name in British Columbia as well, it was never really more than a political gimmick to add lustre to a fairly traditional Conservative program. As for another Albertan, Robert Thompson's brief venture into federal politics as leader of a supposedly national Social Credit Party was more of a regional protest phenomenon than a commitment to Douglas ideals.) Increasingly bitter as he encountered resistance to his ideas elsewhere, Douglas began to advance a conspiracy theory in which international banking interests, Jews, socialists and Freemasons were implicated. Although both Aberhart and Manning rejected this aspect of the Social Credit doctrine, it unquestionably had an impact on some Albertans. It was not long before Douglas's scapegoats were translated into a national context by substituting Bay Street bankers, Liberals and the federal government.

The resentment that followed the federal government's disallowance of several major pieces of Social Credit legislation — legislation which was outside the jurisdiction of the provincial government to enact — only made matters worse, despite the fact Douglas himself had warned Aberhart and Manning that his policies could be implemented successfully only at the national level. After this, the growing sense of Western alienation from the political and economic centre of the country was to become a major theme in all provincial elections.

Western alienation provided further impetus for the province's electoral tendency to one-party dominance. The need to present a united front against the central heartland, especially with a vulnerable commodity-based economy, led voters to support one strong party with one strong leader. Alberta's Opposition parties were small splinters of resistance on the margins.

Not everyone in Alberta supported the Social Credit Party or its monetary policies, however, despite its large electoral majorities. Though opposition was vocal throughout most of the party's tenure in office, it was never organized and consistent. And Social Credit was never really socially acceptable, despite its string of victories. After the Depression, the party's most ardent and public supporters were generally perceived to be outsiders or "down-and-outers" who had little to lose. It became a standing joke that no one in the middle class had ever met someone who voted Social Credit.

Edgar Lougheed, the son of Senator Sir James Lougheed of Calgary, did not vote for a party which made such "foolish" promises, and he did not hesitate to express his views. His elder son, Don, remembered nearly forty years later how upset his father had been when word came of the Social Credit landslide in 1935. His younger brother Peter was only seven at the time, but it was a scene he would not forget either. Thirty years later, he would become leader of the political party that would drive them from office.

One person who openly supported the Social Credit from the beginning was Philip Klein. As a student he had become friends with one of his teachers, Alf Hooke, a man who would later serve as a Social Credit cabinet minister from 1935 to 1970. During the Depression, Philip Klein, a construction worker and part-time wrestler who travelled across the Prairies, seeking work, became a self-described "dyed-in-the-wool" Social Credit supporter. Shortly after settling down in the working-class district of Tuxedo Park, in Calgary, he also became the father of one Ralph Philip Klein.

After Aberhart's early and unsuccessful initiatives, the Socreds, and especially the Manning government, essentially abandoned their commitment to the policies of Major Douglas. Instead they offered traditional conservative policies that did little to rock the boat or disturb the status quo. In fact, Manning was still offering more of the same well into the 1960s, when the rest of the world was becoming restless and ready to move on. His government was also straying further afield from the original principles of the party.

Then, in 1969 Ernest Manning accepted an appointment as a director of the board of the Canadian Imperial Bank of Commerce, a position that might easily have earned him Aberhart's contempt as one of the Fifty Big Shots. By 1970, Alf Hooke, an unrepentant true believer in the Social Credit philosophy, was so disgusted he resigned. A year later Peter Lougheed, the grandson of Sir James, became the tenth premier of Alberta, ending an unbroken thirty-six-year reign by the Socreds.

The Lougheed Legacy

Peter Lougheed is a third-generation Calgarian whose patrician past is evident in his features, yet he could be, and often still *is*, viewed approvingly by Albertans as a self-made man. When many of his grandfather's holdings and the family estate were lost to creditors during the Depression, he learned first-hand the impact of market forces. A ten-year-old Lougheed hid in a closet in the family's majestic home, Beaulieu, and watched its contents being auctioned off for a fraction of their worth before he left in dismay. Confronted by a newspaper reporter on his way out, the young boy did not hesitate to assure him that prices would be better the following day (they weren't), and then suggested the house itself should be converted into a hospital.

Less affected by the Depression than many others, Peter Lougheed nevertheless lived through a time when the effects of the lack of a social safety net on the weak and disadvantaged were obvious, and his suggestion about the hospital showed the impact of his experiences on an impressionable ten-year-old. Even so, Lougheed's upbringing in most respects was typically upper middle class. Forced to leave a private school when the family's funds dwindled, he completed public high school in Calgary and attended the University of Alberta in Edmonton, where he studied law and played a great deal of football. A personable student and natural leader, he also served as president of the student body. Having received his law degree, he could have settled into any number of prominent Calgary law firms. Instead, he went on to Harvard to complete an

MBA, working summers for Gulf Oil in Texas and the Chase Manhattan Bank in New York.

His experience outside of Alberta was further broadened by subsequent career choices. After graduating from Harvard, he spent a short time in a well-known Calgary law firm before he moved on to the huge Mannix Corporation, an international heavy-equipment and construction firm headquartered in Calgary. Rising quickly to the position of Vice-President, Administration, he spent much of his time travelling across North America, conducting high-level negotiations with American executives concerning dams, pipelines, airports and other major projects. In short, by the time Peter Lougheed was ready to enter public life, he had acquired an impressive set of credentials that would prove an invaluable asset for the future premier, particularly during the heady years of rapid expansion and oil development in the province.

In 1965, the Socreds had already been in power for thirty years. The Progressive Conservative party had no leader and no seats. In a contest with only three candidates, the membership elected Peter Lougheed as the new leader by a record 91 per cent of the ballots. The following year, at a party convention, the new leader outlined his political philosophy in broad terms. "We believe in a provincial government which gives strong support to the need in Canada for an effective central government," he declared. In a sentence which could just as easily have been spoken by Bill Davis or other Ontario Tories, he went on to say that, "as Conservatives, we feel strongly that the role of government should be to protect the individual citizens as much as improving the public good." Perhaps the only issue on which the Alberta perspective appeared very clearly was his final point that "God's endowment of this province with such abundant natural resources permits us realistically to set as our objective a society that is not inferior to any province or state in North America." Time would prove all of these points to be highly significant, though they seemed bland and harmless enough then.

The next year a dramatic upset occurred when Peter Lougheed and the Conservative party took six seats in the provincial election. Lougheed became Leader of the Official Opposition. One of the new Tory MLAs, Lougheed's close friend and former football teammate Don Getty, told reporters, "This is the beginning of the end of Social Credit." Most laughed at the time, but they were wrong. In four years, Peter Lougheed and the Conservatives formed a majority government, and the Social Credit Party was history.

There are several important factors in the rapid rise of the Conservatives under Lougheed, all of which can be seen as having an impact on the future political development of the province. First, the Social Credit Party had become the "Manning" party. As the party lacked much in the way of new policies, the strong leadership and personality of Ernest Manning was its sustaining feature. By the end of his time in office, a strong leader had become an essential element in any political party's bid for electoral success in Alberta. As a result, the outgoing premier's attempt to hand over the reins to a nondescript successor (Harry Strom) failed, providing ammunition for the provincial superstition of the "third man" jinx.

A second problem was that the Socreds under Manning had failed to adapt their program and image to the times. Moral conservatism was fast becoming obsolete, while a new progressive element had crept into the programs of Conservative parties elsewhere. In a one-party state, this failure to ensure reform from within was fatal. Voters needed to be reassured they were still getting good government and efficient management from the ruling party, not becoming a backwater the world was passing by. Although he would no doubt be unhappy with the comparison, Peter Lougheed in many respects offered Albertans in 1971 the same things that Pierre Trudeau had offered Canadians in 1968 — a young, attractive, charismatic leader with an infectious attitude of optimism, enthusiasm and national (or provincial) pride. Lougheed convinced Albertans that the possibilities were endless, just as Trudeau had inspired Canadians with the same message a few years earlier.

A third factor in Lougheed's success was his ability to convince Albertans a change from the one-party domination of the Socreds was "safe." He knew voters wanted a more modern outlook from their government, but not a wholesale revision. Lougheed sold the Conservative party to the electorate on the understanding that, while some aspects of government and its programs would be modernized and made more professional and efficient, most of the basic building blocks would remain. This was not to be a revolution, but a smooth transition from one era to another. Reporter Alan Hustak makes a similar argument in a biography of Lougheed. He concludes that the 1971 Conservative victory was primarily "a triumph of style rather than substance — the secular equivalent of a revival meeting — a new minister had been selected to do a better job than the old one, but the faith remained the same."

A change in style may be all the electorate expected in 1971, but it is not what they were given for the next twenty-one years. True, Lougheed did modernize government procedures and enhance the professionalism of the bureaucracy in his first years in office, just as Pierre Trudeau was doing in Ottawa. As premier, Lougheed ran the government much like a corporation. A former management man himself, Lougheed appreciated the value of expert advice. As he explained to his new cabinet, since they were taking power with little or no previous experience in government, they badly needed "a significant staff of senior people involved as back-up resources, much like the privy council in Ottawa."

Not surprisingly Lougheed made sure his cabinet ministers were selected on the basis of competence and experience, not just personal friendships or support for his leadership. In his first cabinet, ministers were not only far better educated than their Social Credit predecessors, but also an average of nine years younger than members of the Strom cabinet. At twenty-two members, the cabinet itself was also the largest ever in Alberta, a clear indication of the expansion of government activity that was to come.

In 1971 there were 18,518 provincial public servants in Alberta; in 1978 there were 48,025. These figures alone tell the tale of the Lougheed years. The Conservative government improved programs and services related to health care, welfare and education; expanded the provincial infrastructure; and provided incentives to industry. One of Lougheed's major themes was the need to "diversify" the provincial economy in the hope of eliminating the boom–bust cycles. Many public/private-sector ventures were initiated to achieve that end, demonstrating yet again the pragmatic and progressive nature of Lougheed's brand of conservatism.

Lougheed was not only efficient, but lucky. As everyone familiar with Alberta history knows, he took over the reins of power at the beginning of an incredible period of economic growth, spurred on by the oil boom.

Times were very good indeed. Nevertheless, a Social Credit government or a more conservatively inclined Tory government would never have taken many of the initiatives the Lougheed government embarked on without hesitation. Every Albertan knows the story of Syncrude, Pacific Western Airlines (PWA), and his greatest achievement, the Alberta Heritage Trust Fund. At the time they were introduced, almost all Albertans approved or, at the very least, were prepared to be tolerant of the government's indulgences. After all, they could afford them. (For some, the nationalization of PWA translated as "Peter wants an airline," but it was almost always said with a smile.)

A larger-than-life figure on the provincial stage for twenty years, Lougheed soon came to be considered a national player, a man the federal Conservatives unsuccessfully courted for the leadership. His battles with Prime Minister Pierre Trudeau on the energy and constitutional fronts were legendary. The irony of this, considering his 1966 speech as the new leader, has not been lost on students of history. Lougheed has always claimed his positions were entirely consistent, pointing to his use of the term "effective." Whatever his motives, however, there can be little doubt that his running battles with Ottawa did much to deepen Albertans' already strong sense of alienation from the heartland of the country. In each subsequent provincial election campaign, Lougheed essentially ignored his provincial opponents and ran a campaign against the federal Liberals. For many Albertans, Pierre Trudeau became the enemy against whom the provincial government must fight relentlessly; elections were simply a reaffirmation that they wanted to present a united front against him.

Tory Troubles

In politics, timing is everything. Just as he knew when to embark on his political career, Peter Lougheed knew when to leave. The economy was heading south fast. Oil prices were plummeting and the boom was about to go bust. Announcing his resignation in 1985, twenty years after taking over the reins of the Conservative party, he publicly urged many people to run for his position so that the party would have a strong presence and an infusion of new blood. Privately, however, he was encouraging his old friend and former Environment minister, Don Getty — now out of politics for six years and happily engaged in the private sector — to go for the brass ring. Everyone "knew" Getty was Lougheed's real choice. Yet, at the convention, Getty's coronation was a near thing, a sure sign that the grassroots were anxious. Those who supported Getty did so more because "Peter wants it," as one delegate was overheard to say, rather than because they felt Getty was the right choice.

The delegates' misgivings were reinforced over the next six years. The Getty era was traumatic for the Conservatives and for Alberta. The premier himself turned out to be the wrong man for the job. Apparently detached and uninterested in the day-to-day affairs of running a government, he also seemed to be a bit of a bungler. Worse still, his love affair with golf and his penchant for holidays down south began to cause enormous concern among suddenly unemployed Albertans whose mortgages and loans were being called in.

To add to the premier's troubles, many financial chickens came home to roost in the province during the Getty years, including a number of projects originally sponsored or supported by the Lougheed government. Every Albertan also knows the names Canadian Commercial Bank and the Northlands Bank, Kananaskis Park, the Principal Group, Alberta-Pacific Terminals, Gainers (of Peter Pocklington fame) and NovAtel.

With the demise of NovAtel alone, increasingly angry Albertans were told the treasury was out some $566 million. Although mismanagement certainly played a role, most of the projects were also victims of a changing international economic order in which a small player like Alberta could not succeed, at least without making substantial changes or further investments. The public neither knew nor cared about these details. As one reporter concluded, after the NovAtel scandal of 1992, "Albertans did not talk much about a changing economy or international investment. They knew someone had lost them more than half a billion dollars. The trail, as usual, seemed to lead to Getty and his pals."

To everyone's surprise, Getty managed to hang on to the premier's job for more than six years. He was actually re-elected in 1989, albeit with a greatly reduced majority and a strong showing by the Liberals. Muttering on the backbenches and among the party membership about the need for a new leader began almost immediately. They would have to act swiftly if they were to revive their flagging fortunes. But by the time Getty finally announced his resignation in the fall of 1992, it looked nearly impossible. After more than twenty years of a Conservative administration, the once-mighty party of Peter Lougheed was sitting at 18 per cent in the polls.

Equally disheartening for the election planners, the Tories' traditional whipping boy of election campaigns, Pierre Trudeau and the federal Liberals, had long since been replaced in Ottawa by the Mulroney Conservatives. Mulroney's record was alienating Alberta voters as much as other Canadians, if not more. As a result the provincial Liberals had emerged as the credible alternative and appeared poised to take over and become the next Alberta dynasty. On that basis, who would want to take the helm of the Conservative party, only to become the victim of the "third man" jinx?

The Maverick of Tuxedo Park

The man who eventually picked up the torch and carried it into the next election for the Conservatives is someone whose character comes close to defying description. Although nothing does justice to his complexity, the term "maverick" seems to fit Ralph Klein the best.

Unlike Peter Lougheed or Don Getty, Ralph Klein did not come from the monied or leisure class. His early years were spent in the working-class district of Tuxedo Park, a few miles but light-years away from the neighbourhood of the Lougheeds. His parents' stormy relationship caused problems for both Klein and his older brother, Lynn. After their divorce when he was only eight, Ralph lived for some years with his maternal grandparents, and also for a while with his father, Phil, the construction worker and amateur wrestler.

A loner and a drifter for much of his early life, Klein appears to have been indelibly influenced by his unhappy and unsettled childhood. Subject to unpredictable mood swings, he is generally gregarious and outgoing but can also be amazingly thin-skinned and withdrawn for a politician. Klein began his political career as an outsider, and this often came back to haunt him on the road to the premier's office. Those who have followed his improbable career also describe him as a chameleon and an opportunist. But the most important element of Ralph Klein's character is the maverick tendency — the fact that he thrives on adversity and enjoys being different. He seems unable to take direction and prefers to do things his way, an approach which almost always involves the unconventional.

At the same time, his desire for structure and stability in his life made him ambitious, and he wanted to fit in and succeed in a conventional sense. This combination of alienation and ambition appears to be at the root of his unpredictable behaviour and complex personality. Along with his deceptively ordinary appearance, these contradictory traits have led most of his opponents to badly underestimate him. Bright and aggressive, he has been able to make up for his lack of formal training and other advantages, primarily through sheer determination. According to Klein's brother, Lynn, the ruthless streak which fuels his ambition was evident from an early age. "Ralph was the marble king at school," he told reporter Mark Lisac, and "you didn't play with Ralph unless you wanted to lose all your marbles."

An indifferent student, Klein left school after grade ten, at the age of seventeen, to join the air force and become a fighter pilot. When this failed to happen (primarily because of his "undisciplined" behaviour and constant run-ins with superiors), he returned to Calgary a year later and married his first serious girlfriend, Hilda May Hepner, shortly thereafter. The marriage was not a success. Although there were two children in quick succession, Klein and his wife were known to have difficulties from the start. There were frequent separations before the final divorce some ten years later, the causes of which provided much fodder for gossip columnists then and throughout his political career. Shortly after the divorce was finalized in 1972, he married Colleen Hamilton, a single parent with an unhappy marriage behind her as well. This second union was fortunately a great success, and his wife has been described as a positive influence on Klein ever since. In fact, many believe his political career would have been impossible without her.

But in 1961, with a young wife, and a child on the way, the nineteen-year-old Klein was far from having a career. His first priority was to acquire an education. Having failed to complete high school, he found that his options were limited, especially with no money and little time.

Klein did what many people in similar situations did in those days. He enrolled at the Calgary Business College, studying Business Administration under the Canadian Vocational Training Program.

This was probably the last ordinary thing Ralph Klein ever did, at least in terms of career moves. For reasons that remain unclear, he was offered a job as a teacher at the college as soon as he graduated. Shortly thereafter he became the principal. For many people with such a modest background, this would have been the pinnacle of their career, but not for Klein. After only three years, he was restless and began looking for other opportunities.

With virtually no relevant experience, he applied for and was hired — largely on the strength of his personality — as the new Director of Public Relations for the Southern Alberta Division of the Red Cross. After a stint there he moved again, to the Calgary United Appeal. There are many anecdotes about his lack of experience and need for a remedial writing course in a job where writing press releases was a key function. Nevertheless, he succeeded, in part because he was a quick study but primarily because of his powers of persuasion and his outgoing personality.

In both of these positions, he came into contact with most of the elites of Calgary. He forged a number of important relationships that would stand him in good stead once he launched his political career. He also developed the primitive roots of his political philosophy while working for these charities. The phrase "Have some fun, do some good" became his personal as well as his fundraising motto. People who knew him then also say that his unconventional work habits (including perennial tardiness, missed meetings and problem drinking) were already well established, but generally tolerated because of his successes.

Six years in the charity business were apparently too much for the ever-restless Klein, who moved on once again. Although his reputation as a public-relations expert would have led logically to a number of attractive options in the business community, he rejected that route out of hand and chose, once again, to do the unexpected. Taking a pay cut and starting from the bottom, he launched himself into journalism, another career for which he had no obvious preparation. This time, however, he made a concession to his limited writing skills and chose a career as a television reporter for a local Calgary station.

Once again an instant success, he was widely respected for his dedicated, innovative and insightful documentary style. For several years Klein covered the city beat, including the civic government, and became an expert on municipal issues and affairs. As usual, his methods were unconventional. His "office" was the beer hall in the working-class St. Louis Hotel. His primary sources were the underclass of the city — the destitute, bikers, prostitutes, drug addicts, urban aboriginals and the homeless — and his stories reflected an innate concern for these outcasts of society and their various problems. (Another of his sources was Klein himself. City officials were frequently chagrined to find Klein reporting on plans or developments which had not been made public. They suspected a leak among staff at City Hall until one day Klein was discovered eavesdropping in a ventilation shaft leading to Council Chambers.)

In 1977, Klein's connections with urban aboriginals helped him land an assignment producing a television documentary on the Blackfoot, to mark the hundredth anniversary of the signing of Treaty 7. In typically unconventional fashion, he chose to spend weeks living with his subjects on their reserve south of Calgary. He also spent a night in the nearby Gleichen jail, for drunk-and-disorderly behaviour, after a fight in a local beer hall. This development appeared to surprise neither Klein's employers nor his colleagues, who by now were accustomed to his frequent disappearances and missed appointments. Even under the steadying influence of his second wife, his drinking continued to be a problem. He was once arrested for impaired driving and later got into a fight with jail guards. But there were no consequences for his career. As a senior reporter, he was basically unsupervised; as long as he produced good material, no one much cared how he did it, a situation which obviously suited Klein's temperament perfectly.

Not only was the finished product of his Blackfoot sojourn one of his finest efforts, but his experience there apparently changed his life. He learned to speak the language, made many friends, and adopted much of the Blackfoot religion, which he still practises to this day. A ceremonial bundle of dried sweetgrass sits in his office in Edmonton and accompanies him on foreign travels. As mayor of Calgary, he once refused to attend an Olympic organizing event in Montreal without his Blackfoot friends, whom he had already invited. ("No Blackfoot, no Mayor" was the curt message he sent to horrified officials, who quickly changed their minds and made the necessary arrangements.)

Most important for his future career path, his experience on the reserve led Klein to become an activist rather than an impartial observer. He began to write about municipal affairs from a much more critical perspective, contributing a monthly column called "The City" to *Calgary Magazine.* He took positions on a number of contentious issues, and became known in the community as a spokesperson for the concerns of ordinary people, the underdog and the taxpayer in their fights against city hall, big business and the developers. Among his more well-known crusades were the fight to save a historic working-class district from "blockbusting" and the wrecker's ball, his campaign to oppose the construction of a transitway extension through a well-established suburban community, and his opposition to a major new civic complex designed to enhance Calgary's "world class" image in support of its bid for the Olympic Games.

All of these crusades became important rallying points for his supporters when an audacious Klein decided to run for the office of mayor of Calgary in 1980. The decision was a bold move for a number of reasons. Klein had no money, no office or workers, and little hope of obtaining any. Even more astonishing was the fact that he entered the campaign *after it had started.* One day he was a reporter covering the race, and the next day he was in it.

Not surprisingly, few people, including his employers or his own father, took him seriously when he announced he planned to throw his hat in the ring. Although his public announcement came late, though, his interest in the position had been growing for some time. His wife and a few close friends, including several who would form the nucleus of the now-famous "Klein Gang," had known of his interest since he seriously considered running for an aldermanic position in 1979.

In an interview shortly after the election, Klein told one reporter that his disgust with deal making and the way municipal politics were tilted in favour of the elites had been growing for some time. "It finally got to the point where I hated even going down to city hall," he told journalist Frank Dabbs.

The story of the mayoralty campaign is the story of Klein's career. He hesitated for a long time before finally making up his mind to enter the race. When he did, he was the underdog, the least likely or qualified of the candidates, but the voters decided they liked him anyway. They liked the man who said he hated to ask for votes because it was "cheap," and they liked the man who had almost no platform except a desire to make everyone feel good about Calgary. He thought people wanted an alternative to the "establishment" candidates, and he was right. His opponents dismissed his candidacy, totally underestimating the man and his determination to succeed once he had set his mind to something.

Several years later, at the start of the provincial election campaign in which he was again the underdog, his handlers scheduled a "Run with Ralph" event in Edmonton one Saturday morning. As Dabbs recounts in his biography of Klein, hardly anyone except his supporters showed up to jog around a track in the park with him, and almost all of them were faster than Klein. Paunchy and awkward, he nevertheless kept going, even after several people lapped him. In the end, slow but dogged, he was the only one left on the track. This graphic refusal to give up was evident from the beginning in Calgary, when his own father told him he was "crazy" to take on city hall. Although the polls indicated the incumbent, Ross Alger, "can lose only if he self-destructs," they failed to take into account what the local media came to call the "Ralph" factor. Building momentum after a slow start, putting together a small and unusual but intensely loyal group of supporters, including his future chief of staff, Rod Love, he steamed slowly but steadily towards the finish line and ended up far ahead of the two favourites. Ralph Klein, the maverick from Tuxedo Park, had become the mayor of Calgary at the age of thirty-seven.

Redneck Ralph

Ralph Klein's stint as mayor of Calgary provides important insights into the man who has become the darling of the neo-conservative movement in Canada. First and foremost, his record as mayor demonstrated that his political beliefs are pragmatic at best. Equally important, his nine years in office revealed many unfortunate character traits which have followed him to the premier's office, such as an explosive temper, unreliability and erratic public behaviour. Last but not least, his considerable ability to recruit supporters and inspire loyalty has meant that many of the colleagues and advisers who support Klein in Edmonton began their long association with him in Calgary, and their influence is considerable.

Ralph Klein was one of the most popular mayors in the history of Calgary. He was also the original proponent of the "Don't worry, be happy" school of political thought. Local reporter Ron Wood described Klein as "the perfect munchkin mayor, brought to power by rainbow dreamers and backfence schemers." Often called the "Happy Face" mayor, he spent his nine years in office being the city's public-relations man rather than its CEO, redefining the post as a political and social rather than administrative one. All the evidence suggests he truly believed his job was to represent the city by being in the public eye as much as possible, both at home with the electorate and when selling the city's merits abroad.

Apart from his many appearances at local events, Klein pioneered a new way of reaching the public — regularly scheduled radio and television "reports" from the mayor. Demonstrating what was to become his trademark skill at using the media to further his own ambitions, Klein became known as "The Master Communicator." As one observer put it, "It was an anti-politician's remedy for politics. Traditional politicians thought he was abdicating his responsibilities. He thought otherwise." More to the point, letting the bureaucrats manage things "fit in well with Klein's evolving conservatism; he distrusted interventionism and believed in the moral limits of politics."

His approach to the job was widely supported by the voters. It was also severely criticized in some quarters, and not just by the elites whom he had replaced. Many in the city's intellectual and cultural community were dismayed. First of all, there was considerable anxiety that he was leaving far too much discretion to the bureaucrats. How would future mayors ever regain control of the reins of power from the bureaucrats once Klein had let them run the show for so long?

There was no question Klein did not consider administrative matters to be his responsibility. At first he avoided the day-to-day operations as much as possible because he was intimidated by the expertise of the bureaucrats. Then, too, there was his well-known aversion to meetings, his inability to keep appointments and arrive on time for scheduled events. But he was also reassured that he could leave administration to the bureaucrats because he developed a close and extremely positive working relationship with his chief commissioner, George Cornish, a man who was the polar opposite of Klein. Competent, efficient and knowledgeable, Cornish not only ran the show in Calgary, but eventually followed Klein to Edmonton.

There was another reason the elites disliked Klein. Put simply, they felt he was a buffoon. At a time when Calgary was trying to make its mark on the national and international stage, they were appalled at the image Klein presented. The man many referred to disparagingly as "Hizzonor" often drank too much at public events. Once he was found by a reporter on his hands and knees in the parking lot of city hall in the early morning, apparently looking for his car keys, a sight that did not inspire them with confidence. Although he amazed everyone by making friends with the redoubtable Juan Antonio Samaranch, president of the International Olympic Committee, and appearing to fit in well with Europe's elites during the run-up to Calgary's successful bid for the 1988 Olympics, he also managed to display the kind of naïveté they found so embarrassing. For many, his request to the King of Norway to fetch his car at the end of a social function was less humiliating than his subsequent and apparently sincere explanation that the monarch's military uniform looked like ones the doormen in Calgary wore.

Klein gave his critics more substantial ammunition in January 1982, just two months after he had won some grudging respect from them for his role in securing the Winter Games for the city. At a dinner meeting of the Calgary Newcomers' Club, where people expected the upbeat "city booster" address he had patented, the mayor suddenly launched into a diatribe against "Eastern bums and creeps" who were ruining the city. He blamed them for the rising crime rate, the high unemployment levels and the extra costs to the city's welfare rolls, and then declared they were not welcome any more. Admitting he was "a bit of a redneck," the mayor then promised to "kick ass of the bad hombres," even if he had to "put them all in jail one on top of another." Delivering the *coup de grâce* to his pre-election image as the people's mayor and the friend of the disadvantaged, he concluded: "It might sound elitist, but

we want highly skilled people, educated people, people with technological skills."

The speech drew widespread and unflattering national attention.
Klein's picture appeared on the cover of *Alberta Report* with the caption
"Redneck Ralph." Federal minister John Crosbie called Klein a "bum"
who had "made an ass of himself." Mayor Mel Lastman of North York
called Klein a "bigot" who "wouldn't make it here [suburban Toronto]
as an alderman or school trustee." Former Supreme Court justice Willard
Estey dismissed Klein as a "nothing" who would be forgotten in ten years.

Across the country the reaction was negative and visceral, yet Klein
managed to turn this public-relations disaster into a huge success for
himself and the city. After a curt apology of sorts the next day, he went
on the attack. He used the publicity generated by his remarks to tour the
country, making speeches in all the right places. Although he continued
to maintain that his remarks were taken out of context and overstated,
he also used another highly successful technique to diffuse the anger. In
what was to become a trademark political tactic in times of trouble,
Ralph Klein simply admitted his mistake, saying "So what? I'm human."

It worked. By the end of his tour, Klein had not only sold Calgary to
the rest of the country as a great city, but charmed the pants off most
Canadians outside Alberta and established himself as a national figure.
Meanwhile, back in Calgary his popularity ratings had soared. As his
executive assistant, Rod Love, told reporters, the mail and calls to the
mayor's office were running eight to one in favour of Klein. When local
alderman Brian Lee accused Klein of being a racist, Klein simply
dismissed him as "a hoser." (A few years later, however, Klein was instrumental in assuring Lee's political demise.) One local entrepreneur started
a rage for bumper stickers that read "I'm a Redneck and proud of it!"
Klein had clearly touched a nerve. The anxiety of middle-class moderates
about their standard of living and their personal safety was felt first in
Calgary, although it would eventually spread to the drawing rooms of
polite society, even in sophisticated Ontario.

If Calgarians loved him despite his foibles and personal failings, they
also forgave him much in terms of his record. In fact, an objective evaluation of Klein's record as mayor leaves the outsider mystified as to what
it was that made him perennially popular. Not only did Klein renege on

several of his pre-mayoralty positions in short order after taking office, but he failed to do anything of much significance on his own initiative.

Having campaigned on an anti-development, "people first" platform, Klein quickly changed his tune once the realities of political decision-making were explained to him. The new civic centre adjoining the city hall was a classic example. Proposed by outgoing mayor Ross Alger and vociferously opposed by Klein during the campaign, it was, as several people pointed out, simply too far advanced to be cancelled. Millions of tax dollars had already been spent, and legal commitments made. Besides, the need for additional office space was undeniable. Only someone as naïve and unfamiliar with the decision-making process and bureaucratic procedures would have thought otherwise.

Klein's solution to this dilemma was to say little and let the issue die. He used the same approach on the proposed Olympic Plaza for the Winter Games, another "extravagance" he had opposed. In both cases the projects took several years to complete. By the time they were ready, almost everyone had forgotten his objections and he basked in the reflected glory of their openings. A similar situation developed with the proposed Saddledome arena. Klein actually accused opponents of this plan of being "misguided academics" and community "activists," apparently forgetting who had elected him, but in the end everyone loved the result and forgot the tirades.

An even more challenging political problem faced Klein on the issue of the light rail transit expansion to the northwest of the city. Having once indicated the route would go through the inner city community of Sunnyside over his dead body, and having received substantial electoral support from that community, he found himself in a quandary when officials explained the necessity of the expansion and the lack of other viable routes. The residents of Sunnyside were not going to forget *that* commitment. Work began instead on the northeast line, while Klein pondered his options. Despite the rational arguments of the bureaucrats, everyone knew the mayor had the power to veto the line if he chose. Would he dare to do it?

In the end Klein was "saved" by the Olympics. Once the city received the green light for the games, opposition to the northwest line somehow came to be viewed as selfish and almost unpatriotic. Klein soon began describing the project as inevitable, and a "soft" intrusion into the community that would have few negative consequences. The people of Sunnyside never knew what hit them. As journalist Frank Dabbs commented, Klein perfected a technique in which he "massaged public opinion in his radio talk shows and public appearances until it was favourable, then emerged, grinning, to cut the ribbon."

Naïve? Pragmatic? Opportunistic? At least one close observer of the Calgary scene concluded that "the Sunnyside flip-flop signaled Ralph the outsider would belong to no political hierarchy but his own ... This was also the first indication that, although he could be innovative and progressive, he was not the liberal many had assumed him to be." This lesson was not learned by either federal or provincial Liberals, however, who persisted in courting Klein in 1988 — either to lead the provincial party or to run as a federal candidate in Calgary.

Apparently they were misled by his support for another "outsider," Sheldon Chumir, a close friend whom he helped win a seat in the provincial legislature as a Liberal. What the Liberals failed to understand was that this was a personal matter for Klein, not a political one. Not only was he pleased to help his friend, but he was even more delighted to work for the defeat of an archrival. Chumir's opponent, Brian Lee, was the same former municipal politician and Ross Alger protégé who had spent years attempting to unseat Klein and make his life miserable before moving on to provincial politics. This time he was vulnerable, and Klein was going to make him pay. (To this day federal Liberals complain that Klein led them on until the last minute, appearing to consider their proposal before finally informing them curtly that it was not on. Many recall Liberal senator Joyce Fairbairn, a co-chair of the Liberals' Election Readiness Committee, confidently assuring them Klein was likely to come on board "any day now.")

Another factor that saved Ralph Klein's reputation as mayor was the dramatic downturn in the provincial economy. With no money available to do significant things and all eyes focused on Edmonton anyway, Klein could continue to boost the city in public, on his radio programs and in places like Hong Kong, where he travelled to encourage Asian markets to view his city as part of the Asia–Pacific Rim. He did it well, and no one expected him to do much else.

During the 1986 mayoralty campaign, some critics did complain about his lack of action on a number of important issues. Others were upset over a pension plan the mayor and councillors had set up for themselves earlier. Klein ignored the optics of spending during hard times and dismissed the criticism out of hand, telling reporters, "The amount of money we're talking here is a fluff in the wind." A local businessman hired a plane to carry an aerial ad across Calgary saying "Ralph, We Love U Just the Way You Are." Apparently most people agreed. Klein won the election, taking 90 per cent of the popular vote.

Eventually the Winter Olympics came and went, with Klein indelibly etched in people's minds as the affable host. Having been mayor for eight years, he found that the restless urge was returning with a vengeance. What could he possibly do to top his Olympic performance? The answer, after much deliberation as usual, was to move on to provincial politics — but as a Conservative, not a Liberal.

A New Conservative

According to the maverick from Tuxedo Park, he never tried to lead anyone on. It just took him a while to figure out where his natural political home was. One day he came to the conclusion that he was simply not a Liberal. His fundamental belief in self-reliance and personal responsibility was the real reason he rejected offers from the federal and provincial Liberals, and eventually accepted an offer from Premier Don Getty to run in Calgary as a Conservative in the 1989 provincial election. This may well be true, but it is difficult to ignore the fact that the provincial Liberals were, in the words of one of their own supporters, "in such a mess even Ralph couldn't have turned them around," while the federal Liberals were as likely to win a seat in Calgary as Klein was to win a beauty pageant.

It is even harder to ignore the fact that Klein also turned down Brian Mulroney, who had earlier offered him a cabinet seat if he would run for the *federal* Conservatives. Although Mulroney's government was returned with a second mandate in 1988, they were much less popular in Alberta than they had been in 1984, and the Reform Party was just on the horizon. Whether Klein could sense the impending Conservative disaster of 1993, or realized he would be out of his depth in federal politics, or whether he simply listened to his wife when she told him there would be no five-hour weekly commutes in *her* future, he bided his time.

Then, in November 1988, he was approached by a beleaguered Don Getty, who had been in political difficulties almost since the day he took over from Peter Lougheed. This initiative was somewhat surprising, since there had never been any love lost between Klein and Lougheed, and Getty was, after all, Lougheed's hand-picked successor. Nor did the two men appear to have much in common. More to the point, Getty was leery of recruiting someone with such an obvious power base who could prove a challenge to his own leadership. But, after an initial meeting with Getty, and a subsequent meeting between the two men accompanied by their wives — a meeting Klein had insisted on, which apparently impressed Getty, the devout family man — the die was cast.

Having been reassured by many friends and supporters that leaving office in mid-term would not prove a political *faux pas*, Klein announced his departure as mayor on January 10, 1989. Since his political future had been the subject of media speculation for months, this came as no surprise. His decision to run in the riding of Calgary–Elbow *was* a surprise, as this was an upper-middle-class riding with little connection to his past. It was also far from the safest Conservative seat in Calgary. Klein had little choice, however, since it was the only one available.

Unlike most other Calgary MLAs, who were intent on staying in power and eventually trying for the leadership, the incumbent in Calgary–Elbow, David Russell, was not seeking re-election. Officially this was because he wanted to return to the private sector while he was still young enough to resume his law career and build a nest egg. Insiders believed it was also because Russell, who had served in cabinet under Lougheed, felt the Getty government was moving too far to the right and was uncomfortable with several of their positions. The events of the next few years reinforced Russell's belief that he had made the correct decision, as Ralph Klein proceeded to take control of the good ship Tory and make a hard right turn into uncharted waters.

Although Klein had the support of the Getty machine and his own riding association, it would be an understatement to say his candidacy appalled many in the party. Some felt he was simply not cabinet material, or even a respectable backbencher. Others bitterly resented the fact he was likely to start at the top if elected, receiving a cabinet post without having spent any time on the backbenches or in the trenches for the party. There were also many who believed Klein was not really a Conservative at all, just an opportunist. In the riding, many long-time Tories were reluctant to work for him or support him, and the outcome was not at all certain. During the campaign there were many occasions on which Klein avoided the standard canvassing techniques and face-to-face encounters for fear of running into traditional Conservatives, not Liberals or NDPers.

Nevertheless, when the dust settled after the 1989 election, Klein was the MLA from Calgary–Elbow and the Conservatives under Getty were back in power, albeit with a reduced majority. Although the premier himself had been embarrassed by losing his own seat, he was quickly elected in a by-election in the rock-solid Conservative riding of Stettler.

Almost immediately, Klein was named Minister of the Environment, an appointment many of his enemies in caucus thought would be the graveyard of his ambitions. In Alberta, Environment ministers often suffered the same fate as federal Finance ministers, a situation which pleased a number of his more ambitious colleagues who were already planning their leadership campaigns in anticipation of Getty's departure.

They were surprised on two fronts. Getty did not leave, and Klein did not fall flat on his face despite their predictions. In fact the new Environment minister, whom many reporters called "the lovable lout," proved far more adept than they expected at juggling the competing claims of the resource sector and the environmentalists. On the one hand, his populist tendencies stood him in good stead with the activists. He opened up the environmental-assessment process to public scrutiny and made a point of visiting various controversial companies or projects himself. The Procter & Gamble toxic-effluent case and the Alberta–Pacific pulp mill problem in the northern part of the province were classic examples of his ability to make personal contact and also to be firm when necessary. Many activists still recognize his contribution in getting environmental-assessment legislation passed and then setting up the Natural Resources Conservation Board, a new super regulatory unit that evaluates all projects except those relating to the oil and gas industry.

On the other hand, he also insisted on promoting some projects of the resource-based industries — epitomized by his staunch defence of the Oldman Dam project — which he viewed as necessary for agricultural interests, and almost always came down on the side of the developer in any prolonged and difficult conflict. But no one seemed to notice when, despite the openness and apparent consultation, the results usually favoured industry.

Shades of the old Ralph Klein appeared now and then along the way, but no one seemed to care about that either. He basically handled himself well and was often described by his bureaucrats as one of the best ministers they ever had — largely because of the intensity of his engagement on the issues and his ability to absorb huge amounts of material quickly and effortlessly. But his drinking continued to be an issue and he still behaved outrageously on occasion.

One such occasion was the big meeting in Athabaska to announce that the Alberta–Pacific mill would be allowed to proceed, albeit with some changes in technology insisted on by Klein to make it more environmentally friendly. Sitting on the platform beside the premier and several other cabinet colleagues, Klein was basking in the limelight, having pulled off this tricky compromise. When an environmental protester in the audience called the compromise a cop-out and gave the dignitaries the finger, Klein blew a fuse. He returned the gesture, a look of pure fury on his face. The moment was captured on film and shown around the province in print and broadcast media for days, but seemed to have absolutely no effect on Klein's image.

Another Klein tantrum, somewhat less public but equally surprising occurred at a dinner in Calgary where the Environment minister was seated at a table with the CEO of Nova Corporation, Bob Blair. Blair, a well-known Liberal who eventually ran unsuccessfully for the party federally, was astonished to find himself the recipient of a blistering and relentless attack over his Liberal ties. An inebriated Klein questioned Blair's credentials as a true Albertan, implying the Conservatives were the only party who could represent the province's best interests. Before things deteriorated further, his visibly embarrassed wife convinced Klein to call it a night and leave. The remaining guests, meanwhile, marvelled at the fierce partisanship of a man who only a few years earlier had not been sure which party he should join.

Despite these occasional lapses, his reputation and media coverage were extremely positive. For many, the fact that this Environment minister was much less close-minded than his predecessors, and not as obviously supportive of the resource sector, was sufficient to make him appear more progressive and reasonable than would otherwise have been the case.

In the three and a half years he handled the Environment portfolio, Klein managed to stay out of political trouble and away from party infighting. This was no mean feat. With each passing year the troubles of the Getty government had multiplied. The megaprojects of the Lougheed years came back to haunt them as the economy worsened, and a number of scandals took the remaining sheen off the Conservative veneer. Albertans were fed up, and Don Getty and his friends were the targets of both justified and completely unfounded anger. The "Getty must go" movement inside the party was becoming mutinous, but Klein kept himself above the fray.

Then, just as many insiders began to fear that Don Getty was never going to resign, the premier finally announced in September 1992 that he was stepping down. The announcement came as a shock to most Albertans, including Getty's own caucus, coming as it did in the middle of the Charlottetown Accord debate. Since Getty had been one of the prominent participants in Brian Mulroney's last-ditch effort, there had been an expectation he would defend it to the end. Of course, he continued to peddle the accord, but as a "lame duck" premier his credibility was severely restricted.

Getty had left it very late. The party was in complete disarray. Money was scarce, fundraising was a disaster and memberships were at an all-time low. The Conservatives were now at an abysmal 18 per cent in the polls. The Liberals under Laurence Decore looked like a sure thing, while the man or woman who eventually succeeded Getty looked like a sure bet to be the next Harry Strom.

Klein managed to avoid the whole debate over Getty, just as he managed to have none of the NovAtel or Principal scandals rub off on him. Some began to think of him as a Teflon man, just like Ronald Reagan. This did not mean he had no interest in the outcome, however. Rod Love, now Klein's assistant in Edmonton, had been checking out support. As one commentator put it, "Ralph was off doing other things. NovAtel did not touch him any more than the pay and perks uproar or the constitution had. He was in charge of an ambitious plan to rewrite Alberta's environment laws. He was also busy accepting speaking engagements all over the province."

Leadership Lessons

As usual, Klein was dithering about whether to throw his hat in the ring. Once again he had no money and no organization. But he had supporters. The "Klein Gang" in Calgary wanted to use their talents to get him elected leader, just as they had helped him win the mayoralty. Almost the entire group of rural caucus members wanted him to put his name forward. So did four of the oldest and longest-serving cabinet ministers, whose roots were in rural and northern Alberta: Ken Kowalski, Peter Trynchy, Ernie Eisley, and former federal MP Peter Elzinga, a disillusioned Mulroney refugee who was serving at the time as Minister of Economic Development.

Opposed to Klein were the younger, more sophisticated and urban caucus members, represented by cabinet ministers Nancy Betkowski and Rick Orman. Getty, meanwhile, had become disenchanted with Klein and his lifestyle, and Klein knew he could not count on any kind of endorsement from him even if it would have been useful. Nor was he supported by Peter Lougheed, whose wife and children were openly campaigning for the traditional Tories who wanted to return to the more progressive brand of conservatism Lougheed had patented. As commentator Mark Lisac put it, the younger caucus members believed that "the cure was to restore the style and the politics of the Lougheed years ... they were socially and politically correct and they had the support of the federal Progressive Conservative establishment in the province. They rejected Klein's politics, feared his power and held him in personal contempt."

With virtually all of the old guard and traditional Conservatives against him, Klein should have given up before he started. But he saw an opening. The most important factor leading to Ralph Klein's eventual success in the leadership race was the party's fateful decision to switch from the traditional delegate-selection and convention format to one in which the leadership was decided by the vote of every member of the party. The move, a misguided attempt to appear more transparent and accountable, was born of a desperation to break the symbolic link with the Getty government and the past.

This "direct vote" process was, naturally, open to various kinds of manipulation, as instant Tories emerged from the woodwork for the $5 price of their membership. More to the point, it allowed countless rural Tories and newcomers to cast an equal ballot with the elites who would have dominated a traditional delegate-based convention. Klein himself told his father, "With an open vote I have a chance." Otherwise, he believed, "the old guard would have simply put in one of their own."

Nine days after Getty announced he was stepping down, Klein took the plunge. It soon became apparent he would be the candidate who benefited most from the changed selection process, since rural Albertans were most easily mobilized and would have a disproportionate effect, despite their smaller numbers. Ernie Eisley and Don Sparrow — cabinet colleagues and supporters — had lined up nearly half of the caucus behind Klein as soon as the race was on, ensuring he would receive almost all of the rural votes to be had. His main opponent, Nancy Betkowski, was an urban Albertan with impressive credentials but no rapport with rural Alberta. Her strength, instead, was in middle-class Calgary and Edmonton. With the direct-vote format, however, this was not enough.

Klein toured the province and appeared in places like Grand Prairie, speaking about canola as if he knew what he was talking about, building up crucial support with the aid of his rural caucus colleagues — people like Walter Paszkowski and Ken Kowalski, who would later find a place at Klein's cabinet table.

In the end it was a two-way race between Betkowski and Klein. The other serious candidates — cabinet ministers Rick Orman and Elaine McCoy — soon fell far behind. In a scenario that would be repeated in the federal Conservatives' leadership campaign nearly a decade later, the race deteriorated into a battle for old membership lists and on-the-ground support.

Betkowski offered a detailed three-year policy plan, while Klein basically refused to talk specifics. As political scientist David Stewart noted, Klein's stock in trade responses were populist phrases about solving problems by "bringing them back to the grassroots" and "using simple, down-to-earth thinking of ordinary people" rather than theories of intellectuals. Nevertheless, hints of the platform Klein would eventually impose on Albertans were evident in his broad support for user fees in medicare and cuts to the public service. He also made a number of spontaneous commitments to rural Albertans to increase spending on agricultural research and irrigation infrastructure. (No one seemed to notice the inherent contradiction of these latter promises, although they would later prove a headache for Klein's treasurer, Jim Dinning, to accommodate within his program of fiscal restraint.)

On the first ballot, Betkowski gave Klein a scare, winning by one vote. But her lead proved illusory. The second, run-off vote showed the first-ballot results were not really reflective of the candidates' overall support. On the second ballot, Klein won easily on the strength of his rural and Calgary support. This support, in turn, was the direct result of the new leadership-selection process. For the first time those eligible to vote were not necessarily supporters of the federal Conservatives. In fact, only 35 per cent of those who voted on the second ballot were members of *any* federal party, and fully 38 per cent of these were members of the Reform Party. For the 65 per cent who held no federal membership, more than half were estimated to be Reform supporters. Almost an equal number were "instant" Tories who had joined the party specifically to vote for a new leader — Klein. The party and its old-line progressive members had been hijacked by a far more radical group of outsiders.

The split between the old guard and the new vanguard of the Alberta Conservatives was evident in the backgrounds of those supporting Klein and Betkowski. Stewart found that Klein's supporters were overwhelmingly rural, low-income males who had not completed high school. Betkowski's supporters, by contrast, were most likely to be university-educated urban professionals. Her support also increased with income. While Klein's primary backers were ranchers and farmers, Betkowski's were most often administrators, health-care workers and students. The apppeal of the two candidates was so different precisely because, with the new procedure, their supporters more closely reflected the divide within

Alberta society as a whole, rather than traditional supporters of the Conservative party.

To no one's surprise, Klein and Betkowski never reached an understanding. At earlier meetings their hostility had been obvious and visceral. At the final meeting in Edmonton to hear the second-ballot results, many people were shocked when Klein turned to her and said, "Wasn't this fun, Nancy?" Although she said little in public, it seemed certain the woman who was Peter Lougheed's more natural successor did not find the remark amusing. Among other things, she had just endured several months of unfounded slurs and innuendo spread by anonymous Klein supporters among rural delegates concerning her alleged socialist leanings and support for lesbians. She demanded and eventually received a written apology from Klein for remarks he had made at one event, but there was no further bridge-building. Like most of the other unsuccessful candidates, she was unceremoniously dropped from the cabinet in favour of the rural caucus members who had supported him with such great effect. One reporter bluntly concluded, "Klein kneecapped anyone who had opposed him."

The leadership was decided on December 5, 1992. On December 12, Ralph Klein, the new premier of Alberta, took over the reins of power in a ceremony at the legislature that looked more like a New Year's Eve party than a staid political event. It also looked like an amateur theatrical production, as confusion reigned and there were a number of miscues. The actual swearing-in ceremony was delayed for more than an hour, apparently because of last-minute changes. When things finally got under way, Klein began introducing the wrong people for the wrong portfolios. At the reception afterwards, there were Indians in the foyer in ceremonial dress, and more people than anyone had expected, judging from the overflow. It was Open House at the Klein Corral.

Ralph to the Rescue

Starting the next day, Klein insisted the door to the premier's office be left open, too, so that everyone could see him working at his desk when they went by. Few could miss the signal Klein was sending out that he was an ordinary guy, and anyone could have his ear. His challenge in the next six months was to make people believe two things — first, that he and his team were reborn Conservatives, unconnected to Don Getty's administration, and, second, that they could handle Alberta's problems. The superficial but highly visible change in management style went a long way towards convincing people of the former, but the latter would be a harder sell.

Still, Klein had a lot more symbolic tricks up his sleeve, and he moved swiftly to implement them and put his own imprint on the government. Some of his tricks were strictly political. Although he and most of his people had been part of the Getty government for several years, he managed to pull the first rabbit out of his hat by firing sixteen ministers from the Getty era and reducing the size of the cabinet from twenty-six to seventeen. Getty's most prominent supporters were out, and Klein's people were in.

Two of Klein's people, Peter Elzinga and Ken Kowalski, were made deputy premiers. Unfortunately, it soon became apparent that neither of them was sufficiently familiar with parliamentary procedures and the business of running a government. There were often painful delays — reminiscent of the first year of the Mulroney government in Ottawa — when the newcomers were caught by surprise and had little idea what to do next. Nevertheless, they managed to hold the fort while their fearless leader toured the province, talking up support for his agenda in preparation for the coming election.

In order to keep the rest of his caucus on side and reward faithful rural supporters from the leadership race, Klein also streamlined the caucus committee system and appointed four of his own people as chairs, promising them real power over decision making. As Stan Schumacher, another disillusioned former federal MP who had returned to provincial politics, said of his own appointment, "I've waited all my political life to feel really comfortable. Now I feel comfortable. I've never had any influence. Now I have some influence."

Next, in order to make a clean break with the past, Klein specifically promised there would be no more NovAtel deals. No more secret deals between government and the private sector, period. (This was a pledge that would eventually come back to haunt him, as the Alberta Treasury Board scandals and the West Edmonton Mall fiasco unfolded in the summer of 1998, but at the time it served its purpose admirably. People believed "Ralph.") Last, but hardly least, Klein made sure his government implemented the planned restructuring of electoral boundaries that would provide greater clout for rural areas.

Then, knowing the Liberals had the advantage with the public on the question of financial competence, and acutely aware that his treasurer, Jim Dinning, would be bringing down a budget in the spring with more bad news on the deficit numbers, Klein decided to strike first. He cut the public service, including several deputy ministers and senior managers. He froze their pay. He put a freeze on government grants and contracts. Careful of his populist image, he also cut the salaries of ministers. When someone asked him why he was doing this in spite of earlier promises that reductions in government spending could be accomplished without such painful cuts, and wasn't he breaking campaign commitments, he answered, "That was then, this is now." If anyone thought this reply strange, they refrained from saying so.

The next rabbit out of Klein's bag of tricks came as a surprise to the government caucus. The premier was opening up the policy process to public consultation. He sensed that most Albertans knew the fiscal situation was bad; they wanted to take their medicine and get it over with. Klein decided it would be easier to sell the inevitable cuts to government programs if it looked as if the decisions on *what* to cut and how *fast* to do so came from the grassroots. As a result the new premier announced there would be a new process — a public "round table" on the Budget — to be held at the end of March in Red Deer.

The event was a huge public-relations success despite the obvious gimmickry. Critics noted the government-invited participants were blatantly unrepresentative, coming overwhelmingly from the business and professional categories, but this did not seem to diminish its credibility. Klein himself did not arrive until the end and spoke only briefly to the participants, saying ingenuously, "This is the fulfilment of a campaign promise ... and I thank you very much for furthering my political agenda."

Predictably the participants said what Klein wanted to hear, and he and Dinning ran with it. More cuts, more frozen grants and no more loans. When a reporter asked Klein if he really thought this would help him win the next election, he looked him straight in the eye and unhesitatingly replied, "Yes, sir. You just watch."

Despite the swagger of Klein's gunslinger pose, few of the pundits believed him. They were sure the urban cowboy who had hijacked the Conservative party was doomed to be the next Harry Strom and succumb to the third man jinx. His clever political gestures had narrowed the gap, perhaps, but it was still too large. The party had no organization, and the Liberals were in fighting form. Ignoring their own philosophical roots in their eagerness to win, Decore's team had actually outflanked the Conservatives on the *right*. Although they began to realize that Klein was regaining some of his traditional support with his cuts and his budget smoke-and-mirrors, they were still not worried. They had another card up their sleeve as well.

As spring advanced, the Liberals sprang the issue of MLA pensions on the new premier, and he blinked. The public, and especially the middle class, were in no mood to hear about the sizable pensions the departing "Getty" Conservatives would receive at a time when their own fortunes were sinking. Klein's first response was to introduce legislation that would scale back the pensions effective after the next election. The Liberals gloated that this would not affect any of the twenty-nine departing Tories who were not seeking re-election, especially the former ministers in the Getty cabinet. Klein replied, quite correctly, that you could not change a plan's benefits retroactively. No one cared about the legal niceties, though, least of all the Decore Liberals, who hammered away at the issue in the legislature to great advantage for days on end.

The strain of the battle was obviously getting to Klein. When the unknown twenty-four-year-old head of the recently formed Alberta Taxpayers' Federation (ATF), Jason Kenney, challenged Klein with numbers on how much the pensions would cost the government in the long run, a "red-faced, spluttering and barely coherent" Klein lost control. He berated Kenney in the lobby of the legislature, where he had been speaking with reporters, accusing the federation of various heinous offences.

Many accounts of the ensuing internal caucus debate have been put forward by the various participants. What seems clear is that Klein eventually decided he could not sell his position, despite manly efforts on radio talk shows and in the legislature. Since he was also sure — unlike most people — that he could win the election if he could put this issue behind him, the matter was all the more critical. At some point he simply decided he was going to lose the election over the pension, and so he reversed himself. He apologized to the ATF and Kenney. Then he stated publicly that he was bowing to the will of the people. The patented Klein strategy of admitting a mistake and changing course was invoked once again.

Meanwhile, in caucus, full-scale internecine warfare broke out between the veteran MLAs and the newer members who had little or nothing to lose. Compromise proved impossible. In the end Klein astonished everyone by not only scaling back the benefits of those leaving, but cancelling the entire MLA pension plan for the future. As he stressed to the media when he emerged, "No ifs, no ands, no buts, NO PENSIONS!"

It may be that Klein could not have won the election without taking such a drastic step. Certainly the Liberals were dismayed, believing they had lost their best issue. Critics, however, argued that Klein had thrown the baby out with the bathwater and set a dangerous precedent. (They were proven right. In years to come, governments across Canada would be urged by right-wing legislators and the Canadian Taxpayers' Federation to "do the right thing" and follow the Alberta government's example. Ironically, this was occurring just as the Reform Party was confronting its own pension crisis, with many of its MPs believing their position had been too hastily conceived.) In any event, the importance of one issue in an election campaign is always difficult to judge, let alone in one where the governing party is returned with a majority after receiving the last rites from the pundits.

In the end it was hardly a contest. It was hardly a typical election either. It became a fight among the Liberals, the NDP and "Ralph." The Conservatives were nowhere to be found on the campaign signs. In an effort to wipe the Getty years out of the voters' memories, there were only signs with Ralph Klein's picture on them. Underneath his photo it said simply: "He Listens. He Cares." The same approach prevailed throughout the campaign. In the televised debate, Klein repeatedly ignored NDP leader Ray Martin's demands that he be specific about cuts to programs. Instead, he turned and faced the cameras. In a move reminiscent of Ronald Reagan at the top of his game, Klein concluded by saying "This is all about trust, folks." Just like Reagan, he then promised the impossible. He would reduce the deficit without reducing spending on core programs in health care or education, or raising taxes. "That, folks, is what you have been saying you want, and that is what we are committed to delivering to you."

And so Klein accomplished the "miracle on the prairies" that Edmonton reporter Mark Lisac had believed impossible. "Ralph" broke the third man jinx and gave the Conservatives another majority government. Not that it was a huge one. They cleaned up in Calgary and in the rural ridings, but they also lost big in Edmonton, where the public service cuts were huge and the unemployment lines were long. It was actually their worst showing since 1971. Yet the Conservatives took fifty-one of the eighty-two seats in the legislature, despite having only 44 per cent of the popular vote. The rural ridings had put Klein over the top with a vengeance.

Now that he had the credibility of an election win under his belt, Klein knew he would have to get down to the real business of government and he also knew he needed help. On the one hand, he needed someone to help him stay on track and keep his supporters in line. On the other hand, the man who once suggested holding bingo games to pay down the province's $47-million debt knew he needed another George Cornish to help him deliver on his promises. Luckily, he knew just where to turn for both.

The Klein Gang

Ralph Klein is no Peter Lougheed, so it came as no surprise to those who knew him well when he brought Rod Love along with him to Edmonton. The former waiter and college drop-out had been insepara-ble from Klein since the beginning of his political career, and no tech-nocrat could replace him. A self-confessed political junkie who cheerfully admitted he was neither an administrator nor a policy expert, Love has been described by many people as the premier's best friend, his alter ego and his closest confidant, after his wife. He has also been referred to as Klein's "minder" and "the enforcer," the bad cop in the twosome's management routine.

Love's influence on Klein was considered so significant that his departure from the premier's office in January 1998 immediately led to province-wide speculation the premier himself was about to step down. One article in the *Calgary Herald* opined that Love's departure would leave Klein "like Wayne without Shuster, Fred Astaire without Ginger Rogers, or — perhaps most germanely — Capt. Kirk without Mr. Spock."

Klein himself handled the announcement of Love's departure with untypical emotion. "Rod and I have been much more than colleagues," he said. "We have been very close friends and I look upon him somewhat as a brother," he continued, pointing out that Love had said he would still like to run the next provincial election for the Conservatives. "He has been a tremendous adviser, particularly as it relates to political strategy, and I am delighted that his advice and counsel will still be available to me."

Although Social Services minister Lyle Oberg referred to Love's departure as "a tragedy," not everyone was sorry to see him go. The man described by Klein biographer Frank Dabbs as "Ralph's air traffic controller, part minder, part gatekeeper, part valet" had managed to trample on several toes and a number of egos during the six years he spent as the premier's executive director. Tall and lanky, with a trademark handlebar moustache, Love was always intimidating. Some would describe him as a bully. Frustrated Tory MLAs knew he often failed to return their calls or pass on their messages. He once came to blows with a furious Jon Havelock, the current Justice minister, over his refusal to meet with Havelock when he was still in the backbenches. Known to party hard and often travel with the premier on vacation, Love was also viewed by some as more interested in the perks of power than in politics or policy.

This was generally a mistake. Like Klein, Love had an instinctive feel for the nuts and bolts of politics, and was frequently the mastermind behind strategic victories, as Klein himself acknowledged. It is widely believed Love was the one who talked Klein into reversing his position on the pension, a move that arguably won the 1993 election for the Conservatives.

Having tried and failed twice to make the transition to elected office, however, Love was apparently beginning to consider his financial future.

After seventeen years with Klein, his departure at the age of forty-four for the private sector was inevitable, as the demands of a growing family and the lack of financial security took precedence. Interestingly, his departure, while certainly a blow for Klein, paved the way for the return to the centre of power of another long-time Klein booster — former federal MP, party president, Klein leadership organizer and deputy premier Peter Elzinga.

Apart from his demonstrated loyalty to Klein over the years, the reasons for the selection of Elzinga to replace Love were apparent from the comments of the premier and those of his newly appointed adviser. For Klein, it was an attempt to build bridges with Edmonton voters and the local government, having been accused for years of overlooking them in favour of his native Calgary, and even of punishing them for their failure to support his team. "Peter has a very high profile in the Edmonton area and I think it will be good for Edmonton," said the premier, whose embarrassing lack of caucus members and ministers from the capital city was becoming more glaring all the time.

For Elzinga, the emphasis was different but equally revealing. "I think I can bring an administrative skill to the office," he offered, when asked why he would leave the private sector. He had been out of active politics since his voluntary retirement in 1993, but had kept his oar in by helping organize the Edmonton area for the 1997 election. "Plus I look forward to working with the premier," Elzinga added, echoing Klein's comment that "Peter's a person I trust."

The people Ralph Klein trusts has always been an issue. There are those who believe he is not the best judge of character, but if he likes someone he will stick with that person through thick and thin. Loyalty is an important component of Klein's make-up. More to the point, he is highly averse to making unpleasant decisions affecting those he likes or trusts. This was the case in Calgary, where even disputes between Love and the mayor's appointments secretary were the source of considerable anxiety for him. "Why can't everyone just get along?" was reportedly one of Klein's favourite sayings.

This was also his initial reaction when two of his leadership supporters, Ken Kowalski and Peter Trynchy, became an embarrassment in their cabinet roles just as he was trying to put forward his new right-wing agenda. The root problem was a clash of cultures and generations. Both men were old-school politicians accustomed to the perks of power, and both expected to have control of patronage appointments in their areas, a definite problem in the new era of transparency and accountability Klein was attempting to usher in, at least in terms of appearances.

In Trynchy's case, the public revelations of an imprudent letter to Kowalski describing how they could split the patronage positions in their ridings, and his hiring of a government contractor to pave his driveway, were too much for Klein to ignore. "Pavement Pete" was gone. Kowalski was another matter. Although the former high-school principal committed highly publicized and politically incorrect *faux pas* on a regular basis, it was internal party problems that finally forced Klein to take action. As a veteran MLA, Kowalski apparently believed he deserved respect from almost everyone else in the system. Not only did Kowalski treat the legislature in an arrogant fashion, but he increasingly abused his authority as deputy premier, making many enemies in caucus and the premier's office. Nevertheless, Klein was extremely reluctant to discipline or penalize his deputy. Although this was primarily because of the loyalty issue, Klein also recognized that he was able to travel around the province — acting as his own public-relations agent — only because he could trust Kowalski to take care of business back in Edmonton.

The open warfare among Rod Love, the other members of the so-called Klein Gang and Kowalski was another problem. Klein's "Why can't everyone just get along?" line failed to do the trick. At one point Klein even arranged a meeting between the Gang and Kowalski — an affair which was cordial but not warm and fuzzy — but little was accomplished in terms of mending fences, except for a temporary truce.

Eventually Kowalski's refusal to give up his control over the proposed Alberta Economic Development Authority proved to be the final straw. As Minister of Economic Development and Tourism, the deputy premier felt the new agency should be an advisory body and report to him. Klein felt it must be independent to have credibility. In the end, Klein asked for and received Kowalski's resignation, but with the promise he would be chair of the Alberta Energy and Utilities Board, a plum patronage appointment. When news of this deal reached the legislature, however, the Decore Liberals jumped on it immediately. They correctly claimed that the minister could not legally accept such a position for at least six months after leaving cabinet. When a report from the provincial Ethics commissioner confirmed the obvious, Klein was obliged to admit he had made a mistake and Kowalski was obliged to return to the backbenches. A visibly uncomfortable Klein had been forced to play the bad cop for once, a scenario he most often left to Rod Love.

Although Klein's handling of the whole affair left much to be desired, what was most interesting about the firing of Kowalski was the role played by the Klein Gang. As Klein biographer Frank Dabbs has outlined, although the public reasons for the deputy premier's dismissal were clear and sufficient, a power struggle was also going on behind the scenes between the Gang and Kowalski. The Gang believed the deputy premier was exercising far too much power over *Klein*, let alone over the government. Certainly Kowalski was unwilling to delegate or share power, either with Rod Love or, more important from his perspective, with a number of unelected advisers in Calgary. The results speak for themselves. Although Klein took the final decision, it was clear to insiders that Kowalski had lost his battle with the Gang.

Since all of the other members of the Klein Gang are unelected and outside the legislative ambit, and their advice is provided in informal settings, it is difficult to evaluate their overall influence. The inside view is that it is formidable. Their influence is also viewed with dismay by many in the premier's cabinet, and outright horror by the "misguided academics" and traditional progressives in the Conservative elite that Klein disdains. Certainly the situation is unusual. While all leaders surround themselves with trusted advisers, few if any have relied so heavily on a brain trust outside the legislature and, indeed, outside the capital city. Even Mike Harris, another new-style leader lacking the usual preparation for public office, has placed most of his key advisers within the premier's office or related agencies at Queen's Park.

Who are some of these driving forces behind the Klein revolution? According to several insiders, at any given time there have never been more than ten or twelve members in the Gang's inner sanctum, a close-knit, eclectic group of individuals who have been with "Ralph" since the early days. Then there are a few additional players on the margins who come and go with each of his career moves. Given Klein's populist image and humble roots, it is interesting to note that long-time members of the Gang are some of the most important figures in the Alberta establishment. Predictably, almost all of them are in the energy business, almost all of them live in Calgary, and almost all of them are men.

The list includes current or former CEOs of such venerable corporations as the Alberta Natural Gas Company, Amoco Petroleum, Canadian Hunter Exploration, SNC Lavalin's Calgary Oil and Gas section, and Peters & Company, a brokerage firm specializing in financing independent oil operations. It also includes a number of prominent lawyers, as well as some friends and campaign workers from the premier's early days in Tuxedo Park. Klein's riding president of many years, real estate developer Hal Walker, is another long-serving member of the group. Former Conservative MP Bobbie Sparrow, and Klein's Economic Development minister, Patricia Black, are apparently the only two women to have gained access to the inner circle, apart from early backers such as his original secretary in Calgary, Isabel Greyston. (Black, it should be noted, scored another victory for the Gang in the fall of 1997 when she succeeded in having MLA Judy Gordon — with whom she was involved in a vicious fight over control of gaming policy — removed unceremoniously from her post by Klein.)

In addition to the perceived influence of this group on specific policies or proposals of the government, several of the members have reportedly been influential in shaping the premier's thinking on a broader spectrum of issues. Norm Wagner, the former chair of Alberta Natural Gas, is also a former president of the University of Calgary. Along with James (Jim) Gray, of Canadian Hunter Exploration, he is reputed to have recommended a variety of neo-conservative authors to the novice premier as he formulated the fiscal-restraint policy that would make up the backbone of his government's re-election strategy and set him on the path to becoming a neo-conservative legend.

These writers included American economists Milton and Rose Friedman, whose *Tyranny of the Status Quo* promotes the same anti-government "cutbacks and tax breaks for the rich" theory espoused by Thatcher and Reagan. Attempting to explain why those two earlier attempts failed, the writers stress the importance of moving quickly in the early part of a mandate, a maxim Ralph Klein obviously took to heart. Other Wagner and Gray favourites included American management consultants David Osborne and Ted Gaebler, whose *Reinventing Government* was handed out by Gray to Klein and all the members of his cabinet. A third work recommended enthusiastically by Gray, *Unfinished Business* by Sir Roger Douglas of New Zealand, is credited with having provided the vocabulary of the Red Deer Budget round table. Terms such as "hit the wall" and "don't blink," for example, made their debut at this event, and have now passed into the common parlance of all Canadian neo-conservatives.

The example of a group of businessmen and industrialists having a significant influence on a political leader is not, of course, new. The Reagan era was not only a classic, but a highly visible case in point, in which several of the president's well-heeled friends and advisers ended up before the courts for a variety of conflict-of-interest and other financial misdemeanours, none of which, remarkably enough, rubbed off on the Teflon Man. In Canada, the broad circle of business friends and acquaintances whom Brian Mulroney often consulted was also well known, largely because of his own comments. Of course, Brian Mulroney was never the populist that Ralph Klein has projected himself to be, and his unabashed references to his close friendships with members of the corporate elite did not help his image either. His self-aggrandizing behaviour actually damaged the perception of policies of his government that might otherwise have been accepted, especially in Alberta. And, unlike Reagan, the scandals involving the business dealings of cabinet ministers and friends such as Sinclair Stevens, André Bissonnette and Michel Cogger took their toll on his reputation.

By contrast, most of the Gang's members are not only well known but highly regarded members of the small Alberta business community, and some, such as Jim Gray, have received numerous awards in recognition of their voluntary activities. The concern of some Albertans about the influence of the premier's Gang has not been about personal gain, but whether these individuals — with their backgrounds in industry and commerce — would be able to perceive the public interest. Or would they, instead, be inclined to view government as a business like any other? Yet most Albertans remain unconcerned. Having bought the populist approach, they have long felt this was "Ralph's" government, not a Conservative one, and certainly not one directed by the elites.

This popular perception was a lucky thing for Klein, not only because it allowed him to put forward the ideas of others, but also because it allowed a number of his inexperienced and unequipped cabinet ministers to shelter behind his image. As a result, several of them survived various pratfalls and miscues that would have finished a politician in most other provinces. The ineptitude and extremism of many in his first cabinet were still remarkable, though, especially after the Lougheed years.

The Cowboy Cabinet

In a scenario that would be repeated a few years later in Ontario, Ralph Klein's first caucus after the 1993 election contained far more rural members than before, and a large proportion of rookies. The reasons for these changes were the same in Ontario as they were in Alberta under Klein. The newcomers were the direct result of so many veterans leaving what they felt certain was a sinking ship, while the rural contingent were the reason the good ship Tory made it to shore after all. Even with these changes Klein's caucus was reasonably representative, however, especially in terms of gender. Nearly one-third of his fifty-one MLAs were women. There were also several visible minorities, apparently reflecting the fact the Conservatives had long been viewed as the mainstream, establishment party in the province. Although there were indeed some long-serving veterans left in the caucus, the average age of caucus members was only forty-seven, following the trend in previous elections (and elsewhere) towards younger legislators.

There were also a large number of MLAs with strong religious views, and their numbers would increase in the 1997 election. The presence of these moral conservatives was a definite problem for Klein. Not only did he not share their views on most of the key "family values" issues, but the issues they wanted to put on the agenda would distract from his "Alberta Advantage" focus on economic prosperity. In almost no time the province would become a hotbed of protest, polarizing the electorate over issues these caucus members were determined to raise, with or without party sanction. Among them were gun control, video lottery terminals, gay rights, religious education in schools and home schooling programs, and the right-to-life issue.

Apparently the premier's desire to reward his leadership supporters and his need to adequately reflect the rural voice that put him in power were his prime considerations in choosing a cabinet. Certainly the balance in caucus was not reflected in the first cabinet Ralph Klein put together after the 1993 election. In many respects it was quite unrepresentative of Alberta society. Some of the numbers were striking. Rural ministers outnumbered representatives of the two major cities by a margin of twelve to eight. The capital had only two ministers, while Calgary had six. In a cabinet of nineteen, only three were women, despite the high representation of women in caucus. Only two were visible minorities, one with a very minor portfolio.

As for the moral conservatives, they were well represented in Ralph Klein's cabinet, although not in key portfolios. Inevitably their presence led to problems, as some sympathetic ministers struggled with the restrictions imposed by cabinet government on their ability to speak out on the issues of most concern to them. Their dilemma grew worse as these issues became part of the public-policy agenda. Although economic and natural-resource troubles were mounting, the public's attention was increasingly focused on these picayune issues, to the chagrin of the more pragmatic and liberal-minded among them.

As one commentator put it, only in Alberta would the cabinet be scrutinized by the media on the basis of their support for "deinsuring" abortion. Yet after the March 1997 cabinet shuffle, for example, several journalists specifically noted there were more moral conservatives in the cabinet than ever before. Lorne Gunter of the *Edmonton Journal* actually calculated that the shuffle represented an increase from three to five votes to deinsure. However, Gunter also cautioned that "before [the pro-lifers and other moral conservatives] start whooping it up they should keep in mind that moderates, or right-wingers who won't rock the boat, hold all the key social portfolios."

One of the most extreme of the right-wing moralists in Ralph Klein's cabinet has been Stockwell Day. His rapid rise in less than five years from Labour to Family and Social Services, House Leader, and finally treasurer, has been most instructive. Highly regarded in his current role as keeper of the purse strings — despite initial fears he could never fill the shoes left by his predecessor, Jim Dinning — Day has nevertheless managed to prove controversial in other ways, lurching from one embarrassing incident to another when expressing his views on unrelated policy fronts.

Earlier in his career there had been reason to believe he would keep his beliefs to himself, or at least exercise some discretion in his public comments. As Minister of Social Services, for example, he had implemented an unwritten policy banning gays and lesbians from acting as foster parents. Although this technique achieved his purpose while keeping him out of trouble in the short term, it inevitably caused problems for the government. It was an untenable bureaucratic situation and one which his successor, Lyle Oberg, was forced to deal with when the unofficial practice became public knowledge.

But the former assistant pastor of the Bentley Christian Centre drew the ire of many more Albertans with his public remarks in October 1997 that convicted serial killer Clifford Olson should be removed from protective custody and placed in the general prison population, where "moral prisoners" could deal with him. Even the usually supportive local media were upset by Day's remarks, which were viewed not only as disparaging the rule of law, but also as demonstrating once again his failure to understand the concept of separation of church and state. As Don Martin of the *Calgary Herald* chided, "The province's top bean-counter is displaying an awkward inability to separate his moral convictions and crusades from growing political clout."

Edmonton Journal reporter Mark Lisac, a rare but vocal critic of the Klein government, went much further. In an open letter to the premier, he accused the Conservatives of having undermined the rule of law and the legislative process repeatedly during the previous four years, to such an extent that Day's offence was hardly surprising. Nevertheless, he urged the premier to either support or disavow his treasurer's comments in no uncertain terms.

Instead, in his typically ambivalent fashion when dealing with colleagues and supporters, Klein said he disagreed with his minister but meted out no punishment. "I didn't ream him out," Klein told reporters after meeting with Day privately. "I said, Stockwell, think before you speak and make these kinds of comments ..." Declaring he was satisifed with Day's explanation that he "spoke out of emotion, and anyone is entitled to misspeak," Klein also indicated that his own solution for Clifford Olson would be the return of the death penalty.

Since then Stockwell Day has become heavily involved in the activities of the federal Reform Party. The man frequently touted as the heir apparent to Ralph Klein has, instead, become involved in the federal "United Alternative" initiative of Preston Manning and right-wing Tories, while his son Logan continues to work for a Reform MP.

Much as Ralph Klein was seen as an outsider in 1992, with all of the Lougheed and Getty loyalists working against him to preserve the "progressive" side of the party, so Stockwell Day is seen by even some right-wing Conservatives as the representative of a dangerous new wave of radical extremists the party has attracted. With Klein having given conflicting signals about his intentions for the next election, there has been the inevitable jockeying for position among the various aspiring caucus members. Ironically it is Jim Dinning, the former treasurer now happily engaged as a private-sector entrepreneur, who is most likely to be Day's chief opposition as the champion of the progressive side of the party in any future leadership race.

According to several sources, Dinning, a supporter of Nancy Betkowski in 1993, ended up in the treasurer's job almost by accident. With Betkowski either dumped or refusing to participate — the version varies — Dinning was the only one of the Getty ministers Klein could call upon to fill a cabinet post and make a tenuous link with the urban sophisticates in caucus who had backed Betkowski. (As Nancy MacBeth, Betkowksi returned to haunt Klein several years later when she took over the reins of the provincial Liberal party. Her incisive criticism of the government has led more than one Conservative organizer to question whether the premier would not have been better advised to keep her within the Tory tent.)

Whether he knew what he was doing at the time or not is anyone's guess, but Klein made the right choice in Dinning. Much as Ernie Eves would later be the rock on which Mike Harris grounded his "Common Sense Revolution" in Ontario, Dinning quickly became the most reliable and efficient member of Klein's cabinet. While Kowalski and Elzinga handled political issues and House business — and not all that competently — Dinning beavered away at the fiscal mess and produced solid results with no fuss and no muss. With little fanfare he essentially became the backbone of the Klein cabinet.

This was lucky for Ralph Klein in more ways than one. Not only was his policy agenda in secure hands, but Dinning's competence — combined with Klein's personality — became the focal point of the government's image with the electorate. As a result, the wild policy speculation and off-the-wall musings of many of his other cabinet ministers in the early days, and particularly of the rural rookies, were initially regarded as aberrations rather than the normal state of affairs.

Apart from the antics of Peter Trnychy and Ken Kowalski, whose free-spending ways infuriated many Albertans before they were finally demoted, several others whom Klein felt obliged to reward also failed to live up to expectations. Worse, they projected an image of rural rednecks and ignorant amateurs that his government could ill afford. Although their views in many cases reflected the opinions of their constituents, or at least of those voters who supported them, they were far removed from the thinking of mainstream Albertans.

One of these hapless gladiators was Diane Mirosh, Klein's first Community Development minister. By January 1993 she had managed to cause quite a stir as the minister responsible for the provincial Human Rights Commission. Initially, Mirosh was concerned about the commission's decision to accept complaints based on sexual orientation, since this was not a category explicitly listed in the province's human-rights legislation. She even asked government lawyers to examine whether the commission was "overstepping its bounds." The commissioners assured her they were on solid legal ground, and explained they felt obliged to act because of numerous court decisions elsewhere, which concluded that sexual orientation was a legitimate ground for complaint even if it was not specifically listed in legislation. Given that all but two other provinces had already included it as a ground anyway, the commissioners felt it was just a matter of time before a legal case would emerge in Alberta and force the government to update its act.

Mirosh first attacked the commissioners for their decision, indicating she had no intention of amending the Alberta legislation to include sexual orientation. "I don't think there should be a law saying they [gays and lesbians] have rights over and above everyone else," the minister declared, thereby demonstrating her ignorance of the purpose of human-rights legislation. "I think everyone should be treated fairly." When told that was exactly what the Individual Rights Protection Act was designed to do, she expressed surprise and said, "Well then, that is something I have to review." Nevertheless, the minister stuck to her guns about not expanding the legislation, saying, "A lot of people who are heterosexual feel uncomfortable about this. And I want people I represent to feel comfortable. We shouldn't overreact to a small lobby group."

The uproar over the minister's comments extended well beyond the Alberta borders, as members of gay-rights organizations and ordinary Albertans expressed their amazement at the government's position. Undaunted, Mirosh reacted to the continuing furore by announcing that, after reviewing the situation, she had concluded that the Human Rights Commission itself should be abolished. Noting the $1.6-million budget for the commission would be saved if it were eliminated, she continued, "So far what I've seen is cases that are basically employment issues ... If employment laws were tightened," she added, "we might not need a commission." Even more astonishing was her suggestion that the Individual Rights Protection Act might also be repealed. "That is certainly something we have to consider, maybe not at this time but certainly in the future," she added.

"This can only add to the false image of Alberta as a redneck province," former commissioner Fil Fraser fumed, noting that Alberta already had the lowest per-capita funding for human rights of any province. When asked for her comments, the former minister, Elaine McCoy (who incidentally had been replaced by Klein after her unsuc-cessful run at the leadership), noted that the act had been introduced in 1971, by Peter Lougheed himself, as the first piece of legislation tabled by the new Conservative government. McCoy went on to say that Mirosh evidently did not realize "the commission's role goes far beyond that of employment dispute arbitrator ... We have 300 agen-cies, boards and commissions," McCoy continued, "why pick on that one which is so fundamental?" Ralph Klein's first response was hardly encouraging. Suggesting the whole issue was a surprise for him, he did not denounce the idea outright but instead asked reporters to "let me have the opportunity of seeing what she has in mind." In the end, the commission survived its near-death experience, but not without major damage to its credibility.

No sooner had the dust settled on this affair when another of Klein's rookies, Family and Social Services minister Mike Cardinal, launched a similar assault on the welfare system. After first refusing to pay the counselling fees for a six-year-old girl who was repeatedly raped by a male babysitter, Cardinal's department finally agreed to cover the costs when the girl's mother — a welfare recipient — appealed to the media and the case became public. Cardinal himself was unrepentant, however, suggesting the rapes could have been avoided and urging parents to "be more careful" when selecting babysitters. With decreased government welfare payments forcing recipients to resort to unlicensed caregivers, the public perceived Cardinal's comments to be grossly unfair. Despite the ensuing furore, Cardinal persevered with his one-liners, asking rhetorically where the girl's father was and implying that single-parent families were the cause of these problems. When it was learned the minister himself had abandoned a mother and child some twenty years earlier, there was a temporary lull in his attacks while he attempted to keep a low profile and stay out of more trouble, as urged by the premier.

Cardinal resurfaced after reports of a decrease in the crime rate in Edmonton reached the Ministry of Family and Social Services in mid-1993. He immediately expressed the view that this was due to the government's decision to remove "young employables" from the welfare rolls, forcing them to get jobs and leaving little spare time for criminal pursuits. Unfortunately for Cardinal, his tendency to shoot first and ask questions later left him looking more than a little foolish once again when it was discovered that the real reason for the apparent decline was a change in the reporting procedures of the police. (The minister later resigned for "personal reasons," to the dismay of those who made a living reporting on his colourful comments.)

This news did not deter others from focusing on the "youth crime" issue, however, including the premier himself. In announcing a Task Force on Youth Crime, Ralph Klein expressed the interesting view that the issue was "bigger than one of jurisdiction." His deputy premier Ken Kowalski followed up with the surprising comment that the Charter of

Rights and Freedoms was contributing to youth crime, since "what the Charter has done is changed the perception in the democracy [sic] from the right of the majority ... to the right of a minority identified as one." Fortunately the Charter was entrenched in the Constitution and Kowalski could do nothing about it, but many Albertans questioned what else the deputy premier might be thinking if these comments were any indication.

It was not long after that Kowalski departed the cabinet, followed by Mirosh and Cardinal. By 1996, Ralph Klein had installed a cabinet that was almost entirely his own, with fewer Getty holdovers and even fewer individuals to whom he still owed favours. While the overall appearance of the cabinet changed to a more youthful image, however, nothing was done to increase the representation of visible minorities or women. Mike Cardinal was replaced by Pearl Calahasen, but as a lowly minister without portfolio. Only three other women were placed in the nineteen-member cabinet, which many viewed as the prelude to the next election.

Although this cabinet could hardly help but improve on the overall ability, education and experience of the previous one, the missteps and political difficulties continued at an embarrassing pace. Apart from the ongoing problems of Treasurer Stockwell Day, the public musings of Justice minister Jon Havelock, Environmental Protection minister Ty Lund and the new Family and Social Services minister Lyle Oberg continued to alternately outrage and bemuse the general public.

Lund's consistent support for voluntary regulations ("to help the oil and gas industry"), and his fiery temper ("If you think Quebec is a problem, just keep shoving things [like the Kyoto Accord] down Albertans' throats"), were matched by Oberg's comical attempts to explain away his department's refusal to allow gays to be foster parents. First, he maintained they were unfit because they were likely to be discriminated against. This line of defence was quickly quashed, however, since his former colleague responsible for the Human Rights Commission had already declared that gays needed no special protection. Then, it was a matter of low incomes. Having agreed with and then denied positions several times in the space of a few weeks, Oberg capped off his performance with the comment, "At this moment, my mind is made up."

Of the three ministers, Jon Havelock's behaviour was perhaps the most surprising. A trained lawyer and acknowledged intellect, Havelock managed to function well as House Leader but quickly became the scourge of the legal community in his role as Justice minister. He began by sympathizing with newspapers which had published the names of young offenders. When challenged on the ethics of these comments as Justice minister, he replied that he supported changing the law, although he did not condone breaking it. He argued that "publishing names may serve as a deterrent," although he also admitted, "I can't give you any evidence which would support that." As one critic put it, once again the motto of the Klein government should be: "We never see a need for evidence to support our views."

The Justice minister's troubles had just begun. Less than a year later he was involved in vicious verbal combat with the judiciary when he suggested they should be placed under government control — apparently despite his knowledge that judicial independence is a mainstay of liberal democracy. Unhappy with sentences he viewed as too lenient, he also mused publicly about the desirability of term limits for judicial appointments, "so there would not be a need for review," ignoring the fact that a lengthy review process occurs in all court decisions.

An outraged *Calgary Herald* called for Havelock's resignation. In an article on November 14, 1997, columnist Catherine Ford decried the fact the minister "has waged a war against judges. He has attempted to use his privilege of speaking out publicly, where the courts cannot, to undermine the trust of Albertans for the judiciary." Alberta's Chief Justice, E.R. Wachowich, evidently agreed. The Justice minister publicly apologized after receiving a scathing letter from Wachowich in which Havelock was accused of "showing utter disrespect for provincial court judges and [tending to] bring the provincial judiciary into disrepute."

In her column, a furious Ford also noted that "judges are the last line of defence against the power of the state. The courts protect all of us against the juggernaut that is majority opinion and emotion-based demands for the blood of those the public deems beneath contempt." Similar fury was unleashed by the Alberta Bar Association, whose president, J.A. Bancroft, published a blistering attack on the minister in which he stated: "The idea that judges would impose harsher sentences if appointed for a limited term of office suggests that judges could be manipulated by outside influences ... As Chief Justice Lamer once commented, while judges should be mindful of public opinion they must never be ruled by it. They must always be governed by the rule of law which is fundamental to a free and democratic society."

Although he pledged to refrain from further comments, it was not long before Havelock was quoted as saying the political process was open and transparent, while "the judicial process is closed to public involvement and is isolated and obscure." The absurdity of these comments did not appear to strike the premier, who not only agreed with his Justice minister, but also described judges as "civil servants," suggesting they should be accountable to the government.

Havelock's next debacle was one the premier could not ignore so easily. In fact, it was Klein himself who pulled the plug on the Justice minister's plans in March 1998, only one day after Havelock tabled the disastrous legislation known as Bill 26, the so-called eugenics case. The bill, intended to provide compensation for victims of government-forced sterilization programs over a fifty-year period, was immediately and universally viewed as draconian, punitive and mean-spirited. If implemented as it stood, it would have capped total compensation for victims at $150,000. It also proposed invoking the notwithstanding clause of the Charter of Rights and Freedoms to prevent victims from challenging the limit in court.

Public reaction was swift and merciless. Ed O'Neill, president of the Criminal Trial Lawyers Association of Alberta, summed up the feelings of many Albertans when he said, "To think they could just take away the rights of the most defenceless, the impoverished and the disabled, with the stroke of a pen like they do in dictatorial regimes — it appalled me!"

Havelock survived the calls for his head largely because of the premier's swift action. Not only did he withdraw the legislation, but he once again used the technique of admitting the government had made a mistake. Although many Albertans were left to wonder how the government could have failed to see that its plan was unacceptable, many supportive comments emerged from the Klein caucus defending Havelock. Various MLAs blamed government bureaucrats and even members of the legal community for the Justice minister's dilemma, claiming he had been misled. Rich Vivone, the editor of the lobbyists'

Insight into Government newsletter, had a different explanation. According to Vivone, "Jon got carried away and forgot he was dealing with real people, not government money and the law."

Another explanation for the debacle centred on the operation of the premier's office and the relationship between the cabinet and the caucus. Bill 26 not only did not go through the standard vetting procedure of the Standing Policy Committee, but it was approved in caucus without individual MLAs having been given a copy of the bill for study. Several veterans attribute these lapses to a concern about information leaks, while others placed the blame on the shoulders of Rod Love's successor. As one MLA put it, "Ralph took care of the politics and Rod watched the details ... Now that Peter Elzinga has Rod's job, you have two guys doing the politics and no one watching the details."

Others, of course, would disagree. They argue the content of Bill 26 was entirely consistent with other regressive policy initiatives of the Klein government since taking power in 1993. They also argue that the way in which Ralph Klein has implemented his right-wing agenda is reflected in Bill 26 as well. Invoking the notwithstanding clause is only the latest example of the authoritarian approach to government which Ralph Klein, the alleged populist, has consistently demonstrated since coming to power. In fact, the man who once said he was prepared to use cowboy techniques in Calgary has actually done so in Edmonton to bring about his neo-conservative revolution, as the next chapter demonstrates.

3

Alberta Bound and Gagged

Normal doesn't live in Alberta anymore.
— Treasurer Jim Dinning, 1994

There isn't a government operation, a government business, a
Crown corporation that is as efficient as the private sector and
indeed [I believe] they're 20–40% less efficient. You don't have
to do a study. You can guarantee it because of the structure in
the way they run their economics. Therefore you don't have to
do a study to save the first 20–40%.
— Municipal Affairs minister Steve West on the government's
proposed 20 per cent spending cuts, 1993

As with so many other things the Klein government has
borrowed from America, it seems also to have borrowed the
right wing's renewed focus on race, immigration and ethnic
diversity ... Klein has recognized the political value of
intemperance and has played on the public's fears.
— *Lethbridge Herald* journalist Joanne Helmer

As anyone who has ever lived there knows, there is no such thing as "the
West." Instead, there are four separate provinces, each with unique
cultural traits. Indignant residents will tell you the province of British

Columbia is actually the "Pacific Region," not part of the Prairies, no matter what ignorant "Easterners" might say. Jean Chrétien found this out the hard way when he attempted to use the old 1971 Victoria amending formula — a formula which lumped all four provinces together for a regional veto — as the basis for a 1995 constitutional resolution he wanted Parliament to adopt.

The four Western provinces were never much alike, and a lot has changed since Victoria. The differences are more obvious now than ever. Even so, Alberta stands out from the rest. In some important respects, Albertans have more in common with people in the United States than in other provinces.

The political culture of Alberta is unique in Canada, and any understanding of the success of Ralph Klein's right-wing agenda can be arrived at only in the context of the province's distinctive character. Although the liberal consensus on the role of the state in education and health care is still well entrenched, the majority of Albertans are considerably more right-wing than their fellow Canadians on a range of other issues relating to state intervention and social policy. Albertans consistently support such measures as the return of capital punishment, harsher Criminal Code provisions for young offenders and stricter welfare eligibility rules to a far greater extent than do their fellow citizens in other provinces. They are also more hostile towards unions and government subsidies, and reject such interventionist "constraints" as environmental regulation, affirmative-action programs or seat-belt legislation far more often than do their counterparts in other parts of the country. Their American-style distrust of the federal government, encouraged by provincial politicians over several generations, is legendary. This, after all, is the province where a sizable minority of residents still believe Pierre Trudeau was planning to turn the old Bowden medium-security prison into a civilian concentration camp for those who opposed the National Energy Program.

Just as Canada's political differences with the United States have been explained in large measure by the varied origins of their first settlers, so the striking differences between the right-wing politics of Alberta and the socialism of its next-door neighbour, the province of Saskatchewan, have been attributed to the different patterns of immigration and the religious and political baggage their immigrants brought with them.

From their earliest days, the Saskatchewan settlers valued the collectivity and the common good, while Alberta's founders focused more on individual rights and personal responsibility. Political scientists such as Seymour Martin Lipset and C.B. Macpherson have speculated that these differences led, among other things, to such political phenomena as the cooperative movement, wheat pools and the creation of the CCF and medicare in Saskatchewan, as opposed to the development of the Social Credit Party and right-wing politics tinged with religious fundamentalism in Alberta.

Evidence of this different approach remains. In the words of Saskatchewan's current NDP premier, Roy Romanow, "Our history, from the Depression years, is to pull together as a community in the face of challenges, whether climatic or fiscal. Our tradition in a crisis has been to rally around the community, the farm and the province." By contrast, ministers in the Klein government talk about the need to take Alberta back to the good old days when real Albertans were fierce individualists and government was small. Or, as *Lethbridge Herald* journalist Joanne Helmer put it, "The sense of community in Alberta is different. Albertans don't cooperate, they compete."

Naturally the dramatic reversals in economic fortunes, and especially the discovery of oil in Alberta, have also played a role in defining cultural differences between the two provinces. For the most part the oil-patch culture, with its dominant American influence, has served to reinforce the existing conservatism and individualistic frontier mentality of Albertans.

By the 1970s, Calgary had become the centre of the oil industry and the epitome of the Alberta culture. In an article that no doubt cost the author many potential local fans, one central-Canadian journalist described Calgary as a city "full of porky pink men in their pink polyester leisure suits," looking smug and self-satisfied. Not a kind portrait, perhaps, but not far from the truth either. This was not a city that wanted to imitate "the East," Bay Street or Ottawa. A navy pinstriped suit would stand out like a sore thumb in those days, but an American-style leisure suit was *de rigueur* for the successful executive.

If Calgarians looked smug, they had reason to be. Oil prices were high and life was good. But deals were made over drinks at the Petroleum Club, not in stuffy boardrooms. The pace of life was deliberately laid back; the culture casual and simple, if not simplistic. Steaks and scotch were the order of the day, not quiche and white wine. Good restaurants, yes, but no jacket-and-tie codes would be tolerated. Success, for Calgarians and Albertans, would be handled on their terms.

As the article went on to suggest, oil and cattle interests seemed to mix well. Memberships in the Cattlemen's Club and the Petroleum Club often overlapped. The new monied elites, heavily influenced by American business partners and colleagues, increasingly focused the public's attention on individual entrepreneurship and corporate success, the classic Horatio Alger mythology of America. In Alberta, Peter Pocklington, the Ghermezian brothers and Ron Southern of the Mannix Corporation were comparable role models.

While the gap between rural and urban Albertans grew, it was not as dramatic as in a manufacturing and industrial province like Ontario. In rural communities the individualistic self-reliance and the moralistic Old Testament ethic of hard work and self-discipline combined to produce the same ideal of the self-made man that the Calgary business crowd was pursuing. For both, being "different" was okay, but speaking your mind, and speaking plainly, was even better, even if you stepped on a few toes. The anti-elite, *arriviste* crowd in Calgary valued industry and success, not where you came from, just as the moral conservatives in rural Alberta did.

The only real exception to this prevailing culture was to be found in the provincial capital of Edmonton. Through much of the 1970s and 1980s, as the size of government grew, and consequently the number of public servants multiplied dramatically, the city began to rival Calgary as the most important urban centre in the province. It also began to develop a different character, based on ideals such as professionalism, compromise and the public good. This alternative viewpoint has continued to the present day, accentuating rather than diminishing the isolation between the provincial capital and the rest of the province.

But Calgary remained the centre of the province in all important respects. The city that hosted the 1988 Olympics reflected the culture of Alberta for the rest of the country, and for the vast majority of Albertans. As such, it is impossible to ignore the fact that Calgary, not Edmonton, has been the home stomping grounds of generations of provincial premiers. Cabinet meetings are regularly held in that city at the McDougall Centre, the government's own version of the Western White House. The fact neither Saskatchewan nor British Columbia has such an arrangement makes this situation even more striking, since the rivalry between Regina and Saskatoon, or Vancouver and Victoria, has been a factor in their respective provincial cultures as well. Yet only Calgary has succeeded in usurping the role of capital city to such an extent. For the others, the compromise of receiving the university or economic centre was sufficient. For Calgary, compromise was a cop-out, and competition was the only game in town.

Alberta's culture has also been far more heavily influenced than its neighbours' by the "boom/bust" nature of its economy. As outlined earlier, major changes in the political climate have been most likely to occur in times of economic downturn. As the oil boom collapsed and the economy of the province deteriorated drastically under Don Getty in the 1980s, Albertans began to retrench both economically and psychologically. Calgarians were no longer smug. A large part of Ralph Klein's success, therefore, was due to having picked the right moment to introduce his dramatic turn to the right. Desperate times require desperate solutions. In Alberta, citizens familiar with hard times were only too ready to believe his argument that they must go further than ever before. In fact, many of them were ahead of him, leading him on.

In a very real sense, Alberta's premiers have reflected the changing nature of the provincial culture. Over time, they moved from the moral conservatism of William Aberhart and Ernest Manning during the Depression and the war years to the modern and progressive conservatism of Peter Lougheed and Don Getty in good times, and then, in another period of severe retrenchment, to the radical neo-conservatism of Ralph Klein. This latest incarnation of Alberta's traditional one-party dominance has arguably been the most significant political development in the province's history. Not only has it restructured much of the government and "re-engineered' the way citizens relate to the state, but it has done so at a time when the rest of the country was watching closely. Unlike the isolation of Social Credit in earlier times and the absence of much national media coverage, the policies of the Klein government have had a direct impact on politics elsewhere in Canada, including their unlikely adoption by the current government of the province of Ontario.

Klein himself has been the subject of numerous articles in *Maclean's* and *Saturday Night* and, even more telling, has been written about approvingly by the American press, including the *Wall Street Journal* and the financial weekly *Barron's*. He has also received awards from several prominent right-wing organizations. In November 1994 he received the Colin M. Brown Freedom Award from the National Citizens' Coalition, and in January 1995 the Fraser Institute presented him with its Fiscal Performance Award — all for his efforts to implement the neo-conservative economic agenda.

Yet, as the previous chapter demonstrates, the path which led Ralph Klein to his date with history has been anything but direct, and many voters could be forgiven for feeling the policies of his government bear little resemblance to the original platform of the one-time maverick from Calgary's Tuxedo Park.

Newt of the North?

Both critics and admirers of the Klein revolution have referred to its author as "the Newt Gingrich of Canada," but they have different ideas in mind. For his supporters, Klein is the man who successfully brought the neo-conservative vision of smaller government to Canada. For his detractors, he is the opportunist who played on the fear and resentment of the public when they were in difficulty. Both groups would have to agree, however, that Klein was a latecomer to the neo-conservative fold.

Few people realize that when Klein stepped down as mayor of Calgary he left the city with a $1.6-billion debt, the second-highest municipal debt in the country. Only Montreal, with Jean Drapeau's legacy of Expo and the Olympics, was in worse financial shape. As mayor, Klein once said he believed the best way to make sure people who had jobs and businesses stayed afloat during a recession was to spend public money. "I think those were brilliant decisions," he told a reporter questioning several of his spending initiatives after he arrived in Edmonton. "The civic debt just doesn't worry me. It's not something new. It's like a mortgage on a house," he said, "a good investment." In short, at the time Klein was actually a closet Keynesian, committed to public spending in bad times and then reducing the debt in the good years.

Klein saw the neo-conservative light only after becoming premier. With the Getty legacy of debts and bad financial management coming hot on the heels of a major economic downturn, it was obvious something would have to be done. Although his grasp of economics was not impressive — having once suggested holding province-wide bingo games to reduce a $43-million shortfall in health spending — the new premier recognized there would have to be some changes made. Even then, however, he did not think they would be as substantial as they ended up being.

In the May 1993 Budget which preceded the election, Klein's treasurer, Jim Dinning, announced no new taxes or tax increases. Instead, the problem of the deficit was to be addressed by implementing "safe" cuts in areas where Albertans — already to the right of centre by Canadian standards — would be receptive. Dinning focused on two key areas, pandering to the public's negative views and especially those of the increasingly insecure middle class. He announced massive job cuts in the public service and major reductions in welfare payments and coverage. (The welfare cuts, which led to a decrease in the number of recipients from 122,000 to 68,000 in a sixteen-month period, would be the source of much consternation in neighbouring British Columbia, where many of the Alberta refugees fled.) As an immediate measure to put on the brakes while figuring out what to do, he also announced a freeze on public-service salaries and a similar freeze on all grants to schools, municipalities and hospitals, the latter despite an earlier pledge to increase funding by 2.5 per cent.

Klein may have thought the worst was over, but nothing could have been further from the truth. It was during the 1993 election campaign, when he realized all of the parties were still talking about reduced spending and the public was insisting on a financial house-cleaning, that he began to appreciate the degree of public concern and the nature of his political problem. With Liberal leader Laurence Decore trying to outgun him on the right by calling for "brutal cuts" to deal with years of Conservative "profligacy," Klein responded by promising even more unspecified but "major" cuts, and assuring voters the $2.5-billion deficit would be eliminated in four years without raising taxes. He also stressed his "ordinary" side, responding in his best populist routine to the comments of voters like a building contractor in Grand Prairie who told reporters, "I'm scared to death because we don't live in the same Canada that we used to ... What we're looking for are people who know what it's like at the grassroots level and know what it's like to hurt."

The cuts were unspecified primarily because Klein did not yet know exactly what he planned to do. After the election he began to consult, but selectively. Apart from the neo-conservative writings on Thatcherism and Reaganomics provided by his friends in the Klein Gang, and the advice offered by the business community through the Red Deer round table, the premier also called on the services of yet another disgruntled Douglas. This time, however, it was not a Scottish engineer selling monetary theories but a former New Zealand finance minister, Sir Roger Douglas, who was peddling the wares of restraint and cutbacks. Having turned New Zealand's economy around and its society inside out, and received a knighthood from the Queen for his efforts, Sir Roger was now touring the world, urging others to heed the call and take the same drastic action. This new messenger of change was actually invited to speak to the Conservative caucus, where he put forward the view that change must be significant and it must be instituted quickly if the liberal consensus were to be broken and the state removed from the marketplace. The government that blinked would fail.

Ralph Klein paid attention. As late as 1997 he told reporter Kenneth Whyte he still worried about losing the political will and falling off the fiscal wagon. In an interview for *Saturday Night*, he said, "It's never far from my mind. I keep asking my caucus are we blinking and they say no, we're not blinking, we're still on track."

With these sources of inspiration, it is hardly surprising Klein decided on his drastic course of action. Between the 1993 election and the end of 1994, Klein and his treasurer oversaw a dramatic reduction in the size and scope of the provincial government. His agenda was so radical that few actually believed him when it was first outlined, and others thought it was impossible even if he meant what he said.

Once again Ralph Klein was being underestimated, and many of his opponents would learn their mistake the hard way. Klein had made up his mind. The province was about to take a hard right turn that would polarize Albertans and lead to unprecedented public unrest and strife. Like Ronald Reagan, Klein was also about to convince many of his victims that these efforts were in their best interests.

Slash and Burn

The first indication of things to come surfaced in the Throne Speech of the new government. In a move reminiscent of the Gingrich Republicans' *Contract with America*, Klein the salesman introduced his "four commitments" to Alberta voters. The first read: "My government's first commitment is to balance our provincial budget within four years and to take the steps necessary to ensure that my government will live within its means." The second commitment was to "create an environment" in which 110,000 new jobs would emerge over the next four years; the third was to "re-organize, deregulate and streamline government" in order to become "frugal and creative"; and the final commitment was to listen and consult often with the people of Alberta.

Of course, this degree of detail came *after* the election, when little could be done to alter Klein's plans, regardless of the fact he had hardly drawn even a thumbnail sketch of these commitments during the campaign. Journalist Kenneth Whyte summed up this problem in a *Saturday Night* article on Klein in May 1994, when he concluded, "Undoubtedly many thought the budget could be balanced by rolling back perks for MLAs, weeding out the lazier public servants, and leaving the core services alone." Klein himself, ever the populist, cleverly shifted the blame for the massive cuts to the public when he acknowledged that he believed Albertans "have been surprised by the magnitude of what *they asked for* (emphasis added)."

What was the crisis Klein and the other party leaders were responding to? Ostensibly it was the substantial deficit and an unprecedented level of public debt. Underlining the public's desire to eliminate the deficit, however, were the anxieties of personal economic uncertainty as the province entered another recession, and the resentment of the Getty scandals and mismanagement epitomized by Principal, Gainers and NovAtel.

Although it could be expected the Opposition parties would take advantage of these issues, Ralph Klein's willingness to decry the record

113

of his predecessors was somewhat less predictable. The political need to distance himself from the Getty government was undeniable, but many of his critics have argued he hardly needed to paint the situation as worse than it was. Refashioning the Conservative party as the party of fiscal restraint did not necessarily mean taking a hatchet to government programs and services.

Yet this is exactly what Klein did. His plan to eliminate the deficit in four years with no tax increases required an overall 20 per cent reduction in government spending, an almost impossible objective if basic health-care and education programs were to be left in place. In the February 1994 Budget, no tax increases appeared, just as Klein had promised. But there were many user fees, increases in health-care premiums for individuals and families and the introduction of premiums for seniors with incomes above $18,200. Another 1,800 public-service jobs were to be cut, and the deficit would be held to $1.5 billion.

By the end of 1995, some 4,500 public servants had been eliminated from the payroll since the Klein government took power, and overall government spending had been reduced by $1.9 billion. Since even the Klein Conservatives recognized it would not be possible to reduce education or health spending by the requisite 20 per cent without massive public resistance, they had opted for a graduated system in which education suffered a 12 per cent reduction but municipalities lost a staggering 47 per cent, so that the overall effect was a 20 per cent reduction in total spending. User fees and premiums continued to escalate, however, and part of the government's "creativity" involved finding an endless number of ways to cut costs and services, even in health care and education.

The cuts that Ralph Klein's government implemented to achieve their objectives were deep and swift, a veritable blitzkrieg of announcements in the first year and a half after the 1993 election. Once again they were following the advice of Roger Douglas and Margaret Thatcher. As one cabinet official confided, "The great thing about what we're doing from a strategy point of view is everyone reacts to us. They respond to what we do. Those who oppose us don't have time to mobilize because when they go to attack on an issue we've moved past it to another agenda." Or, in Douglas's own words, "opponents can't fire at a moving target."

Many interest-group leaders recognized the tactic, but were helpless to respond to it. One of the organizers of the Common Front opposition, Sheryl McInnes, explained that "the restructuring is so fast and so widespread that people are not sure whether to worry about their grandma, their own jobs or the cuts to kindergarten. They don't know where to begin or how to stop the momentum. They feel powerless." The head of the Alberta Council on Aging, Neil Reimer, agreed and noted that another problem is lack of knowledge. "There are quantum changes so vast I would defy anybody, even Klein, to write down a full list," Reimer told reporter Joanne Helmer.

As journalist Mark Lisac attempted to describe the myriad changes, he noted that "there was a whiff of the personal" in some of the government's decisions. "The education cuts were led by a premier and an advanced education minister who had not been to university," he wrote. Moreover, "the liquor stores were sold by a minister who had kept his cabinet job years earlier by standing up in the legislature and pledging he would not drink alcohol as long as he served in government. The social services minister who cut welfare payments and emphasized the responsibility of fathers to their families was revealed to have fathered a child many years earlier by a woman (whom he deserted) who ended up on welfare."

Some areas were lucky. Although there were certainly reductions in assistance for seniors — a mainstay of Conservative party support — they emerged from the cutting exercise less affected than many others. Agriculture, another important source of voter support, was asked to make a symbolic gesture by accepting cuts to certain grants and subsidies, as was Transportation, but neither department suffered the life-threatening surgery performed, for example, on the Environment Department.

Predictably education and health care bore the brunt of the cuts. The government that promised "the best possible education for all Alberta students" would cut $252 million from the Education budget over four years. Alberta's half-time kindergarten system was in danger at a time when most industrialized countries were stepping up full-time programs. In another example of the *ad hoc* decision-making process rampant in the government, Education minister Halvar Jonson first trotted out a paper referring to "thousands" of studies saying kindergarten didn't matter, but later had to change his tactics when the "studies" proved elusive. There was more. School boards were to be merged, and the province would appropriate the education portion of municipal property taxes. (It would also reassess the property tax rates, causing confusion and protest from homeowners and businesses alike.) In the first of a series of dramatic moves towards the privatization of education, it would also allow the creation of charter schools outside the public system.

As for advanced education, not only was $135 million cut from the budget, but tuition fees were slated to rise from 12 per cent of the cost in 1989 to 30 per cent in the year 2000. Worse still, much of the remaining money was tied to dubious efforts. Some $47 million was earmarked as "access" money to ensure needy students could attend postsecondary institutions. Although this appeared both responsible and civic-minded, the problem was that much of the money would be channelled into the coffers of privately owned colleges, many of which had religious affiliations. (The "Bible college" is a well-known phenomenon in Alberta, although little seen elsewhere in the country.)

Welfare, of course, had already been cut drastically in 1992, and the slashing continued as the government found increasingly creative ways not only to reduce benefits, but to remove people from the rolls altogether through more stringent eligibility requirements. Among the most reprehensible were the reclassification of many handicapped individuals as employable ("I know of some paraplegics who can work," said one cabinet minister in an offhand remark), the transferring of others to student-loan programs and those over sixty to the early-retirement benefits provision from the Canada Pension Plan, which meant their income would always be lower than had they been able to wait until age sixty-five. "Able-bodied" single men and youths aged sixteen and seventeen were cut from the rolls, while those remaining saw their benefits drop by more than $100 and their coverage for some other measures, such as medical and school fees, eliminated. In a move eerily reminiscent of Klein's "Eastern bums and creeps" attack in Calgary years earlier, recipients were also offered a one-way bus ticket out of the province, to the chagrin of then B.C. premier Mike Harcourt. Asked what was happening to people dropping off the welfare rolls by the thousands, Family and Social Services minister Mike Cardinal replied he had no idea and no interest in looking into the matter.

Perhaps most important were the cuts to health care. With nearly $300 million slated to be cut from the budget over four years, it was clear that hospitals would be the main target of the Conservatives' cuts, with closures planned across the province. But, as in other areas, the Klein government's lack of advance planning was exposed immediately as it attempted to implement its agenda. Rural areas railed against the loss of their health-care facilities, so that in the end the cities of Edmonton and Calgary bore far more of the burden. Health-care salaries were rolled back, not only for hospital workers and nurses, but for physicians. Yet health-care premiums rose.

Even more ominous was the premier's flirtation with private-sector health care. "Give us a proposal," Klein told Albertan entrepreneurs in response to proposals for American-style clinics for the rich. "We're willing to listen to anything reasonable." A private member's bill, the Gimbel Foundation Act, was introduced in the legislature to allow the establishment of a private eye clinic, and although it was later pulled the government indicated it would consider bringing in its own version of the bill. The premier got into slanging matches with federal Health minister Diane Marleau over his remarks, which she claimed would effectively establish an unacceptable two-tier system of health care benefiting only the rich. In the end the premier backed down on some of the more outrageous proposals for violating the Canada Health Act, but the cuts and mergers continued.

Deficit Deception

Although the cutbacks changed the face of Alberta, they accomplished their stated objective. By 1996 the government had achieved a balanced budget, and since then the surpluses have come rolling in. In 1997–98 the books recorded a huge $2.2-billion surplus, with the 1998–99 forecast predicting a surplus of slightly under $1 billion. Stockwell Day, Jim Dinning's successor in charge of fiscal restraint, was faced with the unusual task of cautioning Albertans that "the era of budget surpluses exceeding $1 billion may be coming to an end," largely because of slumping oil prices. Instead, Day indicated, they might well be reduced to a mere $500–$700 million in future.

Regardless, Day indicated the surpluses would be used primarily for debt reduction, the next big challenge of the Klein government. Lower taxes, in a province with the lowest personal rates in Canada and no sales tax, were another serious priority, according to Day. Under no circumstances would any major spending initiatives be launched, although the 1997 and 1998 budgets did provide for some minor relief for health care and education.

In the February 13, 1998, Budget, Day allocated $585 million to debt reduction and $285 million to tax reductions. By contrast, $70 million was to be "reinvested" in social services, $95 million in advanced education and a total of $380 million *over three years* in education — the total of the three barely equalling the size of the tax break.

While some observers argued the tax break an individual would receive was too small to be worth the bother, critics such as Liberal leader Grant Mitchell decried the fact the government's tax revenues had been trimmed nearly $500 million over three years at the same time that "children are still in huge classrooms and Albertans can't get their parents into adequate healthcare facilities." Mitchell also argued that the money should have been used "to solve red alert problems in the province and hire extra teachers." Others, such as Gordon Laxer of the University of Alberta's Parkland Institute, pointed out that "the numbers sound big but ... they're standing pat with the lowest levels of service in the country." According to Laxer, the additional funds would barely keep up with inflation and population growth. Or, as NDP leader Pam Barrett put it, "They're going to deliberately under-budget people services so they can come up with a surplus that they can apply to their never-ending debt hysteria." Barrett also suggested that eliminating health-care premiums would be fairer and more efficient than offering tax breaks. Meanwhile, in a televised address Klein rejected all such ideas and indicated in future the first billion dollars of any surplus would go towards debt reduction, the next $250 million to expenditures, and any further amount to the debt once again.

Clearly supporters of the Klein Revolution believed the costs were worth it. The books were balanced and, should another severe economic downturn strike, the legislation was in place to prevent the government from trying to spend its way out of recession the way a former mayor of Calgary once did. Yet a growing number of observers who supported the general thrust of the government were beginning to question the wisdom of reducing the debt or taxes rather than reinvesting in health care and education. Others feared a need to make further cuts in the event of another downturn. As reporter Ron Chalmers of the *Edmonton Journal* noted in an article shortly before the Budget, instead of following the Keynesian model, previous governments had spent heavily in good times as well as bad. As a result, "the Klein government then overreacted with spending cuts in both good and bad times."

The issue of spending cuts is particularly important since the Klein government has always maintained "overspending" caused the so-called deficit and debt crisis in the first place. Many experts do not agree, leading to obvious questions about the merits of the government's course of action. If declining revenues — from natural resources, and low personal taxes — were the real source of the deficit dilemma, rather than overspending, then the relentless cuts of the past several years not only were unjustified, but will have done little to prevent a recurrence of the problem. With the next decline in revenue, and with taxes lower than before, critics argue the level of services provided to Albertans will inevitably decline even further along a slippery slope.

Among these naysayers is Kevin Taft, a former public servant and Conservative policy adviser whose devastating exposé of the Klein government's handling of the seniors' file — *Shredding the Public Interest* — first raised the issue of overspending. As Taft noted, the premier himself led the chorus of cabinet ministers repeating this mantra of "overspending" as the rationale for their unprecedented cuts to government programs and services. In early 1994, Klein declared that, "when our new administration took over a year and a half ago ... we saw uncontrolled spending." By late 1996, Klein was still singing from the same hymbook: "We knew we had to get spending under control. We knew it was literally going through the roof." This view was dutifully echoed by his cabinet ministers, including Health minister Shirley McClellan, who commented that health care was rapidly becoming "unaffordable," and her successor, Halvar Jonson, who referred to "spiralling" costs nearly two years later.

Yet, as Taft stressed, the government's own statistics told quite another story. The provincial public accounts and departmental studies, to say nothing of Statistics Canada data, demonstrated that substantial cuts to spending had already been implemented by the Getty government in its final years in response to the dramatic drop in oil revenues. In fact, the last two years of the Getty administration had seen ministers speak repeatedly of a "revenue-loss deficit" which they would have to remedy. As a result, "under the Getty government support for Alberta's public programs went from the highest in Canada to below average."

When Ralph Klein took office, Albertans had already suffered a significant drop in the level of their public services. His proposed 20 per cent cuts, added to the 15 per cent reduction in spending already implemented by Getty, produced a remarkable situation in which the services provided by the Alberta government fell well below the level enjoyed by citizens in the rest of the country. Or, as Melville McMillan, chair of the Economics Department at the University of Calgary, put it, "Alberta is unique and anomalous as being the richest province ... while providing the lowest level of provincial services in Canada."

This determination to reduce the deficit exclusively through expenditure cuts was caused by two key factors. The first was the historically low level of personal income tax in Alberta and the total absence of sales tax. Klein and his caucus were convinced it would be political suicide to impose increased taxes on Albertans. Of course, they did not offer the public the option, nor did they explain in advance the consequences of attempting to eliminate the deficit solely through the use of spending cuts, a point McMillan and Taft make repeatedly.

The second key factor was the dominant influence of the neo-conservative agenda. Since small government was a desirable end — in and of itself — the convenience of using the deficit as the excuse for allowing the Klein Conservatives to reduce the size of the state was irresistible. For reporter Mark Lisac, the fact that Klein was so heavily influenced by the oil-and-gas elites through their membership in his Gang was another added factor favouring the neo-conservative goal. Instead of turning to experts in the bureaucracy, for example, Lisac contends that "Klein seemed to need business friends. He leaned on their judgement. He had no independent training or grounding in economics, and no inclination to look for it elsewhere." And the oil-and-gas industry, having come through a recession by making huge cutbacks in their own backyard, firmly believed government should do the same thing. Certainly it should not raise either corporate or personal income taxes.

Yet Alberta's tax base is larger than those of all other provinces at the same time as its tax rates are lower. The lack of sales tax accounts for roughly 60 per cent of the difference between Alberta's revenue per capita and that of other provinces, but the remaining 40 per cent is due to considerably lower personal income tax. Economists Allan Warrack and Melville McMillan estimate that, with "average" rates for all types of taxes, Alberta would have generated more revenue than all other provinces in every area except alcohol and tobacco taxes. In real terms this would have meant revenues in 1993 of $4,331 per capita, rather than the existing $2,285 actually received. Even more astonishing is the fact that "a moderate level of sales tax could have handled the structural component of the deficit, while leaving all other Alberta taxes at their existing, generally below-average level."

The irony of this has been noted by several analysts. In their article entitled "One Track (Thinking) Toward Deficit Reduction," McMillan and Warrack pointed out the practical consequences of ignoring an increase in tax revenue. They examined the fiscal situations of six other provinces projecting balanced budgets for 1995–96. Although all but British Columbia were have-not provinces, the two economists concluded their per-capita expenditures for government programs and services would be between 9 and 18 per cent higher than Alberta's. This was highly significant since, as of 1993–94, "no province spent less than 10% of the per capita all-province average." Put another way, Alberta's expenditures would be not only the lowest in the country, but up to 20 per cent lower than in other provinces.

The Klein government's planned cuts were originally intended to eliminate only the deficit, not the debt. Although Treasurer Day has been able to use the surplus of recent years to pay off a small portion of the debt, these surpluses — as he indicated in his Budget statement — are likely to fall off since oil and gas revenues are projected to decline for some time. Consequently, many economists conclude that even further expenditure cuts will be necessary if Klein persists in ignoring the "second track" of revenue sources — tax increases.

This was not something the Lougheed government had planned to ignore if things deteriorated under their watch. Although Lougheed left before the bottom fell out of resource revenues, his treasurer, Lou Hyndman, was stressing as early as 1984 that a marked drop in energy prices would mean "there will be no alternative but to look at a combination of service cuts and tax increases."

The province of Saskatchewan did not ignore the two-track approach either, and has achieved better results faster than Klein, a point political scientists Trevor Harrison and Gordon Laxer make in their seminal work on the Alberta situation, *The Trojan Horse*. The authors note that "there are important differences in the way Alberta and Saskatchewan chose to deal with their debt problems." In particular, they point to the fact the Romanow government opted for a mix of options, including "fiscal restraint, planned reorganization in some services, and tax increases including a deficit-reduction flat tax, a rise in provincial sales taxes and a 5 cent per litre tax on gasoline." As a result, in February 1995 the Romanow government tabled the first balanced budget in Saskatchewan in thirteen years.

But Ralph Klein has spent years defending and promoting the "Alberta Advantage" of low taxation, and his government's fortunes may now be irrevocably linked to maintaining this unnaturally low rate, a rate which his government indeed appears to be planning to lower even further, according to Stockwell Day's latest Budget. Klein has indicated many times he still believes that "the way you don't create prosperity is through taxes. That's the stupid way. That's the simple way." The question is, for whom is Ralph Klein creating prosperity?

Going Out of Business

Slashing government spending on programs and services is only the most direct way to reduce the overall size of government. Another favoured method for shrinking the public sector, as Margaret Thatcher demonstrated, is to privatize many of its functions. In this area of the neo-conservative agenda, Ralph Klein and his government have excelled. In just a few short years they have removed a previously unthinkable number of services from the public domain. The government's actions eliminated thousands of employees from the public payroll, many of whom became unemployed while others were forced to work for their new private-sector employers at half their previous wages. Not surprisingly, these actions have also produced the same negative results as in Thatcher's Britain — decreased levels of service, increased costs and higher levels of inequity being the most common complaints. Yet in the beginning there was widespread support for the Klein initiatives, largely because of the unique Alberta perspective on the marketplace.

Albertans may believe they are the most ardent supporters of the free market in Canada, but the reality is quite different. Both the Lougheed Conservatives and the Social Credit before them created a number of provincial Crown corporations and other forms of state ownership in selected sectors of the economy. Like Saskatchewan's, Alberta's small population — spread over a large and formidable space — meant regulation of private-sector monopolies was also necessary if services were to be provided in remote areas and remain affordable. Lastly, provincial government subsidies to businesses and the energy sector have been substantial and ongoing. Kevin Taft concludes: "The Alberta government has spent more on subsidies to the private sector than any government in Canada." Whatever they might think, then, Albertans have benefited from major state incursions into the private sector for decades. Examples of this legacy include the Alberta Gas Trunk Line, the Alberta Energy Company and, as they now know only too well, the Alberta Treasury Branch.

All of this supposedly changed with the arrival of Klein and his neo-conservative agenda. As the premier explained in the legislature on March 28, 1994, at the height of the furore over his government's actions, "the whole purpose of the exercise was to get the government out of the business of being in business." Unfortunately, this ideological motivation was not accompanied by a rational game plan or timetable. Spurred on by the examples of Thatcher, Reagan and Douglas, and apparently oblivious to the fact their earlier efforts had been largely unsuccessful, Klein's Minister of Municipal Affairs, Steve West, championed a massive privatization exercise immediately after the 1993 election. Without benefit of any studies or other evidence, West assured the legislature that the government could proceed in such a hasty fashion because everyone knew the private sector was more efficient. Critics who protested that this aspect of the new Conservative agenda had not even been mentioned during the election campaign were told by Klein that everyone understood privatization was part of the plan, "so there was no need to discuss it."

Once again the blitzkrieg approach adopted by the government served to minimize dissent by confusing the opponents. Virtually every department of government was examining possible areas for privatization, and few observers could keep up with the list, never mind the implications. Public Works was considering "outsourcing" property-management and central computer-processing functions. Agriculture would transfer "pest monitoring" to the private sector, and private veterinary labs would examine animal-health quality assurance. Energy audits were to be conducted by the private sector, and many aspects of environmental protection would be deregulated. In the Family and Social Services ministry, the provision of services to neglected children would be privatized. The Justice minister, Ken Rostad, described the function of provincial jails as "warehousing people" and indicated that an American firm (the Corrections Corporation of America) would be invited to take over the management of at least one provincial institution. Then Transportation minister Steve West announced in 1995 that the design, building and maintenance of major provincial highways would be privatized. What next? was the question on most people's minds.

But the two items on the government's list that would have the most immediate and dramatic effect were the privatization of the Alberta Liquor Control Board (ALCB) and the registry function of the Municipal Affairs Department.

The unprecedented privatization of the registry function occurred in the fall of 1993. Some 229 private agents in more than 150 communities were authorized to provide everything from birth, death and marriage certificates to driver and hunting licences, vehicle registration and land-title searches. One of the stated purposes of this dramatic move was to provide the so-called one-stop shopping approach so popular in modern management theory, but it was never made clear why the provincial bureaucracy could not be reorganized to deliver such service.

Critics almost immediately raised their concerns about confidentiality (of information), competence (of private-sector testers, who were to receive five days' training rather than the one year normal for public servants) and accessibility (for rural residents), to say nothing of dire warnings of increased costs (by greedy vendors anxious to maximize their windfall profits), all of which the government ignored. However, it did announce a multiple fee structure in which some services deemed essential — such as motor-vehicle registration — would have their fees capped, while the fees of those services considered less essential would be at the discretion of the vendor. A complex system of remuneration to the province was also established, in which some services provided hefty revenues for the government and others allowed for all profits to go to the vendor. In the end, the objective was to maintain government revenues at roughly the same level. As Laxer has noted in a chapter on the subject of privatization in *The Trojan Horse*, government revenues remained the same but the cost of the services for consumers increased significantly.

Five years later, in April 1998, the government announced it would allow a 25 per cent increase in the fees charged for the essential services — roughly half of the total number of services privatized — which it had capped at the time the changeover took place. However, none of the estimated $3 million in new revenues would be received by the government. According to the new Municipal Affairs minister, Iris Evans, the private registries needed all of the extra funds to upgrade their computer systems. Her explanation made it clear the priority of the government was to aid the private sector, not increase service. "A one-dollar increase ... should ensure that an average registry agent will be able to operate a financially viable business," the minister concluded in a press release. Meanwhile, as Opposition critics noted in the legislature, a two-tier delivery system was now in full swing. After five years, some rural residents were unable to obtain essential documents without lengthy delays and travel. Others were forced to pay exorbitant, unregulated surcharges for services their urban neighbours could obtain for less than half the cost.

Most Albertans appeared to be unmoved by these difficulties, however. Even among those concerned about the consequences of the government's apparently indiscriminate and *ad hoc* approach to privatization, their wrath was concentrated on the second major target of the government, the Alberta Liquor Control Board. The ALCB case is, in fact, a classic example of the Klein government's tendency to act first and think later, impulsively adopting elements of the neo-conservative agenda without having an overall strategy. The implementation of the ALCB's privatization was fraught with difficulties from the beginning. Not only did the premier and his minister issue contradictory statements within days of each other, but the premier appeared to change his mind on the subject almost daily.

The government got the ball rolling on September 3, 1993, with the announcement that it would remove the state entirely from the "business" of selling liquor. In six months, all of the 210 liquor stores in the province would be sold. The government would not only acquire revenue from the sales, but remove $67 million in annual operating costs from its budget and eliminate more than 1,500 employees. By selling the stores outright, it would also effectively ensure no future government would be able to reinstitute a state-run system.

Within weeks of the announcement, the problems began. Initially the licences were to be issued to small operators (and, as one critic pointed out, anyone without a criminal record). Big chains such as supermarkets were to be excluded, either for four years or for ever, depending on the government spokesman and the time of day. The new owners quickly formed an association to keep things that way, but, by January 1994, the Canadian Council of Grocery Distributors was lobbying hard to change the rules. Within a few weeks Ralph Klein announced that supermarkets would be allowed to purchase licences. Two days later, he reversed himself, in the face of massive public and caucus opposition, particularly from rural areas. Then it was announced that a final decision would be put off until the fall. In the end, Steve West laid down the law by declaring there would be a five-year moratorium on the supermarkets' entry into the liquor business, the clear implication being that five years might be only the beginning. Obviously unaware that this decision was a blatant contradiction of the free-market theory allegedly supported by his government, West answered one critic's question in the legislature by snapping, "That is the free market we have allowed."

Since May 1994, when the last government-owned store closed, polls consistently showed that most Albertans believed liquor costs had gone up and selection had gone down. Independent studies confirmed their perception was correct. Many Albertans were also questioning the safety of shopping at small stores with little security and large cash reserves. Some worried about lax enforcement of age restrictions, particularly as the issue of video lottery terminals exploded across the province. Ironically, few questioned the identity of those who benefited from this dismantling of another government service, despite the fact that special wine-store licences had been granted to a number of well-known Conservatives shortly before privatization was announced.

One person who did question the beneficiaries of the government's privatization drive was Edmonton journalist Mark Lisac. He wrote several articles on what he termed the "red market" the privatization agenda was producing — a legal but vague area in which joint business and private-sector ventures operated with little public control and even less public knowledge. Once again, the government appeared not to recognize how far from the "free market" its policies really were. For Gordon Laxer, meanwhile, the red market was the result not so much of ignorance as of deliberate strategy. In a scathing indictment of the whole process, which he termed "corrupt," Laxer concluded, "It is a new world of political patrons and clients reaching into every community ... Private firms have a monopoly in selling government information. Government awards contracts and licenses without calling tenders. Rural MLA's are powerful people who are good to know. They can get you into large new areas of privatized services."

The degree to which the Klein government's privatization agenda was motivated by a desire to benefit some elements of the private sector was soon evident in another forum, with the introduction in the fall of 1994 of an unprecedented piece of legislation. Bill 57, the Delegated Administration Act, which was described as mere housekeeping legislation when it was tabled, despite the fact it would authorize any minister "to enter into a contract with a corporation under which the responsibilities of the Minister are exercised by the corporation."

Opposition to the bill was swift and vitriolic. Not only the Opposition parties, but the media and the general public perceived the degree to which the government was attempting to remove the decision-making process from public scrutiny. As political scientist Laurie Adkin of the University of Alberta commented, the bill would potentially "transform the Government of Alberta into a holding company for an assortment of private companies which will be selling services previously provided and managed by the government. Specific programs and responsibilities to be contracted out in this way are not named in the Act, leaving no obstacles for insurance, medical or a host of other management corporations to bid for new market territory ..." In the face of widespread outrage in Alberta, and even in other parts of the country, Ralph Klein adopted his famous "I'm sorry, we made a mistake" line and pulled the legislation not once but twice. Having tried to reintroduce it in the spring of 1994, when it received an equally vehement response, the premier then announced, "Until we can fine-tune this thing to address virtually everyone's concerns, this bill will probably not see the light of this legislature."

The act was not the only way in which the government attempted to benefit its friends in the private sector. Bill 41, the Government Organization Act, allowed the Labour Department to go ahead with some of its privatization plans on its own. Shortly after Bill 57 was pulled, the then Labour minister, Stockwell Day, did just that. Beginning with cabinet approval for the Boilers Delegated Administration Regulation, Day announced his intention to proceed with a number of measures which would turn safety, standards, specifications and competency of people working in a particular field — such as the boilers — to outside companies or organizations. He also indicated his intention to consider "privatizing" the administration of all of the province's forty-eight professions and occupations. Declaring that this was simply doing by the back door what the province had been unable to do directly with Bill 57, Liberal labour critic Karen Leibovici warned, "Everything we feared about the implications of privatizing government services can still happen and is happening."

Giving Business a Hand: The ATB Fiasco

Despite the earlier commitment of the Klein government not to pursue any more NovAtel-type ventures, a number of direct grants to the private sector also continued to be dispensed by the government's own bank, the Alberta Treasury Branch (ATB). This was more than a little surprising, since it was Klein's commitment to swear off loan guarantees and other aid to business that helped get his government elected in 1993, a feat which Lisac described as "the biggest political miracle of the half-century."

Certainly such a commitment was necessary in terms of public opinion. Voters were in a foul mood in the months after Klein's takeover of the Conservative party. An independent commission's report revealed the government had lost $2.1 billion in loan guarantees from 1985 to 1992, with another $12 billion being described as high risk. Yet, in December 1993, just months after Klein pulled off his miracle, an article by Christopher Serres in the right-wing *Alberta Report* referred unhappily to a $35-million loan issued to Pacific Western Airlines in September by the ATB, as well as loans of $1 million to Beatrice Foods and $9.2 million to Gainers.

If the public had known what was to come, however, the complaints over such minor amounts would undoubtedly have been much more subdued. As reports of huge losses and irregularities at the ATB began to surface throughout the summer of 1998, two things became clear: Albertans were once again likely to lose considerable sums of money to bad investment decisions, if not outright malfeasance, and the government of Ralph Klein would have to take some of the responsibility.

The most dramatic revelations concerned the refinancing of the huge West Edmonton Mall by the ATB in 1994. With the value of the mall plummeting in 1993, its owners, the Ghermezian brothers, had defaulted on mortgage payments and taxes to the point where both major mortgage holders, Gentra Corporation of Ontario and the ATB, were threatening to foreclose. A restructuring deal had been reached between the ATB and Gentra under the branch superintendent, Allan Bray, before his departure in March 1994, which would have seen Gentra assume control. Instead, that deal was simply ignored by Bray's replacement, Elmer Leahy, and a new agreement was reached that fall with the Ghermezians which mysteriously allowed them to retain control. Under that new arrangement, the ATB assumed responsibility for some $440 million in loans and loan guarantees, an amount which by 1998 it seemed unlikely to recover. Instead, in September 1998 the ATB launched a lawsuit against the Ghermezians and former superintendent Leahy, alleging bribery and other misconduct in arranging the 1994 deal, and demanding the mall be put into receivership pending the outcome of the lawsuit. Leahy responded in early 1999 with a lawsuit of his own against the ATB, Jim Dinning and other members of the Klein government.

Although the various allegations and counterclaims about shopping bags full of money changing hands in dark parking lots captured public attention, the damage to the image of the ATB was not nearly as significant as the effect other revelations appeared to be having on the government of Ralph Klein. The premier who pledged he would not allow any more financial fiascos was accused of having interfered with the arm's-length operation of the ATB by responding to a direct plea from the Ghermezians and writing a letter to the new superintendent. In it he indicated "it would be most helpful" if ATB engaged in "very serious discussion" with the brothers' holding company for the mall, Triple Five Corporation. Although Klein hotly insisted he "offered no direction" in the dealings between the mall owners and the ATB, he also admitted he specifically asked then treasurer Jim Dinning and then Economic Development minister Ken Kowalski to find "an Alberta solution."

Gentra officials, meanwhile, confirmed they had been astonished to learn the deal was off in 1994. In a conversation with Mr. Kowalski (now the Speaker of the Legislative Assembly), one Gentra official claimed to have been told that "no one from Ontario was ever going to own the West Edmonton Mall." When the official pointed out he had a contract, Kowalski allegedly told him, "We'll have a cabinet meeting and overturn it."

While Albertans might sympathize with the objective of keeping Alberta properties out of the hands of "Easterners," they were having considerably more difficulty understanding why the ATB — originally set up by the Social Credit government to help small businesses and rural Albertans in hard times — was in the business of financing millionaire investors in the first place. And, after the Getty years, they had no tolerance for more losses of taxpayers' money, even before the accusations of criminal wrongdoing surfaced. Although the report of Auditor-General Peter Valentine, issued in February 1999, cleared the government of wrongdoing, it severely criticized the ATB's decision to endorse the loan. Critics noted that Valentine's limited mandate prevented him from addressing many important questions. They also noted that the report acknowledged the Klein government's interventions but concluded there was no hard evidence to suggest the interventions made the difference.

More to the point, it appeared that the populist premier who promised openness and accountability had deliberately kept these matters from the public eye. Only with the shift in the ATB's status to a Crown corporation in October 1997 had these events surfaced, leading many Albertans to conclude there was more to come. They were right. In September 1998 another bombshell hit the Klein government when it was learned the cabinet had been aware of other major losses facing the ATB but said nothing about them during the 1997 election campaign. In fact, the day before dropping the writ, Jim Dinning had brought down a Budget which projected a surplus for the ATB of some $23 million. Then, barely three weeks after the election, the government announced the ATB had actually suffered a $124-million loss in the fiscal year just ending. It also announced a deal to sell its 60 per cent share of a northern pulp mill to Millar Western, the previous minority owner, for a further loss of $244.2 million. Once again it appeared the Klein Conservatives were intent on rewarding the private sector at the expense of ordinary Albertans, and even of the rural Albertans who had just re-elected them.

Righteous Wrath

One of the most disturbing aspects of the Klein Revolution has been the rapid descent to the lowest common denominator in public discourse and the increased influence in government of moral conservatives from the religious right. This disastrous combination has led to an unprecedented degree of scapegoating, attacks on minorities and "special interests" by the political leadership of the province. Whether it was Human Rights minister Dianne Mirosh implying that English-speaking immigrants are somehow superior, or backbencher Lorne Taylor denouncing gay "rights," the Klein Conservatives betrayed this bias from their earliest days, and the situation has only worsened over time. Klein himself, though far from a moral conservative, has consistently demonstrated a disappointing willingness to allow these trends to take their course and a distressing lack of leadership. Time and time again, the premier has simply remained silent, stood aside and watched developments unfold, intervening only if he has little or no choice.

The religious right began to take control of the agenda on many unusual fronts. First it was the Alberta Foundation for the Arts, which a number of rural, evangelical backbenchers and cabinet ministers attacked, threatening to revoke its funding if it continued to support events "deemed to offend family values." This was followed almost immediately by the gay fostering issue and Lyle Oberg's dithering, eventually forcing the premier to intervene. Typically, Klein avoided making an unpopular decision, but on this occasion he amazed almost everyone by coming down squarely in favour of leaving the matter to "experts"— in this case, social workers. A similar technique saved the premier from expressing himself on abortion, which he also conveniently left to the experts, the doctors. Given Klein's general disdain for "so-called experts" on economic matters, this sudden conversion on social and moral issues left many critics speechless.

It also left some members of his caucus and cabinet speechless. Apparently determined to demonstrate the strength of *their* convictions, Treasurer Stockwell Day and government MLA Victor Doerksen, the two representatives of the Red Deer area, formally requested the Red Deer and District Museum to return a $10,000 grant it had received from the Alberta Museums Association to study the history of homosexuals in Alberta. Ironically the only real criticism of their position came from the Far Right, with various evangelical groups and the few remaining survivors of the Social Credit Party branding the two legislators hypocrites for staying in the "libertine" Conservative caucus.

The hard-line approach of the government, and the air of moral superiority, were also evident in its approach to the administration of justice. The Justice Department's loss of $40 million, primarily through reduced funding for police and cuts to the Law Reform Commission, were neatly camouflaged by law-and-order rhetoric of the most extreme nature. The premier himself heated up the debate by frequently calling for a return to the death penalty as a solution to various problems, including what to do with Clifford Olson. In April 1994, following on the murder of a young Alberta mother in her own home by three youths, he further inflamed local tensions when he called for the death penalty for anyone convicted of murder, including youths as young as eight. Although much of the talk was about matters of federal jurisdiction, over which the province could do nothing, it served its purpose of distracting citizens.

Certainly Justice minister Jon Havelock was not wasting any time. He introduced a 15 per cent "victim surcharge" fee on the fines for adult offenders to pay for a victim assistance fund. Meanwhile a penniless man convicted of being a stalker was placed on a bus to Victoria, to the chagrin of B.C. Justice minister Ujjal Dosanjh. Havelock also introduced changes to the provincial election legislation which would ban prisoners from voting in provincial elections. When this was struck down by the courts, he vowed to try again. And, still smarting from his sparring match with the Alberta judiciary, in March 1998 he set up a Judicial Selection Process Review Committee which was instructed to "evaluate all aspects of the current appointments process," including the possibility of "alternative mechanisms" that could be used for appointments. Once again the prospect of term appointments and judicial independence was raised, in a clear attempt to convince the public that the arm's-length relationship of the judiciary was either an outdated or an unnecessary concept.

After organizing a Task Force on Youth Crime to look into the federal Young Offenders Act and make recommendations, Havelock focused exclusively on retribution rather than rehabilitation in his review of their report, released in the wake of the murder of a twelve-year-old Calgary girl by her sixteen-year-old brother. Along with the government of Mike Harris in Ontario and the Conservatives of Gary Filmon in Manitoba, Havelock called on the federal government to implement a stringent ten-point plan for young offenders. Their suggestions included lowering the minimum age, using "voluntary" statements as evidence, removing court-appointed lawyers for anyone whose family could "afford" to pay themselves, transferring youths to adult prison once they reached a certain age during the serving of their sentence, and applying the 15 per cent surcharge to young offenders and/or their families. An appalled Sue Olsen, the Liberal Justice critic, pointed out that fewer than 2 per cent of Alberta children were serious offenders, and almost none of those offenders were under the age of twelve. Suggesting rehabilitation was the better route, Olsen said: "Addressing poverty is crime prevention. Let's look at those issues instead of putting a nine-year-old in jail."

Members of the religious right, however, were more than happy with the minister's proposals. For them, the biggest threat to family values was emerging on another front, and one which highlighted the distinction between the economic conservatism of Ralph Klein and his lack of interest in the moral conservatism promoted by many in his cabinet and caucus. Perhaps the most important challenge facing evangelical and family values caucus members has been the Klein government's love affair with video lottery terminals (VLTs). This electronic innovation literally revolutionized the province's revenues as well as its social cohesion. Although VLTs were originally introduced in 1983, the machines only became a major issue when their numbers and locations suddenly increased dramatically under Economic Development minister Ken Kowalski, who authorized widespread distribution in 1992 without any public consultation. By April 1994 there were 4,516 VLTs in hotels, bars and restaurants with liquor licences. Not only did the government rake in revenue — being the sole owner of the machines — but the licensed operators were making commissions of 15 to 19 per cent weekly, per machine. In 1997 the provincial revenue from the VLTs was greater than the revenue from the oil industry.

Both individual Albertans and the Klein government had become addicted to the machines, and public protests were mounting. Rural, religious right-wing Albertans united with socially oriented left-wing Albertans to oppose the machines, which many studies had demonstrated were having a devastating impact on a significant proportion of the population. Suicides, bankruptcies, family violence and child neglect were all on the increase, and the effects of VLTs were blamed for at least part of the problem. As one rural municipality after another took up the cause, the Klein government became increasingly nervous. It authorized a Gaming Commission under MLA Judy Gordon to examine the matter, determined that its $500-million revenue not be jeopardized.

Then at a Conservative party convention in 1997, no less a figure than Canadian Hunter executive Jim Gray, who had become personally involved in the issue, attempted to introduce a resolution calling for the removal of VLTs. Having no success there, he began organizing a petition in Calgary to achieve the same effect by a more indirect route. Soon lobby groups were springing up in many municipalities, all based on the idea of petitions.

In August 1998 the American head of the Mormon Church of Jesus Christ of Latter-day Saints visited Lethbridge, where he delivered a speech urging his followers (an estimated 60,000 Mormons were living in southern Alberta) to work for the abolition of the VLTs. By the fall of 1998 the government could no longer afford to ignore the protests, which had mushroomed into a province-wide movement. Lobby groups were demanding to be consulted directly, and upcoming municipal elections were the emerging battleground.

In the October municipal elections, plebiscites were held on the matter across the province. The Klein government officially remained neutral and uninvolved, but unofficially campaigned hard to ensure a positive outcome. It appealed to Albertans' sense of individualism with its argument that freedom of choice was at stake, and it appealed to their sense of responsibility with its claim that much of the VLT revenue would go in future for charities, education and health-care projects and municipal-infrastructure repair.

While all but seven communities voted to keep their machines, the margins were very narrow, with Calgary's support a slim 58 per cent and Edmonton's a razor-thin 50.1 per cent. This was particularly significant since voters had not been given any compromise options, such as restricting the location of the VLTs to casinos, modifying their performance or allocating more funds for addiction research and rehabilitation. Instead, they were presented with an "all or nothing" scenario.

The results appeared to surprise the premier, who immediately promised that "the concerns [of those who opposed the machines] are not going unheard." The concerns were substantial. As the editorial in the *Calgary Herald* interpreted the results, the "Premier has been given a reprise, not a pardon." Or, as the *Globe and Mail*'s Western correspondent Ross Howard put it, "Mr. Klein has been given a second chance to get it right about gambling in the eyes of many Albertans." It was nevertheless difficult for many opponents of the VLTs to see how Klein would respond to their concerns, since he personally had removed Judy Gordon as chair of the Gaming Commission that was looking into the issue and had ignored a number of their constructive recommendations only months earlier.

If VLTs posed a moral as well as financial dilemma for the premier, the issue of minority rights did not seem to do so. In 1994 the commissioner of the Alberta Human Rights Commission, Jack O'Neil, expressed public concern about the growing public intolerance towards minorities, immigrants and homosexuals, and the increasing tendency of political elites to attack the idea of political correctness through campaigns like that of backbench MLA Lorne Taylor to promote "redneck" values. The situation worsened over the next four years, with a variety of cases raising the temperature of public debate, especially on the issue of homosexual rights.

One of the most important developments was the Vriend case, in which a homosexual teacher was fired from his post because he was gay. His complaint to the Alberta Human Rights Commission was not accepted because, unlike legislation in all but two other provinces, the Alberta act did not list sexual orientation. Vriend then challenged the act in court as unconstitutional, arguing it violated the Charter of Rights and Freedoms. When the court ruled in his favour in 1994, the government appealed the case and the Court of Appeal subsequently overturned the lower court's decision in 1996. Undeterred, Vriend pursued the case to the Supreme Court, where it was heard in the fall of 1997. When this decision also came down in favour of Mr. Vriend, with the Court "reading in" the ground of sexual orientation in the act, Alberta quickly became the scene of bitter and intense debate. Public opinion split on the issue, with those opposed to the decision calling immediately for the government to invoke the notwithstanding clause.

Predictably, Stockwell Day led the charge for the religious right, calling for a province-wide referendum. Many other caucus members expressed fear that the decision would have a broad impact on marriage, pension and other legislation, a fear which Day echoed. Others, such as MLA Barry McFarland, had been much more direct in expressing their views all along. "There's no place for [homosexuality] so why should we have any laws protecting it?" McFarland stated defiantly. In the end, however, the premier took a stand. Having publicly criticized the uncivil nature of much of the dissent, he eventually held a closed-door meeting of caucus at which the matter was debated. In exchange for a guarantee that the government would review the need for additional legislation — to alleviate the concerns about the potential broader impact of the decision — he received the support of the caucus for his decision not to invoke the notwithstanding clause. Of course, it did not escape his critics that Klein was forced to make this decision only because his government had appealed the original ruling rather than accepting it. Perhaps revealing more than he intended about the nature of his thinking and that of his caucus, Klein added, "We've done the right thing *relative to the Supreme Court decision* [emphasis added]. For this government it was a giant step."

In communicating his decision to let the Vriend decision stand, Ralph Klein asked Albertans to "reflect on what it really means to be tolerant and to provide people with dignity in life." His words, while touching, would no doubt have been more believable had it not been for the cavalier attitude he and his government had displayed towards ordinary Albertans for more than six years.

Folksy Fascism

In a speech delivered at a conference at Alberta's Parkland Institute in November 1997, author John Ralston Saul said, "Democracy is alive here. It's just not in control." Ralston Saul's comments came at a time when many — both in Alberta and elsewhere — assumed there was no real opposition to Ralph Klein's agenda. Both politicians and the media tended to reinforce the idea that most Albertans were happy with the new order. "You don't hear the Albertans complaining" was a common phrase among approving right-wing admirers of the Klein government in the early days, as Laurie Adkin points out. Those who did complain, by contrast, were frequently portrayed as a marginal minority – selfish, lazy and not *real Albertans*.

This attitude is not only unfounded, but dangerous in a democracy, as John Ralston Saul suggested. Of course, it was nurtured by Klein himself. Along with his government's authoritarian approach, and its blitzkrieg implementation strategy, it has been impressively successful in stifling debate over the direction the province is taking.

Yet there has actually been considerable opposition to Ralph Klein's agenda from the beginning. His government was elected in June 1993, and by September there were 2,000 Albertans marching on the legislature to protest his cuts to welfare. Little more than a month later, on October 28, it was the cuts to education that had high-school students demonstrating in towns across the province, while 3,000 people gathered in Calgary and some 900 Albertans actually stormed the legislature in Edmonton.

It was not a pretty sight. By 1994 Alberta society had been polarized to a degree unimaginable only ten years earlier, during the heady years when Peter Lougheed was telling Albertans they could have the best of everything. On September 8 of that year, some 15,000 people rallied for the second time to support the Grey Nuns Hospital, which was scheduled to be replaced by a lowly community health centre despite the fact, having been built barely six years earlier, it was one of the most modern and up-to-date hospitals in the province. Health minister Shirley McClellan ignored the protesters and defiantly assured the media she would not back down, no matter how many more rallies were scheduled.

In addition to mass rallies, a number of specific groups targeted by the Klein government's cuts attempted to organize their opposition. The names tell the tale. From the Albertans United for Social Justice Coalition and the Society of the Retired and Semi-Retired to the Quality Education Coalition, the Save Universities Now (SUN) group and the Student Organized Resistance Movement (STORM), it is difficult to find a single sector of Alberta society that has not been affected or outraged by some aspect of the Klein agenda.

This outrage also extended to professional groups such as the medical profession, social workers, teachers and labour unions, and municipal politicians. The mayors of Edmonton have been particularly vociferous in their opposition to the Klein government, largely because their city has been the most badly damaged by them. Former Edmonton mayor Jan Reimer once remarked that the cuts made her "sick to her stomach." Meanwhile, the Catholic Church also entered the fray, as the archbishop of Edmonton instructed his priests to mobilize parishioners in defence of independent separate-school boards.

In short, there is widespread evidence of serious resistance to the neo-conservative agenda. But this resistance has been largely ineffectual, not only in derailing the agenda, but even in raising public consciousness and forging a more broadly based coalition.

Part of the problem has been the blitzkrieg strategy of the government — implementing change so rapidly across such a range of issues that the Opposition is not able to react in time. Another explanation for the lack of focused opposition to the government, however, must lie with the admittedly brilliant handling of public opinion and the media by the premier himself.

There are three elements to Ralph Klein's strategy of opposition "containment." First, he has maintained an aggressive, media-driven campaign to communicate the neo-conservative message. Second, despite his populist facade, he has demonstrated an authoritarian streak — a ruthless willingness to steamroller legitimate opposition through abuse of the legislature and other elements of the democratic process. Third, he has utilized his popularity, and his uncanny ability to present a populist image of an "ordinary guy," to manipulate the existing predispositions of the Albertan political culture.

Klein's use of the media rivals that of Ronald Reagan. The former journalist and television reporter seems able to call on the media whenever he wants, and manipulate them as he pleases. Not only does he make regular use of radio programs as he did when mayor of Calgary, following in the footsteps of other Alberta premiers such as "Bible Bill" Aberhart, but he uses television commercials and special televised addresses with remarkable marketing savvy. One analyst has called Klein a chameleon who is able to change his position on the issues, and his own image, at the drop of a hat, largely because of his communications expertise. As journalist Gillian Steward rightly concludes, "Most politicians can't stretch the canopy of credibility that thinly; their image would shred to tatters. But most politicians haven't learned to use television as well as Ralph Klein has."

At the same time the premier was selling his snake oil on television, however, he ensured his troops were in place to move ahead on the real fronts. The infamous Delegated Administration Act was only one of many examples of the premier's lack of regard for the legislature and the democratic process. He made that clear in February 1995, in answer to a question in the legislature from Opposition Leader Grant Mitchell. Mitchell asked the premier if he would promise no new privatization initiatives would take place without debate in the legislature, the very thing the recently scrapped Bill 57 had tried to do. Having evidently learned nothing from the fierce opposition which had forced him to withdraw the bill, Klein — never one to pull his punches at least — replied, "No, I won't make that commitment. Why should I make that commitment? " The premier should probably have stopped there, but he continued, giving Albertans a very clear idea of his thinking. "Had we had a full-blown debate, we would [probably] not see today the highly successful registries. We wouldn't see that kind of good public service being offered today if we subjected it to ... the nonsense of the Liberal Opposition."

Klein's idea that questions from the Opposition parties constitute "nonsense" was one that should have caused a number of alarm bells to go off in Alberta, but there was more to come. The government then proceeded to avoid debate in the legislature as much as possible through the use of Orders-in-Council regulations, a strategy which one Opposition MLA complained "means important changes are made behind closed doors with input only from Conservative cabinet ministers rather than openly in the legislature with opportunity for debate from all parties." Klein also began to routinely cut off debate through the use of closure. By early 1997 his government had invoked this measure twenty-one times more than any other government in the province's history. (Peter Lougheed, by contrast, used closure only once in all his time in office.)

Even the legislature itself came under attack, as the premier increasingly shortened the sittings and, in the fall of 1997, cancelled *most* of the session entirely, ostensibly to consult with Albertans about future budgetary measures. The so-called Growth Summit, of course, involved only selected participants the government had called upon, just as in Red Deer several years earlier. Certainly it did not involve the elected Opposition MLAs, who were being denied a chance to express the views of their constituents.

Other anti-democratic measures included the decision by the government to remove several laws from the Freedom of Information Act, and Ralph Klein's hilarious statement that the expense accounts of MLAs should continue to be exempt from scrutiny by the Information commissioner. As even the premier must have seen in retrospect (when he promised to "reconsider" his position in the face of public outcry), his reasoning for maintaining the exemption was absurd. The MLAs' expenses, he had said, should be private because the privacy of citizens meeting with MLAs would be protected and, second, Albertans should be content because this situation was better than previously, when there was no law at all.

Another ominous revelation came from former public servant and policy consultant, Kevin Taft, whose book, *Shredding the Public Interest*, chronicled the Klein government's handling of a seniors' report on which Taft had been working before the 1993 election. "Within a week of Klein's leadership victory," Taft wrote, "the release of our report was cancelled even before Klein appointed a cabinet." Worse still, "after a delay of several weeks the order came down to shred all copies of the report." What followed was a bizarre account of several public servants and secretaries spending weeks manually shredding every copy of the lengthy report, which had been printed in the thousands and sat waiting for distribution after its approval by the Getty cabinet. The problem with the report, it seemed, was that it would directly contradict the Klein government's entire strategy in the 1993 election of declaring that program costs and spending were soaring.

Throughout the campaign, Klein and others denied its existence, despite repeated accusations from then Liberal leader Betty Hewes of a cover-up. When the government was finally forced to admit the report existed, months after the election was over, the premier first denied it had been shredded, then said it had been shredded "for recycling purposes," and finally described the report as "full of bureaucratese, too difficult for seniors and the public to read."

The most draconian measure, however, was the government's shameful attempt to invoke the constitutional notwithstanding clause to protect its decision to cap compensation for residents of mental institutions who had been victims of a government-sponsored forced-sterilization program before its termination in 1971 by the Lougheed government.

The public protest in Alberta and across the country was swift and vitriolic. Catherine Ford of the *Calgary Herald* wrote a devastating critique of the Klein government's misguided attempt. Speaking for thousands of outraged and mortified Albertans, Ford declared that "the swift and unequivocal about-face by the government shows just how clumsy and inappropriate the legislation was." She also argued that the public outcry showed "how Albertans regard the tyranny of a majority government when it tried to run roughshod over a defenceless minority."

Anticipating the decision in the Vriend case which would come several weeks later, Ford concluded the matter had not yet been satisfactorily resolved, despite the government's hasty retreat. "Alberta tried to use the notwithstanding clause to escape a moral principle of accountability. There are suggestions that same mean-spirited philosophy ... will come into play if the Supreme Court of Canada rules Alberta must include protection for homosexuals in its human rights act," she thundered. "The kind of thinking [that would invoke the notwithstanding clause] lives on in this government, egged on by an attorney general determined to usurp judicial independence." The same point was eloquently expressed by journalist Andrew Coyne in a devastating critique in the *Ottawa Citizen* of March 12, 1998. He decried the Klein government's use of the notwithstanding clause and argued,"They should be held to account," despite having withdrawn the bill, since "as we have just had demonstrated, any government that insists on the power to override fundamental rights cannot be trusted with it."

Ralph Klein once again admitted his government had made a mistake and tried his "We've listened, we care" line, but it was beginning to wear thin. One of the reasons for this was that his own populist halo was becoming somewhat tarnished after a number of unscripted outbursts. Yet evidence of the iron will under the populist mask had been evident even in Calgary, and nothing had apparently changed. When demonstrators assembled outside the legislature in 1993 to protest his cuts, he responded to the Opposition parties' request that he address the protesters by saying: "Absolutely not. But I'll tell you what. They can stand out there and they can yell and they can scream and they can have all the placards they want and they can have all the billboards they want and they can call me every rotten name under the sun. I ain't going to be there but I'm also not going to blink."

Like the New Right Republicans of Newt Gingrich, the Klein Conservatives also began to criticize some of the more traditional members of their own team. In May 1994, Dave King, another unsuccessful candidate in the 1992 leadership who had resigned to become head of the Alberta Public School Boards Association, resigned from the party to protest what he described as the anti-democratic move by the Klein government to take rights away from school boards. Klein's response when told of the resignation was "Perfect! Now he can whine and snivel and sob and he won't be doing it as a Tory … I don't want to sound pushy or a bully but school boards are there at the pleasure of the legislature."

The third tactic Ralph Klein has used to contain and muzzle opposition to his policies is to play on the generosity and self-reliance of Albertans. Having accused Albertans of profligacy because of previous governments' alleged overspending, he has also convinced them that they now have to take their medicine. They must pull up their socks, rely more on themselves than on government, and keep their complaints to themselves because everyone is sharing in the pain. Both individuals and communities must accept more responsibility after years of irresponsible behaviour.

The beauty of this approach is that it also allows him to create scapegoats. The opponents of his policies are enemies of the Alberta people, or at the very least they are un-Albertan. Not surprisingly, these enemies are also the victims of his policies — recipients of social assistance, teachers, unions, nurses and public servants. They are also women, seniors, the handicapped and the poor. Of course, Klein has different terms for these enemies. Like neo-conservatives elsewhere, he has managed to a considerable degree to marginalize the opposition by portraying them as either self-interested or lazy. Those on social assistance are "welfare bums." Public servants and other professionals are "fat cats." Everyone else represents a detested "special interest."

People admired and respected Peter Lougheed; he was someone they wanted to be. By contrast, they like Klein and forgive him his excesses because he's so nice and ordinary, just like them. As Gillian Steward put it, "Klein is just the right person to deliver the neoconservative cant. If an ordinary guy like Ralph Klein believes in cutting and privatizing health care and education, then it can't be all bad. Only an 'ordinary guy' like Ralph Klein could brag about cutting people off welfare and get away with it."

Others have a different idea of Ralph Klein. Mark Lisac's book on the Klein revolution asked whether Albertans were viewing "the creation of a sugar-coated fascism." Laurie Adkin's article on "Kleinism" was certain they were. Decrying what she described as the "folksy fascism" of the government, Adkin concluded: "In a province where economic freedom is the banner of the regime, basic democratic rights of dissent and speech are in jeopardy, and rights to informed and meaningful participation in decision-making have been eroded." Some members of the public, meanwhile, were beginning to refer to "Ralph" as "King Klein."

Red Tory Blues

On September 10, 1996, the Progressive Conservative Party of Alberta celebrated twenty-five years in power. For twenty-one of those years, Peter Lougheed and Don Getty had been in charge. To mark the milestone twenty-fifth anniversary of their first election victory, the two former premiers and 120 of their closest friends and colleagues from the Conservative party got together at the Palliser Hotel in Calgary on August 30. Premier Ralph Klein, the party's current flag-bearer, was not present. In fact, Premier Klein was not invited.

Although he has been careful not to criticize his successor in public, everyone knows "Peter" is not happy. He speaks indirectly about the situation, criticizing the neo-conservative movement and another of its followers, the Reform Party. "I have a philosophy that's obviously very different," he once said. "I was the leader of an activist government." Criticizing the "authoritarian" and "provincialist" tendencies of the New Right, Lougheed — the boy who lived through the Depression — also has harsh words for Klein's government on the social-policy front, without naming names. "As a Conservative," Lougheed said, "my feeling is that we have to help those who can't look after themselves ... I'm not in public life anymore, and obviously degrees of assistance can be argued, but the basic [Conservative] philosophy of sharing must endure." Pushed hard to expand on his specific views of Klein and his Reform-like policies in an interview with Peter Newman for *Maclean's* in August 1995, after the worst of the Klein cuts had been implemented, Lougheed went so far as to say, "I'm not saying he's sloughing off responsibility for people's

144

welfare, but he's getting to the edge of doing it, and that's my concern."

Don Getty is less concerned about mincing his words. In an interview with the *Calgary Sun* on August 29, 1996, he told the editorial board that Klein was "falling down" on the national-unity file and the government should reassert its former role in economic development. As for the cuts to health care and education, they were "haphazard" and "overly harsh." More to the point, Getty said, "You have to have a plan, because if you ever break the system it'll cost you twice as much to put it back together." Former Lougheed minister Allan Warrack is equally blunt. "Undoubtedly times are different, and, to put it bluntly, we really have a Reform-type government in Alberta." Former minister Dave King agrees. He also decries what he views as the "anti-political" attitude of Klein and many of his cabinet and caucus. "What drove many of them to seek public office was actually an *antipathy* towards politics. They seek to deconstruct the political process," King argues. "They think it's only by a lack of imagination they are prevented from privatizing every function of government, right down to the judiciary." Klein's old leadership foe, Nancy Betkowski, is no longer a Tory either. As Nancy MacBeth she leads the charge against him in the legislature, the new leader of the Liberal party and the Official Opposition.

Meanwhile, the consequences of the Klein revolution are everywhere. Food-bank use more than doubled in 1994 alone. By 1995, Albertans used food banks at nearly twice the rate of their fellow citizens in other provinces. Unemployment in Edmonton soared as public servants — one in eight Albertans — lost their jobs. Calls to the Edmonton Distress Line increased by 33 per cent over six months.

A study by the Edmonton Social Planning Council using Statistics Canada data revealed the number of Albertans living in absolute poverty more than doubled between 1993 and 1995, with the percentage of children in this category rising from 4.2 per cent to 10.4 per cent. Edmonton itself was found to have the largest percentage of citizens living in poverty of any major city in Canada, replacing Winnipeg in have-not Manitoba.

Bankruptcies also soared, especially in Edmonton. In the first quarter of 1995, Alberta led the country in personal and business bankruptcies, a dubious distinction not cited by Ralph Klein as part of the "Alberta

Advantage." In fact, it was doubtful workers or unions thought there was *any* advantage to living in Alberta, as real wages by 1998 had fallen ten points below the 1983 level. Productivity, meanwhile, had risen by twenty-five points in the same period, leading Robert Bragg of the *Calgary Herald* to conclude in a commentary on October 17 that there "is an Alberta Disadvantage," in which "this high productivity/low wage gap has contributed to the province's distinction of having the fastest growing rate of industrial bankruptcies."

Some of the consequences are more visible than others. Line-ups in hospital emergency rooms have grown, and the number of "red alert" situations, in which ambulances are forced to go elsewhere due to over-crowding, has increased dramatically. Seniors have to wait for beds in nursing homes. The death of a two-year-old Edmonton boy in 1995, while being transferred to a distant hospital, sparked a widespread public outcry. In Calgary, 20,000 citizens signed a petition to save a central Calgary hospital. In the summer of 1998 some of those same citizens may have been sitting on a hillside overlooking the hospital in the down-town core as it was deliberately destroyed by the government-hired demolition team. A modern masterpiece of technology refurbished at considerable expense only a few years earlier, it was declared redundant to make way for new development, while citizens were told to use the services of a nearby community clinic in future.

According to Frederick Henry, Calgary's Roman Catholic bishop, the health of Albertans is threatened by many other policies of the Klein government, especially on environmental matters. In a commentary in the *Calgary Herald* on July 24, 1998, Henry accused the premier of "one-dimensional politics being practised again in the province, and the only thing we seem to be concerned about here is the economy." Although the bishop's article focused on Environment minister Ty Lund's recent statements berating the federal government's acceptance of the Kyoto Agreement on greenhouse gases — an agreement which Alberta opposes — environmentalists supported the bishop's statements by pointing to previous studies demonstrating that air, water and under-ground pollution emissions together rose nearly 24 per cent in 1995 alone, despite the "voluntary" guidelines adopted enthusiastically by the Environment minister while pursuing the privatization of the provincial environmental-research centre, the province's electrical-power utilities, the logging of old-growth forests in "protected spaces" and the deregulation of many environmental-protection measures concerning toxic materials.

For many Albertans who oppose the neo-conservative agenda, one of the most disturbing and insidious aspects of Ralph Klein's "success" has been his ability to convince Albertans that there were no other choices. The "ordinary guy" who told them cuts to health care and education were essential convinced them precisely because he was so ordinary. "Ralph" was one of them. Yet Ralph's agenda has hurt many of those people who thought he was like them. They have also hurt the province of Alberta, where the "Alberta Advantage" is helping less than half the population and the other half is becoming disenfranchised. The split in society is deep and painful. Yet this has not deterred others from following his example. Klein's adoption of the neo-conservative agenda — as his many awards and favourable media coverage suggest — has been viewed by the New Right in Canada as a marvellous success story. In fact, Klein's Alberta was literally the blueprint for what was about to happen in Ontario only a few years later under an ardent disciple of Kleinism — Mike Harris.

4

Mike and the Boys

> You have to credit Mike Harris. He has the will. He's really
> committed to doing what he believes is right,
> and damn the torpedoes.
>> — Solicitor General Bob Runciman

> I would think that if you look at the backgrounds, and who we
> consult with and listen to and relate to, I think it's fair [to say]
> Bob Rae is certainly more elitist in the sense of academic. He
> grew up that way though.
>> — Premier Mike Harris

Mike Harris knows he has little in common with Bob Rae, but the self-described populist premier seems surprisingly defensive about it. In a May 1995 interview for *Maclean's* magazine, Harris compared himself with the former premier by saying, "I'm not a bookworm or a Rhodes scholar." When the question was raised again three years later, on the anniversary of his unexpected election victory, Harris replied aggressively, "I grew up in North Bay, in a small business, and relating to more common folk, or the average working stiff. If you were in the Rotary Club, there weren't too many award-winning academics, there weren't too many CEOs. We are who we are. That's how we grew up."

Obviously there is an underlying resentment simmering there, and not just about Bob Rae. Psychologists normally attribute such resentment to unresolved conflict between envy and disdain. In the case of Mike Harris, this resentment appears to be directed at the various elites — social, intellectual and political — of which he has never been a part. His attitude is typical of many self-made men, but more than a little unusual in a politician. Yet the jury is still out on whether the premier from Ontario's hinterland realizes how atypical his background and personality are in comparison with those of many previous leaders of Canada's largest and richest province.

From his comments, it seems unlikely Harris has spent much time worrying about the implications of different backgrounds on leadership styles. He is not an introspective man by nature. On the other hand, Harris came to know four of his predecessors personally, and he had ample opportunity to observe the way they handled the reins of power. Whatever conclusions he may have drawn, Harris has made it clear he feels no need to change *his* style, despite the fact his years in power have been characterized by conflict and confrontation.

The people of Ontario do not seem to be as sanguine. In several recent polls they have sent a clear message to Mike Harris. They are unhappy with his leadership style, and even more dissatisfied with his government's authoritarian approach. Whatever else they expected from the "Common Sense Revolution," it was not a rigid, ruthless and frequently incompetent administration, in which ministers often act in haste and then steadfastly refuse to admit their mistakes or remedy them. For many, the character of the man in charge at Queen's Park is directly responsible for the problems his government has had in implementing its agenda.

Is there such a thing as a typical Ontario premier? Perhaps not, but even a cursory look at four of the men who preceded Harris suggests they have much more in common with one another — despite coming from three different political parties — than they do with the former golf pro from North Bay. Traditional Conservatives John Robarts and Bill Davis, Liberal David Peterson, and Bob Rae of the New Democratic Party may have come to different conclusions about public policy and the role of government, but they moved into the premier's office equipped with a remarkably similar set of tools to do the job.

University-educated, lawyers by profession, and generally well established in their respective party hierarchies before becoming leaders, these men knew what governing was all about before they grasped the brass ring. Although Rae was the first premier to come from Toronto, the others also hailed from the urban core of the province, Davis from Brampton, Robarts and Peterson from London. Each of these men could be described as an urbane, reasonably sophisticated moderate. Many might also call them predictable and rather boring but, as Bill Davis said after winning yet another election for the Conservatives, "Bland works."

The contrast between the images of these former premiers and Mike Harris — a "good old boy" from Northern Ontario whose knowledge of the province stopped well short of the Toronto city limits, a university drop-out, an obscure backbencher in the Davis years, and a stubborn man with an aggressive attitude and a hair-trigger temper whose behaviour was anything but predictable — could hardly have been greater.

Like Albertans, Ontario voters long ago formed a clear set of expectations about the desirable behaviour of their political elites, and Mike Harris was definitely not performing according to those expectations. By the summer of 1998, a majority of Ontario voters believed Harris and his government were simply not managing the affairs of state properly. In fact, the Harris Conservatives were doing things very differently.

If he *had* given the matter any thought, Mike Harris would have found that his predecessors' combination of life experience and personality traits had led them to run their governments in remarkably similar ways, despite their partisan differences. A technocratic, managerial style, cautious decision making and a high degree of consultation and consensus-building were hallmarks of their approach. Even Bob Rae, whose government ultimately became known for confrontations with its own supporters, did not choose conflict by choice. Quite the contrary, Rae as premier went out of his way to accommodate different points of view and interests as much as possible. He made a point of saying he was not there simply to listen to those who agreed with him or who had supported him in the election.

Unlike Harris, who refused to meet with any number of groups and organizations before or after they opposed his initiatives, Bob Rae began his term of office with proactive attempts at bridge-building with the very groups, such as big business, whom he anticipated would oppose his policies. "In the first days after our election," he wrote in his memoirs, "I made a point of reassuring everyone that I wanted to govern in the interests of the whole province, and that this included business." Despite his efforts, Rae concluded he had no hope of either converting the corporate elite to his point of view or convincing them that his government was not incompetent. "As one elder statesman put it to me," Rae recalled, "you have to understand, your becoming premier was never part of my life script."

Rae may be right to conclude that conflict was inevitable during the NDP years. No one would deny the obvious lack of fit between the socialist agenda and the fiscal and economic reality his government inherited. The election of the NDP was a fluke in the first place — an unexpected result of the first-past-the-post electoral system in a province with a strong three-party culture. Certainly the public was shocked by the NDP victory. Rae himself has admitted no one was more surprised, or less prepared in terms of an agenda.

This was hardly the case with the Conservatives. Their election platform had been written a year in advance. They may have been elected by default in 1995, but hardly by accident. Yet conflict and confrontation were the order of the day for the new government, right from the swearing-in ceremony, when more than a thousand protesters staged the first of many "Embarrass Harris" rallies. What was it about the Harris Conservatives that brought on this visceral reaction?

Harris has always maintained it was the agenda of the "Common Sense Revolution," not his personality or his government's style of managing public affairs, that produced four years of confrontation, violent protest and occasional riots in the streets of normally sedate Ontario. He also argues that protest should have been expected with an agenda that changed so much of the way government operated. The premier's belief that resistance was inevitable nicely reinforces his underlying conviction that those opposing his policies are individuals whose careers or self-interest are affected. Put another way, Harris thinks all of the opposition to his neo-conservative agenda has come from undeserving "special interests" or individuals who somehow were receiving an unfair advantage from the government, an advantage which he eliminated.

After four years, it would be hard to find a major interest group that has avoided a direct confrontation with the Harris government. After count-less rallies, protests and "Days of Action," it seems to many Ontarians that their province has become a battleground, and Queen's Park a fortress.

Unlike the premier, most observers believe the conflict between the Harris government and so many of its citizens was far from inevitable. Instead, they lay the blame for much of the heated rhetoric and outright confrontation squarely on the premier's abrasive personality and his government's authoritarian management style. "*La méthode Harris*," as one Quebec journalist described the premier's "damn the torpedoes" attitude, "has been a lethal political mix of ignorance, undue haste, unwillingness to compromise, outright ruthlessness and a cavalier disre-gard for the views of those who dared to disagree."

This approach has been reinforced by the inexperienced but zealous advisers surrounding Harris. It has also been underlined by the ineptness of his cabinet and the lopsided representation in his caucus. At the heart of the problem, though, is the premier himself.

The Boy from North Bay

Who is Mike Harris? First and foremost, Ontario's current premier is an outsider. Apart from Ralph Klein, it is hard to imagine someone for whom this term could be more appropriate. Mike Harris is an outsider geographically, professionally and politically. When Harris won the lead-ership of the once-mighty Conservative party, he did so without any of the typical credentials or preparations for the job, and he won with none of the traditional sources of party support. This factor alone accounts for much of the man's attitude towards government, political power and the fate of individuals.

You may not need a law degree from the University of Toronto to be premier of Ontario, but few people would think a college drop-out from Northern Ontario, who drifted from one job to another for fifteen years, would be a likely candidate. Certainly no one who knew Harris as a young adult thought he would amount to much, including his parents. Harris admitted as much on the night of his election victory, when he departed from a prepared text to muse aloud: "My parents always wondered, I suspect, what would become of me."

Growing up in the north–central Ontario town of North Bay, Mike Harris was raised in a fairly typical middle-class family, despite his subsequent efforts to reinvent himself as a working-class success story. His father owned and operated a welding business in town, where Harris attended Algonquin Composite Collegiate. His high-school yearbook prophetically listed the pastimes of the young "Mikey" as "bowling, curling and antagonizing." After selling the business, Deane Harris bought a resort outside of North Bay, to which the young Michael returned after dropping out of university after one semester. For nearly three years the future premier ran the marina and gave waterskiing lessons while his father handled the overall operation and his older brother, Sid, managed the restaurant.

At twenty-two, Harris married Mary Alyce Coward. The marriage lasted barely two years. After a year, a restless Harris enrolled in a one-year course at teacher's college in North Bay. While still a student, he wrote his wife a letter from a railway camp in Northern Ontario, where he was working for the summer, telling her the marriage was over. Harris basically refuses to discuss the matter, but his ex-wife told a reporter after his election that "the only thing that still bothers me to this day is that after we separated I asked him if he could help me when I went back to college but he said no."

His career in education did not last much longer. After three years as an elementary-school math and science teacher, he returned to work at the family resort, this time as a manager and ski instructor. He also began managing a nearby golf course, and became a certified golf pro. In 1974, at the age of twenty-eight, he remarried. This second marriage, to Janet Harrison, was happily a success.

Still restless on the employment side, Harris was encouraged by a friend to run for a trustee's position on the local school board. Although a virtual unknown, he was successful, very likely due to the typical lack of public interest in such positions. Harris, however, had now found something he liked doing. By 1977 he was the chair of the board. In 1980, at the age of thirty-five, he became president of the Northern Ontario Trustees Association.

This background is particularly interesting in light of Harris's later antipathy towards public education and government funding. Having spent more than half of his working life as a public servant, Mike Harris as premier proceeded to eliminate public-service jobs at a stunning rate, and was particularly hard on those employed by the education system. Personal experience also failed to change his attitude towards the public health-care system. Despite a rare life-threatening disease which he contracted after a bout of 'flu in 1980 — a disease which saw him partially paralysed and hospitalized for more than two months — Harris and his government have embarked on a major cost-cutting exercise which involves closing many local hospitals and reducing the number of nurses, support staff and facilities at others.

After his recovery a year later, at the age of thirty-six, Mike Harris began his long trek to the premiership by running for office in the riding of Nipissing. A card-carrying Tory in a province of apparently infinite Tory election victories, and a long-time critic of Pierre Trudeau (a man whose policies made him more furious by the day), his choice of party was never in doubt. Many felt the election result was less certain, given his lack of party profile and experience. But on March 12, 1981, Harris defeated his nearest rival, Liberal Mike Bolan, by almost 4,000 votes.

While experts attributed his victory to the "coat tail" effect of the perennially popular Bill Davis, Harris himself appeared to feel the victory was due mostly to his own hard work, careful preparation and effective use of the contacts and network he had established during his years on the school board. A man with none of the usual academic or professional credentials for public office, who had never really left Northern Ontario, he had certainly showed everyone. He was going to the big city and the big time. Harris told his new assistant he expected to become a cabinet minister in a short while, and would likely take a run at the premier's job within the next ten or fifteen years. One thing Mike Harris obviously was not lacking was ambition.

With such unrealistic expectations, the rookie MLA was bound to be disappointed. The disappointment was heightened by the fact that Harris perceived his failure to make cabinet as an ideological issue, rather than one of competence. Ignoring the reality that many of his caucus colleagues had far more impressive credentials and relevant experience for public office, he focused on the fact he was a right-winger in a caucus of moderates — a political outsider in his own party. As one observer put it, Harris "found himself on the ideological fringe of a party of the comfortable centre, ruled by an urban Tory elite."

Although he initially tried to toe the line, presumably in hopes of the elusive cabinet post, it did not take long before Harris began to demonstrate his real feelings on a range of issues. By 1985 he supported Frank Miller, the most right-wing candidate for the party leadership, after the resignation of Bill Davis. Not long after the disastrous campaign which saw the Liberals take power and the Conservatives disappear from the radar screen, Harris gave a blistering speech criticizing Treasurer Bob Nixon's Budget. It was the start of his campaign to lower taxes, and the beginning of his "tax fighter" image. In what Harris viewed as the ultimate put-down, he compared Nixon's budget to the ill-fated 1981 budget of federal Finance minister Allan MacEachen. Like the interventionist Liberals in Ottawa, Nixon's Budget "attempted to say, I think in a very arrogant way, that government would tell companies how to spend their money and how to create jobs ..."

By the time Harris won the leadership in 1990, the party was broke and hopelessly mired in last place in the polls. The "tax fighter" had won a dubious prize, primarily through lack of interest on the part of the heavy hitters in the party. But there was another reason for his victory. With the defeat of the Tories in 1985, the vaunted Big Blue Machine — the cadre of political advisers, election strategists and all-around "backroom boys" who had guided the party to victory for decades — had started to crumble. Harris and his supporters took advantage of this weakness, just as Ralph Klein had done in Alberta.

As was the case for Klein, the Tory leadership race in Ontario in 1990 was conducted for the first time on the basis of a one-member/one-vote system, not the elite leadership-selection process the Big Blue Machine had traditionally controlled. This meant Harris could appeal to the extreme right of the party, the "conservative" component of the "progressive conservative" coalition. It also meant that, when he won, Harris owed nothing to the party elites or the old guard.

Fresh from his leadership victory, neither he nor the party was prepared to face an election, which is why Premier David Peterson called one. Although the "tax fighter" theme garnered some support for Harris, the party finished a dismal third once again. The only thing that really saved Harris from a quick exit as leader was the fact that no one else wanted the job. So, between 1990 and 1995 Harris toured the province, raised funds and reorganized, essentially rebuilding the party in his image.

Despite the fact they were in no position to quibble, his critics within the party were legion. For one thing, his caucus felt he did not spend enough time in the legislature. Of course, this was probably a blessing in disguise, since Harris was no parliamentarian. With all his years in office, his knowledge of procedure, to say nothing of his speaking skills, had not improved. Viewed by many in the caucus as well as the media as a loose cannon and a misfit, he was further hampered by the widespread belief he simply did not have the intellectual equipment for the job. The media dubbed him "Flintstone," and the moniker caught on with almost everyone who knew and disliked him.

Harris persevered. His middle-class roots rapidly fading from memory, he worked hard at creating an image as a populist, a "just plain folks" guy-next-door, whom the "working stiff" would feel happy voting for. Given the recent public rejection of political elites in the referendum on the Charlottetown Accord, the timing could hardly have been better.

But there were already indications the real Mike Harris was not quite as folksy as he appeared. His attitude towards welfare, which many saw as small-minded and mean-spirited, was highlighted in 1993 with a cheap publicity trick in which he publicized the plight of a single mother of two, Helle Hulgaard, who felt forced to quit a low-paying job and go on social assistance because of the high cost of housing, prescription drugs and other items covered by welfare, and the lack of similar assistance for the working poor. The incident demonstrated two things about Harris: his visceral dislike of social assistance recipients, whom he viewed as the authors of their own misfortune, and his general ignorance of public policy. Unwilling to seek or accept advice from experts, and inclined to trust his instincts or gut feeling, Harris maintained that Hulgaard would actually receive as much or more income on welfare, an error which departmental officials were quick to point out.

Since taking office, Mike Harris has continued to show voters both sides of his personality. The right-wing ideologue and populist are evident in the scripted moments, while the rigid authoritarian with the petty streak appears when the premier strays from his game plan. Interestingly, no one who knows him well disputes the existence of the second, less flattering set of character traits. His long-time assistant Bill King has confirmed what everyone already knew, that Harris has a terrible temper. His wife, Janet, actually referred to his mean-spirited side when she volunteered in an interview that "I've attempted to make Mike a little bit more romantic, a bit more compassionate ... I've always said politics is really good for him in getting him to mature. But some of that has come from me too. I'm more sensitive."

The premier's lack of empathy and rigid commitment to the neo-conservative agenda are nowhere more evident than when he discusses the effects of his government's cutbacks on the disadvantaged. In one interview, he volunteered his opinion that "homelessness is generally people who have made a decision, and for whatever reason we regret they make it." Asked about the increased use of food banks since his government's welfare cuts were implemented, he replied, "I think times are tough. I think some of the adjustments ... has had an impact on food banks. We acknowledge that. We hope it's temporary." Then he added that he had just made a donation at a food bank the previous day.

He has even kept his temper and responded nonchalantly to accusations that his tax cuts were "blood money," paid for by the welfare cuts. "If there are some people who have money that is more than they feel they need and they would like to see that go to a worthwhile cause, gosh, we really encourage that," he offered somewhat ingenuously. In one interview he turned his answer into a diatribe against "government dependency" as opposed to hard work. The impact of his argument was somewhat lessened, however, when he concluded with the statement: "I can't tell you how many millionaires started out with minimum-wage jobs."

Harris reappeared at a news conference in November 1996, called to announce a government-sponsored school breakfast program. To the horror of his advisers, he managed to turn a carefully scripted "good news" story into a public-relations disaster. The announcement was designed to soften the premier's hard-hearted image, an image reinforced by Bob Rae's "Chainsaw Mike" label. The press plan featured Harris discussing the benefits of hot breakfasts for children. Warming to his subject, the premier departed from the prepared text. He declared that working mothers were to blame for more children going to school hungry, not the high unemployment rates, or the 21.6 per cent reduction in welfare payments imposed by his government. "If you go back 30 or 40 years ago," he mused, "where it seemed to be that mom was in the kitchen with a hot breakfast cooking as everybody woke up in the morning, that's not the normal situation today." The pack of mesmerized reporters standing on the steps of the legislature could hardly wait to report this latest sociological finding, which brought predictably shocked responses from welfare and social-action groups, feminists and just about everyone else.

The premier's lack of formal education and intellectual pursuits were the source of another embarrassing press conference shortly after the government announced a second round of cuts to cultural agencies, including a cumulative 44 per cent cut to the Ontario Arts Council, whose budget was reduced to 1974–75 levels. Earlier, Mike Harris had refused to accept any responsibility for the demise of a number of Canadian literary publishers — including the prestigious Coach House Press — after his government cut funding and/or refused to guarantee loans for publishers of Canadian works. In his usual cavalier fashion he told reporters, "If they can't compete in the marketplace ... if their reaction is to blame somebody else, that probably speaks to their management capabilities."

Harris was in trouble on this one to begin with, since he had promised categorically during the leadership debates that there would be no cuts to culture. Putting two and two together, the press asked the premier to name his favourite Canadian book. "Uh, probably, uh, I'm trying to, yeah, you've caught me here, I wasn't ready for this," he replied sheepishly. No doubt sensing a loose-cannon scenario coming on, the press persevered. What book had he been reading lately? "I don't know. Lately, uh, uh, I guess it's, uh, there's been a book called *Mr. Silly*. And it's one of [his son] Jeffrey's favourites and I wish I could give you the author ..." His advisers were not amused, and wanted to cut it short. One or two looked slightly ill.

Allegedly trying to be helpful, another reporter lobbed Harris an easy one. What was his favourite book of all time? "I don't have one clear favourite," he replied somewhat more carefully. "I mean, I love reading.

As a boy, I mean, I read all the Hardy Boy books ... I read *He Shoots, He Scores,* was an all-time favourite of mine through [my] teen years, you know, a hockey book ..."

If this was the premier at his most vulnerable, he was at his worst in the first three years when dealing with those who confronted him on his agenda. At a party convention in Hamilton, Harris joked about the 75,000 protesters who had converged on the legislature earlier to voice their opposition to the government's plans for massive cuts to the public service in Bill C-26. "If you took away all of the government employees," he declared, "the other four or five may have had a point to make." On a more serious note, he suggested to reporters that, "by and large, I think the mainstream marchers were union-organized." To the convention delegates, though, Harris referred to them as "union goons." When a delegate asked if he had ordered the police presence, which had resulted in several injuries, he unwittingly demonstrated his ignorance of the fundamentals of democracy by retorting, "I don't control the police. You see, that's the great thing about a parliamentary democracy — the separation between the police and the state."

Unable to stop there, he tried again to dismiss the whole event as unimportant by marginalizing the participants. There were no "ordinary" Ontarians in the march. They were all public servants, unionists or other "special interests." Asked about these so-called special interests by a reporter, Harris said, "If you saw the banners going by from some of the Communist parties, as I saw, and I guess the Iraqi group and Iranian group ..."

Exactly what the premier meant by these comments was not made clear, but protests from the Canadian Arab Federation forced him to issue a written apology the next day. It was the first of many apologies Mike Harris would make as premier, all of which were the result of his penchant for off-the-cuff remarks based on his "gut instinct" and his "common sense."

All of these events were still to come, though, when Mike Harris unveiled his "Common Sense Revolution" in 1994. At the time the future did not look at all promising. In a scenario strangely reminiscent of Ralph Klein's first campaign as the new Tory leader in Alberta, there was less than a year to go before the Ontario election, and the

Conservatives had been written off as having no chance of forming the next government. Nevertheless, by the time the 1995 election rolled around, the party was far more prepared than in 1990, both financially and ideologically. This was largely thanks to the efforts of Harris and the new group of like-minded advisers he had assembled. Most important, the party had a platform that was a detailed blueprint for change and, as the events of the roughly six-week campaign (thirty-seven days) demonstrated, it was a strategic masterpiece.

The election was not a cakewalk, however, thanks to the electoral musings of the leader in his unscripted moments. Having planned the "Common Sense Revolution" so carefully, his advisers were in despair more than once at the gaffes and bloopers he delivered in unguarded comments. Within the first two weeks, the would-be premier had mused aloud about the need to do away with tenure for university professors while campaigning in London, the home of the University of Western Ontario. He followed this up a few days later in Windsor with the thought that maybe the government should close the local casino, a widely supported source of municipal revenue. Before the halfway point in the campaign, his advisers decided there could be no more off-the-cuff comments from the leader, and the "policy consistency" adviser took a firm grasp on the reins.

As a result of their actions, the campaign, and the premier's chair, were saved. Having started the election in third place, the Conservatives soared to the top by the end of the campaign. The morning after his astonishing election win it was hard to know who were more surprised — the Liberals, who had thought they were a sure thing; the voters, who had not expected such a majority; or the Conservatives themselves. For Mike Harris it was a sweet vindication. The boy from North Bay was about to become premier.

Mike's Whiz Kids

As more than one observer has noted, Mike Harris lacks the "intellectual rigour" to convert gut instinct into a saleable political platform. What turned the obscure backbencher into the leader of the Conservative party, and then the premier of Canada's largest and richest province, was a combination of luck and shrewd choices. Nowhere was this combination more evident than in his choice of advisers, the people who would form his inner circle and accompany him on the long journey from the Opposition benches to the premier's office. Without these advisers, Queen's Park veteran reporter John Ibbitson argues, Harris "would today most likely still be railing from the opposition benches at his more sophisticated and successful opponents."

Like Harris, virtually all of his closest advisers were political outsiders. The importance of this alienation was reflected in a speech delivered to the right-wing Fraser Institute in September 1995 by Tom Long, the campaign chair for the election earlier that year. In his remarks on the reasons for the Tory victory, Long referred disparagingly and often to "the opinion elite," the "smart set," and the "self-reinforcing, centre–left consensus among influential members of the media, the political and the business elite."

Unlike Harris, his new advisers had a good understanding of mainstream Ontario, despite their youth and relative inexperience. They also had a much better grasp of neo-conservative ideology. In fact, it was their passionate commitment to the Far Right that had made them political outsiders within the Conservative party during the Davis era. Nevertheless, their knowledge of the nuts and bolts of the party organization, as well as their Southern Ontario urban perspective, helped give Harris the more rounded image and policy depth he needed to persuade the party grassroots he was not too marginal to be the leader.

Every politician has staff members who are part of his entourage because of long-standing relationships or connections. For Harris these included Bill King, a former reporter from the *North Bay Nugget* who became his assistant as soon as he was elected in 1981, and David Lindsay, a career political staffer who had earlier worked for Dennis Timbrell and joined Harris in 1985, becoming his executive assistant when Harris won the leadership in 1990. Another important confidant was King's uncle, Bill Farlinger, a successful Bay Street executive who was instrumental in raising money for Harris and the Conservatives, and served as co-chair of the Conservatives' transition team with Lindsay in 1995. (Farlinger was later appointed head of Ontario Hydro by Harris in recognition of his contribution.)

But Harris does not have someone like Ralph Klein's Rod Love. The political advisers who would prove instrumental in the transformation of Mike Harris from loose cannon to serious contender were active on the far right of the party long before he came along. In the beginning, they were driven more by ideology than by personal loyalty. Some people might even argue that they used Mike Harris to accomplish their own objectives, rather than the other way around. Certainly they had no hope of implementing their neo-conservative agenda while Bill Davis was premier. On the other hand, if they could find the right diamond-in-the-rough and shape him to suit their purposes, they could take the party leadership and move into Queen's Park to play in the big leagues.

Who were these right-wing *Wunderkind*? The oldest and probably the most dedicated of the young neo-cons was Tom Long. A self-described political junkie, Long enjoyed his first taste of politics as a child accompanying his mother on door-to-door canvasses for the local Tory candidate in Sarnia. He attended the University of Western Ontario, became active in campus politics and set out to take control of the Conservative party's campus club. A bitter opponent of the Davis government's "Red Tory" policies, and especially of the human-rights legislation introduced in 1980, Long was constantly on the outs with the party hierarchy. By 1982 he was engaged in guerrilla warfare with the party executive and successfully managed to out-manoeuvre them to take control, with his cohorts, of both the campus and the youth wings of the party.

Long and his neo-conservative friends subsequently used their positions to influence the debate at several party policy conventions. They also were instrumental in ensuring the victory of a young Montreal lawyer, Brian Mulroney, over the hopelessly moderate Joe Clark in the federal Tory leadership race in 1983.

With the resignation of Bill Davis in October 1984, it looked as if Long might have a chance to play kingmaker provincially as well. Unfortunately, although he chose the right horse in Frank Miller, Miller went on to lose the election almost immediately, and the Tories found themselves on the outside looking in. The leadership race proved useful in one way, however, since Long and the member from Nipissing found themselves on the same side in the leadership race, became acquainted and realized they were in agreement on many issues.

During the next few years, Long served as party president while his neo-con colleagues threw their weight behind Larry Grossman after Miller resigned in the wake of the disastrous electoral defeat. Although they had control of both the party and the leadership to some extent, it did little good since they remained in Opposition.

By 1989, Long spearheaded a campaign to have the party elect its next leader by a new one-member/one-vote system. Grossman had already resigned after the party's second defeat in 1987. Long believed a more grassroots, anti-elite approach to decision making was essential if the Far Right was ever going to achieve success within the party. The immediate and negative reaction of the party hierarchy, including such long-standing Davis backroom advisers as Hugh Segal, Norm Atkins, John Tory and John Laschinger, proved Long was right. Virtually all of the party's big guns campaigned against the idea, and they still lost by a three-to-one margin. Most disappeared shortly thereafter. As one member of Long's coterie, Alister Campbell, put it, "The grown-ups basically left — retired, quit, lost interest or went to Ottawa."

This left Long in control of a party that was broke, leaderless and in third place in the polls. Undeterred he launched his own campaign for the leadership, a campaign that ended several months later with his reluctant conclusion that he had neither the personality (too aggressive) nor the experience (at thirty-two, too young for most Conservative voters) to capture the brass ring. Long left active political life for Bay Street, and watched from the sidelines as a number of his former youth-wing colleagues decided to throw their lot in with Mike Harris.

In May 1990, the youth brigade secured the leadership of the Conservative party for Harris. It was a dubious victory. The party was broke, and many people were telling the new leader he should declare bankruptcy. The leadership contest itself had been bitterly divisive. Virtually all of the remaining Davis party elite had supported the only other serious candidate, MPP Dianne Cunningham, a Bill Davis disciple, in a vain effort to prevent Harris from taking control. As Harris adviser Alister Campbell put it, "In the final months of the campaign ... when it shook out to just the two contenders, it split ideologically." The bottom line was that few of the Big Blue Machine veterans were prepared to stay around and work with the Harris team, and they weren't asked. The new guard were on their own.

In addition to Campbell, other members of the neo-conservative youth group who stayed and supported Mike Harris were Tony Clement, Mitch Patten, and the lone woman in the Harris boys' club, Leslie Noble. They had all been active in campus politics, and all of them had been involved in unpopular, far-right activities totally out of fashion at the time. Campbell and Clement, for example, had first joined forces at the University of Toronto in the late 1970s to take control of the Conservative association on campus, while Patten had been involved with the Tory group at Wilfrid Laurier University. Campbell had actually attended Republican campaign events, including the 1981 national Convention. Clement, who like Long had spent his youth canvassing for the party with his mother, had publicly and enthusiastically supported the policies of Ronald Reagan and Margaret Thatcher in campus debates. All of them had been given a wide margin by the mainstream membership of both federal and provincial Conservative organizations because of their extreme views. This included their firm belief that most social programs should be abolished — a position which was simply anathema to the Davis/Clark/Stanfield school of Conservative thought at the time.

Although they were unhappy with the trend of Conservative policies, there is no suggestion they were ever motivated to leave the party. Instead, they were constantly searching for ways to "capture" the organization and bend it to their will. One of the reasons for this determination to overcome obstacles from within may have been their visceral hatred of the alternative, the Liberal party and the policies of Pierre Trudeau.

At a time when the rest of the country was enchanted with the charismatic prime minister and his vision of Canada, simply being a Conservative was an unusual choice. To be committed to the neo-conservative agenda of Thatcher and Reagan during this period was nothing short of suicidal, politically speaking. For this group of committed and aggressive young turks, their decision to support the candidacy of the honourable member from Nipissing — the only backbencher who openly loathed Pierre Trudeau and everything he stood for, despite the warm relationship between Ontario premier Bill Davis and the prime minister — was both natural and possibly inevitable.

During the 1990 provincial election that followed so closely on the election of Harris as party leader, his youthful advisers concentrated on holding on to seats, including the leader's. With virtually no campaign platform except tax reduction, they depended heavily on Harris and his "tax fighter" image to get them through. This one-note refrain did the job, but just barely. The morning of September 6 found them in third place in the legislature once again, with twenty seats and 23.5 per cent of the popular vote. Although his own father, Deane Harris, would tell the media his son "wasn't ready" to be premier yet, almost no one else thought Mike Harris would have a second chance.

With most of the old guard either sidelined or in disarray, the party was as intellectually bankrupt as it was financially. This proved to be a silver lining for the young turks guiding Harris. As all of them saw immediately, it was the perfect opportunity for them to take the helm of the party platform, steering it far to the right.

They succeeded because, quite simply, no one else cared or was paying attention. Between 1991 and 1994, the same small group of dedicated right-wingers worked hard at rebuilding the party's finances, restructuring the organization and, most important, building on the one-note tax-reduction theme. Tony Clement became the party president at twenty-nine, and took on the organizational tasks along with an executive whose membership included no one over forty.

By 1994 Leslie Noble, Mitch Patten and Alister Campbell — all of whom had been pursuing business careers — began to plan election strategy. Noble was hired full-time by Harris as the party's Election Readiness director. Tom Long, who had watched developments approvingly since 1990, also came back on board for the platform exercise which David Lindsay, as the leader's principal secretary, technically quarterbacked. The group's regular meetings at the Bradgate Arms Hotel were well known to party insiders, who dubbed the strategists "the Bradgate Group."

The platform they drafted was to be a manifesto of the New Right, a revolutionary document that would, in the words of Tom Long, "fundamentally move the goalposts" of Ontario politics. Despite all the careful planning, the document introduced to the world as the "Common Sense Revolution" would acquire its popular title by accident, thanks to a now-famous comment by Harris executive assistant Bill King. Listening to the others discussing the revolutionary nature of their platform proposals, King reacted to the term by saying "Mike's not about revolution. He's about basic things, like common sense." By putting the two ideas together, the team had a title which was a perfect blend of populism and the neo-conservative agenda. It appealed to everyone, including the leader.

The content of the "Common Sense Revolution" (CSR) was no surprise to anyone who knew Harris's young advisers well. Nor were the roles played by the various members. Long, who began the writing exercise, predictably concentrated on ideological rhetoric. His first draft actually contained several notations to "insert policy here." Campbell, as the real intellectual of the group, had a more substantive input, while Noble whipped things into shape. Harris himself simply stressed the outcome — he wanted a plan that produced a balanced budget and a tax cut — and left most of the content to them. His own contribution, in the final stages, would be to set the tone and follow his instincts to ensure the populist context of a "you" and "we" approach. Of course, he knew his people and they knew him. He knew he could count on them to produce sufficiently right-wing proposals, and they knew he would approve.

One of the reasons they all knew this was because they had already explored some radical right-wing options together, south of the border. One of Tom Long's closest friends happened to be Mike Murphy, an American political consultant who later ran right-wing extremist Lamar Alexander's unsuccessful bid for the Republican presidential primary. In 1993, however, Murphy was advising another Republican, Christine Todd Whitman, in her successful campaign for the governorship of New Jersey.

Whitman defeated a popular Democratic incumbent, Jim Florio, primarily on the basis of a Murphy-inspired campaign using a "common sense" slogan and pledging a 30 per cent tax cut. Since her victory, the activities of her government in implementing this plan had been carefully charted by Harris aide Bill King. In March 1994, Harris actually travelled to New Jersey to meet Whitman and discuss strategy. Two months later, the "Common Sense Revolution" with its 30 per cent tax cut was unveiled.

Another close American friend of Tom Long's was in the news when it was discovered Harris had hired him to direct the thirty-second campaign ads for the $600,000 CSR media launch. When Harris was asked by a spokesperson for the Association of Canadian Film Craftspeople why he would pick an American director, cameraman and crew for the ads — when Toronto was an internationally recognized film centre — the unrepentant Conservative leader replied that the director was a friend of his campaign manager, the cameraman was a friend of the director, and he had no idea about the crew because "I didn't check [their] passports. I'm a free-trader ... I'm after the best and the brightest."

Interestingly, many of those associated with the CSR and still involved with the Harris government have attempted to minimize the importance of the American influence on their thinking. Yet the connections between individuals and the similarities in platforms and policies are impossible to ignore. Nor was Whitman the only American neo-conservative who inspired the Harris team. Similar admiration was directed towards Michigan governor John Engler, New York's governor George Pataki, and a clutch of other Republican politicians, including Republican House Leader Newt Gingrich.

Some of the rhetoric in the CSR comes directly from Gingrich's *Contract with America*. Several of Engler's policies ended up in the 1995 platform, and the state of Michigan was mentioned by name in the CSR as an example of a model jurisdiction, in which privatization and deregulation had had a very beneficial effect on the economy. (After the election, Michigan's environmental standards — which are much lower than those of Ontario — were cited as the ideal by the government, in a protracted debate among bureaucrats, business interests and environmentalists.) The focus south of the border is also obvious in the explanatory documents accompanying the platform. Many stress North American rather than Canadian contexts, and there are almost no references to other provinces.

The one province mentioned in the Tories' manifesto is Alberta. This was hardly surprising. Klein advisers had been briefing the Harris team since well before the election. In fact, the number of flights back and forth from Edmonton to Toronto had led one wag to suggest they should hire their own plane. Alberta's economic strategy under Klein was discussed in some detail in the CSR, but the manifesto went out of its way to demonstrate how it differed from the Klein plan, in case anyone thought its authors were simply copying the Alberta approach.

Klein may have felt imitation was a sincere form of flattery, but the Ontario neo-cons wanted to stress their differences, as if they were afraid the world would notice the similarities. "It should be noted," they declared, "that the CSR, unlike the Klein plan in Alberta, takes as its starting point the measures to reduce tax rates and eliminate barriers to growth." Given this disclaimer, it is also interesting to note that Klein's people were consulted after the election as well. In addition, Finance minister Ernie Eves actually made an unpublicized trip to England to discuss the mechanics of privatization with some of the Thatcher bureaucrats who had recently completed the same exercise there.

During the 1995 election, Long and Noble served as the campaign chair and manager, respectively. Bill King and another young right-winger who had been involved in the 1990 campaign, Guy Giorno, were the speech writers. Alister Campbell's job was to ensure policy consistency, monitoring the "message" put out by the leader and others on a daily basis — a task, as noted earlier, that would prove very demanding. Mitch Patten was the campaign secretary. David Lindsay and Debbie Hutton, a young aide in the leader's office, were on the leader's tour, travelling with Harris around the province to the various campaign events. Another adviser was Jamie Watt, a communications expert who, like Giorno, had helped out in 1990 and in this campaign proved highly effective at derailing the opposition. Among his notable contributions was a devastating campaign advertisement portraying Liberal leader Lyn McLeod as a weathervane.

When the dust settled on the morning of June 9, Harris turned to many of these same advisers to staff the premier's office. In a move reminiscent of Brian Mulroney's approach, the premier-designate decided to favour loyalty over experience and dance with the ones that brought him. Despite the fact that none of these young turks had any experience with government, *they* were the ones who moved into the premier's office in Queen's Park, not the remnants of the Big Blue Machine.

Yet, because ideology rather than close personal friendship had been the reason for their involvement in the first place, many of the team chose not to work on the inside after the election. Long, Noble and Campbell all returned to the private sector, but remained close to the Harris government. According to at least one insider, they actually continued to influence decision making through regular, almost daily contact with those who worked in the premier's office, and meetings with David Lindsay every few months. According to reporter John Ibbitson, Lindsay "was regularly queried [by the premier] on what 'the campaign team,' as the premier still called his young advisers, was recommending on key issues." Meanwhile Tony Clement, who had been the Tory candidate in Bill Davis's old riding, found himself on the government backbenches. (By 1997 he would join the cabinet as Minister of Transport, replacing the hapless Al Palladini.)

David Lindsay stayed on as the premier's principal secretary, Mitch Patten became the deputy, Guy Giorno was the new director of policy planning and Debbie Hutton the legislative assistant. Bill King was given the task of caucus liaison, while Jamie Watt was to have been the director of communications. (This last piece of the staffing puzzle was undone shortly after the appointments were announced, when some unsavoury episodes from Watt's past came back to haunt him, and he was forced to resign before ever really assuming his post.) The position went through numerous incumbents in a short period of time, remaining vacant at one point for nearly a year, and proved to be a major, ongoing problem for the Harris team. Eventually a former Davis staffer, Ab Campion, came on board, and the team was complete.

The youth and inexperience of Harris's advisers were the subject of much speculation among veteran Queen's Park reporters. Of the senior staff in the premier's office, every single one was under forty and some, like Giorno (twenty-nine), were under thirty. Caution was not their strong suit. How would Harris manage without any moderating influences from those around him?

Of course, Harris and his team felt there was no need for moderation. In fact, that was precisely what they were trying to avoid. They were highly committed to the neo-conservative agenda, and now they were in a position to do something about it. Nothing and no one was going to stop them. The results were predictable. On the one hand, the new guard provided the unifying sense of purpose for the government from the day it took power. On the other hand, as reporter John Ibbitson concluded, "They would also, in their more strident moments, convey the sense of ideological fervor, of harshness, of lack of compassion or forethought, that would darken the government's record and alienate some of its core supporters."

The combined effects of zeal and inexperience resulted in some departures from the office by 1998, and some new faces being added to the line-up. Yet the replacements were, if anything, younger and less experienced than their predecessors. John Toogood, for example, was another Tory youth-wing product who, as a protégé of the youthful Mr. Giorno, was described as looking "too young to shave."

Guy Giorno himself continued to play a crucial policy role as director of strategic planning. Viewed by ministerial aides as a "true believer" who toiled at the centre of the web, he could be rigidly inflexible if departmental initiatives failed to conform to his expectations and/or the CSR priorities. It was not long before he was given the nickname "Rasputin" by *Frank* magazine and opposition MLAs. (After more than three years at Queen's Park, the man whom a departing Ab Campion described as the "intellectual heart" of the Harris government was still unknown to many, including Liberal House Leader Jim Bradley, who allegedly asked to have him pointed out at a Queen's Park Christmas reception.) With an operating style completely opposite to the highly visible and omnipresent Rod Love's, Giorno managed to keep the kind of low profile more typical of public servants. His influence, however, appears to be at least as great.

Meanwhile, Deborah Hutton, who remained as the premier's legislative assistant, was given the nickname "Jabba the Hutt" by ministerial aides terrified of her legendary tantrums. One of these aides, like all of those working for the Conservatives, was willing to be more specific only on the condition of anonymity. According to the disgruntled staffer, Hutton was and remains "a one-person Blitzkrieg against party morale. She guards her access to Harris jealously, and frequently speaks on his behalf."

More than three years after the election, the small band of true believers who steered the party back to power evidently can't let go. Despite their unrestricted access to bureaucratic expertise and information, the political outsiders who handed Mike Harris the premier's office continue to behave like the Opposition. Their "us" versus "them" siege mentality is so ingrained that it applies to ministers of their own government, not just hapless bureaucrats. According to veteran MPP Morley Kells, still languishing on the backbenches at the time, "The direction of this administration resides almost totally in the hands of the political operators in the premier's office."

The dictatorial and centralizing tendencies of the premier's office led government insiders to refer to "the centre" in ominous and disparaging tones. What "the centre" wanted the centre had better get, or heads would roll. After nearly four years, the fear and loathing of some members of the premier's team, and the relentless way in which the remaining whiz kids still attempted to control all aspects of policy implementation, led one journalist to prepare an in-depth analysis of the premier's office entitled "Inside the Harris Kremlin." Needless to say, it was not a flattering piece.

The Throwback Caucus

The significance of the problems in the premier's office was magnified by the lack of depth and experience in the cabinet. Although some might blame the results of the 1995 election, this unhappy situation was caused more by bad judgment than by bad luck. True, the election dealt Mike Harris an unusual hand. Cabinets must be drawn from the caucus the voters elect. Many of the best and brightest Tories of the Davis era, having spent nearly ten years in Opposition, simply did not choose to run again in 1995, especially since the polls early on predicted yet another humiliating defeat. Former cabinet ministers and potential leadership candidates who were no longer on board included such well-regarded moderates as Dennis Timbrell, Larry Grossman and Alan Pope.

As a result, some 60 of the 82 seats the Conservatives won in 1995 were held by new members with no experience in government. What was more, many of the new Tory MPPs had only been recruited to run with great difficulty, since it was thought the Conservatives had little or no chance of winning those seats. This inevitably resulted in a candidate profile for these rookie members that differed from the typical background of Tory candidates in the past, especially in ridings where the party nomination was a sure route to public office.

Simply put, many of the Conservative MPPs in the class of 1995 were older and less educated than their predecessors. There were far fewer professionals, and — although Margaret Thatcher would no doubt have been delighted — the fact that the new Tory caucus was overwhelmingly a group of shopkeepers meant it was not a promising talent pool from which to draw cabinet ministers. Given the traditionally high representation of lawyers in any party caucus, the Conservatives' mere fifteen lawyers, for example, were a striking contrast to the thirty-seven "small businessmen," eight farmers, and one veterinarian they had elected.

The caucus was also noticeably unrepresentative of the face of modern Ontario. With only one visible-minority member (Dave Tsubouchi, a third-generation Canadian of Japanese origin) and twelve women (a mere 14 per cent of the caucus), the Conservative caucus was a throwback to an earlier time.

Given the nature of their electoral victory, which was based on a rural/suburban coalition, the caucus also lacked any significant representation from the major urban centres of the province and, most strikingly, Toronto. Just as in Alberta with Ralph Klein's first victory, the rural dominance of the caucus meant an unusually large number of Harris's Tory MPPs came from the conservative wing of the party. This was especially true for the 1995 recruits, many of whom had decided to run precisely because of Mike Harris and the "Common Sense" platform.

Unlike their leader, however, many of these right-wingers were also religious fundamentalists. Their inspiration was the Moral Majority faction so prominent in the American radical right. Mike Harris, like Ralph Klein, is a social conservative on the law-and-order and welfare issues, but definitely not a moral conservative. More important, the Ontario electorate are not receptive to moral conservatism either. (This, of course, is a major reason why Reform has made so little headway in the province, as a later chapter demonstrates.) As a result these "family values" MPPs were a potentially serious problem for Harris. Like Brian Mulroney, the new premier felt he would have to accommodate some of them in the party hierarchy, or risk internal revolt. One of the ways in which he managed this issue was to appoint several of the more extreme backbenchers to special committees or task forces, such as the Ontario Crime Control Commission. This kept them out of trouble but also out of the cabinet.

Although these constraints certainly made the cabinet-selection process more difficult, the new premier still had enough options to create a reasonably balanced, experienced and representative cabinet if he had wanted to do so. In the end, the cabinet's weakness was caused less by the results of the 1995 election than by the premier's biases and the choices he made. Once again he ignored much good advice and proceeded to make appointments primarily on the basis of loyalty, friendship and degree of commitment to the neo-conservative agenda. Once again, those that came to the dance with him would prevail over others with far more experience or competence.

Using these criteria meant there were some notable exclusions from cabinet. More than a few eyebrows were raised when neither Morley Kells nor Chris Stockwell — veteran MPPs with solid credentials and a record of performance in the legislature — made the grade. Virtually no one believed it was a coincidence that both men had never been Harris supporters and were far to the left of the neo-conservatives running the show. (Stockwell's exclusion from cabinet came back to haunt Harris with a vengeance when the veteran MPP became the Speaker of the Legislative Assembly, and promptly ruled several times against the government in a series of embarrassing incidents.)

A similar pattern of bias can be seen in the appointments Harris made from the class of '95. Derwyn Shea is a case in point. While Shea was a rookie MPP, so were more than a third of the cabinet appointments Harris would make. Yet, Shea, an Anglican minister from an inner-city Toronto riding — with four earned degrees and a lengthy list of management credentials with hospital, educational, social and cultural agencies, as well as the Metro police and Hydro commissions — was passed over in favour of several other newcomers, all from rural Ontario, whose education and experience paled in comparison. Three years and two cabinet shuffles later, Shea still had not made the grade. Given Harris's lack of bench strength from Toronto (only two of his original cabinet held Toronto ridings), this omission seemed all the more glaring.

With the type of criteria Harris was using to make his selections, many people felt it was only a matter of time before his government began to look like the gang that couldn't shoot straight.

The Harris "Boys' Club"

Just before his departure from the Transport portfolio in the fall of 1997, Al Palladini offered reporters this explanation of his position on the proposed Hamilton expressway: "Right now, all we basically have is a bridge that we don't quite know how to walk across it, we might need one paddle, we might need two. I'm going to leave the door wide open."

While Palladini was being shuffled off to the less demanding Tourism post, his sidekick Dave "Tuna" Tsubouchi was being extricated from Community and Social Services and sent to purgatory in Consumer and Commercial Relations. Tsubouchi was the man about whom one Liberal insider had earlier joked, "That's one minister we'll never ask to resign! Why should we?" Meanwhile, Jim "Tiger" Wilson was heading off to the obscure Industry, Science and Technology portfolio, leaving the Health ministry in tatters for Elizabeth Witmer to fix up, and John "Crisis" Snobelen had vacated the Education post in disgrace to be replaced by cabinet heavyweight Dave Johnson. The cabinet shuffle that produced these changes was no surprise. The real mystery was how any of them had survived for so long.

Who made the grade in 1995 and found themselves at the cabinet table? First and foremost, Mike Harris chose people like himself. This meant white, middle-aged men. It also meant self-made men were in, and well-educated upper-middle-class ones, for the most part, were out.

In addition, Harris picked a third of his cabinet from rookie MPPs with no experience in the legislature, let alone the cabinet. The advantage, for Harris, was that they would always perceive themselves to be in his debt. After all, they had been elected on *his* coat-tails, not those of Bill Davis. The combination of these two selection criteria alone was likely to cause serious problems for the government, but Harris did not stop there. Ignoring conventional wisdom once more, he deliberately (and some would say perversely) placed individuals in portfolios for which they had no relevant experience or training.

His theory was unique, but understandable if one considers his neo-conservative perspective. Normally, ministers function as spokespersons or advocates for the "constituencies" they represent through their departments. The minister's role, around the cabinet table, is to put forward legislation benefiting these client groups, or to express concerns about the proposals of other departments which might have adverse implications for their constituencies. The Minister of Agriculture, for example, would be expected to speak up in the interests of dairy farmers, arguing for increased revenue or greater assistance in the face of American challenges to the marketing system, not calling for a reduction in the number of farmers and lower prices for consumers. In the end, of course, the cabinet collectively decides in the best interests of the public as a whole, with the premier taking a lead role and, if necessary, making the final call in the event of an impasse. At least, that is the traditional theory.

But Mike Harris has a different view of government, and so naturally his view of the role of ministers is also at odds with tradition. In his mind, his government was elected to reduce or eliminate much of the existing structure of government. The role of his ministers, then, would be to enforce these cutbacks in their various areas of responsibility. If they were to have any hope of implementing their ambitious and radical agenda, no minister could be allowed to be captured by client groups, any more than by self-serving bureaucrats. The Minister of Education and Training was not supposed to be a friend of the teachers, but their nemesis. As one observer put it, Harris "didn't want his Transportation minister becoming a pawn of public transit or road safety advocates ... his Social Services minister was there to cut social services, not expand them," and so on.

The premier's view of the cabinet's role helps to explain John Snobelen, a man with a grade eleven education, ending up in the driver's seat at the Ministry of Education and Training. It also explains Dave Tsubouchi, a Markham lawyer and councillor, becoming Minister of Community and Social Services; Al Palladini, a Toronto car dealer, being appointed Minister of Transportation; and Al Leach (a man with some actual experience in transportation policy as a former chair of the Toronto Transit Commission) receiving not Transport, but the Municipal Affairs portfolio.

Even the men in question openly expressed surprise at some of Harris's choices. As he later told Queen's Park veteran John Ibbitson, when Mike Harris phoned to offer him the Transport post, Al Palladini thought the premier had misdialled. "Mike, this is Al *Palladini,*" he said, assuming the post should have gone to Leach. But Harris did not think he had made any mistakes, at least not at the time.

The premier did not ignore all of the old guard in his selections. Instead of Davis supporters such as Morley Kells or Chris Stockwell, though, he chose to elevate three long-standing veterans who had never been considered serious cabinet material during the Davis years. All from rural ridings, all self-made men and all right-wingers who had shared a brief moment of glory with Harris during the Miller interregnum, these were people whom Harris understood and trusted to follow his script. Norm Sterling, who had been in the Tory caucus for nearly twenty years and managed only a one-year stint as a minister without portfolio, was appointed to Consumer and Commercial Relations. (Having managed to stay out of trouble there, he later moved on to the more important Environment Department, where his major role was to eliminate regulations and positions.) Noble Villeneuve, a farmer and franco-Ontarian from eastern Ontario, was given the Agriculture portfolio and responsibility for francophone affairs, while Bob "Mad Dog" Runciman was given the solicitor general's post, with responsibility for Correctional Services.

As the above list of names suggests, the Harris cabinet has been a male domain. Despite two subsequent shuffles, this has remained the case. In 1995 there were only four women in a cabinet of nineteen. Their numbers rose to five in 1997, but the cabinet increased to twenty-three members. The addition of Isabel Bassett as Minister for Culture and Recreation in 1997, for example, was negated by the earlier demotions of Brenda Elliott and Marilyn Mushinski. As for the premier's former leadership opponent, Dianne Cunningham, her role in cabinet was purely symbolic and her portfolios of Minister responsible for the Status of Women and Intergovernmental Affairs have been so unimportant as to be irrelevant.

Meanwhile Elizabeth Witmer's appointment as Minister of Labour was fortuitous for the government, as she proved herself steady and capable during endless rounds of labour strife. This competence did much to enhance her status at the cabinet table until, in the most recent round of cabinet shuffles, she ended up with the Health portfolio. However, many insiders believe this move had as much to do with optics as enhanced responsibility, as the government looks to soften its image heading towards the next election. Opposition critics were quick to seize on this ploy.

NDP leader Howard Hampton described the move as "political damage control," while Liberal Dalton McGuinty declared, "The government has hired the well-known public relations team of Witmer and Johnson ... to spin a softer line. They are very capable and convivial, very gentle in their demeanour. But we're still heading down the same path."

Arguably the only other really important woman in the Harris cabinet has been a second-round draft choice, Janet Ecker, in the crucial Social Services portfolio. No doubt Ms. Ecker was able to learn from the trials of her predecessor, Dave Tsubouchi, but she already had far better credentials than the hapless Tsubouchi in the first place. Yet she was forced to wait in the wings as his parliamentary secretary for two years. An obvious explanation for this delay is that her background as a university-educated member of the urban elite did nothing to endear her to the premier, in addition to the drawback of her gender. Many believe she was also hampered by the perception that she was too soft or "Red Tory" in her outlook. Since her elevation, however, she has made up for lost time and made quite a name for herself as a tough, uncompromising neo-conservative of the Margaret Thatcher school. In short, she has become "one of the boys."

Perils of a "Common Sense" Cabinet

"What I know about housing you could write on the head of a pin and still have room for the Lord's Prayer," Al Leach exclaimed to reporters after being sworn in as the Minister of Municipal Affairs and Housing. Unfortunately, the same could have been said for many of his cabinet colleagues. Mike Harris's penchant for self-made men would prove to be a recipe for incompetence, if not disaster.

Almost from the first day, the trio of Palladini, Snobelen and Tsubouchi were in trouble, barely taking time to open their mouths before changing feet. Al Leach and Jim Wilson were not far behind. Yet most of these ministers remain in the cabinet to this day, having merely had their hands slapped or their portfolio changed. Like Palladini, Dave

Tsubouchi and John Snobelen retained their place in cabinet despite their many gaffes, although Tsubouchi suffered an obvious demotion.

By contrast, Brenda Elliott and Marilyn Mushinski, appointed primarily to give some semblance of gender balance, lasted barely a year before being dropped from the cabinet altogether. Mushinski's failings were obvious. This was the Culture minister who showed so little enthusiasm for her portfolio that, when forced to defend it, she could only manage the limp "Culture is not a frills ministry. There is not a government in the Western world that doesn't have a ministry of culture." When pressed, she also displayed a dazzling lack of knowledge of Canadian artists, reminiscent of her boss's knowledge gaps. Unable to name a single Canadian movie, for example, she volunteered the title *Mortal Beloved* as a guess. (The film, about the German composer Beethoven, was actually titled *Immortal Beloved.*) Elliott, on the other hand, appeared to be no more incompetent than most of the men in question, leading many observers to wonder whether gender did not play an even more important role in cabinet selection than the low numbers alone would suggest.

For many of the neophytes, the lack of knowledge of their portfolio was accentuated by their lack of parliamentary experience. For almost all of them, the neo-conservative values they espoused were an additional problem, since these values were not shared by most of the electorate. As a result, on many occasions their biggest mistake was simply speaking their minds

Worse still, many of them seemed to be as insular and parochial as their leader. It was not long before references to the cabinet's apparent lack of contact with the real world began to appear. For a group of alleged populists, this was the unkindest cut of all, but one that seemed to fit with their self-made success stories. In an article for the *Globe and Mail* in November 1995, columnist Murray Campbell summed up this anomaly by suggesting that "anyone looking to confirm the existence of parallel universes need look no further."

The Minister of Transportation was a classic example of all of these problems. From the beginning, the affable Al Palladini was a godsend for the Opposition parties and the media. The owner of a well-known suburban Toronto car dealership ("Any Palladini's a pal of mine"), with no other obvious qualifications for public office, Palladini had just been elected for the first time when he found himself in charge of the Transportation ministry. He also found himself with a chauffeur and a driver he had no intention of giving up. When he heard from reporters that the premier was proposing to eliminate these perks as a symbolic nod to the massive cuts to municipal transit the government had just imposed, the new Transport minister unhesitatingly replied, "Fighting the traffic to come downtown, I'm not used to. I wouldn't want to do it every day. It's rough."

A few well-chosen words from the premier convinced Palladini to change his mind, but not his outlook. Before long he was in hot water again. When it was learned the government was eliminating the Emergency Traffic Patrol as part of its cost-cutting measures, the public as well as the Opposition was shocked. Liberal MPP and Transportation critic Mike Colle told Palladini the service was too important to do away with — some 1,500 motorists had been rescued in the previous month alone — and the savings would be negligible in any event. Why would the minister want to endanger public safety?

The minister's reply brought the house down. It was up to motorists with cell phones, not the government, to rescue stranded motorists, he said. "Most people have a cellular phone in their car," Palladini began, but was cut off by Opposition pandemonium. When Colle questioned this answer, saying "How many of us nowadays can afford cell phones? Let's get real. This is not a practical way of dealing with emergency problems!" the minister responded that there were always auto-club towing services and radio traffic reports to assist motorists in distress. A frustrated Colle suggested the minister "take a long ride up to Wawa in his limo with a cell phone and let him try to phone in and tell us how he's doing."

Unfortunately, the next round of trouble for Palladini came from his personal life, not his department. Faced with a paternity suit and the revelation he had been paying $1,500 monthly for child support for several years, the minister decided to lie low. This was a wise move in a caucus with a significant "family values" wing, although Harris himself, as noted earlier, does not subscribe to that approach. With several second marriages and other minor misdemeanours in the cabinet ranks, the palimony "scandal" was something the premier was rightly inclined to ignore as unrelated to the minister's performance of his duties.

By the time of the 1997 cabinet shuffle, however, even the premier could see that it was time for Palladini to move on, if not out. The politically sensitive legislation on truck safety was finally passed, but only after a special one-day recall of the legislature during the summer recess. (The legislation had languished on the order paper during an embarrassing series of delays which not everyone felt was the fault of the minister, and the minister himself had given up trying to explain the reasons for the delays.) Palladini's move, which many saw as a demotion, also allowed former Harris adviser and neo-con stalwart Tony Clement to take over the reins at Transport as Palladini moved on to become Minister of Economic Trade, Tourism and Development. In announcing the shuffle the premier nevertheless chose to accentuate the positive, describing Mr. Palladini as "the best salesman in government" and declaring he had "the energy, enthusiasm and commitment to market Ontario around the world."

By 1998 Mr. Palladini was up to his old tricks again. Rather than selling Ontario to the world, he was busy lambasting the cab drivers of Ottawa for "shoddy" vehicles and incompetent service. Residents of the nation's capital, always attuned to slights from the provincial capital, responded with their own gibes at the hapless minister. Finally, the mayor of Ottawa, Jim Watson, managed to put the matter in perspective by pointing out that the issue of licensing was a municipal, not a provincial, responsibility in any event, and that he didn't "think we need a royal commission on the matter."

The uproar over his broadside had barely subsided when the minister was widely quoted for his enthusiastic reply to a reporter's tongue-in-cheek question about the state of the economy and recent buoyant liquor and condom sales. "I think they go hand in hand," the minister replied, apparently serious. "I think it's great ... I hope they give Mike Harris's government the credit for all the partying that's going on, and all the positive things that are happening in our economy. I think it's all tied in. It's all one and the other." There was no official word on the reaction of the Tories' "family values" caucus, but it seems unlikely they were amused.

Certainly the general public was not amused by the handling of the social-services file by Palladini's colleague, Dave Tsubouchi. The self-made man from Markham was another early victim of political foot-in-mouth disease, as he attempted to square the government's 21 per cent reduction in welfare rates with the essential facts of life, such as eating. The public had been given an example of his political naïveté just a few days after the initial cuts were announced in July 1995, when he eagerly agreed with a reporter that the climate in British Columbia was much better than Ontario's. This comment immediately led to sensational stories that the Harris Conservatives were planning to encourage welfare recipients to leave the province for other jurisdictions, as Ralph Klein had done in Alberta. Luckily for B.C. premier Glen Clark, the public outrage prompted a "clarification" from Tsubouchi the next day and the potential B.C. exodus was averted.

The tone had been set, however, and the new minister fared even less well once the legislature began sitting in the fall. As *Globe and Mail* columnist Murray Campbell concluded in an article on Mr. Tsubouchi's troubles on November 11, the minister "has an uncanny ability to deliver self-inflicted wounds ... [which] call into question his basic competence." Having passed regulations cutting the welfare benefits of thousands of disabled people, he rescinded the cuts when they were made public, indicating they had been a mistake and he hadn't realized what he was signing. Next, when asked how single welfare recipients could survive on a monthly food allowance of $90.21, he replied they could buy tins of tuna for $0.69. Informed by the Opposition that tuna could not be purchased for less than $1.29 at the time, he suggested recipients should bargain for a better price.

By now the minister was a laughingstock in the legislature. Tsubouchi made matters worse in response to a question by NDP leader Bob Rae. "Instead of obfuscating, the way most politicians do when answering questions," a reporter noted, the minister "indicated he had a shopping list showing how to live within the limits imposed by the government's cut, and he would be happy to share it" with Mr. Rae. Having publicly revealed its existence, Tsubouchi then stalled for weeks before finally offering it to Mr. Rae alone, apparently believing he could keep it from the media and the public at large.

Needless to say, debate over the list and its contents made for continuous coverage in most provincial newspapers for weeks. With bologna featuring prominently on the frugal list, Tories attending a fundraiser found their cars pelted with the menu staple as they arrived. Diners in posh Toronto restaurants debated whether tuna could be found for *less* than 69 cents (one businessman claiming he had seen it advertised for a mere 63 cents in Leamington), and a *Toronto Sun* columnist actually followed the menu for a month and reported on it. Tsubouchi never recovered from this fiasco. He was demoted barely a year after his appointment, to the much less demanding Consumer and Commercial Relations portfolio, and has rarely been heard from since.

A similar fate awaited John Snobelen, the third member of the trio of loose cannons whom everyone predicted would cause Harris problems. The self-made millionaire with the grade eleven education, whose fortune came from a waste-transport business, was evidently a fan of business-management theories and jargon. Seen musing on video with departmental officials about the need to "invent a crisis" in education, Snobelen did himself irreparable damage shortly after taking office, damage which no amount of explanation about the context could remedy. Certainly not the minister's own explanation that to invent a crisis was "not just an act of courage, there's some skill involved." Likewise his use of the term "tool kit" to describe his department's proposed $400 million in reforms produced much hilarity, but little action.

His alternatively unctuous and aggressive manner also did little to repair his image. His failure to deliver on the promised reforms, and unwillingness to communicate with stakeholders, were a major source of frustration. One Ottawa trustee, infuriated by the uncertainty, actually bought a ticket to a Tory fundraiser in order to confront the premier on the issue. Ted Best told reporters, "I've been a trustee for 23 years and I've never, never seen such a lack of communication. I don't know if it's arrogance on Snobelen's part or ineptness, but they're losing credibility fast."

The minister's subsequent battles with the teachers over Bill 160 — the government's plan to centralize control of education at Queen's Park and drastically reduce both the number of teachers and overall expenses — became legendary. By the end of his tenure, the two sides were barely speaking. In the end Harris was obliged to send in his one of his few heavy hitters, Dave Johnson from Management Board, to salvage what was rapidly becoming a very damaging situation for the government. Nevertheless, Snobelen survived, moving on to Natural Resources rather than out of the cabinet entirely.

Another problem minister proved to be Al Leach, a man with respectable credentials as the former manager of the Toronto Transit Commission (TTC). Leach was evidently misplaced in the Municipal Affairs and Housing portfolio, as he himself suggested. His difficulties showed up early on, when he was attempting to defend sections of the government's omnibus bill relevant to his department. "I had that right there to read back to you," he started out in answer to an Opposition question. "Completely lost ... Mr. Speaker, give me two minutes ... That's another one I'm going to take under advisement," he concluded, to general hilarity on the Opposition benches. In fairness, Leach was attempting to respond to questions on a bill which would later suffer the indignity of more than 160 *government*-sponsored amendments, the first and most painful example of the inexperience of the premier's office and the ineptness of his cabinet.

However, Leach's ability to recognize his limitations was commendable. Having taken on the Housing portfolio, he initially planned to implement the "Common Sense Revolution" platform commitment to sell off social housing ("We will end the public-housing boondoggle") as quickly as possible. No fan of public housing himself, he thought he could get rid of "the bricks and mortars business" in a few days. "I thought, Oh that's pretty easy. Wonder what I'll do tomorrow?" But as he told reporters, it turned out not to be so simple.

Having sent Ernie Eves to Britain to examine Margaret Thatcher's privatization scheme, the Harris government slowly began to realize there were a number of constraints they had not anticipated. This was only half the story, however, since the Canadian situation was very different from the one in Britain in the first place. As Don Richardson, the chair of the Metro Toronto Housing Authority, put it, "They didn't research it. They 'knew' they had a social housing problem and they figured, Thatcher did it so why can't we?" As Leach himself put it, "The more you get into it the more you find that these issues are very complex, and they're very volatile because you're affecting people's lives." Perhaps the most interesting thing about this comment is the fact that it came from a politician, or someone who presumably would have entered public life to affect people's lives …

Lack of political judgment appears to be a major problem with Leach, who also ran afoul of the Speaker and parliamentary procedure on three separate occasions in his first two years on the job. Although the first incident, in which he supported an aide's inappropriate intervention in a legal action, earned a mild rebuke from the Speaker, the second incident caused an uproar. By this time the Speaker was none other than the spurned aspiring cabinet minister Chris Stockwell, but it is unlikely a different Speaker would have produced a significantly different result. As the Opposition parties correctly pointed out in outrage, the minister's misdeed was irrefutable. Before legislation had been passed in the legislature, he had approved and distributed a series of advertisements describing the measures as a *fait accompli*. The Speaker, in a highly publicized and embarrassing decision, found the minister in contempt of the legislature.

The minister's third offence was to write a letter to the quasi-judicial Health Services Restructuring Commission. This action, according to Integrity commissioner Greg Evans, had "flagrantly" violated the Members' Integrity Act. Amazingly, the minister's defence was ignorance of the act, although the premier in his defence of the minister countered that actually Leach had contravened the act because he thought he was entitled to.

Another explanation that was offered for Leach's behaviour came from the Integrity commissioner himself. According to Evans, the TTC management system "has traits similar to a peacetime army. It is a well-established system based on power and control — in other words, authoritarian — and makes no pretense at being a democratic institution." Presumably the conclusion Evans had drawn was that Leach was having trouble functioning in a democracy. (This conclusion, of course, was not unrealistic, given the behaviour of the Harris government in its first term, an issue which re-emerges frequently in the next several chapters.)

A similar incident occurred less than a year later. This time, however, it involved the solicitor general, Bob Runciman. In an effort to highlight the government's accomplishments to date, the Throne Speech prepared for the return of the legislature in April 1998 trumpeted, among other things, the "success" of the Tories' hard-line approach to youth crime. Using information provided by Runciman's department, the speech read by Lieutenant-Governor Hilary Weston referred to the parents of a young offender and cited their appreciation for the boot camp which "gave us back our son." Unfortunately for Runciman, by identifying the parents by name in the speech, he had apparently contravened the federal Young Offenders Act, which prohibits the publication of any information that could lead to the identification of a young offender.

This regulation, of course, is not an obscure one. And Mr. Runciman, as solicitor general, should surely have been expected to be familiar with the provision. Yet, when questioned by reporters about Opposition calls for his resignation, Runciman declared, "I don't have any plans to resign." Instead, he told reporters, his actions were legal because the ministry had obtained a waiver from the mother of the young offender. The following day the minister was obliged to retract his statement. "I was informed ... that we had a waiver signed and that there was a legal opinion," he said, "but I now understand that wasn't the case." According to several legal experts, the issue of consent was irrelevant. "Only a court order can lift the ban on publication of information identifying a young offender," said Nicholas Bala of Queen's University. Professor Bala, the author of a text on the act and a leading authority in the field, added that the speech "appears to be in violation of the Act, and it's not a mere technical violation."

In the end, the minister resigned several days later, after a morning meeting with the premier and his aides. In the legislature, Runciman indicated he was resigning out of "respect for the office I've held for the past two and a half years, and my high regard for the laws of our country," but he also emphatically denied any wrongdoing and expressed confidence that he would return to his post after a public inquiry. The premier, meanwhile, told the legislature that he had "lost from cabinet today somebody who cares deeply about law and order, about justice in the province, who takes his role very, very seriously."

Runciman was later reinstated after an inquiry found that, although the minister's action was undoubtedly a breach of the Young Offenders Act, it was taken without intent to commit a crime and, more important, was protected by parliamentary privilege. The author of the offending Throne

Speech, whiz-kid Guy Giorno, was similarly protected, the inquiry found, a point which NDP leader Howard Hampton viewed with considerable scepticism. If this is permitted under the guise of parliamentary privilege, he asked pointedly, what else will be encouraged?

Few in the legislature would have disagreed with the premier that Bob Runciman took the issue of law and order very seriously. It was the *legislature* that both he and the Harris government did not seem to respect. Runciman had initially refused to resign and Harris had supported his decision until the issue became too hot to handle. By now it was obvious to everyone that the authoritarian mindset identified by the Integrity commissioner as one of the reasons for Al Leach's difficulties was, in fact, a cabinet-wide problem in the Harris government. It was also one with which the general public was becoming increasingly unhappy.

Given the Harris team's collective lack of experience and preparation for public life, the question most often asked by outside observers is "Why would anyone have been surprised at these developments?" Like his fellow authoritarian populists, Newt Gingrich and Ralph Klein, Mike Harris and his self-made cabinet exhibited an entirely predictable combative approach and inflexible attitude. True believers in the neo-conservative agenda — and lacking the relevant education, training or parliamentary experience to appreciate that politics is the art of the possible — the Harris team was programmed to proceed aggressively with its implementation. Once elected, they could be counted on to do what they said, regardless of the consequences, unless their incompetence derailed them.

Unlike Ralph Klein, however, the Harris Conservatives made crystal clear their radical agenda nearly a year before the election, when they released their election platform, the "Common Sense Revolution." The next chapter examines the evolution of this neo-conservative manifesto, and the election strategy that allowed them to put it into practice.

5

The "Common Sense" Revolution

Common sense appears to be only another name for the
thoughtlessness of the unthinking. It is made up of the preju-
dices of childhood, the idiosyncrasies of individual character
and the opinion of the newspapers ...
— W. Somerset Maugham

We seldom attribute common sense
except to those who agree with us.
— La Rochefoucauld

If those voting for Mike Harris and the Conservatives in 1995 thought
they were getting a "new and improved" version of the Bill Davis years,
they were in for a shock. Mike Harris was no Bill Davis, and the Tory
platform was like no Conservative blueprint Ontario had ever seen
before. As Harris himself said, "I'm not talking about tinkering, about
incremental changes, or about short-term solutions. We need a revolution in this province, a Common Sense Revolution of practical ideas."

Even the timing of the release of the Harris platform was revolutionary, coming as it did a year before the eventual election call. Trailing a
distant second in the polls, with the Liberals under Lyn McLeod — a
leader hardly anyone could name — securely in first place and poised to
take power whenever the writ was dropped, the Conservatives decided

extreme measures were called for. As old-time Liberal advisers began to measure office space in Queen's Park and veteran Liberal spin doctor Pat Gossage was seen parking his car in space allocated for the government, the Conservatives realized they had nothing to lose.

At the same time, Harris and his advisers astutely recognized the public was in a foul mood. In the aftermath of the Charlottetown debacle and a decade of Brian Mulroney's brokerage politics, voter cynicism was at an all-time high. The situation deteriorated during the chaotic Liberal/NDP interregnum, from David Peterson's perceived arrogance to Bob Rae's hapless attempts to reconcile socialist goals with fiscal realities. By 1994, Ontario voters were in no frame of mind to listen to vague commitments or condescending platitudes.

With this in mind, the Tory strategy of releasing the full platform so far in advance of the election was intended to repeat the phenomenal success of the federal Liberals the year before. In October 1993, Jean Chrétien and his advisers had parlayed their *Red Book* promises into a stunning majority victory. Like Chrétien, Harris and his team knew voters were disenchanted with glitz and wanted to see the beef. As one senior Liberal described the *Red Book*'s role in their electoral success, "It was the whole story. Period. Leadership didn't enter into it, except negatively. The funny thing is, I don't think it mattered a damn what we put in there. They wanted us to put our promises in writing, so they could hold us to them, but I don't think they cared what those promises were, so long as we stuck with them."

That may have been true, but it was also clear to anyone who actually read the *Red Book* that it was a classic liberal package. If anything, it emphasized the return of the federal Liberals to their centre/left roots, positioning them to regain the voter coalition created by Pierre Trudeau that had brought them nearly twenty years of power. The "Common Sense Revolution" (CSR), by contrast, was taking the Ontario Conservatives into uncharted waters on the extreme right. It was a far cry from the "Red Tory" progressive/conservative coalition that George Drew, Leslie Frost and John Robarts had constructed, and that Bill Davis had carefully tended at Queen's Park for nearly the same length of time as Trudeau held sway in Ottawa.

The Origins of the Big Blue Machine

As the largest and richest province, Ontario has an image as a stable, middle-of-the road society — one the whole country shares. Unlike in the West, where massive change took place in a very short space of time, Ontario's transition, both economically and socially, was slow and steady. Its culture was ideally suited to a centrist political party promoting a balanced approach to issues, one favouring pragmatic solutions and cooperation over ideology and conflict. The Ontario Conservatives since the Second World War had done exactly that, and the voters had rewarded them for their efforts.

Balance was a key factor in the success of the Tory strategy, since the province and its people were never as homogeneous or single-minded as its tranquil postwar history might suggest. In fact religious differences, an agrarian protest movement and the evolution of numerous special interest groups had all been potential sources of conflict over time. So was the very real but minority right-wing sentiment of rural and Loyalist Ontarians, who favoured a more "minimalist" government. But the Conservatives, under Robarts and Davis, had brilliantly managed to keep these tendencies under control. They were able to do this primarily through their assiduous attention to what political scientist Sid Noel has called the "operative norms" of the Ontario political culture.

Of these norms, the most important is "managerial efficiency," or the electorate's expectation that, once in power, a political party will run an efficient and almost non-partisan administration. This expectation, while unusual, is remarkably similar to that of Albertans. However, the similarities end there. In Ontario, competence is expected to enable the governing party to deliver the goods on two more operative norms that Albertans certainly do not share: maintaining the province's all-important economic dominance and ensuring its pre-eminent role in the federation. These objectives reflect an underlying theme of Ontario's political culture — the perception that the province is the centre or heartland of the country. Put bluntly, Ontarians believe their province's interests are synonymous with the national interest. Nowhere is this perception more evident than in their tendency to define themselves as Canadians first, and Ontarians only as an afterthought. Needless to say, these views are strikingly at odds with those of Albertans.

These perceptions naturally have electoral consequences. As John Wilson, an expert in Ontario voting behaviour, has concluded, "The one side of this dominant pattern of values, stressing the necessity of competent leadership and efficient management, is very conservative." At the same time, the other dominant pattern of balancing competing claims and "focusing on fair play for everyone" is clearly progressive. The conclusion Wilson and others have drawn from this behaviour is that Ontario "is best described as a 'red tory' province, quite different from any other part of Canada."

There can be little doubt the postwar Conservative leadership in the province understood this progressive/conservative dynamic of the political culture. Managerial competence was always a theme of their campaigns. From Leslie Frost's view of government as a family-run business ("Government is business, the people's business") to John Robarts's updated image of himself and his cabinet as the CEO and board of directors of a corporation ("I'm a management man myself"), the notion that the party should check its ideological baggage at the government door was always recognized and respected.

As a result, successive Conservative governments pragmatically and efficiently used the tools of the state to modernize and industrialize the provincial economy. They poured public money into massive infrastructure programs such as highways and electrical power. They also expanded the role and size of government through commissions, boards and agencies, and promoted manufacturing through industrial incentive and support programs. For Bill Davis, ensuring Ontario's continued economic domination meant a "pragmatic balancing of public–private sector interests that our present-day capitalism seems to indicate." A "proud capitalist," Davis nevertheless invested heavily in state enterprises and created a modern educational system that included community colleges and a network of regionally based universities.

Although the Conservatives were aggressively pursuing their economic goals, they never lost sight of the need to maintain the balance between competing economic and social interests. This shared appreciation of Ontario's political culture led each of the Tory premiers to emphasize consultation over confrontation, and assume certain social responsibilities as the proper role of government. For Leslie Frost, the progressive/conservative balance was "a partnership between the two philosophies of economic advance and human betterment." By the Davis era, the "progressive" side of the Tories' balancing act produced such untypically conservative policies as rent controls; a human rights code; a women's commission; and the government purchase of Suncor, the provincial equivalent of Trudeau's "window on the energy sector," Petro-Canada.

For many, Bill Davis was the consummate Ontario politician, pragmatic and flexible. For some, he was too flexible, too cautious and too concerned with consultation. His apparent lack of any real ideological commitment and well-known willingness to compromise were a constant source of frustration for his opponents. If the term "Teflon man" had been in use in his day, Bill Davis would have been its poster boy. Yet most agreed with a former colleague, Hugh McCaulay, who argued that the Davis legacy of a prosperous and stable Ontario was only possible because of these traits: "We've had a minimum of strife and a maximum of progress and change. I don't see how we'd have gone as far under any other kind of leadership, because the 'do it my way and do it now' kind of approach won't work in Ontario."

One of his former caucus members, Morley Kells, recounted how "the boss never talks about philosophy, at least not to caucus anyway. He talks about the art of politics, the art of getting elected ... He says if you can't get elected you can't do what you want to do." Of course, Davis was also viewed by many in his party as the quintessential Red Tory, far on the left of many of the Conservative party's grassroots supporters. Certainly it is true that Davis sometimes was obliged to modify his positions, because of opposition not from the public, but from within the right wing of his own caucus.

Although he usually attempted to play down "this left–right thing" in public, he had been known to express his frustration with "some of my very right-wing Tory friends." Former cabinet minister Sally Barnes confided to his biographer that the normally tolerant Davis "can't abide the far right politically, and he can't abide it personally." Especially from a political perspective, Barnes continued, the right-wingers made him "angry" because he saw them as dangerous for the party and for the future of the coalition the party had created. "He feels right-wingers are immovable ... and that's contrary to what he thinks is proper ... He knows hard-line views won't work."

Nevertheless, by 1995 the right wing had taken charge of the once-mighty Conservative party, as the previous chapter demonstrated. This had not been too difficult, of course, since ten years in the political wilderness had left the party broke, leaderless and in third place in the legislature. For backbenchers like Jim Taylor, a former cabinet minister who once said, "Pragmatism is the enemy of democracy," the Harris approach to politics was much more attractive, and the "Common Sense Revolution" was what platforms and elections were supposed to be all about: hard-line views and straight talk. "That might get you defeated, but so what?"

Defeated is what everyone expected Mike Harris to be. The "tax fighter" had gone much too far this time, with a radical platform no one in his or her right mind would try to sell to the Ontario electorate.

Changing Course

Undaunted by their decision to abandon the party's traditional winning formula, the Harris team pressed on with their plan to replace pragmatism with the ideological "higher ground" of the Far Right. The "Common Sense Revolution" was a form of manifesto, and its publication was a figurative "throwing down of the gauntlet." As if to stress this dramatic change in party policy, the Harris team decided to drop all references to "Progressive." In fact, almost no mention was made of the Conservative party, since it was felt Brian Mulroney had done irreparable damage to the party's image. Instead, throughout the CSR text and in the election campaign that followed, voters were constantly urged to support the "Mike Harris Team."

Harris and his advisers were convinced that by staking out their ground ahead of time they would have the advantage, regardless of the content of their message. They also believed their views accurately reflected the concerns of a "silent majority," not a fringe minority.

The question was how to reach this large group in the electorate and raise their consciousness. By releasing the platform so far in advance, the

Conservatives felt they would have a year to communicate their radical new message and familiarize the electorate with their plans. Even better, they would be able to put the Liberals on the defensive, once the election was under way, by exposing what they were sure would be that party's lack of firm alternatives to the CSR.

True to form, as soon as Premier Bob Rae called the election, Liberal leader Lyn McLeod and her party launched a traditional-style campaign, trying to be all things to all people. This earned them the dubious title of "the big Liberal sponge in the centre," a description offered by one analyst shortly before the writ was dropped. Political scientist Nelson Wiseman went on to predict the Liberals would take as many as 100 of the 130 seats, since "the NDP is discredited and ... the Conservative right-wing appeal isn't working." In fairness to Wiseman, his expectations were shared by almost everyone in the province. Only the Harris Tories continued to have faith in their strategy.

The wheels started to come off the Liberal machine shortly afterwards. Their pale pink imitation of the federal Liberals' *Red Book* was a hodge-podge of policy options that was immediately ridiculed by virtually everyone who read it. As the campaign unfolded, the Liberals found themselves constantly clarifying their positions and often contradicting themselves. Meanwhile, the Conservatives stuck to their basic message, reinforcing their revolutionary platform commitments with hard-hitting, unequivocal campaign speeches.

Initially the Conservatives met with considerable resistance, not only because Harris himself was still seen by the media as a loose cannon, but also because the high degree of voter cynicism had created a credibility gap. The Harris team expected some voters to reject the neo-con agenda outright. These voters likely would have strong attachments to other parties and could not be won over in any event. For the critical swing voters the Tories were courting — no longer committed to any particular party — the issue of credibility was crucial.

On April 30, Mike Harris was confronted with the issue head on. "Your plan sounds wonderful and I want to vote for you," declared Peter Judd, a Toronto resident, when he met Harris mainstreeting in the west end of the city. "But I'm afraid that, when you get in there, you'll just say the same things as all the rest." Ironically, in what may have been a revealing glimpse into the ability of Harris's populist style to overcome substance, Judd went on to say, "You'll just say there isn't enough [money] to do what you planned." Since the CSR was not planning to spend any money, but rather to *cut* spending, this last remark suggests a lack of familiarity with the details of the Tory platform, a situation that may well have worked to the party's advantage. The message was clear: Harris and his team would have to work hard for the rest of the campaign to convince voters that they meant what they said.

Apparently they succeeded. Time and time again during the campaign, the media predicted the Tories would stumble and fall. Their "Common Sense Revolution" was just too extreme for Ontario, too right-wing and bizarre. Instead, the Conservatives picked up steam in the second half of the campaign while the Liberals collapsed, their leader and platform in disarray. Days before the election the Conservatives went from being in a tight race with Lyn McLeod to leading the pack. On June 8, Harris and his party came in from the cold, winning an upset victory and a majority of seats.

As reporter John Ibbitson admitted in his account of the election, he and his colleagues "were certainly flummoxed" by the Harris victory. Ibbitson describes the electoral strategy of the Harris team as a "modern masterpiece of voter divination," focusing on their populist appeal to "a well-spring of discontent, impatience and longing for change." Yet while it was clear that Harris and his team had benefited from voter discontent as much or more as from the Liberal collapse, it was much less clear whether their victory reflected a real shift in majority voter opinion or merely a temporary fit of pique. This was an important distinction since, unlike Ralph Klein's clear-cut victory in Alberta, Harris had also benefited from the split opposition to his right-wing agenda that resulted from Ontario's three-party system.

The question was academic, however, and certainly not one that would interest Mike Harris. As far as he was concerned, he had a mandate for change. After their come-from-behind victory it soon became obvious these new-style Conservatives really meant everything they said (or almost everything). What was more, they were in a hurry to prove it. With almost unseemly haste, they proceeded to ram through some key elements of their plan, demonstrating that at least the second half of their platform title was not just an ad-man's gimmick. A revolution they had promised and a revolution they delivered, one that was neither bloodless nor quiet.

For many Ontarians the immediate shock was how ruthlessly the Harris team set about implementing their promises. But over time, as the implications of their sweeping changes began to sink in and become visible, the radical nature of the CSR agenda itself began to trouble more and more. This was certainly not "tinkering" at the margins, just as Mike Harris had warned. Unfortunately, it appeared many voters had not read the fine print in the CSR manifesto, while others had not expected what they viewed as campaign rhetoric to be taken literally.

Even reporters who had been covering Harris for years were taken aback by the hard right turn in policy direction. When Southam veteran Jim Coyle suggested the platform had actually been a successful ploy to head off the fledgling provincial Reform movement, and that the Tories would soon return to the centre of the political spectrum, he was informed in no uncertain terms by key Harris adviser Tom Long, "We're not coming back. This *is* the new centre."

What followed were three tumultuous years of political upheaval. By 1998, much of the infrastructure of government in Ontario had been changed, perhaps irrevocably. By 1998, Mike Harris and his Conservatives had also plummeted in the polls. They were consistently trailing the front-running Liberals under their new leader, Dalton McGuinty, a man whose views resembled those of Bill Davis in more ways than one. The same polls revealed that more and more voters were being turned off by the extreme nature of the neo-conservative agenda, while those who still supported the general direction of the agenda had serious concerns about the ability of the premier and his cabinet to implement and administer it.

In just a few short years, Ontario had become a leaner, meaner place to live. Polarized by deep divisions in society, the winners and losers of the "Common Sense Revolution" were becoming plain to everyone, and many did not like what they saw. The question on everyone's mind was "How did this happen in Ontario, of all places?" After all, this was not Alberta, but Canada's largest, most cosmopolitan and tolerant province.

Troubled Times

If ever the conditions were ripe for the success of the neo-conservative agenda in Ontario, it was in 1995. To begin with, the province had endured a recession longer and deeper than that faced by most of the rest of the country, seriously challenging its status as the economic engine of Canada. Especially for voters accustomed to using economic success as a measure of their government, this was a major crisis.

Ironically the federal Conservative government was the source of this crisis, although it escaped blame for some time. According to a 1993 study by the Institute of Policy Analysis at the University of Toronto, the recession, which began in Ontario in late 1989, was caused primarily by the series of tax increases imposed by the Mulroney government in Ottawa. These taxes, which "tended to push up inflation just as the Bank of Canada was trying to reduce it," were the "single most important factor" in Ontario's steep decline. The study's authors concluded the increases not only plunged the Ontario economy into a far deeper slide than would otherwise have been the case, but *slowed its recovery as well.* The resulting combination of high interest rates and less disposable income hobbled the middle class and severely curtailed the consumer spending which might have alleviated the economic pain.

Yet for most Ontario residents it was the successive tax increases imposed by the Peterson and Rae governments, which admittedly made matters worse, that were the primary target of voter frustration. With their economy further devastated by the one–two punch of globalization and free trade, much of the manufacturing sector in shreds and the unemployment figures still appalling — especially in a province accustomed to economic stability and job security — the citizens of Ontario in 1995 were anxious and unhappy, to say the least.

At the same time they had endured nearly a decade of relentless political "education" about the importance of deficits and the debt by politicians at all levels as well as by a sympathetic media. By now even previously complacent Ontarians were convinced something needed to be done about the soaring Ontario deficit. Their concern increased after Bob Rae's socialist government did an about-face in mid-term and introduced the "Social Contract," especially when the premier himself

196

declared this was an effort to restore investor confidence and avoid having the province hit the so-called debt wall. (One can only imagine what the public mood would have been if they had known NDP supporters such as Bob White of the Canadian Labour Congress had actually suggested that the province declare bankruptcy if necessary, a startling revelation made by the former premier in his memoirs.)

By 1995, Ontario voters had tried and rejected all three mainstream parties in less than a decade. Angry, disenchanted and fearful, the electorate was now extremely volatile. Voters were both cynical about the upcoming election and receptive to any new party message that might offer improvement in their personal situation after a decade of economic upheaval. Supporters of the federal Reform Party were seriously talking of forming a provincial wing. This was nothing short of remarkable in a province where voter attachment to political parties had been the most stable in the country for nearly fifty years. The Harris Conservatives, more than any other party, took advantage of this extraordinary situation.

In classic populist language, the CSR manifesto spoke directly to the individual voter. It was Harris himself who insisted on the use of "you" and "us" in the text. This allowed him to describe the changes he was proposing as "the same types of changes all of us have had to make in our own families and in our jobs." In a direct steal from *Contract with America,* the CSR continued: "For too long government has grown larger and still failed to meet the needs of the people. We will put people first."

By presenting the "Common Sense Revolution" as the outgrowth of popular input, of "the message you sent us" in "town hall meetings, in living rooms and around kitchen tables," Harris was able to claim that he was *agreeing* with "you, the people" that "the system is broke." It was "time for us to take a fresh look at government, to re-invent the way it works." While this language might have led some readers to conclude that a positive program of action was being proposed, nothing could have been further from the truth. The party that had been so closely identified with government for so long was now reinventing itself as the *anti-government* option, just as Ralph Klein's Conservatives had done in Alberta.

The CSR's focus on reducing the deficit, lowering taxes and creating jobs was both politically astute and entirely predictable. In fact, all three political parties attempted to emphasize deficit reduction and job creation. The Tories actually placed less emphasis on deficit reduction than the Liberals, but the Liberals and NDP were prepared to use the instruments of the state for job creation, while the Tories were not. Only the Tories pledged to reduce taxes as well, a plank that was to become both a major selling point during the campaign and a major headache for them afterwards. (The Liberals, in a desperate attempt to respond to the Harris juggernaut, actually proposed a number of complex and incomprehensible tax deductions and credits, but these were both minor and too specific, unable to compete with the simplicity of the Harris commitment to an across-the-board tax cut of 30 per cent.)

What really distinguished the Tory platform from the others was how they proposed to go about accomplishing their objectives of deficit and tax reduction. Even Bob Rae had been prepared to make some cuts to government expenditures. Both the NDP and the Liberals had mused about the possibility of streamlining some government services and programs, especially ones delivered by the municipalities. But the similarities ended there. While the two mainstream parties were proposing a moderate mix of remedies, including selected tax increases, over a four- or five-year period, "Chainsaw Mike" was planning to make big cuts, fast.

The "Common Sense" Agenda

The neo-conservative agenda promotes a negative option, not a positive one. Its goal is dismantling the state and removing it as much as possible from the marketplace. Not surprisingly, then, the "Common Sense Revolution" proposed to reduce the deficit *and* lower taxes solely by cutting back dramatically on the expenditures — the programs, services and activities — of the provincial government. Declaring that "Canadians are probably the most overgoverned people in the world," the CSR also set out to privatize, deregulate, restructure and "do better with less," all within the first two years of their mandate.

The CSR's plan was classic neo-conservative economics. Based on the trickle-down theory made popular by that quintessential neo-conservative Ronald Reagan, it argued that "reducing taxes stimulates consumer spending and investment, a direct boost to job creation. In fact, *taxes must be cut if we want to create jobs.*" Of course, this theory of indirect job creation resulting from tax breaks, known as "supply-side economics," was not new. But apart from Ronald Reagan's ill-fated experiment — in which taxes were lowered but the deficit ballooned and job creation stalled — it had rarely been promoted in such an aggressive fashion, with such specific numbers attached. Even Ralph Klein, the Canadian role model for the Harris team, had not tried to lower taxes while tackling the Alberta deficit.

It was difficult for the media to locate any mainstream Canadian economists who felt the Harris team's economic package was feasible, particularly in light of their commitment to cut both taxes and the deficit. True, some American economists continued to support the "supply side" theory, arguing that Reagan had simply failed to implement it correctly because he allowed government spending to increase dramatically. But even these stalwarts found the Harris plan "overly optimistic" or, as Professor Roberto Perotti of Columbia University put it, "brave."

Not surprisingly, there were many critics of the Conservatives' economic plan, some of whom felt it was deliberately misleading. The plan's credibility hinged on an endorsement by Mark Mullins, who was described in the CSR manifesto as "the Chief Economist at Midland Walwyn, one of Canada's most respected securities firms." Mr. Mullins's endorsement was somewhat suspect, however, since he was the author of the plan and a member of the Harris team.

The critics' charges of deliberate misrepresentation found further support in the text of the manifesto itself. Although the language of the CSR social-policy planks was straightforward and even provocative, the language promoting the neo-conservative economic agenda could only be charitably described as "carefully crafted." Presumably this was intended to avoid offending moderate sensibilities as much as possible. Some might even say it was a masterful effort to disguise an iron fist in a velvet glove. For example, instead of focusing on government cutbacks, deficit reduction, or even tax cuts, as the ultimate objective, the CSR maintained all these proposals had one overriding objective, the creation of 765,000 new jobs. In the era of the "jobless recovery," this was a message that would make voters sit up and take notice.

Where would these new jobs come from? According to the

Conservatives, they would result from the CSR's five-point plan for economic recovery:

- first, to cut provincial income taxes by 30 per cent over three years (a direct copy from the platform of New Jersey governor Christine Todd Whitman)
- second, to eliminate "government barriers to job creation, investment and economic growth"
- third, to reduce the size of government
- fourth, to cut "non-priority" government spending by 20 per cent in three years
- fifth, to balance the budget in five years

Put another way, a careful reading of the CSR revealed that the 765,000 new jobs Mike Harris was promising were expected to materialize in the private sector, without any direct help from the government, in part as a result of their plans to eliminate "barriers" and "red tape," and in part as a result of balancing the budget. But as the Conservatives' own background document admitted, their tax cut and massive reduction in government spending would start out by *decreasing* employment. The average voter might well have failed to grasp this point from the tortuous way in which this admission was worded. "We do not make any claims on how the CSR will affect growth," the document stated, "other than by diminishing it in the short term because of deficit reduction–induced economic drag."

By 1998 very few Ontarians would remember the stated overall objective of the CSR was to "implement a five-point Job Creation Plan," but they could hardly forget the five points. This was because the Harris government pursued these points with such vigour, while all talk of job creation had long since been downplayed, and with good reason.

As for the first point in the CSR's economic plan, the much-vaunted promise to cut income taxes by 30 per cent, this move could be expected to be popular with voters in theory, but, as an article in the early days of the election noted, many were sceptical. Of course, what the electorate distrusted was the claim by Harris that he could cut taxes *and* the deficit without having to make serious cutbacks in government spending, cutbacks in areas the public viewed as "untouchable," such as education and health care. Ontario voters wanted a tax cut, but not at any cost, and probably not before the deficit was brought under control.

The voters were right to have been sceptical, as the events of the next several years demonstrated. Certainly it was this commitment to a 30 per cent tax cut that caused the Harris government the most trouble in the years after their election, and actually forced them to modify their agenda. As Liberal Finance critic Gerry Phillips remarked during the campaign, "If it looks too good to be true, it probably is." Of course, the promises to cut the size of government, reduce "non-priority" spending and eliminate government "barriers" to growth were as carefully worded as the job-creation pledge. The 20 per cent cut in government expenditures, for example, would be accomplished "without touching a penny of Health Care funding. Other priority areas of law enforcement and *classroom funding* for education will also be exempt [emphasis added]."

While funding for health care was considered politically untouchable, the Harris team found a way around this dilemma by creating the concept of a "Fair Share Health Care Levy." Despite the fact this was an obvious tax grab, and one which would seriously reduce the benefit of the promised tax cut to the middle class, the measure received little attention before or during the election campaign. One explanation may be the CSR's promise that "under this plan [the levy] there will be NO new user fees." After several years of these indirect tax increases, Ontarians may have simply preferred a more direct, comprehensive approach to the inevitable. Certainly their tolerance for all forms of taxation was far greater than that of Albertans, giving Mike Harris more options than were available to Ralph Klein.

As for the use of the term "classroom funding" to qualify the Conservatives' commitment on education, the significance of these words would become all too evident in two years' time as massive cuts were introduced to almost all other elements of the educational system.

The same could be said of the term "barriers." While it was obvious from their manifesto that the Tories planned to privatize certain Crown corporations, notably TVOntario and the Liquor Control Board of Ontario, other aspects of government "red tape" they were planning to eliminate were not spelled out, the better for the Harris team to interpret this pledge any way they chose after the election. For those who followed political developments abroad, the shape of things to come could be surmised from the description of Michigan and Margaret Thatcher's Britain as models of right-thinking jurisdictions. Nevertheless, for many Ontarians the Conservatives' subsequent decisions to "decontrol" Ontario Hydro and eliminate many fundamental environmental, transportation and labour regulations were unexpected.

One thing was crystal clear. The Harris team was determined to eliminate the NDP's "job killing" labour legislation outlawing replacement workers and strengthening unions. While individual voters may have been indifferent to this issue, the business community was not, and the Conservatives wanted every one of those votes. Bill 40 was doomed if the Harris team won, and they wanted everyone to know it.

The exemption of law enforcement from spending cuts was somewhat surprising. Ontarians were unhappy with the handling of the Bernardo murder trial, which was unfolding in tandem with the election campaign — a situation the Tories shamelessly exploited — but the issue of police funding was not part of the broader public debate. In fact, only Tories were talking about this "issue." Many critics believed law enforcement was exempted for purely political reasons, to attract the support of the far right by emphasizing the Conservatives' commitment to "get tough" on crime, and especially youth crime.

Political considerations undoubtedly influenced the Tories' decision to avoid spelling out which "non-priority" areas would suffer the 20 per cent cut. Not only did this prevent voters from fixing on any particular area and objecting, but it essentially allowed the Conservatives to make some of the tough decisions at a much later date. Since the health, law-enforcement and education envelopes together accounted for the lion's share of the total Ontario budget in 1995, the task of imposing a 20 per cent cut in overall spending would actually mean imposing far more draconian cuts on the remaining government programs and services — or, as one critic of the Harris government put it, "taking a meat cleaver" to them.

Unfortunately, all the talk about the feasibility of the numbers in the CSR manifesto precluded any serious discussion of the assumptions on which it was based. This was a lucky thing for the Harris team, since many were incorrect, incomplete or simply false. As journalist Thomas Walkom later wrote, "The Common Sense Revolution set out to solve a set of problems ... that by and large did not exist."

Take the issue of taxation. The 30 per cent tax cut the Tories were promising was little short of astounding, and was obviously based on the assumption that existing provincial tax rates were far too high. To prove this assumption, the CSR relied on the statement that "our tax rates are currently among the highest in North America." The trouble with this statement is that it is simply irrelevant. Any comparison of tax rates is fraught with difficulties, but this example was worse than most. First, there are many kinds of taxes, and only a comparison of the total tax burden in different jurisdictions is meaningful. Even then, the comparison will not necessarily be useful if taxes are used to support different types or levels of services.

Using *North America* as the basis for comparison meant Ontario tax levels were being compared to those of the United States, a country out of step with almost all other Western democracies in terms of the level of public services provided to citizens with tax dollars. True, American taxes were lower than those in Ontario, but, for that matter, they were lower than those in all other Canadian provinces, and all other OECD (Organization for Economic Cooperation and Development) countries. The tax rate in Ontario was being compared to that of a country with no universal public health care, a dismal public education system and prohibitive university tuition fees, to say nothing of the higher crime rate and growing cost of private security for the middle class.

A more helpful comparison would have been with other Canadian provinces. Here, of course, the situation of the Ontario taxpayer appeared much less onerous. This was especially true if one compared marginal tax rates. For example, in 1995 an Ontario taxpayer earning $12,500 would have paid the second-lowest rate in country, while someone earning $50,000 would still be paying the third-lowest rate (behind British Columbia and Alberta). Put another way, only individuals earning more than $75,000 would be paying a rate that was the second-highest in the country. Yet the tax "burden" was always portrayed by Harris as something from which all Ontarians, and especially the middle class, needed relief.

Another interesting comparison of the Ontario tax situation can be made by examining the tax revenues of provincial governments relative to their gross domestic product (GDP). As Walkom has pointed out, on this basis Ontario was well below the provincial average in Canada for the entire period from 1981 to 1994. "Ontario's tax burden was consistently lower than that of neighbouring Quebec or well-to-do British Columbia. What's more, it was lower than Alberta's throughout the period." In fact in 1994, under the NDP, whom Harris accused of "tax and spend" excesses, "Ontario's provincial taxes as a percentage of GDP were not much higher than they had been thirteen years earlier when the Tories were in power."

But Mike Harris, as we have seen repeatedly, was not someone who would let the facts get in the way of a good plan. Certainly many of those who voted for Mike Harris in 1995 could be forgiven for having failed to grasp the extreme nature of his neo-conservative *economic* commitments, veiled as they were, and often concealed in reassuring populist rhetoric. On the other hand, for the true believers who had always been there on the conservative end of the Ontario Tory coalition, the language was clear enough to bring out some enthusiastic campaign troops who had rarely been visible since 1985.

The CSR did not stop with the ultra-conservative economic agenda. If it had, the election might have produced a different result. Despite winning 82 of the 130 seats in the legislature, the Conservative victory was hardly the majority mandate for change the Harris government has since claimed. Indeed, with 44.9 per cent of the popular vote, the Conservatives might as easily have concluded more people opposed their program than supported it.

The New Conservative Coalition

The Conservative victory resulted from a large number of factors, ranging from the most important — the total collapse of the Liberal campaign and the lack of any other viable alternative to the NDP — to such minor developments as the low number of incumbents from other parties who were seeking re-election. (Incumbents traditionally have an edge in elections, especially in closely contested three-way races, which was the case in many of the new Tory ridings.) But while they may have been lucky, the Harris team also had a plan, and judging from the election results it largely worked.

The source of the Conservatives' electoral support is the key to understanding this plan. While they recaptured most of the small-town seats in eastern Ontario they had held for generations, they did not regain their traditional levels of support in Northern Ontario or the City of Toronto, where immigrant, francophone and low-income voters were concentrated. Nor did they make gains or recapture seats in the other major urban areas, or among communities with large numbers of public servants. In short, they lost much of their traditional support.

These failures were more than compensated for, however, by their greatly increased support in southwestern Ontario and the suburban areas around Toronto. Here they took all seventeen of the fringe ridings of the Greater Toronto Area (GTA), and all but four of the twenty-eight rural and small-town ridings in the south. This so-called doughnut effect of the "905" area code is particularly instructive, for it is here that a large component of the affluent urban population had been relocating for some time. (With the electoral redistribution introduced by the Conservatives in 1998, the effect of this population shift will become even more pronounced, and can only be expected to benefit them in the next election.)

In short, while some elements of the traditional Conservative coalition remained, the Harris team actually fashioned a new coalition of voter support to win the 1995 election, one based almost exclusively on rural and suburban ridings, and one that excluded most urban voters and minorities. Another interesting demographic trend was the greatly increased support for the Tories among young and first-time voters, with some 46 per cent of those under twenty-five claiming to have voted for Harris, as opposed to 28 per cent for the Liberals and 15 per cent for the NDP.

What prompted this realignment? An analysis of voting results suggests the success of the Conservatives in forming a new coalition is directly related to the appeal of the two major elements of the CSR — its neoconservative economic and social agendas.

As political scientist Geoffrey Hale has discussed in his review of the volatility of party support in the 1990s, the correlation between income level and party choice in Ontario appears to have been greatly heightened by the severe economic dislocation of the previous decade. While the Conservatives could be expected to retain their stranglehold on upper-income ridings (winning twenty-six of twenty-nine with income levels at 11 per cent of the provincial average or more), a key component of their success in 1995 was their ability to take middle-income ridings away from the Liberals. Although most evident in the suburban GTA, another area of their success with middle-income voters was their breakthrough in industrial centres such as Kitchener, Oshawa and Cambridge.

This success, in turn, can be explained in part by these voters' receptivity to the Harris attack on high taxes and the deficit — the CSR's neoconservative economic agenda. But the social planks of the CSR also appealed to these suburban, middle-class voters, as well as to rural and small-town Ontario and the young. Not for nothing had Mike Harris and his team spent considerable time in their manifesto on a number of the "hot buttons" of Ontario political culture at the time. The Tories' response to these issues was a classic form of *social* conservatism, which, along with Harris's populist image, allowed the neo-cons to exploit voters' fears for electoral gain.

It was this second element of the CSR that cemented the Tory victory with many of their new-found supporters. Their right-wing social planks returned crucial rural ridings to the Tory fold — primarily by cutting in half the support for fringe parties such as the Family Coalition Party and the Confederation of Regions Party, which had siphoned off Conservative votes in the 1990 election and cost them many three-way races. In addition these planks helped Harris capture the suburban vote by offering a politically acceptable outlet for the growing frustrations of the economically endangered middle class and their adult children.

What were these so-called hot buttons? In Ontario in 1995 there were four: welfare, employment equity, young offenders and photo radar. Separately, none of these issues was important enough to make a difference. Taken together, they offered a potent weapon. While these issues may *seem* unrelated, there was actually a common thread running through them. What the Harris Tories intuitively understood and took advantage of was the public's underlying concern about a lack of balance, or "unfairness."

Equally important was their growing frustration with the government's failure to respond to their concerns. Not only had successive Liberal and NDP governments refused to recognize these concerns in any meaningful way, but, worse still, they had basically dismissed them as unfounded. Unlike the Davis Conservatives, neither the Liberals nor the NDP appeared to understand the governing imperative of consensus-building and conciliation. For middle-class, middle-of-the-road Ontarians, this was not acceptable behaviour from their government.

Some of these issues had been brewing for some time, while others had emerged more recently. For years a significant minority of the taxpaying public in Ontario had been uneasy about what they perceived to be growing abuse of the welfare system. In times of economic distress, the essential unfairness of undeserving individuals taking advantage of the system rankled more than ever. More recently this group of anxious moderates had also been alarmed by what seemed to be an increasing number of random acts of violence committed by juveniles. Their anxiety grew after media coverage highlighted the disdain of some accused for the judicial system, and especially for the Young Offenders' Act. To many, this legislation appeared to be giving wayward juveniles an unfair means of escaping the consequences of their acts.

As if to add insult to injury, the moderate-middle-class backbone of Ontario watched in disbelief as Bob Rae's government implemented sweeping employment-equity legislation that appeared to discriminate unfairly against the sons of white, middle-class Ontarians, many of whom were looking for employment in the middle of a recession. The photo-radar legislation, meanwhile, simply appeared to many Ontarians as a sneaky, underhanded and basically unfair way for government to proceed, if not a fundamental violation of citizens' rights.

Whether these concerns were well founded or "justified" is, in a sense, beside the point. Like many small-l liberal governments elsewhere, the Rae and Peterson regimes took the liberalism of their electorates for granted. They failed to sense the degree of quiet concern lying just beneath the surface. As a result they also failed to respond to it, either by making minor changes to accommodate legitimate concerns, or by dispelling misconceptions and explaining their policies in a clear, non-patronizing fashion that responded to the public's need for better information. In some cases, by rejecting even moderate criticism of their programs as marginal or politically incorrect, they alienated the very liberal voters they were counting on to support their measures. Left to simmer, this growing frustration was ripe to be exploited by the neo-conservatives.

By simply articulating these concerns publicly and loudly, the Harris Conservatives captured much of this large pool of discontented moderates. Disregarding evidence that violent youth crime was *not* on the increase and welfare fraud was *not* a significant problem in Ontario (most estimates placing it at less than 1 per cent), the Tories reinforced the public's fears. The "Common Sense Revolution" was a lightning rod for these concerns and, even if the solutions the Conservatives proposed were more radical than many expected, at least they proved someone was paying attention.

Even so, the Harris team tried to present their radical solutions in language that would be acceptable to as many voters as possible. Their handling of the welfare issue was a classic example. On the one hand, they aggressively pushed the hot-button issues of welfare fraud and "overreliance" on the part of able-bodied individuals. Their manifesto promised a mandatory Workfare program and "a province-wide computer system, coupled with a strictly enforced program of photo identification for all welfare recipients." They also claimed some $500 million would be "saved" through "improved management techniques, stricter eligibility requirements and fraud reduction," even though they knew almost all of the savings would come from eliminating thousands of recipients through the changed eligibility rules.

On the other hand, after claiming that welfare rolls had "swollen" because Ontario benefits were among the highest in North America — a statement they did not even attempt to justify — they went on to describe their planned $1-billion cut in benefits for those still eligible as "setting welfare benefits at 10 per cent above the national average," an initiative which would be "fair for all involved."

The message Mike Harris conveyed on the hustings was less carefully phrased, however, and his handlers had to rein him in on several occasions.

As the Helle Hulgaard case had demonstrated the year before, Harris truly viewed welfare as the last refuge of the shiftless, lazy and undeserving.

The tendency of all social conservatives to focus on law-and-order issues was given free rein in the Harris team's approach to the perceived increase in youth violence. Ignoring all evidence to the contrary, the Conservatives launched an assault on another non-existent crisis. Unable to tackle the Young Offenders Act itself, since it was a federal responsibility, they came up with a solution that appealed to the most hard-line elements of their support. Borrowing another page from the American right, they promised to set up a number of military-style boot camps for juveniles.

Although the Tories' opposition to photo radar was, at least on the surface, an obvious contradiction of their tough "law and order" approach, this inconsistency was rarely raised by their critics. This was probably because the general public mostly agreed with the Harris team that moderate speeding was not a serious offence. Of course, for Harris and his supporters there was a neo-conservative principle at stake — government was already far too intrusive in the lives of ordinary citizens — but there was also a political motive. The ominous radar-gun vans, located on major highways such as the 401, affected primarily the very rural and suburban voters Mike Harris was trying to attract.

As for employment equity, it was not directly mentioned in the CSR, since the Rae government had introduced the legislation shortly before the election call. In fact, the bill was not scheduled to come into force until September 1995. Nevertheless, it had provoked an immediate backlash upon being tabled in the legislature. Mike Harris capitalized on this public discontent early in the election campaign by pledging to scrap the NDP's "quota bill." The NDP never recovered from this clever assault on Bill 79, which in reality did not mention quotas at all.

Although designed to enhance employment opportunities for minority groups, women and disabled people — an objective with which most Ontarians probably would have agreed in principle — its poorly defined terminology, repeated reference to numbers and other statistical data, and broadly based application destroyed its credibility and gave critics much to target. Political scientist Brian Tanguay believes Bill 79 "generated more controversy than almost any other piece of NDP legislation," an impressive claim, given the widespread resistance to the "Social Contract." More important, Tanguay stresses that "the manner in which the bill's advocates conducted debate over the law — by branding opponents as racists or worse — needlessly polarized and inflamed public opinion on this subject."

Even more revealing was the comment of a former consultant to the Employment Equity Commission, who concluded that the bill's emphasis on numbers, if not quotas, was fatal. In her words: "The numbers became a proxy for *fairness.*" The clash over Bill 79 revealed the underlying concerns of a sizeable minority of the population about the fairness of the whole concept of affirmative action, a concept liberal politicians and activists thought had been widely accepted more than a decade earlier.

Once again, the Harris Conservatives had recognized and taken advantage of an emerging social issue that resulted from liberal overconfidence. Together with the other three hot-button issues in their social program, it proved an irresistible package for many discontented moderates.

Indeed, the dual themes of fairness and common sense, which were emphasized throughout the Conservative campaign on both economic and social issues, were a perfect fit with the mood of many Ontario voters. On the one hand, the anxious middle class was desperate to find ways of reducing their financial problems and economic uncertainty. The "common sense" approach of tax cuts and less government seemed the right answer. On the other hand Ontarians, unlike Albertans, would have been unwilling, or even afraid, to choose this option had it not been for the accompanying political promises about fairness. They certainly did not want to see their province become a battleground between government and its citizens, as had happened in Ralph Klein's Alberta.

Hearing that key social programs like health care and education would not be cut, and having their negative stereotypes about welfare reinforced by political leaders, many voters felt reassured. They had, in a sense, been given permission to choose self-interest, knowing they would not be causing too much pain in exchange for the hoped-for gains. On June 8, the "Common Sense Revolution" became a reality.

6

Ontario Undone

The goal of the Common Sense Revolution was to "put people
first." Who are the people this government has chosen to serve?
Who are the people being put first? Even those who support a
strong hand in financial matters must be aware of the fear,
the suspicion and the polarization growing in the province.
— Bishop Terence Finlay

The government's options are decidedly limited. It has gone
too far to turn back ... and must therefore go forward. If it is
correct in its belief that Ontarians will eventually appreciate the
necessity and the wisdom of the Tory revolution,
its reward will be another victory in the next election.
If it is wrong, its days are numbered.
— Sid Noel, *Revolution at Queen's Park*

On the evening of September 4, 1984, a whimsical Brian Mulroney
turned to friends and advisers gathered at a cottage in Baie Comeau to
watch the election results roll in. "Okay, we've won," he said. "What do
we do now?" His comment was all the more amusing since his victory

that night had been a certainty. The only question left unanswered until the final polls closed and the votes were counted was the size of his huge majority.

For Mike Harris and the Ontario Conservatives in 1995 the situation was very different. Coming from far behind, fighting until the last day of the campaign and then winning with 44 per cent of the vote, the Harris team might have been expected to catch their breath and rest on their laurels for a few days. With so few of his caucus members and advisers having experience in government, and given Mulroney's disastrous example, Harris himself might have been expected to move slowly. Why make hasty decisions he might later regret?

As the NDP advisers helping with the transition soon learned, nothing could have been further from the premier-designate's mind. Mike Harris was determined to establish his government's credibility with voters. This meant implementing some of his key election promises as soon as possible. There was a strategic as well as a political reason for haste. Harris was convinced by his pre-election consultations with Ralph Klein's advisers that he would have to move very fast to implement such a radical agenda. Any delay would heighten the risk of being bogged down by an "uncooperative" bureaucracy or the protests of the innumerable "special interests" negatively affected by his program. Making sure this did not happen was the Harris team's top priority.

Two senior members of the Tory transition team, Bill Farlinger and David Lindsay, held their first meeting with the NDP's David Agnew, the outgoing cabinet secretary, the morning after the election. At that meeting they surprised Agnew by presenting him with a list of six deputy ministers with whom Harris wanted to meet as soon as possible. As one member of the NDP transition team remarked, his party "assumed office but never took power. These guys are taking power even before they have assumed office."

Knowing the Harris Conservatives' dislike of bureaucrats in general, the deputies had no idea what was in store for them when they arrived at the Park Plaza Hotel in downtown Toronto the next morning. It turned out they had nothing to worry about. They were on the A-list, having been identified as competent and sympathetic to the new regime. One of them — Rita Burak from Agriculture — was selected to become the new cabinet secretary, and was in place at her new job before the week was out. Another nine deputies were not so lucky, receiving pink slips shortly thereafter. By Wednesday of the following week, a new deputy minister of Finance, Michael Gourley, had been brought into the bureaucracy from the University of Western Ontario. The Harris Conservatives meant business.

Pretend Populists

"We are the people of Ontario," an organizer told an estimated crowd of more than 2,000 people outside the legislature at Queen's Park. They were gathered there — teachers, grandmothers, housewives, union leaders and social activists — to protest as Mike Harris and his cabinet were sworn in. Although few would have believed it at the time, the event was only a sample of things to come. The province that had cultivated "bland" politics for fifty years was about to become a tangled bramble of protest and discontent.

Unlike previous occasions, when the ceremony had taken place on the lawn of the legislature complex with the public in attendance, the swearing-in of the Harris cabinet took place in the privacy of the legislative chamber. The buildings were closed to the public for "security reasons." The group of somewhat annoyed and unhappy ministers was sworn in while the crowd outside could be heard chanting "Mike should be embarrassed." It was a bad beginning for the government, and one that set the tone for its mandate.

June 26, 1995, marked the beginning of a new era in Ontario politics in more ways than one. Over the next three years, the "Common Sense Revolution" would change the shape of government. During the same time, the combative approach of the Harris Conservatives in implementing their agenda would change the fundamental relationship between the provincial government and its citizens.

For a self-proclaimed populist government, the Harris Conservatives made more than their share of enemies in their first three years in office, and the situation showed no signs of improving in 1999. In fact, the prognosis for more of the same was inevitable, given the projects the government intended to complete before calling an election. Yet a truly

213

recalcitrant Premier Mike Harris indicated in several interviews during the summer and fall of 1998 that he had no regrets about the course of action his government had taken. If people disagreed with his agenda, so be it. They were free to protest, and he was free to ignore them.

Harris first demonstrated this attitude on May 1, 1996, on the eve of yet another mass rally to highlight his government's cuts to social programs and education. The two-day protest in St. Catharines, the *tenth* in a series of rotating Days of Action sponsored by organized labour, was described by the premier as "foolish." According to him, there was no need for people to protest in the streets "when a letter to me would express it just as well." But Wayne Samuelson, president of the Ontario Federation of Labour, disagreed, saying that the premier's door is closed and "there are barricades around Queen's Park most of the time ... The reality is this government doesn't care what people think. This is an opportunity for people to have a voice and a say ..."

Samuelson could hardly be blamed for coming to that conclusion after the events of the previous year, many of which were unprecedented. The protest at the cabinet's swearing-in marked the beginning of a long, hot summer in which the government managed to raise the ire of doctors, nurses, teachers, environmentalists, social activists and organized labour in general — partly because of the radical measures it introduced, but even more because of the high-handed way in which it announced them. For much of its first term of office, the Harris government not only failed to consult with the various stakeholders affected by its plans, but refused to meet with them even when they asked to do so.

For Mike Harris, consultation seemed to mean speaking with those who agreed with his views. As journalist Thomas Walkom noted in one article, when the Tories decided to deregulate the provincial building code, "only the home builders' lobby was consulted. The environmental lobby, even the insulation manufacturers' lobby, was ignored." Even more striking were the government's efforts to impose major changes on the powerful health and legal professions and organized labour. "In the health field, the Tories' Bill 26 took on the province's doctors. Among other things this omnibus bill gave the Minister of Health unprecedented authority to determine where doctors would practise [and] this was done without consulting the furious doctors."

Lack of consultation is one thing, however, and physical confrontation is another. In typically staid Ontario, it takes more than one or two unpopular measures to provoke much dissent, and a great deal more to produce the steady stream of protest marches, sit-ins and rallies that have characterized the Harris mandate to date. As veteran Liberal MPP Sean Conway pointed out, "Harris has taken a real relish in combating people that Bill Davis or David Peterson or Bob Rae would have accommodated."

The results have been unsettling, to say the least. The rally at the swearing-in ceremony in June was a peaceful if unusual event. The protest organized on the steps of the legislature for the Throne Speech on September 27 was expected to follow the same course. But things went terribly wrong. By the time it was over, police using truncheons had bloodied several demonstrators — many of them women — and photographs of the event were splashed across the front pages of newspapers across the country.

At the same time, questions were being raised in the legislature about security matters. Deputy Liberal Leader Sean Conway and several other members had been refused entry to the building at the height of the melee, and missed the Throne Speech entirely. Meanwhile, former premier Bill Davis and other invited guests at the event were being prevented from *leaving* out of concern for their safety. A bomb threat eventually forced everyone to exit the building by an underground tunnel, leaving the protesters surrounding an empty building. The questions about security matters were taken seriously by the Speaker, Al McLean, under whose jurisdiction the matter fell, and the fallout from this incident would set the stage for future violence at Queen's Park.

If there were any lingering doubts in the bureaucracy that Harris and his team intended to move on their election commitments, and move fast, these doubts were removed when Harris spoke to a closed-door session of all senior bureaucrats on June 27, less than three weeks after the election. In that speech the new premier assured them he intended to "change the way government does business." Clearly unfazed by the ugly protest the day before, he warned them this would mean "gut-wrenching" changes to the bureaucracy, but he expected "their absolute commitment" to the government's political agenda. The message was clear: Anyone who didn't like the message knew where to find the door.

Not long afterwards, the Conservatives really began to take charge. Although they could only reverse certain NDP decisions over the summer — ones that did not require the approval of the legislature — the Tories managed to find enough programs to cancel to show the voters they were on the job.

After a cabinet meeting on July 5, Harris emerged to tell reporters that photo radar was dead. At the same time he indicated another NDP initiative (the Interim Waste Authority, set up to examine the problem of Toronto's garbage and find a long-term solution for its disposal) was also being canned. Entirely consistent with the neo-conservatives' view that the provincial government should do less, not more, Harris announced that from now on each municipality would be responsible for finding its own waste-disposal solutions. The gasps from the environmental community could be heard as far away as Ottawa and North Bay.

The following week Harris did it again. With considerable relish he announced the elimination of several planned government agencies to administer long-term health care. Not only would this matter be left to the private sector, but it would become more "competitive." Instead of being the purview of voluntary non-profit agencies such as the Victorian Order of Nurses (VON), it would be thrown open to competition by allowing for-profit groups to compete for government contracts. Since for-profit agencies could be non-unionized and pay minimum wages, it seemed likely they would take over in this field, a move decried by most health-care experts but applauded by small entrepreneurs.

Then, on July 21, news came from Finance Department officials that the deficit for the current 1995–96 fiscal year would more likely be $11 billion than the $8 billion estimated before the election. This shortfall, they explained, was due primarily to much lower tax revenues than expected. The Tories moved quickly to salvage their economic agenda. The deficit could not be allowed to balloon out of control, or all of their calculations for their tax cut and spending reductions would be undermined. Fledgling Finance minister Ernie Eves issued a financial statement, or mini-budget, in which he accomplished two things. First, he implemented the CSR promise to cut welfare benefits by more than 20 per cent, a move which he expected to save the government some $469 million by the end of the year. Second, he cancelled outright a number of infrastructure projects across the province, including municipal transit projects in Ottawa and a key subway extension in Toronto, and ordered all government departments to find another $500 million in savings.

Although the welfare cuts had been loudly trumpeted during the election campaign as part of the CSR agenda, the coupling of these cuts with other measures to keep the deficit under control made an unfortunate impression on the public. This impression was reinforced by countless social-interest groups who argued the welfare cuts were being made, not just to reduce the deficit, but to ensure the Tories could still make their 30 per cent tax cut. Try as they might, the Tories were unable to shake this connection, which was reinforced by subsequent events.

On July 25, for example, the Tories moved to implement their promise to eliminate subsidized housing in a province with one of the highest shelter costs in the country. According to Al Leach, his announcement of a moratorium on new construction was only the first step in their plan to sell off existing stock and "get Ontario out of the housing business once and for all." Predictably, the non-profit-housing and social-action groups accused the government of reducing the deficit on the backs of low-income earners and single parents. Predictably, the government ignored them.

Less easy to ignore were the complaints from private-sector builders. Many of them had begun work on the 503 new projects already approved, and their losses would be considerable, to say nothing of the fact that their contracts would have to be ripped up to impose this ban. Since many of these same small contractors had just voted the Conservatives into power, this did not seem a fine idea. The "compromise" announced by Al Leach was to cancel 118 of the new projects outright and establish a "close-out" system to allow the government to "buy its way out" of the remaining 385. An attempt to have the contractors waive their right to sue for damages or lost income before receiving these payments was aborted when the courts ruled in favour of one contractor who challenged the plan. The government did not reveal the final cost of cancelling the projects. "When you get into it, you find these issues are very complex," a chastened Leach explained.

The issue of who would benefit from the Conservative victory was raised again when Health minister Jim Wilson announced in early

September that he was restoring full OHIP medical coverage for Ontario residents who spend winters in the United States. Only the year before, the Canadian Snowbird Association had lost a court challenge of the Rae government's decision to reduce their coverage to $100 per day. In explaining his decision, Wilson was quick to point out that it "covers all age groups," but most observers were equally quick to make the connection between the predominantly middle-class seniors who voted for the Conservatives, and the vast majority of "snowbirds." That this announcement was made shortly before other planned cuts in OHIP coverage — the delisting of procedures — did nothing to dispel the view that the Harris government was busy taking care of its own at the expense of others.

The Axe Falls

By early fall, the Tory axe was in full swing. The infamous "quota bill" on employment equity was killed, as was Bill 40 on replacement workers. Workfare was announced. With the hot-button social issues largely out of the way, the Harris team turned its full attention to the neo-conservative economic agenda. Having temporarily staved off a deficit disaster with their July announcement, they could now proceed with their five-point plan in three stages — the first almost immediately, and the next two within eighteen months.

Given the almost childlike naïveté and impetuousness of Mike Harris and much of his cabinet, it is perhaps not surprising that the initial legislation implementing their economic platform would be so controversial. Obsessed with the need for speed, these new-style Conservatives were not about to consult anyone. They were even less interested in bureaucratic excuses about why their plans could not be instantly put in place. After all, their platform had just been approved by the public in an election. What more did bureaucrats or Opposition parties want? Ignoring concerns expressed privately by some bureaucrats that their approach verged on the undemocratic, the Tories insisted on trying to do almost everything at once.

In November they tabled an omnibus bill — Bill 26, the Savings and Restructuring Act — which not only began to implement their economic agenda, but also provided the means for them to adopt other measures quickly, overriding standard legislative procedures.

The government was now turning its attention to the "MUSH" sector — municipalities, universities, schools and hospitals — where it was once again proposing radical surgery. The bill, which affected some forty-seven separate pieces of legislation, was an obvious attempt by the Harris government to accomplish as much as possible in the shortest time possible. In fact, having tabled the bill on November 29, Tory house leader Ernie Eves indicated the government wanted the bill examined by committee and returned to the legislature before Christmas, so that final passage could take place by the end of January.

In parliamentary terms, this was a breakneck pace. In normal times it would have been difficult for a government to push any single legislative measure through the House in such a short period. For the Harris government to try to ram this massive bill through was like waving a red flag in front of a bull. Groups who would have to prepare themselves for testimony before a committee, and Opposition members who would have to study the legislation in a clause-by-clause analysis, were outraged. They knew that the Harris government had done this deliberately to prevent them from making an impact, taking a page from Ralph Klein's blitzkrieg book.

The Conservatives refused to budge. Invoking the myth of the majority mandate, and their very real majority of seats in the legislature, they forged ahead with the bill despite massive and sometimes violent public opposition. One day the legislation was referred to as the "bully bill" by a journalist, and the epithet was quickly adopted by all opponents of the government's strong-arm tactics on Bill 26.

The bill was a blatant violation of parliamentary practice and, in the eyes of many parliamentarians, demonstrated a lack of respect for the democratic process. For many veteran observers of the political scene, the government's action was eerily reminiscent of Bill C-84, the newly elected Mulroney government's attempt in 1985 to overhaul most federal financial legislation in one swift thrust. (The Mulroney omnibus bill — which proposed to amend the Income Tax Act, the Unemployment Insurance Act, the Canada Pension Plan, the Financial Administration Act and the Petroleum and Gas Revenue Tax Act — also met with intense resistance from Opposition parties, and set the confrontational tone for the remainder of that government's mandate.)

Not surprisingly, the Opposition parties tried a variety of tactics to delay the passage of Bill 26, while they attempted to draw media and public attention to the impact its measures would have. The very day after the bill was introduced, the Speaker expelled no fewer than six Opposition MPPs from the legislature for "unparliamentary" language. Among them were Liberal leader Lyn McLeod, Deputy leader Sean Conway and Health critic Elinor Caplan, all of whom accused Harris and his government of lying to the people of Ontario when they promised they would make no cuts to health care.

In keeping with other CSR election commitments, Bill 26 first eliminated many of the "barriers" and "red tape" the Harris Conservatives believed were limiting private-sector growth and job creation. These so-called barriers included a wide range of measures related to environmental protection (such as corporate clean-up regulations), public safety (notably the "privatization" of elevator inspections) and health care (including the deregulation of the cost of prescription drugs under the provincial drug-benefit plan). In addition, a wide range of industries, from travel agents to car dealerships and real estate agencies, would now be "self-regulating." To ensure this drive to simplify things for business continued, the government also set up the aptly named "Red Tape Commission," whose job was to identify further areas in which the government could fold its tent and slip away into the night.

The second and even more contentious objective of the omnibus bill was to provide the Harris government with unheard-of powers — powers which would essentially give the government *carte blanche* to implement the rest of their agenda in the weeks and months to come. And so, at one fell swoop, the way was paved for the Conservatives to impose user fees for a whole host of government services, establish road tolls and privatize maintenance of highways, close hospitals and even tell doctors where they could practise. Drafted with the knowledge of exactly what cuts and transfers of responsibility they planned further down the road, Bill 26 also provided authorization for municipalities — legislative creatures of the province — to raise their own new sources of revenue through user fees and tolls, as well as to dismantle local environmental, health and safety boards.

Then, on December 6, when the Opposition parties found they had no hope of convincing the government to delay the committee hearings on Bill 26 until after Christmas, they tried another tack. Refusing to vote on a government motion, some thirty Liberal MPPs were obliged by the Speaker to leave the chamber. But former Housing minister Alvin Curling refused to leave his chair. As reporter John Ibbitson recounts, when the Speaker ordered the sergeant-at-arms, Tom Stelling, to remove Curling by force, Curling's colleagues in adjacent seats linked arms with him to prevent his removal. A nonplussed Stelling looked to the Speaker for direction in this unprecedented situation. Realizing that Stelling had no back-up assistance, Curling simply sat there and said, "We have a long wait here, Tom." Speaker Al McLean called a recess, and everyone but Curling left.

The former minister had not taken leave of his senses. Knowing the rules of procedure, he had decided to stay in his seat overnight, aided by various colleagues who ferried supplies and offered moral support. Shortly after ten o'clock the following morning, when Curling left to the cheers of supporters and a flurry of media coverage, he had accomplished his objective. His delaying his departure until after 10:00 a.m. meant that the legislature was prevented from sitting that day. Since it was a Thursday, and the legislature could not vote on bills on a Friday, all debate on Bill 26 would now have to be postponed until the following week, the last scheduled week of legislative sittings before the Christmas recess.

Ernie Eves's plan to have committee hearings completed before then was in shreds. Either the government would have to hold hearings over the Christmas recess, or debate would be delayed until January. And so the Liberals, represented by House Leader Jim Bradley, cut a deal with the government. In exchange for a full month of hearings in January, they would drop their demand that the bill be broken up into several smaller pieces of legislation. Realizing he had little choice, Eves agreed.

The next week it was the NDP's turn. For four days they attacked the contents of the "bully bill" in a detailed, precision strike that left ministers dazed. Sloppy drafting allowed former premier Bob Rae to raise a host of unanswered questions about the consequences of the bill. For example, Rae noted that it appeared municipalities would be able to introduce sales taxes, gasoline taxes and perhaps even a poll tax. Is that what the government intended? The hapless Al Leach, as noted earlier, was reduced to taking several questions under advisement because he simply did not know the answers. At one point a flustered Leach actually referred to Bob Rae, now the leader of the third-place NDP, as "the leader of the Opposition coalition."

The problem was simple. Not only had the bill been drafted in the premier's office by the whiz kids — so that ministers were not familiar with its contents or properly briefed — but it had been compiled in great haste. As subsequent events demonstrated, this would become a trademark of the Harris government. Journalist Carol Goar referred to this trait of the Tories as "the almost child-like quality in the way Premier Mike Harris and his colleagues go about policy-making." Listing several other measures the government had implemented with similar difficulties, Goar concluded, "They decide what they want. Then they get so impatient for results that they set impossible deadlines, make unreasonable demands and barrel ahead at breakneck speed." Tony Clement, the former whiz kid and a backbench MPP at the time, disagreed with this interpretation. In his view, the haste and the confrontation were worth it. "The way we've decided to run the government is revolutionary," he told John Ibbitson. It requires "change first, then consolidation. We can't put things off because we'll get too close to an election and we'll lose our nerve."

When the legislature resumed sitting in January, the Opposition parties made good use of the public hearings to bring out the many consequences of the bill. As a result the government was obliged to bring in some 160 amendments to its own act, an unheard-of situation and a great embarrassment to a government that had prided itself on its pre-election preparation.

This extensive preparation, in the form of their CSR manifesto, was actually part of the problem as well. With not only Harris, but his advisers and most of his ministers having so little experience in government, they seemed unaware of the very real difference between election platforms and government policies. Worse still, they seemed to believe there was *no* difference between policy development and implementation. In politics, saying you plan to do something is one thing. Deciding *how* to achieve it is another. Bureaucrats, trained experts in the fields covered by their departments, are hired precisely so they can assist politicians in deciding how to achieve their objectives. But the Harris team was not interested in the advice of bureaucrats or anyone else.

In their analysis of the 1995 transition period, political scientists Graham White and David Cameron recount how they were "struck on several occasions to find political interviewees voicing what to our minds was a naive distinction between policy and implementation. Policy was what was in the CSR," they were told by several people in the new premier's inner circle. "The election meant that the policies of the Tories had been approved by the electorate and now implementation could begin. There was no need for policy committees of cabinet, no need for papers presenting options or exploring the costs and benefits of alternative courses of action ... Public servants were simply to get on with the job, and politicians were there to see the job was done." As White and Cameron rightly predicted, "It is not difficult to see how this conception of the distinction between policy and public administration could lead a government to serious errors in judgment and vexing political problems."

Sledgehammer Democracy

The vexing political problems began shortly after the bill was passed. On February 7, in another dubious first, some 2,000 university students staged a sit-in at Queen's Park, protesting the government's cuts to post-secondary education. Higher tuition fees, larger classes and fewer course options were just some of the concerns the students were raising as Ontario universities struggled to cope with severely decreased budgets. Like the rally at the time of the Throne Speech, this one started peacefully. Like the previous one, it ended in violence. When the dust settled, four students had been charged by police, windows were broken and the doors of the legislature were smashed in as students entered the lobby. The total repair bill for the damage came to more than $20,000. The government's response was summed up nicely by another backbench MPP, Ed Doyle, who told reporters, "I find it a little disturbing that people think that by getting out of hand, they can make changes ..." Once again invoking the myth of the majority mandate, Doyle continued, "If you don't like what we're doing, remember when it comes time to vote."

223

Few in the general public took the students' violence seriously; it had been a small minority who caused the damage, and the issue of university student fees was an elitist one. Then, on February 24, an estimated 100,000 people marched through the streets of Hamilton as provincial Tories held their convention. Safe behind police barricades at the convention site, Premier Mike Harris assured the party faithful that no "union goons" would stop him. He received a standing ovation from his supporters that night, but the general public was by now less complacent. What was happening in staid old Ontario these days?

The confrontation continued to escalate when, only two days later, the province's 60,000 public servants went on strike for the first time in history. Not only was the walk-out anticipated by the government, it had long been expected. Some might even have said it was encouraged. Negotiations between the Harris government and the union leadership, OPSEU (Ontario Public Service Employees Union) president Leah Casselman, had been dragging on for some time. With their salaries frozen for the past several years, the public servants were not even asking for a wage increase, but rather were focusing on job security. This, however, was something the government was not prepared to give. Actually, it was not prepared to give anything at all. When the government's chief negotiator told Management Board chair Dave Johnson that the government's refusal to offer some concessions would lead to a strike, Johnson replied, "So be it."

This time almost every resident of Ontario, and not just those living in Toronto, could see the results of the government's confrontational approach. Roads and highways went unploughed in the dead of winter. Many routine services — marriage licences, drivers' licences, birth certificates, liens against automobiles and the transferring of property after sales — all became difficult if not impossible to obtain. Although the government attempted to minimize the impact by temporarily suspending a number of regulations, the citizens of Ontario began to appreciate the enormity of the strike. Even food shortages were anticipated, although this proved to be a false alarm, and various safety concerns arose as government inspectors walked off their jobs.

But Mike Harris, mindful of Ralph Klein's advice, did not blink. In fact, he made matters worse with another one of his uncensored comments.

Speaking to reporters before a cabinet meeting, he suggested the strike was really the fault of the NDP government that preceded him, since they gave public servants the right to strike. "They were given this candy, this new tool, by Rae and they are determined to go and use it ... and I'm not sure there's anything we could have done to stop them." Coming as it did after someone in the premier's office leaked the (unfounded) story that the government was prepared to use up to 5,000 replacement workers to maintain essential services, the union personnel were furious.

Whether these two incidents should be seen as the direct cause of the riot at Queen's Park on March 18 is debatable, but certainly they added fuel to the flames. With each passing week, the government's intransigence and the vigilance of the picket lines in front of all government buildings had increased. By March 18, when the legislature was scheduled to resume sitting at 1:30 p.m. after the winter recess, the patience of many picketers had worn thin, and so had the tolerance of the government. More important, Speaker Al McLean was determined to ensure that no repetition of the Throne Speech debacle occurred. All of the MPPs would be able to enter the legislature for its opening, or he would know the reason why.

Responsibility for security at Queen's Park, much like the security on Parliament Hill in Ottawa, is a confused issue. In Ottawa, the Commons and Senate have their own force of security guards inside the buildings of the parliamentary precinct. On the grounds outside the buildings, however, the RCMP has the responsibility for security. The Mounties may not enter the Parliament Buildings, while the local Ottawa police force and the Ontario Provincial Police cannot even venture onto the grounds. (During an incident when a mentally unstable protester drove his Jeep up the steps of the Centre Block itself, the inadequacies of this system were painfully exposed for public scrutiny.) Similarly at Queen's Park, six OPP officers reporting directly to the Speaker have the primary responsibility for security within the legislature buildings, while the Metro Toronto Police are responsible for security on the grounds. In the event of a strike or rally, therefore, the Metro police would normally be in charge.

The Speaker, however, still wounded by criticism of his handling of the Throne Speech melee, had taken an unprecedented step in the days before the opening, and requested the OPP to produce a "battle plan" for ensuring that all MPPs would be able to enter the building unobstructed. The OPP had done so, calling on the services of their riot squad, the Crowd Management Unit.

As retired justice Willard Estey later found in his report on the incident, the principal reason for the chaos that ensued on March 18 was a stunning lack of communication. For reasons that remain unclear, the Speaker did not inform anyone else of his plans. Not even the Metro Police were aware of the battle plan or the presence of the riot squad. Since the long-standing policy of both the Metro and regular OPP forces was to avoid the appearance of taking sides in such situations, by assuring orderly proceedings but not assisting anyone to cross picket lines, the addition of the riot squad as a new factor in the security equation was bound to cause problems.

Nor was the government aware of the Speaker's plans. In fact, Management chair Dave Johnson was busy making plans of his own, to request a court-ordered injunction if things got out of hand. In the past, OPSEU had respected such injunctions, and he apparently believed they would do so on this occasion as well. Meanwhile, OPSEU, which had been picketing the legislature every day for the past several weeks, was assuming that it was business as usual on March 18. The MPPs, like government employees, would have to wait in line at the one entrance which the picketers had not closed. MPPs, like employees, would be allowed to enter in small groups at intervals of ten or fifteen minutes, after enduring a fair amount of name-calling and other verbal barbs. The Metro police, as usual, would stand by but not interfere.

Anticipating difficulties, some government MPPs and ministers had actually stayed in their offices in the building overnight, rather than choosing to run the gauntlet. Others arrived early and, for the most part, were able to enter with only minor delays. At a certain point in the late morning, the delays and the lines of those waiting to enter became longer. When the riot squad perceived that MPPs were being prevented from entering, they emerged in full battle gear to the horror of not only the strikers, but the Metro police, who had been handling things without serious incident until then.

With the engagement of the riot squad, the picketers were faced with truncheons and shields. Many strikers claimed they distinctly heard police officers threatening to "whack 'em and stack 'em." One protester, rendered unconscious by a blow to the head, fell directly across the path being cleared for MPPs escorted by the riot squad. That night, TV screens across the country featured videos of Ontario legislators *stepping over* the prostrate form of the protester.

If they had been unhappy about their exclusion from the legislature before, the Opposition members were furious about the measures taken to ensure their entry this time. As NDP MPP Peter Kormos put it in a point of privilege raised with the Speaker, "We are seeing here, within your scope of jurisdiction, I submit, a most undemocratic and violent utilization of police power to obstruct and interfere with lawful picket lines ... very specifically to facilitate the entry of Conservative MPPs into these buildings." Although the government was not directly at fault, the aggressive approach the Harris government had taken during the strike, and the premier's well-known hostility towards unions, meant the Tories would be identified with the riot regardless of where blame was eventually assigned. They knew it. After two days of unrelenting criticism, a chastened Speaker suggested a parliamentary inquiry. When the Opposition rejected that option as a "whitewash," the premier quickly overruled McLean and his own advisers and agreed to a public inquiry, headed by former justice Estey, in order to divert attention away from the government.

The tactic worked. The union eventually was forced to settle with the government after a five-week strike, gaining little but claiming a moral victory. A few weeks later, the entire matter appeared to be forgotten, at least by the general public. Several polls suggested most people had little sympathy with "public servants" and agreed with the government that the unions were in the wrong. What the poll failed to measure, however, was the public's long-term retention of a negative image of the government as aggressive and inflexible, if not downright authoritarian.

The Other Shoe Drops

By March 1996, the Harris team had completed the first stage of their plan to revolutionize government in Ontario. The other shoe dropped barely two months later, in early April, when Management Board chair

Dave Johnson tabled a sixty-two-page document outlining where the government planned to make its cuts. The document contained all the favourite neo-conservative buzzwords. Johnson told MPPs in the legislature, "We are downsizing operations, saving money in administration, reducing waste and duplication, streamlining and transferring services and taking a more businesslike approach to government."

As Johnson noted, these cuts were fulfilling the Tories' campaign pledge to reduce "non-priority" spending and "cut the size of government." Most of the Conservatives' targets came as no surprise, although the severity of the cuts was unexpected. The bigger surprise, at least for many voters, was learning that *increasing government revenues* was also part of the Harris plan. Apparently the price of cutting taxes and balancing the budget would be not only massive cuts to government services and programs, but an increase in government revenues through almost every other means *except* personal income taxes.

In total, the package would reduce spending by $3 billion within two years (by the end of the 1997–98 fiscal year) and eliminate 10,600 public-service jobs. What did this mean in real terms?

Despite the length of the document, this was still not very clear. Each government department had been assigned a target for expenditure and personnel cuts, but in many cases the details of how those cuts would be implemented were not available. Instead, the so-called business-plan format simply stated that the required savings in each department would arise from "unspecified efficiency moves."

Opposition leaders termed this approach "irresponsible," but actually it was worse than that. By forcing bureaucrats to make the tough decisions, the government was still free to criticize any unpopular moves and claim there had been no need to take such action. (Harris would later do the same thing to municipal politicians, cutting their transfer payments while assuring citizens that there was no need for any increase in property taxes if municipal politicians were diligent and efficient.) Like their counterparts in Alberta, Ontario's public servants would find themselves in a Catch-22 situation where "doing better with less" meant they must implement massive cuts without causing any obvious decrease in service — an impossible task.

Despite the lack of details in many areas, there were some specific programs and regulations the Conservatives had not hesitated to target. By far the most important of these was, once again, welfare. This time, the government was cutting more than 17,000 people off welfare because they were attending postsecondary institutions. (The fact they were doing so as part of a program established by the department to upgrade their skills and find employment apparently was of no concern to the government, which proposed instead that these individuals should apply for student loans.) The department responsible for administering welfare, the Ministry of Community and Social Services, was expected to save $189.7 million because of the anticipated drop in the social-assistance caseload resulting from these and previous changes the Tories had made to the eligibility criteria. In a move that left many critics speechless, the department would also "save" another $8.9 million by reducing funding for people with developmental disabilities.

Many of the cuts in other departments would result from privatization or outright elimination of programs. Among the targets were agricultural research and education programs (transferred to the University of Guelph); the Ontario Training and Adjustment Board (eliminated); and a number of arts, culture, heritage and library programs (encouraged to become "self-sufficient"). Several government buildings would be sold, along with an unspecified amount of public housing. Among the most dramatic and controversial moves was the decision to privatize the operation of fifteen provincial parks.

A clearer picture of the government's deregulation plans emerged from the document's approach to environmental matters. Environmental-assessment procedures were to be "simplified," and the department's laboratory testing facilities were to "get out of routine, high-volume analysis." This did not appear to leave much for the department's employees to do, so that some 752 positions could be cut, for a saving of $25.3 million. As one horrified critic concluded, "The forests are basically going to be transferred to the control of people who cut down trees. The people who like having trees around aren't going to have any say at all."

As for the unexpected decision to raise revenue, the government left few stones unturned. It would raise fees and/or impose new ones on a variety of services, from marriage, liquor and fishing licences to

229

entrance fees at tourist attractions such as Ontario Place and the St. Lawrence Seaway.

Meanwhile, a close reading of the document suggested the Harris team was playing fast and loose with their commitment to maintain spending on health care, law enforcement and education. The Health ministry was to cut some $40.5 million in spending *annually*. Although $23 million would allegedly result from "streamlining" of overhead, fully $17.5 million was slated to be cut from "emergency health services and laboratory services." An *additional* $39.5 million was to be saved through an across-the-board 5 per cent reduction for district health councils and other advisory bodies. The Harris government's definition of law enforcement, meanwhile, apparently excluded courts, halfway houses and the legal-aid system, all of which were targeted. In the first of many such moves, the Education portfolio was also being severely cut, this time by eliminating some $265 million in capital expenditures. In addition, universities would lose some $400 million in grants, but would be allowed to increase tuition fees by 20 per cent. This last point was a risky move indeed, since most of the students in postsecondary education would be the children of the middle class on which Harris was now so dependent.

Although the taxpayer was supposed to be the "winner" in the "Common Sense Revolution," the government's approach to fiscal policy seemed to be geared to helping some kinds of taxpayer more than others. As the vice-president of the union representing provincial employees, Bill Kuehnbaum, responded when he had seen the document, "It's quite obvious that there is a big winner here, and that's big business." As if to counter this view and demonstrate that the burden was indeed falling equally on all citizens, the document also announced further cuts to "business subsidies," but the effect of this "balance" was diminished somewhat when it was discovered that enterprises such as an aboriginal community radio station would be affected.

The Opposition parties were predictably outraged, and the tone of their comments suggested their concern was deep and visceral. Speaking in the legislature, former premier Bob Rae went out of his way to contrast the Harris regime with that of his Conservative predecessors. "Mr. Davis had a sense of proportion and balance," Rae declared, "which the right-wing zealots who have taken over this party have completely and utterly lost." For Lyn McLeod, still the leader of the Liberal Opposition, the measures introduced by Johnson revealed "the cold-hearted face of Mike Harris's Ontario. The most vulnerable get trampled in order to find the dollars to pay for a tax cut for the rich."

In the face of this criticism, Harris just shrugged and said, "You have to understand that a lot of these politicians and bureaucrats [who opposed him] are going to lose their jobs, and that's unfortunate. But the fact of the matter is we have too much government, too many politicians, too many bureaucrats."

The tax cut to which McLeod referred was, of course, still the centre-piece of the CSR platform. Its introduction the following month in the Budget would mean that four of the five points in the Tories' neo-conservative economic agenda had been implemented.

As indicated earlier, it was this promise of a 30 per cent tax cut that caused the Harris Conservatives the most difficulty. With the deficit situation and the provincial economy worse than they had expected, the new government was finally obliged to abandon its rigid determination to do everything at once and move more slowly than planned on this key commitment. The CSR had originally promised a 15 per cent tax cut in 1996, followed by cuts of 7.5 per cent in 1997 and 1998. The first budget tabled by Finance minister Ernie Eves in May 1996 provided for the cut to be phased in more gradually, with roughly 3 per cent coming in 1996, 12 per cent in 1997 and the remaining 15 per cent "sometime between 1997 and 1999."

One problem with this new approach was that most voters would hardly notice the 3 per cent cut the first year, especially those middle-income earners who would also have to pay the "Fair Share" Health Care Levy. Yet they could hardly help but notice the fuss being raised by organized labour, lawyers, doctors, judges, and just about every other category of worker, to say nothing of the advocates for women, the poor, the disabled and the elderly.

Mega Madness

A less committed government might well have changed course at this point. The confrontations showed no sign of decreasing, and the political credit would likely be slow in coming. Yet the Harris Conservatives not only stayed the course, they pursued it aggressively. If Mike Harris ever had the slightest doubts about his plan, he never expressed them publicly. Apart from a few minor concessions, such as the ones made in response to protests by judges and the Law Society, the Harris government did not blink.

In fact, the second half of 1996 found Harris and his cabinet hard at work on the plans for the third and final stage of their agenda, which they euphemistically termed "disentanglement." To the rest of the world, it would be known as the "Megaweek" announcements. Implementing the remainder of their promises to reduce the size of government and "do better with less," the Tories introduced a string of bills in the legislature covering a multitude of issues. From the strategically named Fewer Politicians Act (Bill 81) to the Fewer School Boards Act (Bill 104), the neo-conservative agenda of reducing the role of government in society was plainly visible in all of them.

For those who thought the reaction to the omnibus "bully bill" set new standards for public protest in Ontario, the winter of 1997 brought a whole new meaning to the term. One reason for the virulence of the opposition to this new offensive by the Harris government was the scope. So many people were affected by the wide-ranging proposals, and their collective opposition was channelled into a very short period of time. In addition many of the groups directly affected, such as the teachers, were already highly organized and could respond quickly.

Another reason for the intense opposition to disentanglement was the fundamental — in fact, revolutionary — nature of the changes being proposed. While the measures the Harris team had implemented in the first two stages of their plan were certainly extreme, they could still be reversed by a future government if it chose. Welfare rates could be raised again, eligibility could be expanded, environmental or safety regulations could be rewritten. It might not be easy, but it could be done. The Megaweek proposals, by contrast, would change the underlying structures of government. The sheer magnitude of the changes, the cost and time it would take to implement them, and the very real pain they would cause, would mean that, once implemented, they would be nearly impossible for a future government to alter. As one critic described it, "The

Harris government is proposing not to renovate Ontario's large and sprawling house, but rather to bulldoze it and build a new and smaller structure according to its own blueprint."

As before, the Tories had identified a genuine concern and then built on it to suit their purposes. Many people were concerned about the quality of education in the province. Hardly anyone in Ontario would have claimed the existing web of shared provincial and municipal fiscal responsibilities was perfect. In fact, the previous NDP government had appointed a special commission, headed by former Toronto mayor and federal Tory David Crombie, to look into the matter and suggest ways in which the system could be rationalized.

The key word was "rationalized." While some financial savings might result from a more coherent arrangement, no one else was proposing to eliminate programs or save enormous amounts of money. Rather, the Crombie commission was set up to apply solid managerial techniques and a coherent framework to programs and responsibilities that had grown like Topsy and were no longer either as efficient, or as fair and equitable, as they might be.

Not surprisingly, the Crombie commission soon became known as the "Who Does What" exercise. The Harris government, meanwhile, went to work on their own plan. When the Crombie report was issued, some of its recommendations were used selectively by the government to demonstrate support for its own proposals. Others were ignored. Eventually Crombie was moved to voice his disapproval publicly. Despite his Tory connections he disowned the Harris plan, parts of which he bluntly described as "wrong in principle and devastating in practice."

What exactly was at stake? In a breathtaking pre-emptive strike that took almost all the stakeholders by surprise, the Harris government was proposing to assume almost complete responsibility for the educational system in the province. In exchange, the municipalities would have to assume complete or greatly increased responsibility for social services such as welfare, public housing and child care, as well as public transit. All were areas which to date had been jointly funded by the province and municipalities. According to the Tories, their primary purpose was to ensure quality education for students. Most important, they argued that this restructuring, or "disentanglement," would also simplify administration and result in significant savings, so that the total effect of the transfers would be revenue-neutral.

The problem with their argument was that it had no basis in fact. Apart from David Crombie's loud protestations, the roars from municipal administrators in all the large urban centres could be heard across the province. They knew this proposal would result in additional expense for their citizens through their property taxes, and none of them believed the result would be "fair and equitable." Rural areas would be the big winners, since the social-service costs for urban centres are much higher, as is the cost of public transit. Suburban areas would also likely benefit. In the case of Toronto, for example, the city would be forced to absorb the huge public-transit and welfare costs while the surrounding suburbs would benefit from the services and still see property taxes reduced. (For Torontonians, already reeling from previous examples of the Harris government's disdain for the province's capital, this appeared to be nothing short of vindictive — punishment for not having supported the Conservatives in the 1995 election.)

Initially many rural areas recognized they were in the most favourable position and said little. With almost no social services to fund, they would benefit from the province's decision to absorb the entire cost of education and distribute it "equally" among the province's boards, rather than allowing the boards to raise money themselves through local taxes. While Toronto's or Ottawa's well-funded and well-equipped schools would suffer a dramatic decrease, rural areas would have greatly improved educational facilities.

The next announcement from Queen's Park hit rural and urban areas equally. Overall provincial spending on education would decrease significantly. What was more, the province was planning to reduce the number of boards, the number of trustees on those boards, and their remuneration (from as much as $48,000 to a uniform $5,000). The final blow was the proposed creation of an Education Improvement Commission that would have the power to reverse the decisions of the elected boards. Now everyone understood the real importance of the omnibus bill introduced the previous year, and the extraordinary powers it had given the province were certainly being exercised.

Working to the Tories' advantage was the fact that the scope of the proposals was simply too great for the average citizen to grasp. Without a detailed knowledge of the workings of the educational system, the changes being proposed there were unclear to most people, including parents.

While the public may not have grasped all the details of the proposed transfers or their consequences, they certainly understood the issue of property-tax increases, and it was here that the Harris government was most vulnerable. During the campaign and in the "Common Sense Revolution," Mike Harris had bluntly stated, "There is only one level of taxpayer. You. We will work closely with the municipalities to ensure that any actions we take will not result in increases to local property taxes." Despite Municipal Affairs minister Al Leach's constant declarations that the whole exercise would be revenue-neutral, the overwhelming opinion of municipal administrators, experts and academics was that this was simply not so.

Although the government had admittedly put aside some money for a "transition" fund to cover the extraordinary start-up costs of the municipalities, it was clear to everyone except the government that the municipal shortfall could not be rectified over such a brief time. But for the Tories, this was merely municipal whining. In an unguarded moment in the heat of a press scrum, Al Leach revealed the real thinking of the government when he declared that, if some municipal politicians couldn't balance the books with the one-time extra provincial funds, they should simply "cut expenses" or "not bother running for re-election."

No doubt the last person the cabinet expected to have difficulty with over these proposals was a man well known for his own right-wing tendencies and anti-elite views. Yet before the dust had settled on their proposals, the Harris government found itself firmly in the sights of none other than the flamboyant and fiery mayor of North York, Mel Lastman. "You screwed Toronto, Mr. Premier. You are cutting the heart out of the city," the mayor-elect of the new City of Toronto bellowed at a press conference at Metro Hall. Vowing to campaign to defeat the Harris government in the next provincial election, Lastman continued, "Mr. Premier, you and your cabinet promised revenue-neutral. Mr. Premier, you lied to me and you lied to the people of the City of Toronto."

What was Lastman so worked up about? Having decided to run for the new post of mayor of the proposed amalgamated City of Toronto, Lastman had campaigned on a platform of zero tax increases, and won. This platform, in turn, had been based on the assurances by Leach and Harris that the whole downloading exercise from the province to the municipalities would be revenue-neutral. When it became clear that this was not the case, Lastman went ballistic. He knew he was in trouble with his electors before he took office. Officials were predicting a minimum 12 per cent property-tax increase to cover an estimated shortfall of nearly $164 million.

One after another municipalities began to speak out, including those that might initially benefit. Mayor Ann Mulvale of Oakville, one of the wealthiest municipalities in Canada, pointed out in a *Toronto Star* article on January 26 that, while it might not affect her town in the short term, "we know that if there is another economic downturn we could be badly hurt."

Critics argued that the government knew this as well. While the long-term costs of education in the province could be expected to decrease, the social-services costs could only escalate, and future downturns would be inevitable. What the province was really doing, the critics agreed, was downloading its financial commitments. Of course, with a budget to balance and a tax cut to pay for, this latest move on the part of the Harris government did not come as much of a surprise for the opponents of the neo-conservative agenda.

The conflict escalated when many municipal politicians threatened to pass on their increased costs to their taxpayers, along with a note in their tax bill clearly identifying the provincial government as the culprit. The Harris team actually responded by tabling legislation to make this illegal. Then Mel Lastman raised the stakes again with his "liar" comments, to which the premier responded, "Mel is Mel. That's the way he sold refrigerators and furniture and quite frankly, screaming and yelling and ranting and raving doesn't have a great impact with this government."

Cooler heads finally prevailed, and the province was able to achieve a compromise through negotiations with the Association of Municipalities of Ontario (AMO), the body which was speaking on behalf of the municipal politicians and officials. Here, finally, the Harris government did make some significant concessions, such as agreeing to continue to pay 80 per cent of the welfare bill. However, while the details of the restructuring may have changed, the true objective of limiting total provincial expenditures did not. When a deal was reached in early May that both sides could live with, Al Leach revealed this objective when he explained that "the size of the pot had to remain the same, but if we could mix the ingredients a little differently to come up with the same answer, we could do that." (Lastman eventually apologized for his comments, but only after another special fund was allocated to ease the burden on the new City of Toronto.) The property-tax problem was not eliminated by this solution, but it was certainly reduced. When coupled with the province's new reassessment plans, though, it would return to haunt the Harris government in 1998, especially with businesses and much of the Metro Toronto region slated for huge increases. The situation was so confused that municipalities delayed mailing out their final property-tax statements for the year — losing vital revenue in the process — and advised citizens they would receive their notices "sometime later in the fall."

Yet Harris himself appeared unfazed. The issue was simple, really. There was no doubt in his mind that he was on the right track. His opponents were more concerned with their careers than the alleged "problems" they kept raising. "Those who are proceeding in good faith, with the same objectives as we have, are not having significant difficulties," he maintained. The problem was entirely with "those who believe it's in their interests to create confusion where there is none."

Toronto Redux

Throughout all of this long winter of discontent, the protest over the restructuring issue had completely overshadowed a parallel and equally heated protest taking place in the Metro Toronto area over Bill 103, the proposed amalgamation of the six Metro Toronto municipalities into a megacity. In one sense this lack of public attention was not surprising, since the rest of the province traditionally does not relate well to the capital. In another sense it was amazing, since Metro is home to a fifth of the province's population (22 per cent) and is the single most important factor driving the provincial economy.

True, Mike Harris was an outsider with the anti-Toronto mindset so typical of his rural/suburban caucus members, but his Minister of Municipal Affairs, Al Leach, was not. One of only two ministers to come from Toronto, Leach certainly had the background — as a former manager of the Toronto Transit Commission — to appreciate what was at stake. Yet Leach appeared truly surprised when former Toronto mayor John Sewell started crying "Shame, shame!" as Leach unfolded the amalgamation plan at a breakfast meeting with invited guests of the Toronto Board of Trade.

As those who lived through the winter of discontent will remember for some time, opposition to the government's megacity plans was not only widespread, but visceral and determined. Led by John Sewell, the opponents of Bill 103 worked up a religious fervour the like of which had not been seen since the glory days of the Maple Leafs.

Rallies were held in local churches, packed with 1,000 to 1,500 supporters every night. The city was awash in letter-writing campaigns and protest Web sites. In a new twist a referendum was organized by the six municipalities, which was eventually passed by some 76 per cent of participants. The Harris government, however, dismissed the results as invalid, citing both poor methodology and low voter turnout (roughly 30 per cent of eligible voters). At one point Metro Toronto chair Alan Tonks implied that violence might once again be imminent. In the legislature the Opposition parties rallied to the cause, staging a filibuster based on the use of thousands of computer-generated amendments. During the debate on these amendments, the government once again indicated it was taking a "damn the torpedoes" approach. A furious Liberal MPP and former Metro councillor, Mike Colle, condemned the government's refusal to respect the results of the referendum and demanded, "Where did you get the right to suspend democracy and ram this down the throats of the citizens of Metro?"

By the time the bill finally was passed, Leach and Sewell would have further acrimonious encounters, including a face-to-face meeting at Leach's house over the Easter weekend. According to at least one report, the exchange prompted Leach's wife to refer to Sewell as a "wingnut" and Sewell to declare that "it was like talking to a crazy person." At the height of the "crisis," churches in the Metro area were the site of regular rallies organized by Sewell's Citizens for Local Democracy group, attended by 1,500 angry supporters or more at a time. With plans for a Metro-wide plebiscite and a constitutional challenge being drawn up, the anti-amalgamation forces appeared to have the upper hand, at least with the media and the public. Perhaps even more important, for the first time the government was acquiring an image of uncertainty and incompetence.

Many critics have suggested that Mike Harris fell into the amalgamation plan by accident. Certainly it was not part of the "Common Sense Revolution." During the campaign Harris had responded to a question about Metro with an answer that implied he had given the matter little or no thought. On the one hand, he believed the "fewer politicians the better." On the other hand, in an obvious contradiction he apparently did not see, he also stated government should be as close to the people as possible.

Before the 1995 election, Premier Bob Rae *had* given the matter some thought, and had set up a task force chaired by the head of the Toronto United Way, Anne Golden. She was to present proposals on how to remedy the classic urban problem that Toronto had been encountering for some time — the hollowing out of the core. As with many other large North American centres, it was losing its tax base to the suburbs due to the high cost of land and services in the city centre. The resulting need for even higher property taxes to pay for these services — many of which were used by suburban residents — produced a vicious circle of a larger exodus to the "905" suburbs.

Harris and his team were finally forced to give the matter some thought when Golden tabled her report in January 1996. Following the solution adopted by many other jurisdictions, she recommended giving greater powers to the local municipal level, and then creating a larger regional administrative unit to pool tax revenues for specific region-wide concerns such as transportation, infrastructure and economic planning. In the case of Toronto, this would mean eliminating the existing Metro organization in favour of a broader regional body covering the entire Greater Toronto Area (GTA), which included the 905-suburbs. For Golden and her fellow commissioners, this solution was a happy one which allowed Toronto to keep its local political identity, while providing a better redistribution of the service load to all the taxpayers who benefited from it.

Initially very receptive to her recommendations personally, Municipal Affairs minister Al Leach soon discovered the 905-code MPPs in the Tory caucus were not amused. Neither were their constituents, who had formed the backbone of the Tory victory. And so, once again ignoring the advice of experts, the Harris government decided to move in the opposite direction. Flying in the face of the Golden recommendations, Bill 103 proposed to eliminate the *municipal* level, not the Metro level, and combine the six municipalities into the megacity of Toronto, while leaving the outlying 905 suburbs untouched. There would be one mayor. Forty-four councillors would replace the existing 104 councillors and be elected for the same areas as the twenty-two federal ridings. The numbers of bureaucrats from the six municipalities would be "streamlined," and the potential savings would be considerable. How this plan would remedy the "hollow core" problem was not specified.

Not surprisingly the six local mayors objected strongly, but so did thousands of other individual citizens and interest groups, for almost as many reasons. Financially, historically and logistically, the problems with the Leach/Harris scheme appeared to be horrendous.

Opposition to the plan was visceral and widespread, but, unlike the province-wide opposition to the disentanglement exercise, it was confined to a small geographic area. In addition, the "take no prisoners" approach of the anti-amalgamation organizers was tactically unwise, leaving them and the government with little room to manoeuvre. Only when some of the government's own MPPs and supporters began to express their reservations did the premier decide to cut Toronto some slack. A few concessions were made, but they were modest. In the end, another twelve councillors were added to the plan, and their wards were reorganized on the basis of Metro regions rather than federal ridings. The whole plan then moved ahead despite its overwhelming rejection in the disputed plebiscite, and a last-ditch Opposition filibuster in the legislature.

When the City of Toronto Act was finally passed, newly elected Liberal leader Dalton McGuinty decried the government's "sledgehammer democracy." John Sewell lamented, "That's literally the end of democracy." Some opponents were still not ready to give up, however, and launched a petition asking Lieutenant-Governor Hilary Weston to refuse to sign the bill into law. Others launched a lawsuit. (Similar desperation tactics were employed by other groups concerned about the government's downloading exercise — alias "disentanglement" — including a court challenge questioning the constitutionality of the proposed measures, but these too were ultimately unsuccessful.)

For many Toronto residents, the one–two punch of the City of Toronto Act in December 1996 and the restructuring legislation in January 1997 produced a siege mentality. It also linked the two plans inextricably, so that opposition to one tended to be viewed as opposition to the other. When the president of the Board of Trade for Metro, George Fierheller, called a press conference to denounce the disentanglement plans, the Harris government listened. Fierheller argued either the welfare and transit burden on Toronto would become impossible, leading to an American-style city with all of the attendant problems, or the tax burden on businesses would become impossible. Either way, it would greatly reduce the city's appeal as a place to do business. After Mel Lastman, at that point still the mayor of North York, publicly and repeatedly accused the Harris government and the premier personally of lying, the need to compromise became obvious. Shortly thereafter, the province's negotiations with the AMO took on a more positive note and the agreement outlined above was reached.

But the troubles with the restructuring package were not over. The dust had barely settled on all of these problems when Labour minister Elizabeth Witmer tabled one more piece of legislation, Bill 136. Witmer cunningly described the bill as merely "housekeeping" to pave the way for the various dislocations that would occur as boards were merged and disentanglement unfolded. Nothing could have been further from the truth. The bill essentially violated municipal collective-bargaining agreements by creating an entirely new structure of employer–employee relationships and binding arbitration, as well as a number of new independent "commissions" which would arbitrate in cases of dispute. It was followed in August by Bill 160, which emasculated local school boards and centralized control over decision making in the Ministry of Education and Training.

For the people who had protested against several of the previous bills related to education, Bill 160 proved to be the final straw. The subsequent teachers' strike and the nationwide coverage it received did nothing to enhance the image of the government, particularly as comparisons were frequently drawn with labour unrest in the previous two years. "First the doctors, now the teachers, who next?" was the pointed question posed by one letter writer to the *Globe and Mail* who found the new, uncompromising face of the provincial government more than a little disturbing in a society where tolerance and compromise had always been highly valued.

After a two-week walk-out in November, the teachers eventually returned to work, but the matter was only dormant, not resolved. A lawsuit was planned to challenge the constitutionality of the government's plans, and passive resistance continued at many levels within the system.

After the megaweek proposals were implemented, the pace of change introduced by the Harris government appeared to fall off. Legislation and regulations continued to decrease the role of government, but, after three hectic years, the Harris regime appeared to be nibbling at the margins. Their game plan had been followed, and it was apparently time to consolidate and present a "kinder, gentler face" to the electorate.

By the summer of 1998, on the third anniversary of the Conservatives' election, Mike Harris began to muse aloud that he, too, had children, and they would have to pay for university tuition. He, too, had parents, and they would need medical attention. It was as if what had happened to Ontario over the past three years had simply occurred, rather than been imposed on its citizens by the Harris Conservatives. On the other hand, the premier and other members of his cabinet were quick to take credit for the greatly improved economy.

After three years, few people doubted the Harris government's commitment to its neo-conservative agenda, but many people were beginning to ask themselves what else the "Common Sense Revolution" had accomplished, and at what cost.

A Runaway Government

By the summer of 1997, the Harris government was the subject of an unprecedented number of lawsuits launched by unhappy citizens, all of whom the premier would dismiss as special interests. In July alone, the Ontario Public School Boards Association, several Toronto hospitals and a hospital in Pembroke were in various stages of the legal process. At the end of the month, Justice Stephen Borins ruled on the claim of the six Toronto municipalities that the provincial government's actions were a violation of the Charter of Rights and Freedoms, and hence invalid. While the judge rejected their claim outright, he apparently did so with considerable regret. In his own words, there was no Charter guarantee of protection from "government chutzpah or imperiousness." In addition, the judge noted that all of the traditional methods of consultation had been ignored by the government. Not only had the Toronto amalgamation plan not been part of the CSR, but "Bill 103 simply appeared on the government's legislative agenda," he wrote in his decision, "with little or no public notice, and without any attempt to enter into any meaningful consultations with those people who would be most affected by it — the more than two million inhabitants of metro Toronto." In essence, the judge agreed with their claims that the Harris government was behaving in an authoritarian, almost anti-democratic fashion, but concluded their only redress was to vote for someone else in the next provincial election.

This theme of an authoritarian government was outlined a few months earlier by political scientist Robert Vipond of the University of Toronto in an article in the *Globe and Mail* on December 10, 1997. Vipond noted that extraordinary appeals to the federal government (to disallow legislation), the lieutenant governor (to withold assent) and the courts (to rule legislation invalid) had all been tried in recent months by opponents of the Harris regime, to no avail. He then raised the obvious question. What other means could be used to "corral" a runaway government or, as he put it, "to check a government that prides itself on upsetting the traditional rules of the game"? According to Vipond, with a majority government there are almost none. When an election is near, this may not be a problem. When one is much further down the road, with a government barely at its mid-term, the problem is more pressing. His own suggestion, to develop a limited provincial constitution, was evidently one that he knew was a non-starter, judging from the defensive tone in which he advanced his idea.

The only remotely successful protest against the actions of the Harris government to date has been that of provincial educators. Upset by the "bully bill," they joined in the general rallies and Days of Action, but were no more successful than others at deterring the government from its plans. Then, when the Harris government introduced Bill 160, an act which expressly removed autonomy from local school boards and centralized it at Queen's Park — allowing the government to cut overall education expenditures, fire teachers, remove principals and vice-principals from unions and increase class sizes at will — both the teachers and the school board trustees had had enough.

For two weeks in October 1997, the province went through another wrenching strike, this time of the teachers. When the various teachers' unions voluntarily decided to return to the classroom at the end of two weeks, it was only a temporary truce. Shortly thereafter, both the teachers and the school boards launched court challenges of the legality of the government's actions in Bill 160. In the weeks following the strike, a series of rotating protests continued to hold the government's feet to the fire.

On November 18, some 1,000 demonstrators gathered in Guelph outside a Holiday Inn, where the new Education minister, Dave Johnson, was about to attend a Tory fundraiser. As one of the protesters, twenty-three-year-old student Sarah Vance, soon discovered, the concept of a peaceful protest appeared to have little meaning for the more than one hundred provincial and local officers assigned to "handle" the event. Within fifteen minutes of her arrival, she had been arrested along with fourteen others, transferred to a regional detention centre and strip-searched. According to Ms. Vance, a veteran of several anti-Harris protests, she was astonished at this treatment primarily because she thought she knew from experience what would be seen as acceptable behaviour from the perspective of law-enforcement officers. "We had been picked up for conducting a peaceful demonstration, and our treatment was completely excessive ... It was completely humiliating and designed to intimidate."

Well-known civil rights lawyer Alan Borovoy, of the Canadian Civil Liberties Association, responded to the news of the student arrests by saying, "When it comes to protests under Bill 160, there seems to be an unduly uptight response [on the part of the government and the police] to critics and criticism." Then Borovoy put his finger on the nub of the problem — the government's unwillingness to consult, and its high-handed approach to policy decisions. "Few governments have been as reluctant to meet with pressure-group critics as this government has," Borovoy stated. "This is not a partisan opinion," he stressed. "In the past, governments of all three political parties seemed much more responsive to meetings than this government is. And what's happening as a result of this apparent reluctance to meet with critics is a lot more heated protests."

The government was "uptight" for good reason. Convinced it had a mandate to act on the commitments in the CSR, the Harris team had remained oblivious to opposition until then. This was the case partly because they believed they were doing the right thing, but also because they were convinced that the majority of voters supported their actions. The teachers' strike and the subsequent protests over Bill 160, as well as the threat of a province-wide general strike by labour leaders opposed to a related bill on unions (Bill 136), began to make the Harris Tories question the accuracy of their thinking. Internal polls showed that a majority of Ontario voters sided with the teachers and the unions, not the government. This trend was reinforced by the revelation that the government was planning to introduce further spending cuts to the education envelope, something it had earlier denied and now was forced to admit and hastily dismiss as merely an option that had been considered and rejected.

Yet the Harris government did not really learn much from this experience, or perhaps it learned the wrong lesson. By the fall of 1998, it was just as authoritarian, just as impetuous and just as mean-spirited as it had always been. There was the disastrous handling of the Dionne sisters' file by the premier in April. The premier's petty and rigid stance had outraged just about everyone in Ontario as well as the rest of the country, and forced him to issue yet another apology. In May, Mike Harris made off-the-cuff remarks comparing nurses — losing their jobs as a result of his government's cuts — to the obsolescent Hula Hoop, another bit of candour for which he paid dearly in the form of a public apology. (By now the phrase "I did not mean to offend anyone, but if I did ..." was becoming all too familiar to Ontario residents.)

This was followed in June by the school textbook fiasco in which the government, intent on making changes *fast*, had no option but to choose *American* textbooks because Canadian publishers had not been given sufficient notice to update their texts. In July the government lost whatever credit it might have earned for a well-intentioned piece of legislation — a new Disability Act — by stubbornly refusing to carry out any meaningful consultations with stakeholders or accept their proposals for improvements. In the end, the bill was withdrawn.

Polls consistently showed that a majority of voters were extremely concerned about the Harris government's high-handed approach to governing, regardless of their views about the government's policies. According to an Angus Reid poll in late December 1997, more than 43 per cent of voters believed the Tories were on the right track in terms of policies, but "their style of governing is wrong for the times." Another 34 per cent believed the "government's policies and its style of government are mostly wrong." Even more important, the poll found some two-thirds of Ontario voters "believe the government is making changes too fast."

In a series of interviews marking the third anniversary of his election, the premier expressed neither concern nor regrets. He merely shrugged and said that change is always hard. Instead of focusing on the voters' concerns about his government's style, he wanted to talk about the policies that had been implemented. In fact, he stressed that his campaign team were already beginning to map out the contents of a new election platform, the "Common Sense Revolution II."

For Mike Harris and his government, the situation was clear. They had delivered. They had kept their promises to reduce the role of government in the economy and eliminate citizen's dependency on government services and programs. But they still had a way to go before the "menace" of state intervention was eliminated once and for all. They would need a second term to complete the dismantling of so much unnecessary bureaucracy. Having kept their promises, they apparently believed a grateful electorate would support them, despite their authoritarian approach and occasional lapses in competence.

For many of the citizens of Ontario, however, and especially those who did not live in middle-class suburbs, the "dismantling" of the government had produced untold hardships and a decreased quality of life. They saw no reason to reward the government for its dogmatic attack on "special interests" and its unwillingness or inability to balance competing claims fairly.

Even more significant was the growing evidence that many Ontarians evaluated their governments as they always had. The ability to manage competently and the ability to balance competing interests fairly were still two of the most important criteria for good government as far as many citizens were concerned. As political scientist John Wilson speculated, "Mike Harris and the 'reformed' Conservatives [will] pay the price if they continue to act as though leadership means telling other people what to do without any discussion ... They may be admired for sticking to the guns they laid out in their election manifesto. But there are two sides to the Ontario political culture, and if the new government is perceived to be overstepping the bounds of fairness and propriety ... which have been every bit as important as the demand for managerial efficiency, it will suffer [the consequences]."

By the end of 1998, Harris's third year in office, the previously stable Ontario political culture had been shaken. Worse, the province was rapidly becoming polarized — between urban and rural, have and have-not, winners and losers in the Common Sense Revolution. Yet the consequences of the Conservatives' actions were only beginning to be appreciated.

One reason for the delay in assessing the impact of the government's agenda was, ironically, its authoritarian style. Focusing on the Tories' "sledgehammer" approach to governing had led many observers to overlook the full impact of the neo-conservative agenda itself. Yet, after three years, the "Common Sense Revolution" had certainly had an impact.

A second and more important reason for this time lag was the strong economic recovery which had occurred during the government's first three years in office. This was a lucky break for Mike Harris, since he was hardly responsible for it. The successful deficit-reduction policies of the federal Liberals, and the boost to exporters brought about by the falling value of the Canadian dollar, were the primary reasons for Ontario's striking recovery. Had the economy not turned around for Harris, as it did also for Ralph Klein in Alberta, his government's ratings after three years would likely have been very different. Appreciated or not, however, the Conservatives were determined to stay the course.

Tax Cuts and Other Fables

As far as Mike Harris was concerned, by June 1998 there could be no doubt that he and his government had done almost exactly what they said they would do in the CSR's five-point economic plan. Government expenditures and the number of public servants had been reduced by more than 20 per cent, and the deficit was expected to be eliminated by fiscal 2000–01. Personal income tax reductions had been phased in and were scheduled to reach 30 per cent shortly. A massive deregulation and privatization exercise had removed the provincial government from much of the transportation, environment and public-safety domain. In short, there was certainly less government in Ontario in 1998 than when the Harris Conservatives took power in 1995.

But these measures were not supposed to be an end in themselves. The CRS manifesto had promised these planks would bring about economic recovery and create jobs, some 725,000 of them. Had they done so? As usual in economics, the answer is yes and no.

A glossy eight-page flyer distributed to all Ontario residences in late April trumpeted the government's tax cuts, the elimination of five hundred government regulations and the creation of 341,000 jobs in the previous two and a half years. In case any readers missed the link, the title of the document was "Creating Jobs Through Tax Cuts."

Critics were not prepared to accept the government's version of reality at face value. For one thing, almost all economists agreed that Ontario was benefiting from the nationwide economic recovery. This recovery, in turn, owed as much or more to booming international markets and a federal restraint policy that had produced low inflation and stable interest rates. While Ontario was admittedly reducing its deficit, the Harris government had tackled this problem later, and more slowly, than the federal government and many other provinces. In fact, as Liberal leader Dalton McGuinty pointed out, Ontario was going to be the last province in Canada to balance its budget.

More to the point, according to McGuinty the deficit could have been eliminated in 1998 if it had not been for the CSR commitment to a tax cut, which cost roughly $5.6 billion a year and added $14.8 billion to the debt. Critics also pointed to the obvious imbalance in the tax cuts.

The government's own brochure indicated the maximum benefit for a middle-income earner at $54,040 would be $1,710, while someone earning more than $177,000 would receive $6,030 and those with incomes over $255,000 would find themselves $15,540 richer. As former premier Bob Rae put it in an article marking the third anniversary of the Tories' election, the "rising tide" of the old liberal economy was designed to lift all boats, while the neo-conservative economy "lifts yachts and BMWs but swamps small craft."

If the well-to-do were benefiting most from the tax cuts, business was certainly the winner in the Harris government's deregulation sweepstakes. "Just contact the Red Tape Commission about a red tape problem affecting your business," the flyer urged. The government-appointed commission had already made 132 recommendations for regulatory reform, and the Harris Conservatives had followed through. With 11 of 17 "red tape" bills already passed, the government had eliminated 45 "unnecessary" acts and amended another 181.

Nowhere were the winners and losers in the deregulation exercise more clearly identified than in the fields of environmental and transportation policy. For business, the elimination of these "barriers" was a godsend. For those interested in environmental protection or consumer safety, they were a potential nightmare.

The Conservatives' fast action on many environmental regulations revealed the extent of their antipathy to these "restraints." In short order after their election, the Harris government had lifted the ban on incinerating garbage, removed responsibility for the Niagara Escarpment from the Environment Department, "relaxed" regulations on the disposal of PCBs and heavy metals, and proposed reductions in everything from smog standards to the number of soft drinks in reusable containers.

Although the outcry from environmental groups moved the government to pull back on a few of its more extreme proposals, a package of additional measures tabled by Environment minister Norm Sterling in November 1997 still caused much concern. According to Paul Muldoon of the Canadian Environmental Law Association, even with the changes the government had agreed to, the measures "still leave Ontario behind where it was when the Conservative government took office in 1995." Muldoon also said there was "a huge sense of frustration [among environmentalists] that we had to work so hard to maintain what [concessions] we got."

This frustration had been publicly evident for several months, as a result of comments made by the premier to American governors gathered for the annual Council of Great Lakes Governors. Addressing the issue of cross-border air pollution caused by American industries, Harris had not only urged the governors to do more, but assured them that "we are moving aggressively in Ontario and planning to become far more aggressive." For environmentalists this was the last straw. They angrily denounced the premier for his "unfounded" claims and "total lack of credibility" on environmental matters. Several demanded he explain what "much stricter emission controls" he had been referring to at the meeting.

Mike Harris was unfazed by these attacks, and the deregulation process proceeded apace. In February 1998, it was learned that the Environment ministry was raising the limits for two companies unable to meet existing standards for effluent discharges. While a ministry spokesperson assured reporters the increased limits did not present any health or environmental hazard, he also stated that "regulations must balance the economic requirements of industry with environmental protection." For environmentalists, however, the issue was not so much the specific case as the signal it sent to the business community. Stating the obvious, Mark Winfield of the Canadian Institute for Environmental Law and Policy said "It opens the door to other companies seeking these types of changes. It makes it clear that, if the limits become inconvenient, the ministry will move them."

The issue came to a head in April 1998, when the business and environmental communities became embroiled in a public debate over another package of government proposals for deregulation and relaxed enforcement. Arguing that many special events, such as car races, should be exempt from standard environmental permits, the government was proposing to create a new category of permit called a "certificate of approval." It was also proposing to establish "standardized" approvals for events with "predictable, controllable and/or well-understood impacts" on the environment. Among the activities for which the government proposed to issue standard approvals were the operation of municipal waste-transfer stations, the application of sewage sludge on farmland, and the "temporary" use of groundwater.

While the environmentalists accused the government of attempting to minimize its oversight and enforcement functions for activities with "potentially very serious effects on the environment," the business community was up in arms about the department's failure to introduce far more sweeping changes. Accusing the Harris government of reneging on promises, the Alliance of Manufacturers and Exporters Canada issued a statement in which they decried the government's failure to adopt the lower standards in place in Michigan. "The proposals do not even approximate the wholesale reform of the approvals process which the Ministry of the Environment had promised to Ontario industry," the report stated.

Predictably, the business community prevailed. But the environmentalists, like the teachers, were not prepared to roll over and play dead. Instead, in the next three months the Ontario government was bombarded by negative reports and press releases issued by various environmental groups. In late April, the Sierra Legal Defence Fund and the Wildland League both filed applications under the Ontario Environmental Bill of Rights, accusing the government of failing to enforce forestry regulations and permitting logging in the protected Algoma Highlands area. A few days later, the World Wildlife Fund (Canada) issued a report in which Ontario was accused of having the worst record of all the provinces in protecting endangered species and wilderness areas. In releasing the report, Fund president Monte Hummel said the province "has a blind spot on the environment" and "we are losing ground, not just marking time."

The groups' attempt to focus public opinion on the impact of the government's environmental policies was given an unexpected boost when newspapers across the province carried a front-page story about the fundraising efforts of three Ontario ex-premiers. What would it take to get three former premiers, from three different political parties, to put aside their differences and make common cause against the current government? An unlikely scenario, and yet there they were, posing for the cameras — Bill Davis himself, the Liberals' David Peterson and Bob Rae of the NDP. As the news coverage made clear, the three were reduced to raising funds privately to complete the construction of the Great Lakes Institute for Environmental Research, after the Harris government withdrew an earlier funding commitment.

The attack on the government's record continued with the presentation of a report to the premier by the Ontario Environmental Working Group in June. Based on information provided from government agencies such as Environment Canada, Statistics Canada and the Ontario Fire Marshall, the report concluded the Harris government's actions since 1995 had actually made pollution worse. In four key areas — acid rain, smog and air toxins, waste management and emissions — the government's record was judged "wholly inadequate to address the problems." The report also noted that fines against polluters had fallen, from an average of $2.6 million in the 1980s to less than $1 million in 1997, and questioned whether this could possibly be the result of decreased pollution activity. Even more embarrassing, the report continued, was a court decision to fine the province's Ministry of Natural Resources for ignoring provincial forestry regulations.

Perhaps the most effective of all of these critical assessments was the annual report of the Ontario Environment commissioner. After a scathing denunciation of budget and staff cuts to the Environment ministry that "completely hobble" any attempts to monitor conditions or enforce regulations, Commissioner Eva Ligeti stated that Ontario "has turned its back on the environment" In her damning conclusion, Ms. Ligeti argued the government's "focus needs to change from one of granting regulatory relief for polluters to improving its commitments to the environmental health of its residents and the natural environment." Although both Norm Sterling and the premier had defended the government's accomplishments in the face of the attacks by environmental groups, whom they claimed were "eco-extremists," neither one commented on the commissioner's report.

As for the jobs which the elimination of all these regulations were supposed to help produce, barely half of the promised 725,000 new private-sector positions had materialized by April 1998. Not surprisingly, the government carefully did not refer to this promise in its brochure. Instead, it simply argued that its tax cuts were "helping boost retail and housing sales, which put more people to work." Since Mike Harris had promised to resign if his government did not keep all of its commitments, it looked as if the next election might have to be fought on this issue unless the Tories could find a way around it.

By May 1998 there were not just fewer regulations in Ontario, but far fewer government programs providing far fewer services, contrary to what Mike Harris liked to claim. The 1998 Budget numbers, according to the Ontario Budget Alternative Working Group, were seriously misleading. Total spending on services and programs was actually $3.4 billion less than in 1995. The group's spokesperson, Hugh Mackenzie, claimed net spending had also declined, from 15 to 12 per cent of GDP. The May 5 Budget attempted to "camouflage" some of these spending decreases through creative accounting, and it was for this reason that Mackenzie's group — comprising numerous social agencies as well as former NDP supporters — had prepared their own version of the Budget numbers.

One reason the decrease in spending was not apparent was because the province, while taking credit for education spending as part of the disentanglement exercise, was also still taking credit for spending on the services transferred to the municipalities. "The spending figure for the current fiscal year is inflated by the fact that nearly $2.3 billion in services ... still show up on the province's books, even though the municipalities are bearing the costs," Mackenzie stated. In addition, the Working Group identified money allocated but never spent, or allocated to unspecified contingency funds, all of which totaled more than $6 billion in decreased expenditures.

One obvious reason the Conservatives would want to avoid drawing attention to their expenditure cuts was made clear in an example given by Mackenzie to reporters. According to his group's calculations, the government's "total education commitment for 1998–99 is roughly a billion dollars below the commitment for 1997–98." The "Common Sense Revolution" had carefully promised not to cut "classroom funding," and it was difficult to imagine how a cut of such magnitude would not affect classrooms.

Apart from total spending, however, the impact of the Harris government on the key education and health sectors could be seen in a variety of statistics closer to home. By 1998 many Ontarians were seriously concerned about the level of health care provided by the province's hospitals. Television viewers were frequently treated to scenes of line-ups and overcrowding at emergency rooms around the province. Despite his attempt to blame federal cutbacks for these problems, Mike Harris failed to convince voters that his commitment to health care remained sincere. Since taking office, his government had cut $870 million from annual hospital budgets. In a direct contradiction of the CSR manifesto, it had also introduced user fees for prescription drugs for seniors and delisted many OHIP services. Despite his election promise in the leaders' debates that "I can guarantee you, it is not my plan to close hospitals," a great many hospitals around the province were being merged or closed, ranging from two in Sudbury to three in Ottawa and eleven in Toronto.

The Tories' attempt to get around their pledge to maintain "class-room funding" without attracting much attention had also failed. Few voters missed the massive spending cuts. Nor did they agree with the measures severely reducing or eliminating funding for such "frills" as junior kindergarten, special education, adult education, early-learning programs and, unbelievably, school buses. In the Tories' zeal to find other means to reduce their spending on education, even school oper-ating and maintenance funding was cut, by 5 per cent per square foot. For most people, "classroom funding" was affected by these cuts, as well as by the reductions in the numbers of principals, vice-principals and teachers, through the ruse of "decreased teacher preparation time."

Clearly there were two types of promises in the "Common Sense Revolution." There were the "positive" ones the Harris Conservatives made because they believed in them — such as the five-point economic plan — and these they implemented with righteous wrath. Then there were "negative" commitments they made to placate voters or avoid losing support — such as their pledge to avoid cutting health care and education. These they either did not care about, or actually did not believe in. They were not part of their agenda, and therefore could be fudged, if not ignored.

This distinction appears to hold true on social policy issues as well as economic ones. Certainly the Harris government's zealous pursuit of its hot-button issues and its social conservative agenda is readily apparent in a review of its record after nearly four years in power, and nowhere more so than in the case of welfare.

Winners and Losers

"What we're doing, we're making sure that those dollars don't go to beer," Mike Harris told some mildly astonished reporters in the spring of 1998 when asked to explain why his government — which had already imposed a 22 per cent cut in welfare payments and removed tens of thousands of people from the welfare roles by changing the eligibility criteria — was now eliminating a $37 monthly food supplement for pregnant women.

For those covering Queen's Park on a regular basis, the surprise was not the latest cut, but the callous way the premier explained it. From Workfare and electronic fingerprinting of recipients to demanding receipts from the homeless, changing disability criteria, cutting dental benefits for the working poor and depriving low-income seniors of their canes and walkers — nowhere had the mean-spirited side of the Harris Conservatives been as visible as in their approach to welfare. Even coming from Mike Harris, though, the stereotypical attitude revealed by his statement was a bit of a shock to many.

Three years in government evidently had not changed the premier's view of welfare recipients as lazy, shiftless and dishonest, a view he had demonstrated so clearly in the unfortunate Helle Hulgaard affair in 1994. And because he truly shared the neo-conservative perspective that the poor are basically to blame for their lot, his government's record on welfare and social services during the prior three years was nothing short of draconian.

It certainly came as no surprise to the government's critics when Social Services minister Janet Ecker reported in June 1997 that some 250,639 individuals had dropped off the welfare rolls. The surprise was that Ecker appeared to believe this was a good sign. Although she admitted she had no idea where all of these people had gone ("The municipalities keep those figures. You'll have to ask them"), Ecker nevertheless attempted to take credit for the return of so many people to the productive workforce.

The nonplussed Liberal critic, MPP Sandra Pupatello, finally replied that "seeing people fall off welfare when you have no idea where they've gone is no reason to celebrate."

Since the jobless numbers in Ontario had risen over the same period, from 499,000 to 500,000, it seemed unlikely many of these individuals could have found work. Social-welfare advocates pointed to much greater use of food banks and shelters for the homeless. Waiting lists for social housing were skyrocketing, as was the incidence of family violence, spousal abuse and the placement of children in foster care.

Perhaps the truest measure of the government's commitment to a socially regressive agenda was its relentless pursuit of Workfare. As it was part of the CSR, the Harris Conservatives were obliged to make some attempt to fulfil their election commitment. But when the plan was first announced in April 1996, it was widely criticized for being not just morally offensive, but unworkable.

Faced with evidence that a less ambitious Quebec project had been abandoned as pointless after nearly six years, the Harris team might have wanted to reconsider. When they were presented with the facts of the failed New Zealand experiment, the whole plan clearly should have been shelved as a bad idea whose time had not come. The former Employment minister of New Zealand, Maurice McTeague, told reporters, "Quite frankly, with the Workfare thing, we didn't succeed." Mr. McTeague, who happened to be serving as New Zealand's high commissioner to Canada in 1996, added that "the biggest problem [was] finding jobs for people."

Undeterred, the Harris government forged ahead with its plan, intent on finding the kind of "'jobs" for these involuntary "workers" that would not take paying jobs away from anyone. Although the plan was scheduled to begin that fall, its implementation was often delayed and then carried out as pilot projects, since very few social agencies or other non-profit organizations agreed to participate, and a number of municipalities refused to do so until required by legislation.

By February 1998, nearly sixteen months later, Workfare was described by several critics as "a flop," and for exactly the same reason given by Maurice McTeague when it was introduced — a lack of jobs. According to one report, there were 68,000 able-bodied individuals eligible for Workfare positions in Toronto, Hamilton and Ottawa alone. Yet a total of only 116 welfare recipients were actually filling unpaid jobs.

For Ms. Ecker, it was "too soon to tell" whether the program was in trouble. But she also indicated she would consider allowing private-sector employers to take some of the recipients. "We now have a bottom line that Workfare cannot displace people in paid jobs," Ms. Ecker said. "But if that rule can be observed and we can have private-sector placements, we will be prepared to do it."

At the same time, Ms. Ecker released a new package of regulations related to the "work-for-welfare" plan, measures which seemed not only draconian, but petty and vindictive. One of these was Mike Harris's $37-a-month cut for pregnant women. Others meant welfare recipients living with parents would lose their benefits entirely. Recipients taking in boarders would have benefits reduced. Those on welfare for more than a year would have a lien placed against their house by the government. Most striking was the plan to give welfare officials police-like powers to lay charges against individuals — friends, family or neighbours — who refused to provide information to them about recipients.

As of May 1, the province would also no longer fund medical devices (wheelchairs, hearing aids, walkers, etc.) or funerals for the working poor and low-income elderly, but only those on welfare, forcing municipalities to pick up the tab. In Ottawa–Carleton, this would result in a saving to the province of roughly $850,000 per year, according to Alex Munter, chairman of the region's Community Services Committee. "What kind of incentive is this?" Mr. Munter queried. "If people are on minimum wage and need medical devices they should get them. Otherwise there is no incentive to get off welfare." Meanwhile, Dick Stewart, Social Services commissioner for Ottawa–Carleton, said, "The government's new rules for this program are incomprehensible. This is a classic example of a government program that is hard to access, difficult to understand, and doesn't serve those it is intended to help."

NDP critic Peter Kormos said the changes demonstrated "the lack of knowledge the Tory government has about the poor. Sure it is going to reduce welfare costs, no two ways about it, but it fails completely to understand the real issues ..." Referring to the changes as "nickel and dime," Ian Morrison, a lawyer and social activist associated with the publication *Workfare Watch*, described the changes as "like pulling wings off flies. There is no policy rationale discernible here, except to be mean to people."

But the Tories did not blink. Nor did they change their minds on social housing, another "luxury" which low-income Ontarians obviously did not deserve. By early 1998 the Ontario Housing Corp. (OHC) announced it would sell off 1,864 social housing units, despite the fact that demand was increasing and waiting lists were longer than ever. Worse still, it was planning to sell the best units, ones integrated into neighbourhoods rather than high-rise complexes.

In his own words, Dino Chiesa, CEO of the OHC, provided the motive for the sales. Mr. Chiesa, a Tory appointee, proudly declared, "The big thing is the dollars that can come out of the sale. Many of these assets are valuable. If you can sell 100 units for between $100,000 and $200,000, that's $20 million." It is interesting to note that the board postponed a vote on the matter in June 1997, and only voted again, this time in favour of the sale, after six of the eleven board members were replaced by Tory appointees in December.

Fundamentally opposed to any provincial role in social housing, the Harris government had originally pledged to sell off the OHC itself. Finding themselves unable to do so for various reasons, they downloaded social housing to the municipalities instead. According to David Hulchanski, a professor at the University of Toronto and former board member who opposed the sale (and whose appointment was not renewed in December), "It's stripping off the best assets of these local housing authorities prior to their being downloaded to the municipalities." In short, the Ontario government was preparing to take the money and run, saddling the municipalities with run-down units and huge costs.

A similar story unfolded with respect to child care, another program the Harris Conservatives did not consider valid. In the CSR they had promised only to "encourage the private sector to provide child care for working parents." Once in power, and having rejected an offer from the federal Liberals to co-finance additional child-care spaces, the government of Mike Harris instead became the first in the history of the province to actually cut funding for child care. By May 1998, there were 30,000 Ontario families on waiting lists for child-care subsidies.

Clearly the Harris social agenda was not designed to benefit single mothers or children living in poverty, both of whom were somehow "undeserving." In fact, the social agenda was not about providing assistance at all. Instead, it was all about removing unfair benefits that were already being provided, and, in the case of the legal system, punishing the guilty.

This enthusiasm for retribution had been obvious in the Harris government's approach to young offenders, as its boot-camp pledge had demonstrated during the campaign. For these new-style Tories, minimizing the role of government did *not* include reducing the punitive powers of the state, despite overwhelming evidence retribution does not work, especially with young offenders.

A classic example was the response of Solicitor General Bob Runciman — a philosophical clone of his Alberta counterpart, Jon Havelock — to widespread public concern following a highly publicized rape case involving an eleven-year-old boy. Fanning the flames rather than allaying the public's fears, the Ontario solicitor general called on the federal government to immediately lower the minimum age in the Young Offenders Act, and increase sentences. Yet both of these remedies had already been proven ineffective, as the minister should have known. More to the point, the minister should have known that incidents involving ten- and eleven-year-olds had actually *decreased*, from 1.4 per cent of the total youth offences in 1983 to 1.2 per cent in 1992.

In response to the minister's actions, Susan Eng, former chair of the Metro Police Services Board, publicly criticized the Ontario government's approach, pointing out that "criminal justice research repeatedly shows the threat of heavier sentences does little to deter youth." According to Ms. Eng, the remedy which had proven most effective was the "restitution initiative." She went on to explain that "restitution initiatives tried elsewhere involving teachers, parents, police and victims have been proven conclusively to reduce recidivism [repeat offences] ... However, this kind of long-term approach requires a commitment to intervene that is absent from the zero-tolerance approach in Ontario ..." By 1996 Ontario's per-capita rate of youth court cases was already four times that of Quebec, which preferred to use restitution or other diversion options whenever possible and had met with considerable success.

None of this deterred the minister, who continued to accuse the federal government of being "soft" on young offenders.

Another predictable item on the Harris agenda for the administration of justice was the plight of victims of crime. Like their neo-conservative counterparts in Alberta and the Reform Party, the Ontario government was able to find considerable resources for deserving citizens such as these, even when funds were scarce. And so Attorney General Charles Harnick announced a $10-million fund for victims of crime, and Solicitor General Bob Runciman announced the creation of the Ontario Crime Control Commission — only a short while after they had suggested the province might not honour unpaid legal-aid lawyers' bills because of the large deficit in the legal-aid plan.

This funding "crisis" was only averted when the Law Society, which administered the plan, agreed to reduce the total number of certificates from 225,000 to 80,000 per year in 1996, and specifically targeted family law for a reduction (a 75 per cent cutback from 1992–93). The results were entirely predictable to those working in the field. By November 1997, the legal-aid plan actually reported a surplus of $24 million, which its administrator suggested could rise to $60 million by the end of the fiscal year. Robert Armstrong of the Law Society of Upper Canada speculated that the "windfall" was the result of two things: many lawyers refusing to take legal-aid cases at all (fees having been frozen at impossibly low levels for a decade) and many discouraged eligible clients not bothering to apply. Meanwhile, the courts increasingly were bogged down with cases where the accused represented themselves — a time-consuming and one-sided process in which the defendant rarely prevailed.

The situation had deteriorated further by December 1997, when the report of the government-appointed review panel chaired by John D. McCamus proposed a fundamental redesign of the legal aid system, an approach that reflected the Harris Conservatives' inherent dislike of legal aid.

The report was criticized by the Ontario Criminal Lawyers Association (CLA) as "repulsive" and "naïve." They argued it was a "destructive" and "misguided" attempt to save money, whose recommendations would turn courts into "guilty-plea factories." Among other things, the report actually suggested that the ever-expanding number of accused appearing before the courts without representation was the result of personal choice, not a crisis of funding. In its formal response to the report, the CLA declared, "If the justice system in Ontario is to become a Wal-Mart style operation with clearance rates, loss leaders and block contracting, we will have achieved the ultimate in sacrificing quality justice on the altar of expediency."

By February 1998 the government and the Law Society agreed to a compromise package based primarily on the McCamus report. It included a large one-time cash infusion and provided for the establishment by April 1999 of an *independent* corporation (rather than one controlled by the government as it would have liked) to administer legal aid. An article in the *Globe and Mail* on February 26, 1998, reported that Attorney General Charles Harnick was "so keen to wrest legal aid away from the law society" that he agreed to this halfway measure, although he admitted he would have difficulty selling the agreement to several of his cabinet colleagues, who were "openly hostile" to the very idea of legal aid.

This unseemly fight over legal aid was not the only case in which the government attempted to favour retribution over rehabilitation and fairness, but it was the most public. A year earlier it had cancelled another progressive measure, the highly regarded Bail Program, with little fanfare and less public attention. The cut would probably have gone completely unnoticed if the government had not decided to ignore legal procedures in its enthusiasm to eliminate the plan as quickly as possible.

On March 22, 1997, the solicitor general and Correctional Services were essentially accused of breaking the law, by unilaterally changing judicial release orders. This accusation was made by Neil Webster, director of the Bail Program, who claimed the minister's attempt to scrap the entire program by March 31 was fraught with legal difficulties. When informed by his officials that it could take several months to actually wind the program down, the minister had apparently decided to ignore their advice and do administratively, by letter, what would normally require a lengthy and complicated legal solution in the courts. If the correct legal route was pursued, every bail order would have to be changed individually by a judge. Instead, Correctional Services simply advised Webster that all of his 450 clients should report to police stations as of April 1.

This procedural tempest in a teapot unfortunately tended to over-shadow the importance of the government's decision to shut down a program that was an eighteen-year success story. As the program was always fully booked, owing to scarce resources, many experts had advo-cated its expansion rather than its elimination. In support of this case, Webster produced a court transcript for the media which quoted a judge saying "There unfortunately being no other form of release I can consider ... the accused will have to be detained ..."

The cancellation announcement prompted "rare consensus" among judges, Crowns and defence attorneys, who lobbied together to save the program to no avail. The irony was that neither cost-effectiveness nor public safety could be used by the government to defend its decision. Although the ministry claimed it would save $1.9 million annually, experts stated that the cost of incarceration (at $116 per day, versus $4 per day for bail supervision) clearly demonstrated the practical value of the program. Lawyer Paul Calarco also warned that "the government is jeopardizing public safety by eliminating the program."

Neil Webster pointed to the obvious inequity of the government's decision, saying, "There's no question about it. People will be held in jail simply because they're poor." A response from Solicitor General Runciman, in typical neo-conservative fashion, simply stated that "super-vising accused people before their trial is not part of the ministry's legislative mandate."

By June 1998 the government's blue-ribbon panel of backbench Conservative MPPs, the Ontario Crime Control Commission, tabled its first report, on youth crime. To no one's surprise, the commission, mandated to "find new ways to fight crime and improve public safety," advocated moving even further in the direction already taken by the Harris government. The commission's chair, Scarborough West MPP Jim Brown, stressed the need to "get tough on crime" repeatedly during a press conference to discuss the report. Among the report's major recommendations were a "safe school act" promoting zero toler-ance, legislation to hold parents financially responsible for damage caused by their children, and the creation of "citizens' courts" to "hand out appropriate punishment." (This last idea proved the most controversial, with many critics arguing it was a frighteningly short step from the promotion of "voluntary tribunals" to vigilante enforcement tactics.)

The commissioners also enthusiastically recommended following the lead of several well-known American law-and-order advocates, such as Mayor Rudolph Giuliani of New York City, in pursuing a "broken windows" approach to crime control, in which police aggressively pursue minor infractions in the hope of preventing major ones. This would include allowing police to use civil court injunctions to limit antisocial behaviour such as loitering, vandalism, prostitution or drug-related offences. Such a move would circumvent the need for evidence, as required to prosecute offenders under the Criminal Code. Among the success stories of the New York City approach, according to the report, was the "virtual elimination" of the homeless from the city's downtown core. (The report did not explain where these individuals were subsequently located. It also failed to note two other important but unrelated factors in the decreasing crime rate — namely, shifting demographics, including the dramatic decrease in the number of young males resident in the city, and the economic recovery, which had greatly alleviated the unemployment problem for many youths.)

This "tough on crime" theme was already evident in the commission's earlier activities, which included hosting an international conference of "the world's top crime-fighters" in Toronto, and presenting awards to "top Ontario crime-fighters" in February. By early April 1998, several news articles indicating the government was planning to target "immigrant crime" as a priority in its upcoming Throne Speech had appeared. According to one source, "It addresses the government's belief that Ontarians are fed up with immigrants who break the law, and with sponsors of immigrants who fail to live up to their responsibilities." Ontarians had given no evidence of being fed up, but the premier certainly had. Only a short time earlier he had made numerous public comments criticizing the federal government for their "open door" policy on immigration, a theme he repeated when Ottawa was in the midst of negotiations with the United Nations to accept political prisoners from Cuba.

Reactions to this leaked draft of the Throne Speech were swift and almost universally critical. Church groups, immigrant-support groups and various groups of immigrants themselves all roundly attacked what they perceived to be an outrageously negative approach. "It's typical of the divisive, victimization politics practised by Mike Harris," said one critic. NDP leader Howard Hampton said, "It's the old saw. It's the rhetoric this government goes back to when the well is empty." Liberal leader Dalton McGuinty went even further in his condemnation of the proposal: "In order to make people feel better he finds a scapegoat. Welfare people were the enemy before, and now he's found some others, apparently. It's unbecoming for a premier, but typical." Putting his finger on the likely reason for the government's renewed interest in crime-fighting, McGuinty continued, "People out there aren't talking about new Canadians or immigrants committing crimes. They are talking about people being stacked up in hospital corridors."

The negative response is undoubtedly why the final text of the April 23 Throne Speech did not refer to immigrant criminals, although the section on "Personal Safety" remained a highlight of the document. Having apparently run out of any other specific ideas, the speech instead contained a lengthy section devoted to Priscilla de Villiers, president of CAVEAT (Citizens Against Violence Everywhere Advocating Its Termination), as well as a recognition of a police constable shot in the line of duty ("We will do everything necessary to support the law enforcement officers who protect our lives"), and a meaningless pledge to "continue to press the federal government and Parliament who actually make the laws the provinces enforce."

McGuinty's comments on hospitals, meanwhile, reflected the string of polls showing the Harris government was most vulnerable on the subject of health care, and that this was an issue of intense interest to the people of Ontario. Not surprisingly, the Throne Speech contained a lengthy section on "Health Care for All" in which it tried to convey the impression the government was not only aware of people's concerns, but hard at work attempting to rectify them. More money was promised for long-term-care beds and community care, but this promise had been made before and still had not materialized.

As if unable to prevent itself from reverting to its negative perspective, the government's speech then veered off onto the social-conservative agenda again, announcing a plan to introduce a "smart information system" and "enhanced investigation" to "help address health care fraud" — subjects which no polls had revealed were occupying the general public, but evidently were weighing heavily on the minds of Mike Harris and his cabinet.

With the "immigrant criminal" issue a non-starter, the Throne Speech was essentially a non-event, except for the comic touch added by the resignation of the solicitor general while the OPP investigated the role played by his department in revealing the identity of a young offender in the text of the speech. Nevertheless, the debate over the contents of the speech had reinforced the government's negative image with many of its critics, and especially with church groups.

Mike Harris vs. God

The rift between the churches and the Harris government had been growing for some time. It was a significant development in a province where spiritual and political leaders had traditionally been very supportive of each other. Indeed, unlike in Western Canada, where fundamentalist religious groups have themselves been considered "outsiders" and frequently hold anti-state views, organized religion in Ontario had always been an important element of the traditional elite class. (Some observers have argued that it was Bill Davis's appreciation for the long-standing political support of Toronto's Catholic leader, Emmett Cardinal Carter, that was the deciding factor in the former premier's move to award full funding for the separate-school system in the province, a move which ironically cost the Conservatives an election.)

The unusual church–state dispute had become embarrassingly public a few months earlier, when a broadly based multifaith coalition issued an open letter and press release roundly criticizing the Harris government for its policies and their effect on the disadvantaged. The conflict led the *Ottawa Citizen* to run a major article on the issue on May 24, 1998, entitled "God vs. Mike Harris." In it, Bishop John Sherlock of the Ontario Conference of Catholic Bishops declared that the premier's government "runs a very great risk of being unchristian."

In their open letter to the premier, representatives of the Catholic, Anglican, United, Lutheran and Mennonite churches, as well as the

Jewish, Buddhist and Islamic faiths, deplored the "moral crisis" they saw unfolding in the province. "We are alarmed," they wrote, "by a trend which we perceive to blame immigrants, welfare recipients, those who are unemployed, the disabled, those who are on workers' compensation, and those forced to live on the streets, as responsible for their own suffering." This attitude on the part of the government, they continued, "has led to ... a lessening of civility, the abandonment of compassion, and an abandonment of our mutual responsibility to meet the needs of our neighbours."

The letter and accompanying statement came after a string of cancelled meetings with the premier, and a subsequent press conference in which Harris referred to certain leaders of the coalition as unreasonable, intransigent and politically biased because of their refusal to cooperate with the government on the mandatory Workfare program. In response, the multifaith group noted that "the current approach to social services by this government is directly contrary to the recommendations that have been made by various publicly appointed and well-respected bodies during the past ten years."

The resulting furore over the appropriate role of religious leaders in the political sphere was heightened by the publication of a blatantly critical work on the Harris government by Quaker prison-reform activist Ruth Morris, entitled *Listen Ontario! Faith Communities Speak Out.* The book was endorsed by the former primate of the Anglican Church in Canada, Edward Scott, who wrote in his foreword that "this volume could be a valuable source for members of the government. It would help them come to a deeper awareness of the human values that are affirmed or ignored in legislation, and of the very real danger of creating moral and spiritual deficits of which they seem to have been unaware as they focus their attention primarily on overcoming the financial deficit very rapidly."

Perhaps Mike Harris was somewhat chastened by this latest attack on his government's record, or perhaps he merely concluded he would have difficulty dismissing the church groups as marginal extremists in the same way he had rejected the criticism of labour, professionals, environmentalists and other "special interests" with whom he disagreed. In any event, it was a more subdued and less confrontational Mike Harris who met with a number of reporters in late May and early June 1998 to discuss his government's accomplishments after three years in office.

When asked if the next year or two before an election would prove as hectic, for example, he indicated that "the legislative priorities [for the remainder of his mandate] aren't as significant as they were in the first half." However, he was not about to accept criticism or hesitate to assign blame for problems that had occurred along the way. When asked by one reporter whether he felt his disentanglement and megacity initiatives were proving to be difficult to implement, the premier replied, "There may be one or two or three per cent of difficulties in determining exactly what's there, but I think those who are proceeding in good faith with the same objectives as we have are not having significant difficulties."

His testiness reappeared when asked whether he planned to implement many of the recommendations of the Crime Control Commission's report ("Well sure, we didn't set up the commission to simply go hear what people had to say and then ignore it"). Even more telling was the premier's inability to find fault with his government's record. Asked to identify anything he would take back from his agenda of the last three years, he replied, "I don't look at things that way. There's lots of things that don't come out exactly as you may have hoped, but I don't analyse them and I won't say you should take them back."

As for the next election, it would likely come "sometime between the fourth and fifth year," but "I haven't turned my mind to it and ... it's a fair ways off as far as I'm concerned." Then the premier concluded on a much more conciliatory note, with repeated pledges to restore funding for health care and introduce new legislation to better provide for those with permanent disabilities.

A Kinder, Gentler Mike Harris?

With the premier musing pensively about the plight of people with disabilities and the possible reinvestment of funds in education and health care, it might have appeared that Ontario, after three years of the neo-conservative agenda, was about to see a return to a more tranquil and traditional form of Conservative government. This momentary illusion was quickly dispelled, however, with the government's introduction of two blatantly anti-union bills that could only be expected to result in further confrontation between the government and many of its citizens.

The first, tabled in late May, was aptly named the Prevention of Unionization Act. The purpose of the bill was straightforward and simple: to prevent Workfare participants from organizing. The main opponents of the bill were the public servants who feared, understandably, that the next place the government was going to impose Workfare was on the broader public sector.

The second, Bill 31, the Economic Development and Workplace Democracy Act, was presented in mid-June. The Orwellian Newspeak did not fool anyone, and certainly not the unions against whom it was directed. There appeared to be many objectives to this legislation, all of which would tilt the field against labour unions. One provision exempted "all non-construction employers from having to abide by province-wide construction contracts on building projects." Another clause prevented the Ontario Labour Relations Board from being able to certify a union if it was found that employer intimidation had been a factor. This was the so-called Wal-Mart clause, introduced expressly to prevent a recurrence of the board's earlier decision to certify a union at a Windsor Wal-Mart store after evidence of blatant employer intimidation tactics had been presented.

A third provision of the bill was more problematic, as several critics were quick to point out. Dubbed "the Olympics clause" by one analyst, its purpose was to allow no-strike clauses in contracts for "major industrial projects." The irony of this, as several labour experts noted, was that it might very well end up benefiting union workers. Years earlier, a similar attempt at strike prevention in B.C. under W.A.C. Bennett, for the Peace River and Columbia power projects, had actually resulted in the province's having the highest union wages in the country.

By the legislative recess in late June it was looking as if the summer of 1998 would be long and hot for the Harris government. Apart from the anticipated union demonstrations and rotating strikes in the construction industry, the teachers' unions were returning to the fray. Their continued opposition to Bill 160 led them to unite with school boards to launch a constitutional challenge of certain provisions of the legislation, to be heard in late June. At the same time, teachers' unions across the province were holding strike votes and warning that they would consider staying off the job in September if changes to the bill were not made concerning their terms and conditions of work.

The dispute became more personal in late June, when parents in the Toronto District School Board (TDSB) sent out a newsletter under the auspices of the board, attacking the government's actions. The government responded the next day, with a full-page ad that began "Get on With It" and ended "Isn't it time for the TDSB to stop playing games?" Toronto parent Kathleen Wynne, a member of the parent group that had drafted the letter, saw the government's prompt and vicious response as a sure sign the Harris Tories were getting worried. "They're mad because we've interrupted their 'good news' announcements," Ms. Wynne declared, referring to the stream of recent statements by Education minister Dave Johnson on funding and curriculum changes, all of which began, "I'm here today with another good-news announcement for the students of Ontario."

For Liz Sandals, president of the Ontario Public School Boards Association, the situation could only deteriorate further for the government, once the full impact of the changes had sunk in. "There's still mass confusion," Ms. Sandals stated, adding "people (and especially parents) won't know the full impact until the fall and into the next year or two."

The mass confusion escalated on July 22, when the courts ruled in favour of the legal challenge of the Ontario English Catholic Teachers Association. The ramifications of the decision were breathtaking. The government could hardly leave the situation as it was or their budgetary provisions would be in chaos. Nor could they ignore the fact that this put the Catholic school boards, still a minority in the province, in a different legal position from the majority Protestant boards. For their part, in the midst of re-evaluating their property-tax assessments, municipalities now faced the possibility that school boards would attempt to levy their own component of the municipal taxes. Faced with such a challenge to its plans, the Harris government took the only logical action open to it and appealed the decision. (Meanwhile, in Alberta, Ralph Klein and his government were watching anxiously, knowing full well they were facing a similar legal challenge for making almost identical reforms to their own education system in 1994.)

As for the government's health-care reforms, and especially the mergers of hospitals in many urban centres, they were proceeding at a snail's pace, especially in comparison with the school-board issue. Cynics noted that, unlike the educational system, health care was a subject in which every citizen had both a vested interest and an understanding of the issues. Terrified of negative publicity — such as the coverage of ambulances being turned away and deaths in emergency wards that had plagued the Klein government's efforts — the Harris Tories were definitely putting the brakes on and taking another look at their plans. If Al Leach had thought dismantling social housing was "more complicated than he first thought," this was nothing compared with the Ontario Conservatives' discovery that the delivery of health-care services was a hugely complex area in which they had virtually no expertise or insights.

In Ottawa, the public-relations disaster over their earlier attempt to close down the Montfort Hospital — the region's only French-language facility — had caused them to cave in several months before. As summer turned to fall, the residents of the nation's capital began to realize the full extent of the government's disarray when another hospital slated for closure, the Riverside, appeared one morning sporting a banner describing it as a "branch" of the Ottawa General, one of two local hospitals which had been spared. This was clearly another exercise in damage control, since the Riverside had undergone a major and hugely expensive renovation only two years prior to its announced closure, and Ottawans were fuming about the government's apparent lack of logic in making these decisions. Meanwhile, in downtown Toronto, where chaos in the emergency wards was looming large and few practitioners understood what changes would be occurring, or when, one physician was overheard warning his friends they should not even consider going to a hospital on a Saturday unless they wanted to end up dead by Monday.

In the new "megacity" of Toronto, all was not going well either. The practical and logistical problems involved in merging and administering a population of 2.5 million — problems that had been identified by opponents of the government's plan months before — were becoming all too evident barely four months after the merger was imposed. As Councillor Jack Layton remarked sarcastically, "I think there's only 11,000 bylaws that have to be brought together. We can easily finish it in a decade."

With the new Toronto council of fifty-seven members having the final say on all matters, council agendas, meetings and decision making were also running out of control. For political scientist Edmund Fowler, a specialist in local government at York University, the problems were entirely predictable. As Fowler pointed out, "The council is larger than some provincial legislatures, but without the organizing principle of political parties." While agreements might be reached among some members at the committee level, these agreements disintegrate when the issue goes to full council, where "there are too many members, all with their own ideas about what should happen. The result is council meetings that are a circus."

By June 1998, routine decisions on tree-cutting were still taking up the time of full council, and individual grant applications were debated for nine hours. The prospects were not good for the speedy resolution of more important issues, such as the implementation of the provincial government's new property-tax-assessment scheme. With literally tens of thousands of Torontonians furious about the impact of the Harris tax plan, it seemed unlikely the summer would be tranquil in the provincial capital, despite the absence of provincial MPPs from Queen's Park on their summer recess.

Just before leaving, however, the Conservatives introduced two additional pieces of legislation which would also prove highly controversial. The first was a bill to "decontrol," or essentially break up and partially privatize, Ontario Hydro. This groundbreaking legislation naturally attracted considerable media and Opposition attention. But if the Tories had hoped to divert attention from their second initiative, to amend the Ontario Election Act and the Election Finances Act, they were singularly unsuccessful. Opposition to these measures was so intense, and debate so chaotic, that the legislature was actually adjourned for an hour, and eight Opposition MPPs were removed for refusing to abide by the rules of procedure.

Why the fuss? As Queen's Park reporter Ian Urquart succinctly put it, "It's called stacking the deck." The changes, introduced by Management Board chair Chris Hodgson, were ostensibly to "save taxpayers' money" and "modernize our rules." However, all of the money saved would come from the switch to a permanent voters' list, one of the few non-controversial parts of the package. As the financially embarrassed Opposition parties realized immediately, the real thrust of the bill was to allow the Conservatives to spend far more money in the next election.

Flush with cash while the Opposition Liberals and NDP had empty war chests, the Harris government saw its chance to take advantage. Among its proposals were the raising of the spending limit for individual candidates as well as for the central party campaign, and the exclusion of polling and travel costs from the limits. In addition, the proposal to shorten the election from thirty-seven to twenty-eight days clearly favoured incumbents — in this case, the governing Conservatives.

Urquart noted that "past changes to the election rules have been made only when there is a consensus among the three parties. By moving unilaterally, the Tories are violating that tradition." Opposition anger intensified when the government announced it planned to ram the changes through before the legislature adjourned in less than two weeks, and without holding public hearings. The final vote, on June 24, took place in an atmosphere even more raucous than the debate two weeks earlier. Liberal MPPs broke into a rendition of "The Star Spangled Banner." Two of their colleagues placed a sack of fake money on the desk of the premier and unfurled an American flag with the words "Governor Harris" stamped on it, before being ejected from the legislature. NDP MPPs tossed Monopoly money in the air at their desks.

Liberal House Leader Jim Bradley, who called the legislation the "Buy-the-Election Bill," said he feared the measures would make Ontario susceptible to the same problems Americans now face. "We'll discourage people without money from running ... And political parties, at least the Conservatives, will cater to the most wealthy people because the payback will be large political contributions." Clearly not amused by the Opposition's antics, Premier Mike Harris first accused them of being "disrespectful" of the Speaker, the legislature, and even of democracy. He then maintained that "the limitations here are still much more restrictive than in the United States," and concluded by saying, in his view, "There's no big money that's going to tip the balance in Ontario elections."

Money may not have been on the premier's mind, but elections certainly were. Despite his end-of-session interviews dismissing the prospect of a fall election, the premier and his advisers had evidently become concerned with polls showing continued Liberal strength (41 per cent of decided voters, according to an Angus Reid/ *Globe and Mail* poll of June 25) and a persistent gender gap (48 per cent disapproval rating of the government by women, as opposed to 32 per cent by men). Worse still, although many Ontarians supported the general direction of the government's policies, they were increasingly inclined to dislike the government's style and methods, and still believed it had moved too fast. The youth vote was slipping away from the Tories, who were left with core support among older, affluent males. Not surprisingly, that support continued to be heavily concentrated in suburban/rural areas, while their limited urban support had actually dropped.

Even less surprising was the flurry of letters to the editor provoked by the premier's self-congratulatory end-of-session interviews. Refuting his claim that his government was "on the right track" and Ontarians were now far better off than they had been in 1995, writers critical of the Harris government most often mentioned its lack of balance and social conscience. A typical response came from Michael Lundholm of Toronto, who wrote: "Dear Mr. Harris, No, you are not on the right track!" For Mr. Lundholm, who assured the premier he was "not active in politics, nor am I aligned with any one political party," the Harris government's unbalanced "vision of Ontario based exclusively on economic perfor-mance will lead to a barren and boring future for all of us."

The depth of voters' feelings, and the fundamental issues of balance that Lundholm and others raised should have been of serious concern to the premier. Noting that he had "deep roots in Ontario and [had] lived under governments of all three political parties in various parts of the province," Mr. Lundholm concluded: "While I have from time to time disagreed with particular policies or programs ... never before have I felt so completely alienated and offended by my government."

A similar level of alienation was expressed by an eighteen-year-old student, confirming that Harris was going to have difficulty keeping the support of young voters in the next election. In a letter entitled "Don't expect the youth vote, Mr. Harris," Oakville high-school student Peter Miller stressed that, while he objected to the government's education policies, they were only part of the reason for his disenchantment with the Harris Conservatives. Putting his finger on the same "Who benefits?"

argument raised by the churches and the unions, Mr. Miller concluded, "It seems that the interests of the rich and the elite are being protected in Ontario ... In the next election, I will not be voting for the Conservative member in my riding. In the next election, I will cast my vote in favour of real common sense, not the Harris kind."

When Mike Harris appeared on the podium to say a few words of introduction at a SkyDome reception for visiting South African president Nelson Mandela, the boos and catcalls were so loud he was unable to be heard over the din. These displays of ongoing public discontent came only weeks after many residents of the province watched in disbelief as John Snobelen, the former Education minister now presumably safely out of harm's way in the Natural Resources portfolio, came under heavy criticism for two improbable decisions. First, the minister announced that he was raising the quota for sport fishermen in certain areas of the province "so their experience would be more enjoyable." Then he explained that it was perfectly reasonable to allow twelve-year-olds to obtain hunting licences so they could enjoy an important experience with their fathers. As one letter to the editor exclaimed, "Are there no limits on the rights of individuals under this government? What happened to the public interest?"

As the fall session of the legislature opened, the teachers' strike that had been looming on the horizon became a reality, and the government was eventually forced to cut a deal with the Opposition parties and bring in back-to-work legislation. It was a solution which resolved little, especially as school boards across the province were soon expressing their outrage over Education minister Dave Johnson's remarks about school closings. With the province now holding the purse strings, and having informed boards arbitrarily how many spaces it would pay for in each district, using a ridiculously inept formula, board officials calculated there would have to be up to 600 school closings. Boards were particularly hard hit in Ottawa and Toronto, where some 130 schools alone would have to close and many students would have to be bused to distant schools. Yet Johnson, ever combative, tried to blame the closures on the boards themselves, ignoring the fact the province was forcing the issue and stressing it was up to the boards to decide which schools to close.

Premier Harris waded into the issue as well, accusing the administrators of the Toronto District School Board of being a bunch of "fat cats" who were closing schools because they were unable to trim administrative costs to bring them in line with other boards. He also implied their books were closed to the public, and with good reason. Furious at and frustrated by the government's blatant efforts to make her a scapegoat, Chair Gail Nyberg turned the tables on the premier with a brilliant public-relations move. Inviting reporters to tour inner-city Toronto schools that would have to close under the government's new formula, she pointed out the many flaws in the government's simplistic "one-size-fits-all" plan, with Toronto's older schools, higher operating costs and expected *increase* in enrolment playing havoc with the board's efforts to adjust to the $362-million shortfall. Within days a muted Harris withdrew from the fray having had his bluff called. He announced more money and a one-year delay in implementation, while officials "re-examined" the government's impetuous plan. Nevertheless, many officials pointed out the compromise would not prevent eventual closings, but merely postpone them, presumably until after a provincial election.

Election Countdown

Entering the home stretch in its first term, the Harris government was facing a classic dilemma of its own making. Having committed itself to no cuts in core education and health-care spending, it appeared to be doing exactly the opposite, despite several attempts to portray its moves differently, including a surprise announcement by Health minister Elizabeth Witmer that the government would go it alone and compensate Hepatitis-C victims who had been excluded from the original federal–provincial settlement agreement. While voters may have agreed with the government's move, they were not distracted from their concerns about the state of the provincial health-care system. Worse still, the increased anxiety and anger over government cuts were highest among the middle-class suburban voters Mike Harris had just attracted to his new coalition in the 1995 election.

At the same time, inspired in the last election to move to the extreme right to maintain traditional rural votes and stave off incursions by the Reform Party into provincial politics, the Harris government was also alienating much of its traditional "progressive" Conservative support. Yet any attempt to move back towards the centre (even if it had wanted to do so), by presenting a "kinder, gentler" face to the electorate, would not only appear opportunistic, but also risk alienating the social conservatives in their caucus and open up the possibility of a right-wing split with Reform in the next election.

This dilemma left the provincial Liberals under Dalton McGuinty with an enormous opening to assume the mantle of the traditional Conservatives by demonstrating moderation, competence and balance in their positions, while distinguishing themselves sharply from the Harris neo-cons. Their failure to do so by the end of 1998, however, left the Conservatives with an opportunity to regroup. The same Angus Reid poll that demonstrated continued Liberal strength also showed the Conservatives with a solid 40 per cent base of support, and an almost equal approval and disapproval rating among decided voters. In fact, probably the most significant trend revealed by the poll was the degree to which many Ontarians had not yet made up their minds about the Harris government. Like Peter Judd, who had asked Mike Harris in June 1995 whether he would keep his promises, and who indicated in June 1998 that "the jury is still out," many voters in Ontario appeared to be torn between their admiration for the government sticking to its agenda and their dismay at the impact the agenda was having on society as a whole.

The myth of the majority mandate could be at the root of this ambivalence. Although Mike Harris and his advisers never questioned their mandate, it may well be that the Conservatives succeeded in 1995 because their supporters agreed with the *problems* identified in the "Common Sense Revolution," rather than the extreme solutions proposed.

In addition, many of the swing voters who supported the Conservatives in 1995 — the discontented moderates threatened by economic uncertainty and dislocation — may well have become more sanguine as the Ontario economy rebounded strongly. If so, once the full effects of the neo-conservative agenda on women, and on poor, elderly and disabled people (and on policy areas such as education, the environment, culture and health care) are more widely seen and understood, the balance for many undecided Ontario voters could well be tipped away from the "Common Sense Revolution."

This is even more likely, given the traditional focus of Ontario voters on federal, rather than provincial, politics. With some 90 per cent of Ontario residents describing themselves as Canadians first, and Ontarians second (as opposed to in Alberta, for example, where the numbers are almost the reverse), it is a fact of life that provincial politics in Ontario holds less interest for its citizens than those of the alienated hinterlands.

With the Mulroney Conservatives in power in Ottawa, voters opted for David Peterson's Liberals and Bob Rae and the NDP provincially. While this was in part a response to the traditional voter concerns about leadership and efficiency — neither of which the provincial Conservatives were demonstrating at the time under the hapless Miller — it was also a response to the growing unpopularity of the Mulroney Conservatives. With the Liberals back in office federally, voters were free to focus almost exclusively on their traditional concerns about managerial competence and a balanced approach to the issues. Although no one could deny that Mike Harris and his new-style Conservatives made their positions on the issues crystal clear in the election of 1995, it is less certain that voters were paying close attention. Since then, however, they have had considerable opportunity to view first-hand the cavalier attitude and incompetence of the Harris neo-conservatives as well as the negative consequences of their agenda.

Certainly former premier Bill Davis has indirectly revealed his own concerns about the direction Mike Harris has taken the Conservative party. Although more cautious even than Peter Lougheed in his criticism of Ralph Klein, Davis has demonstrated by deeds rather than words his unhappiness with the imbalance of the neo-conservative approach taken by Harris. His picture in newspapers across the province sitting with former premiers Rae and Peterson — to support an environmental project whose funding had been cut by the Harris government — was worth more than a thousand words. So was his support for Hugh Segal, the federal Conservative leadership candidate most closely aligned with the progressive tradition of Ontario Conservatives, and a former Davis aide. Segal was the one candidate Mike Harris had publicly and vehemently opposed, and Harris operatives were part of a group committed to stopping him and Joe Clark.

By the end of 1998, the strategy of the Harris team for the next provincial election was already evident. First, there were the unprecedented and costly media advertisements attacking Dalton McGuinty and the Liberals for their alleged lack of clear position on the health-care issue. Second, there was the announcement by the premier in a year-end interview that 1999 would be the "Year of the Middle Class" in Ontario, an announcement which his critics felt was merely a statement of the obvious, but which was apparently intended to reassure his new coalition supporters that more tax breaks and other benefits of the neo-conservative agenda were on their way. (In an apparent effort to ensure that his legacy remained in place even in the event of an electoral defeat, Harris also introduced a remarkable bill at the end of the 1998 session which, in effect, would guarantee that his successors would not be able to introduce tax increases or reverse his deconstructionist trend. As one Liberal wag put it, "He wants to prove you *can* take it with you.")

The third and most important aspect of the Tories' pre-election strategy was a widespread series of attacks by cabinet ministers and the premier on labour unions. Social Services minister Janet Ecker, for example, accused the unions of "blackmail" to explain her department's inability to place welfare recipients in jobs and defuse the Workfare debacle. Meanwhile, the Education minister and several of his cabinet colleagues were taking on the teachers' unions in an attempt to blame them for all the woes associated with the implementation of the government's controversial cutbacks.

With the infuriated unions vowing to spend considerable sums on advertising during the next campaign to bring down the government, it appeared they had handed the Harris government a new weapon in their strategy of opposing "special interests" to win votes. As reporter Ian Urquart concluded after covering the party's annual convention in Ottawa, "The Harris Tories need a bogeyman to run against. In 1995 it was welfare recipients. This time it's the hated unions." With most of the caucus and party supporters coming from the small-business and agricultural communities, their ignorance of unions and their readiness to accept this strategy were foregone conclusions, despite the fact previous Conservative governments had made a practice of maintaining amicable relations with all of the province's major unions. The social peace of Bill Davis was, it appeared, about to be traded in for a permanent state of siege.

Meanwhile, the unions were also in a classic dilemma, with Canadian Autoworkers' leader Buzz Hargrove speculating that it might be advisable for his members to vote strategically in the next provincial election, supporting Liberal candidates rather than the NDP in ridings where the Liberal party was the only one likely to be able to defeat the Conservative incumbent. His comments drew predictable ire from staunch NDPers, and also left the political elites from all parties marvelling at the remarkable change in dynamics that had occurred in the province in such a short period of time.

As journalist Thomas Walkom has noted, the kinds of changes brought in by the Harris government have upset the traditional Tory balance in many areas of Ontario's political culture — the balance between "private and public enterprise, state and market forces, and business and labour" — as well as widening the gap between rich and poor. In short, the Harris Conservatives' policies and methods in many respects have been truly revolutionary. But for the neo-conservative agenda to succeed in Ontario in the long run, the underlying political culture of the province must also have changed dramatically as well. Such change is possible, but highly unlikely in so short a period of time. While there has obviously been some movement on certain issues during the Harris government's tenure, there is little hard evidence to suggest the population of Ontario has moved significantly to the right, despite the concerted efforts of the Conservatives. In fact, there is every reason to believe little has changed in the underlying values and beliefs of the majority of the province's citizens. If such a massive sea change has not taken place, the Harris government's efforts to duplicate Ralph Klein's achievement and create a new right-wing dynasty in the Canadian heartland are likely doomed.

7

Reformers:
Uninformed and Proud of it

If the Canadian political situation continues to degenerate and
if the cause of conservatism continues to suffer and decline ...
a whole new party committed to the social conservative
position [will emerge].
— Ernest Manning, 1967

We are not a party of racists, radicals and religious kooks.
— Preston Manning, 1987

We keep positioning ourselves so that when the next wave
comes along we can ride it higher and longer.
— Preston Manning, 1993

In the early 1960s, most young adults, even in sedate Alberta, were
breaking with the past. They were wearing their hair long and their
clothes casual. They were listening to the Beatles, JFK and Allen
Ginsberg. At universities across Canada they were exploring Marxism,
Sartre and the New Left. At the University of Alberta, however, the
sixties counterculture was less advanced. Something of the rural still
permeated the campus, giving it a small-town atmosphere in which
protests and rallies had little place. Nevertheless, the sight of a gawky

young man with neatly combed hair, dark-rimmed glasses, and a shirt and tie was more than a little unusual.

Those who knew him well were aware the young man who looked like Buddy Holly and excelled at physics and mathematics was actually the son of Alberta's premier, the dour Ernest C. Manning. Manning's father had already ruled Alberta with a heavy hand for nearly twenty years. Before that he had been "Bible Bill" Aberhart's first student at the Calgary Prophetic Bible Institute, his protégé in politics and his right-hand man in government, finally taking over the reins of power himself in 1943. A charismatic speaker who often involved the young Preston in sermons on his "Back to the Bible" radio program, the premier was a rigid thinker with unbending principles and high expectations for his son. His mother, Muriel, was a perfect foil for the premier and was also busily engaged in church work, directing the choir for the premier's radio program and writing columns for the "Busy Bee" church bulletin. Having such parents immediately explains the younger Manning's demeanour. Solitary if not actually anti-social, Preston Manning evidently had been warned by his father to avoid associating with the other students lest they prove a bad influence.

His father, by contrast, was an enormous influence on Preston Manning all his life and even after his death, shaping his religious convictions and his political perspective. (Years later, as head of the new social conservative party his father had hoped for and predicted, Preston Manning made sure his father received appropriate recognition for his contribution to the creation of the Reform Party. He established the Ernest C. Manning Award for "the Canadian who has demonstrated an outstanding commitment to the promotion and practice of democratic principles" and promptly awarded it to his father posthumously. By 1998 the party had not seen fit to present the award again, leading one Ottawa wag to conclude the next winner would be Preston Manning himself.)

Not surprisingly, then, the young Preston Manning was out of step with the times in his thinking on partisan politics as well as in his appearance. While campus activists were singing the praises of left-wing liberalism, Manning staunchly defended Social Credit policies and, even more telling, attacked what he described as the "rampant socialism" threatening Canadians. In one of his few extracurricular activities, he participated in a series of Model Parliament debates, decrying the creeping rot within the Conservative and Liberal parties at every possible opportunity. In a debate on February 7, 1964, reported in the campus paper, *The Gateway*, Manning indicated, "We believe that Canada is drifting towards socialism even though the majority of Canadians are opposed to collectivism and the welfare state."

In a move that presaged the future direction of his political activities, he also declared that "Canadian citizens who believe in free enterprise must band together," regardless of previous partisan affiliation. For his efforts, Manning was jeered and mocked unmercifully. Yet his hopelessly out-of-place appearance and lack of friends did not seem to bother the young man, who concentrated on his studies to the exclusion of almost all other activities. Having graduated from high school with a 93 per cent average and several awards, he knew how much was expected of him and he intended to live up to those expectations.

Then, in 1962, in recognition of his hard work and promising career, a family friend arranged for the budding scientist to spend the summer working at the San Francisco research laboratories of Bechtel, the giant American multinational corporation. For several months Preston Manning worked on projects related to lasers and other newly emerging technologies, toiling alongside some of the best and brightest from Stanford and Berkeley, as well as the scions of the California Republican establishment. At the end of the summer the young man's favourable evaluation by the personnel team meant the company would sponsor him at any one of the country's best graduate research programs, guaranteeing him a job in their labs on graduation.

As biographer Frank Dabbs has noted, the younger Manning's decision to forgo a promising future with Bechtel was ironically motivated by his need to work with people, something a career as a research physicist in a sterile laboratory did not offer. Having earlier rejected a religious ministry as his calling, Preston Manning spent an agonizing fall deciding what it was he actually wanted to do with his life. In this respect, at least, he was typical of most young adults, but his options and his final decision were hardly typical. First, he decided to switch from physics to economics, and went on to complete his Honours BA in 1964. Then, despite his equally successful foray into this new field, he again confounded his academic mentors by deciding against a graduate degree of any kind. Instead, he decided to follow in his father's footsteps and run for public office.

Like Father, Like Son

With no provincial election in the offing and a desire to strike out on his own, the younger Manning chose to represent the "national" Social Credit Party of Robert Thompson in the 1965 federal election. Although the situation was hopeless from the beginning, with the incumbent a well-established Conservative virtually certain to be re-elected, Manning decided to throw his hat in the ring in the riding of Edmonton East. He was twenty-three but looked eighteen. Even if his ideas had not been anathema to the voters, his apparent youth sealed his fate. Not even the family name could save him from defeat.

The family name was, in fact, beginning to lose its lustre in some quarters, as increasing criticism of the Social Credit government's social policies were beginning to take their toll. For others, however, the Manning government was the only one in Canada following the appropriate right-wing path. A number of wealthy industrialists attempted to prevail upon Ernest Manning to leave provincial politics, where they felt things were well in hand, and move on to the federal scene to rescue the floundering federal Conservative party. According to various reports, including one by former Aberhart minister Alf Hooke, Manning gave the matter some thought before deciding it would be easier and more effective to encourage all "right-thinking men" including Social Crediters to infiltrate the federal Tories. What was really needed, he believed, was "a realignment of political thinking in order that the Canadian people may have a clear-cut alternative" to the socialism of the federal Liberals.

Some of the wealthy industrialists decided a right-wing think-tank was also needed, to promote Manning's ideas, and in 1965 they quietly set up the National Public Affairs Research Foundation (NPARF). Although most of the backers preferred to remain silent, it was known that the driving force behind the NPARF was R.A. (Bobby) Brown, president of Home Oil. Much has been written about this unassuming organization, whose first act was to hire the newly defeated Preston Manning as its researcher. An article by Don Sellar of the *Calgary Herald* on July 1, 1967, stressed the fact: "The NPARF name is not even painted on the door and their office secretary contributes to the secrecy by answering the telephone 'Preston Manning's office'." As author Murray Dobbin has noted, Manning's job with NPARF was "the first of many research jobs over the years that were characterized by two things: unusual secrecy and employers who were almost always conservative governments or corporations in the oil and gas industry."

Preston Manning's first project was a "White Paper on Human Resource Development" whose turgid prose and technocratic vocabulary failed to conceal the same Social Credit ideals of individual responsibility and self-determination that had marked the beliefs of Ernest Manning for decades. The younger Manning's penchant for systems analysis was clearly visible as well, though, and gave many of its readers pause for thought as they learned the Alberta government now proposed to "apply new and advanced techniques, initially conceived for industrial application, to the analysis of social problems."

Manning's second assignment at NPARF was to help his father write the book he had been planning for years. *Political Realignment: A Challenge for Thoughtful Canadians* appeared in 1967 to largely negative reviews. It also stirred considerable controversy at the national Conservative leadership convention, where 30,000 copies were mysteriously distributed by anonymous benefactors. Despite several other efforts to market the product, it became obvious even to the Mannings that their brand of social conservatism was simply not acceptable to most Canadians. Of course, from their point of view the theme of a radical right-wing coalition in one united party was simply a good idea whose time had not yet come, rather than a fundamentally unacceptable vision Canadians would never embrace.

And so, while waiting for the right time and the right wave, Preston Manning continued to work for NPARF. Shortly after his father's book appeared, he left Calgary on another assignment, once more with an American technology conglomerate. This brief period is one Manning is reluctant to discuss, and his continued reticence has led to endless speculation about the real nature of his work for the TRW Corporation. Given the company's connections with the military and its work in Southeast

Asia, many have surmised Manning's activities in the United States at the height of the Vietnam War were far less innocent than he would care to admit. Authors Murray Dobbin and Trevor Harrison have both noted the company had a number of government clients, including the CIA. In his early work on the party, *Preston Manning and the Reform Party*, Dobbin refers to the mysterious "fact-finding" mission Manning and his wife, Sandra, somehow took to Southeast Asia in the middle of a war zone, and questions whether the study Manning prepared for TRW could have been linked to the "rural pacification" projects the American government was sponsoring through a number of research organizations to counter the "domino effect" their agents were predicting if the war was lost. TRW employee Frank Booth is quoted by Dobbin as saying his internal inquiries led him to conclude that "it seems likely that Mr. Manning worked for one of the government agencies" that regularly used TRW, such as the CIA, rather than directly for TRW.

Whatever the purpose of Manning's venture, it was wrapped up by the time his father had announced his intention to resign as premier. Shortly afterwards, Ernest Manning established the consulting firm of M & M Systems Research Limited, and hired his son as his first full-time employee. At the same time it soon appeared the former premier was calling in his markers with the business community. In short order, Ernest Manning accepted seats on the boards of a number of major corporations — several of which were located in Eastern Canada — a move which infuriated many hard-core Social Credit supporters and mystified others. Among the positions Ernest Manning accepted were seats on the board of the Canadian Imperial Bank of Commerce and the National Citizens' Coalition, the fledgling right-wing lobby group which at the time was heavily influenced by Conrad Black. Manning also did the unthinkable and accepted a Senate appointment in Ottawa, all the while continuing to receive a pension from the Alberta government, a situation a number of Liberals pointed out many years later when the Reform Party — led by his son — began to accuse former Liberal cabinet ministers of double-dipping. (On his death Ernest Manning was reputed to have left a multimillion-dollar estate, apparently acquired through his corporate consultancy and the sale of the family estate after his departure from politics.)

Among M & M's clients over the next several years were the newly formed Business Council on National Issues (BCNI) and the Canada West Foundation, for which Preston prepared a number of studies. One of their first projects recommended "the provision of social programs by private industry." Another, for the BCNI, promoted the inclusion of an American-style "property rights" clause in the Constitution. The firm eventually acquired a broad range of clients from business and the resource industry, and the younger Manning was exposed to much of the country's corporate elite through his father's connections.

Perhaps the most controversial of his projects, however, was Preston Manning's long-term association with Slave Lake Developments Ltd., described in Reform literature as a "community development" company of which Manning was the president. Just as Brian Mulroney's self-description as a labour lawyer annoyed those who worked on the side of the unions rather than the employers, so Manning's choice of the term "community development" to describe a commercial real estate enterprise consisting primarily of oil-company interests left many observers frustrated. This was especially galling since the development was often described by Manning as a "partnership" with aboriginal peoples, despite the fact only a few Native people ever appeared to benefit from the company's efforts. Even more exasperating for some were the seemingly endless accusations of conflict of interest and exploitation that swirled around the company and its president, without effect, until the day he left in 1986 to launch his third and ultimately successful attempt at catching the wave.

Church and Family

Unlike Ralph Klein and Mike Harris, Preston Manning evidently knew what he was looking for in a wife and succeeded on his first try. It was not that difficult a task, perhaps, since the girl he eventually married was practically the girl next door. Shortly after Manning joined his father at M & M Research, he married Sandra Beavis, a young woman whose father, Gordon Beavis, was a highly successful businessman who also happened to be the tenor in Muriel Manning's choir for the "Back to the Bible Hour." The two had met at weekly get-togethers of the

Fundamentalist Baptist Church's Career and College Club. Sandra, two years younger than Preston, was studying nursing at the University of Alberta, having already attended the Prairie Bible Institute in Three Hills and obtained a BA in Music.

Married in March 1967, the two were often described by friends and acquaintances over the years as "Mr. and Mrs. Perfect." Certainly the marriage appears to have been a great success, weathering both economic and political stress, and producing five children in relatively short order. Sandra Manning, who remained at home to raise the family, has often been described by political advisers as an invaluable asset to the Reform leader, demonstrating an aptitude for politics and a "humanizing" effect on her husband's image. She has also demonstrated an independent streak, having begun a successful career in real estate once the children were older. A close confidante who shares her husband's strong religious and political views, she is a frequent speaker at Reform gatherings and has taken on a mentoring role for the wives of Reform MPs. Manning himself has said, "The wisest decision I ever made, from the standpoint of my own well-being and that of my family — and in terms of my business and political career — was to ask Sandra to be my wife."

The perfect couple have been described by many of their closest friends as kind, generous to a fault and exemplary role models for the tenets of their evangelical religion. Not only did they engage in numerous charitable activities, but they were constantly providing financial assistance, and even free accommodation, for individuals in crisis, often total strangers. Several people who knew the Mannings were amazed at the steady stream of visitors and sometimes even more permanent guests who shared their home. A case in point is that of Sam Okaro, a Biafran refugee whom Preston Manning met on a plane to Edmonton one day and invited home, helping him to find work and accommodation, and later subsidizing his wedding. Similar stories abound concerning Sandra Manning. Despite taking primary responsibility for the children, while her husband travelled much of the time on business and political matters, according to Manning biographer Frank Dabbs she nevertheless found time to engage in a variety of other activities, on one occasion even rescuing a young girl from an abusive home environment and financing her university education.

Almost all of the Mannings' friends came from the same close-knit religious community, and it was the focal point of their limited social activities. Manning's religious beliefs were also a prime motivating factor behind his desire to enter politics. At one point he actually organized a group of former colleagues from his Intervarsity Christian Fellowship days to discuss ways in which Christianity could be incorporated into politics. Manning himself wrote several papers for discussion by the group, in which he consistently argued that "one's faith should have an effect on one's public service."

According to Frank Dabbs, at the same time, "Preston understood he would have to be more circumspect about his faith than his father [had been] ... He did not proselytize the way his father had and he expressed himself in contemporary idioms, not biblical prescriptions." As impartial observers have noted, this would be an essential concession if he was to be acceptable to most Canadians, since his evangelical religion stresses the literal truth of the Bible, the immorality of homosexuality, and the subservient role of the wife to the husband as the head of the family.

The early years of the Mannings' marriage were not easy from a financial point of view. Preston Manning appeared more interested in developing ideas than in pursuing wealth. He was also frequently absent, at behind-the-scenes political gatherings of like-minded right-wing activists. As his former policy adviser, political scientist Tom Flanagan of the University of Calgary, has noted, Preston Manning never abandoned hope that the populist wave would arrive and allow him to seize the opportunity to pursue his alternative agenda. In fact, he twice mistakenly believed the time had come, before his third and final effort succeeded.

Along with the publication of his father's book, *Political Realignment*, Manning's first attempt to catch the wave was to establish a Social Conservative Club. This effort was a dismal failure, however, and he waited more than a decade to try again. His second attempt came in 1978, when Pierre Trudeau and the Liberal government seemed about to lose control of the national agenda. With his father now a senator in Ottawa, Manning was regularly in the nation's capital and felt he had a much better grasp of political events. He and his father were sure the Liberals were heading for electoral disaster, and they wanted to be ready with their alternative.

Manning's Movement for National Political Change was founded in 1978 , at what he and his father believed was the right moment to catch the next populist wave. The movement was first of all intended to promote "political education." It was supposed to engage "Canadians from all walks of life interested in studying national issues in the hope of bringing about change or reform."

In September 1978, Preston Manning, as the executive director of the movement, issued a statement under the heading "Something New Is Being Born." (This, of course, was the phrase Manning would use many times in the future when his third effort, the Reform Party, was launched.) The statement proposed three things: a restructured economy, a renewed federalism, and the movement itself, which would "either radically transform one of the existing political parties or produce a viable new political party capable of displacing one of the existing entities." Manning indicated he wanted to acquire an initial membership of 1,000 and organize regional conventions to discuss future directions for the country.

The Liberals did go on to lose the 1979 election to Joe Clark but, as all Conservatives remember only too well, the new prime minister from Alberta promptly threw away their first chance at power in many decades, allowing the Liberals and Trudeau to return for another four years. To the Mannings' dismay, this second effort also foundered almost immediately, with Clark's election and subsequent defeat. Neither the members nor the conventions materialized, and Manning was left once again holding an empty bag.

After two false starts, a lesser man would surely have given up. Yet Preston Manning never lost sight of his objective. According to Edmonton journalist Don Wanagas, "My boss would come in all excited, talking about some guy who was ready to start another political party in Canada, or someone across the table at lunch would have the same story in a totally different context. The guy always turned out to be Preston Manning." Author Murray Dobbin has marvelled at the amazing single-mindedness of father and son during this lengthy self-imposed waiting period. "The sheer determination of the Mannings," Dobbin wrote, "and the unchanging nature of their goal characterized them as almost marginal to the Canadian political process."

Preston Manning apparently did become somewhat anxious after the second failure, expressing concern on several occasions about his ability to actually enter politics after such a lengthy absence, should the right time ever emerge. According to one source, Manning would confide in his wife his fears that "I'll forget how. I haven't given a speech in years." His wife, meanwhile, encouraged his activities despite the toll they took on family life, believing he would always regret having failed to rise to the occasion when it presented itself. Of course, the occasion did finally arise, but not as Manning had expected.

Early Converts

It was not the Liberal government of Pierre Trudeau but the Mulroney Conservatives who finally stirred up Western unrest sufficiently to create Preston Manning's third wave. Like the Klein and Harris Conservatives, Manning was the beneficiary of widespread public discontent over the patronage, scandals and economic mismanagement with which the Mulroney government had become irrevocably identified. At the same time, he was able to benefit from something the two future provincial premiers could not — the heightened sense of Western alienation. With Liberal governments in Ottawa, many Westerners had assumed their problem was a partisan one. They were voting for the wrong party. When Brian Mulroney's Conservatives swept to power with a huge majority, these same Westerners immediately assumed things would change for the better, and quickly. When this did not come to pass, they began to conclude the problem was not partisan preference but system failure.

In response to Western alienation, a number of extremist fringe groups had surfaced in Western Canada over the years, and particularly since the implementation of official bilingualism and the National Energy Program, but none had much legitimacy. Most were transitory, with few members and a short shelf life. Several were the purveyors of blatantly racist views, while others were clearly the lunatic fringe. Some were attempting to persuade Westerners, and especially Albertans, of the need to separate from Canada altogether.

Western separatists were not taken seriously either. Most were malcontents who were seen to have ulterior motives and much political baggage.

One proponent of Western separation, former Saskatchewan Conservative party leader Dick Collver, actually advocated union with the United States rather than outright independence. Collver eventually moved to the United States when he found little support for his ideas. Doug Christie, a disgruntled former Manitoba monarchist and unsuccessful Tory candidate, set up the Committee for Western Independence (CWI). Another prominent separatist was a millionaire car dealer from Edmonton, Elmer Knutson. His loss to Tory incumbent Doug Roche in a 1979 nomination battle, and the subsequent re-election of the Trudeau Liberals in 1980, led him to form the Western Canada Federation (WCF). Knutson's marginal views, which had already been expressed publicly many times, included "increasing police powers, ending bilingualism and tightening immigration policies." These various fringe groups mutated several times. Christie's group was incorporated with others, and renamed the Western Canada Concept (WCC), shortly before a rancher named Gordon Kessler won a 1982 provincial by-election under the WCC banner, replacing a Lougheed Red Tory. Kessler himself took over the WCC at one point, after other members of the leadership left amid accusations the organization had become dominated by right-wing Mormons such as Kessler. By late 1983 most of the other fringe groups had disappeared, and separatists consolidated in the WCC under yet another leader, former RCMP officer Jack Ramsay, another future Reform MP.

Although the separatists' efforts would come to nothing in the end, some Alberta federalists became anxious when Kessler won his by-election, but not Preston Manning. Instead, this blip on the political radar screen sparked renewed interest rather than concern on Manning's part, and he actually met with Kessler, apparently hoping to see whether the next wave might have arrived. In the end he decided it definitely had not, and ended his contacts with the WCC abruptly.

The same by-election produced another result which had long-term consequences for Manning. An old acquaintance from the Social Credit days, Ray Speaker, was sufficiently concerned about the separatist movement and Peter Lougheed's handling of the constitutional file that he decided to form a federalist provincial party. Speaker, a well-regarded former cabinet minister, established the short-lived Representative Party expressly to counter both the Western separatists and the Lougheed Red Tories. While Speaker's efforts also did not produce much in the way of tangible results, it led Manning to conclude that things were beginning to come together and the wave was building nicely. He later found numerous recruits for his Reform movement in the membership of Speaker's stillborn party, and Speaker himself would, of course, go on to become a Reform MP and Manning's right-hand man in Ottawa.

By 1986, two additional developments gave Manning the impetus he needed to begin a major push towards the establishment of his political alternative. The first was the increasing interest in alternative visions of federalism expressed by Dr. Francis Winspear, a wealthy former Edmonton businessman who had once been a bagman for Lester Pearson. Winspear, now retired and living in Victoria, was exceedingly unhappy with the nature of all government policies coming from Ottawa. While the eighty-four-year-old millionaire was busy funding a number of private policy meetings to explore the federal alternatives to Western separatism, a radical right-wing journalist, Ted Byfield, was busy writing about them in his magazine, *The Alberta Report*.

Both had heard of Manning and become interested in the ideas he was expressing. On August 25, 1986, Byfield published a major article entitled "The West Needs Its Own Party." At roughly the same time, Francis Winspear put up $50,000 and called on another former Liberal in B.C., Stan Roberts, to organize an event supporting a federal alternative.

Stan Roberts was someone Winspear knew well. An economist, former Manitoba Liberal MLA and head of the Canada West Foundation, past president of the Canadian Chamber of Commerce and vice-president of Simon Fraser University, Roberts had strong credentials and experience in both the academic and business communities. He began to pull together an organizing group, calling on the services of an old friend, Calgary oil-patch lawyer Robert Muir, and a young consultant who had just published an article entitled "A Western Reform Movement: The Responsible Alternative to Western Separatism." The consultant, naturally, was Preston Manning.

Manning, meanwhile, had sent copies of his paper far and wide, inviting comments from such diverse individuals as Ted Byfield, Dr. David Elton (the new president of the Canada West Foundation), Fred Mannix

Jr. of the Mannix Corporation, Calgary oilman Jim Gray, construction company owner John Poole, oil-company lawyer Diane Ablonczy and tax lawyer Cliff Fryers of Calgary, and an obscure municipal politician named Cliff Breitkreuz, all of whom had expressed an interest in the subject. (Breitkreuz and Ablonczy also went on to become Reform MPs, while Fryers later ran the Reform Party executive before moving to Ottawa to become Manning's chief of staff.)

Things were definitely coming to a head, but a catalyst was still needed to get Manning's reform project off the ground. With the Mulroney government's stunning decision to overrule their own bidding procedures and award the CF-18 maintenance contract to a Montreal firm, rather than Winnipeg-based Bristol Aerospace, the second defining event had arrived. As Frank Dabbs underlines in his account of these developments, "The angry response from the west was instant and intense ... Preston Manning and the nascent Reform movement had their *cause célèbre*."

By November 1986, Manning was making a presentation in Jim Gray's boardroom before many of the same Calgary players, on a "Proposal for the Creation of a Western-Based Political Party to Run Candidates in the 1988 Federal Election." Shortly thereafter, Winspear held a meeting in which he called on Roberts and Manning to head the Reform Association of Canada and organize a major event in Vancouver in May 1987. Roberts and Manning agreed to co-manage the association and arrange speakers for the conference, which was billed as a "Western Assembly on Canada's Economic and Political Future." Ted Byfield meanwhile agreed to publicize the event through his magazine.

Although the event attracted considerable interest in Western Canada, it was predictably ignored by most of the national media. Held in the Hyatt Regency Hotel in Vancouver on May 29–31, it has been variously estimated to have attracted anywhere from three hundred to six hundred participants. The vast majority were extreme right-wing Conservatives, although a number of disgruntled Liberals and interested NDPers attended as observers. Edmonton journalist Don Wanagas concluded, "In spite of Preston Manning's efforts to present the new organization as something else altogether it was clear it was dominated by old-time Socreds dying for one more kick at the political can." *Globe and Mail* reporter John Cruickshank wrote that "while Mr. Manning and Mr.

Roberts spoke ceaselessly about creating a 'broadly-based party' their delegates were almost uniformly social and economic conservatives."

It is particularly interesting to note that, even at this point, the organizers (which is to say Preston Manning) were concerned about screening participants. Although the event was widely publicized as one which anyone who paid their $25 registration fee could attend, the coverage of the meeting in Byfield's *Western Report* of June 8 underlines the fact that "the delegates were handpicked by Assembly organizers to weed out the extremists and cranks." For many observers the definition of extremist was unclear. One of those deliberately excluded was the WCC's Jack Ramsay, who had been branded an extremist. (Mr. Ramsay, in turn, accused his future leader, Preston Manning, of being a "political opportunist trying to take advantage of the rising tide of Western alienation.") Yet, June Lenihan, an anti-abortion advocate, was received with open arms despite her declaration she was "one of the people in this room willing to admit that I'm an evangelical, right-wing redneck, anti-socialist, ultra-conservative, fundamentalist Christian."

The Reverend Philip Mayfield (yet another future Reform MP) opened the session with a short prayer which highlighted why most of the delegates were there. "Some people have come here with great anger," he said, and "some people have come here with great frustration." Indeed, as political scientist Trevor Harrison has demonstrated, for many delegates the issue of Western alienation was increasingly taking a back seat to their frustration with the direction of the Mulroney government on economic and social policy. Harrison concludes that "the continued de-alignment and disintegration of the Tory alliance realistically threatened many on the right with the possibility that their worst nightmare — a social democratic government in Ottawa — might come true. The creation of a new right-wing party was thus intended, at least in part, as a solution to that potential problem."

Although Ted Byfield was the keynote speaker, it was Preston Manning's speech to which the crowd responded most warmly, and the one Byfield's journal would later enthusiastically report. While many observers felt Manning's speech was simply a reformulation of his father's social-conservative views, it had the added advantage of convincing many of the delegates that a new political party was the only solution to their concerns. By the end of the Sunday meeting, some 76 per cent of the delegates had voted in favour of Manning's call for a new party. A founding meeting, with the selection of a leader as its first order of business, would be held sometime in the fall. Together Winspear, Manning and Roberts were in charge of fundraising and organization. As Manning himself would later say, something new was indeed being born.

The Loner

If Ralph Klein is a maverick and Mike Harris is an outsider, Preston Manning is probably best characterized as a loner. Nothing demonstrated this better than his attitude towards the leadership of the new Reform Party. From day one, he was not only firmly in charge, but essentially a one-man band. Those around him would do things his way or head for the doorway.

At the Vancouver convention he had been careful to address not only the reasons for creating a new party, but the criteria for selecting its leader. Rejecting the need for a "charismatic, Messianic leader" — which he all too clearly was not — Manning instead stressed the desirability of the delegates' selecting "the person who renders the greatest and most effective service to the party over the next three or four months." Or, as one delegate was heard to say, "In other words, nominate Preston." Put another way by Adrian Berry, a former Calgary alderman and Reformer, "It wasn't a party picking a leader, it was a leader picking a party."

Manning left nothing to chance. He was determined to defeat his only opponent, Stan Roberts, who was not only more charismatic and eloquent but better known and better equipped financially. Reluctant to enter the race, Roberts was finally convinced by Winspear that a leadership contest was necessary to ensure the legitimacy of the outcome. Roberts also was becoming increasingly concerned about the direction the fledgling party's supporters appeared to be taking, fearing it was becoming too extreme on both economic and social policies. He also was greatly concerned that the anti-French sentiment of some of the delegates in Vancouver was being given free rein.

Once Roberts entered the race, only a few weeks before the founding convention in Winnipeg in November, he ran a classic leadership campaign. Manning, meanwhile, had been running hard for the leadership for four months but focusing almost exclusively on delegate selection. At the end of the day, Manning's approach paid off. The hall was filled with his people when, nearly a day ahead of schedule, Manning urged the organizers — including the chair, staunch Manning supporter Diane Ablonczy — to cut off registration of delegates. When Francis Winspear took the floor to protest this action, moving a motion to reopen registration and noting many of Roberts's delegates had not yet arrived, he was soundly defeated by the Manning forces. Astonished and shaken, Winspear left along with a furious Roberts, who later withdrew his name.

In an angry press conference the next day, Roberts not only accused the organizers, and implicitly Manning, of "compromising" the new party's commitment to "honesty and integrity," but also alluded to a significant sum of missing funds and accused Manning's supporters — almost all of whom were from Alberta — of being "a bunch of right-wing Christian fanatics." Ted Byfield, meanwhile, carefully reported on the event and the selection of Manning as leader in glowing terms, while ridiculing Roberts unmercifully. "Mr. Roberts went down in flames, embarrassing himself and the party," said Byfield's article in the November 9 *Alberta Report*. "He announced to the convention that he was quitting the leadership contest and stomped out of the convention hall, his entourage of 20 — apparently all that was left of his support — in tow."

Manning appeared unconcerned about Roberts's departure, and many of Manning's supporters essentially said "Good riddance." Frank Dabbs concluded that, in the party's "first crisis," Manning "had failed the test of reconciliation." Roberts's departure was the first and most highly public clash of party members with the new leader, but it would hardly be the last. From policy director Tom Flanagan to such well-known MPs as Jan Brown, Jim Silye and Stephen Harper, it soon became obvious Manning was not the type of leader to tolerate dissent, nor to encourage the grooming of a successor. Behind the scenes within the Reform Party the same scenario unfolded with organizers and volunteers, although many of their clashes and departures were carefully kept from public view. Yet Manning routinely attached the blame for these departures to a lack of commitment to the cause, rather than his own rigidity.

Another reason for Manning's solitary style was his lack of relevant experience for the job of leader of a political party and, ultimately, of the Official Opposition. His work experience, as we have seen, was highly unusual. Apart from his father, he had never had work-related colleagues. As a consultant to big business and the powerful energy sector, he was singularly insulated from much of the rest of the "real world." Despite his evangelical faith, he did not participate in a number of collective charitable or community activities either. This was not a man who organized a Boy Scout group or directed a local United Way campaign, although these would have been entirely normal pursuits for many business people. Instead, his acts of faith, like his consultancy, were primarily solitary ventures.

Author Murray Dobbin, admittedly a critic of Manning and the Reform Party, pointed out the obvious about Manning's political career when he wrote: "Manning is in the unusual position of seeking the highest post in the land without ever having held any office." In fact, "before he founded the Reform Party he was rarely involved in organizations with formal structures." Dobbin's assessment received strong backing from an unlikely source — a close friend of Manning's and a former Reform supporter, Brian Hay. Hay's remarks, made in 1991, would take on particular significance six years later, when Manning would run his third election campaign as Reform leader on a platform that attacked Quebec and the French-speaking politicians who had led the country in the past. Although Hay stressed he still had "the highest regard for Preston Manning personally," he, too, was deeply concerned that "Preston Manning has never held public office, whether at the municipal level, the school board level or the provincial level. I have trouble envisioning him playing a leadership role in holding the country together or, conversely, building a new country out of the pieces that might be left."

Whether it was some former members of his church group reviewing his papers, or friends and colleagues of his father to whom he was presenting his ideas for a new party, Manning always carefully selected those with whom he worked. His "hand-picked" delegates to the 1987 Vancouver Assembly were typical of his desire to micro-manage and control events. Not surprisingly, then, Manning was only comfortable working in the Reform Party with an executive he trusted and a caucus he could control. Predictably the people Preston Manning trusted were people who were with him from the beginning, such as Cliff Fryers and Ray Speaker.

The Inner Circle

Speaker went to Ottawa with Manning in 1993 and became the Reform House Leader and finance spokesperson, but was often unhappy with the way in which he was forced to toe the party and the leader's line. There were several occasions when the party's position on fiscal matters was enunciated by Speaker and then contradicted by the leader or other Reform finance spokespersons. There were other times when the behaviour of his own colleagues made him look distinctly uncomfortable. There were also personal attacks on his position as a former Alberta minister receiving a pension while earning an income as a federal MP. Although he dismissed such attacks, and continued to be a steadying influence on the party in the House of Commons, his influence with the leader appeared to decline, and his interest in federal politics certainly did. Not one to criticize publicly, he simply announced he would not be seeking re-election in the 1997 campaign. As one of the few MPs with any legislative experience, he had been an invaluable asset to Manning in Question Period, especially in the early years, and his maturity and experience would be missed in the undisciplined Reform caucus.

Unlike Speaker, Cliff Fryers had no interest in becoming an elected representative. A prominent Calgary tax lawyer who had supported Manning from the beginning, he soon became the party's chief fundraiser. Over the next few years he assumed a number of key positions on the party executive, becoming the chair of the Executive Council and the party's chief operating officer in 1991. Virtually everyone familiar with Manning and Fryers described this appointment as representing a consolidation of Manning's control of the party, and a redoubled effort to raise party revenues through corporate donations. They were right on both counts. Fryers used his contacts to increase the party's standing with the business community and kept an iron grip on the head office for years. He also played a key role as an internal troubleshooter and strategic planner.

When Manning's leadership appeared to be in serious difficulty after the near caucus revolt following the London convention of June 1998, Fryers was convinced to leave his lucrative law practice in Calgary to serve full-time as Manning's new chief of staff. (His predecessor, Darrel Reid, had left earlier to become the head of a special-interest group, the conservative Focus on the Family.) Described by former party insider Tom Flanagan as "the party's hardest-driving administrator and toughest enforcer," Fryers was obviously called to Ottawa by Manning himself in an attempt to bring his MPs — whom he was *not* able to hand-pick — into line. A self-made man from humble beginnings, Fryers was seen by the grassroots membership as both ruthless and single-minded. Known to party insiders derisively as "Mr. Warmth," Fryers was described by another member of Manning's inner circle, MP Diane Ablonczy, as the practical complement to Manning's theoretical, systems-analysis approach. "Preston is a man who is highly effective at dealing with public policy issues on a conceptual basis," Ms. Ablonczy said tactfully, while "Cliff's skills will be in execution of a strategic plan to implement that vision."

Certainly Manning has always seen himself as his own best policy adviser, which is no doubt why both of his two former directors of policy — Stephen Harper and Tom Flanagan — are no longer with him. In the beginning Manning had high hopes for Harper, whose speech to the Winnipeg founding convention was described by Manning as one of the best and most influential. A former political aide to Conservative MP Jim Hawkes and a disillusioned Mulroney Conservative, Harper was adamant about the need for a Western perspective on economic and constitutional issues. But the Ontario-born economist, whose pre-Reform career was spent working in Calgary in the oil patch, soon ended up clashing with the leader on a number of fronts.

As the party's first director of policy and charter member of the executive, Harper was responsible for drafting resolutions and manipulating delegates to the party's assemblies, something for which his experience in Ottawa proved invaluable. He was always extremely adept at handling the media and articulating the party's policies to the public. However, he was also an economic conservative largely uninterested in the social- and moral-conservative issues beloved of the leader and so many of his supporters. Harper frequently wanted to place the emphasis on economic issues, which others were happy to leave rather vague. At the same time, his intellectual rigour and commitment to participatory democracy clashed with the leader's increasingly obvious top-down style of management and inability to tolerate competition.

In 1991, opposed to major revisions to the party structure which Fryers and others were proposing, Harper left the director's post and returned to the private sector, but he still continued to work on preparing the platform for the next election and retained some influence through the executive. This influence proved crucial in 1992, when Harper's calm but unequivocal opposition to the Charlottetown Accord, coupled with that of his successor, Tom Flanagan, forced Manning to reverse his earlier decision to support the "Yes" option at the instigation of another adviser, Rick Anderson. There can be little doubt that Manning's and Reform's opposition to the accord almost single-handedly propelled the party to its stunningly strong third-place finish in the 1993 election. Equally, there can be little doubt that if Manning had stood by his initial inclination to support the accord, the party would have been consigned to oblivion.

Harper's time in Ottawa as a Reform MP was inevitably no less controversial. He clashed with Manning on everything, from the leader's secret expense allowance to fiscal policies and the constitutional position of the party, and was reprimanded by the Manning-controlled executive. Worse still, many members of the media and the general public began to compare Harper's positive performance in the House with his leader's lacklustre efforts. Harper's image as the heir apparent increasingly rankled with Manning as much as Manning's inconsistencies in dealing with the extremists in caucus annoyed the disenchanted Harper. After months of public speculation Harper announced nearly a year before the 1997 election that he would not seek re-election.

As the new head of the right-wing National Citizens' Coalition, Harper has since been openly critical of the party and the leader on several occasions, and was courted by the Blue Tory wing of the Conservative party to put his name forward in the 1998 federal leadership race. Having refused to do so out of apparent concern for his reputation with his former Reform colleagues, he is still believed by many to be the logical successor to Manning if the party survives to fight another election.

Harper's successor at head office, Tom Flanagan, suffered a similar fate in a much shorter period of time. Recruited in 1991 on Harper's departure, Flanagan lasted less than two years in the Calgary lion's den. The somewhat controversial political science professor from the University of Calgary had always been more interested in a consistent right-wing message than the so-called populist element of Manning's platform, and trouble developed between the two almost immediately. As Flanagan detailed in his own book on Manning and Reform, *Waiting for the Wave*, the chaos at the head office was not confined to policy. The Finance and Administration section had also seen a series of arrivals and departures. Hal Kupchak, hired in June 1991, lasted only six months, until January 1992. With no executive director in charge of the staff, and the elected members of the Executive Council — to whom Kupchak technically reported — also working as paid employees under him, the situation was a managerial recipe for disaster from the beginning.

Another problem was the party's unsuccessful but highly revealing foray into the world of consultants and professional party organizers, which resulted in the hiring of American pollster Frank Luntz. Luntz had worked briefly for the Reagan administration and later went on to run Pat Buchanan's unsuccessful run for the GOP nomination. According to Flanagan, Luntz's ultimately brief relationship with Reform had nothing to do with his credentials or citizenship, but rather was tied to the fact that Rick Anderson opposed his hiring. The leader himself was ambivalent about including yet another individual in his plans. Put another way, "bringing in newcomers at that point ... overstretched Manning's capacity to trust others." Despite repeated requests by Luntz to spend time with the leader and familiarize himself with his thinking, he was never able to break through the Loner's isolation and need to remain in control of events. As a result the party ended up "flying blind" during the crucial 1992 referendum debate, having paid dearly for the Luntz experiment.

Meanwhile, in the misnamed Policy, Strategy and Communications unit to which Flanagan was appointed director in 1991, on Harper's departure, the emphasis was definitely on communications rather than coherent policy development. Flanagan recalled, "Supposedly these functions were unified so that policy would always drive communications

... but in practice the opposite came closer to the truth." The problem, once again, was Manning himself, who "managed around me rather than through me as Director. Anything he was really interested in, he directed himself." Since "Manning's deepest interest was and still is communications," according to Flanagan, "to the extent that Manning functioned as the real Director of Policy, Strategy and Communications he naturally conveyed his concern with communications to staff, leaving little time for serious policy development." The result was entirely predictable: "Any policy development that did take place was usually impelled by the needs of the moment. Manning would decide that he ought to make a speech on a certain subject, or that he had to have an answer to a question that someone had asked, or satisfy a demand from within the party to enlarge on a point in the Blue Book. Staff would then scramble to pull some ideas together. The driving force was always communication."

Flanagan recounts a hilarious example in which Manning worked endlessly on his cherished communication slogans and "hooks" for the party's "Zero-in-Three" deficit reduction plan before finally settling on "The Deficit Hole" as his key phrase. He was truly horrified when staff presented him with a line graph showing the debt and deficit *rising*, and insisted on reversing the chart to show the line dropping, so that he could use the slogan "When you're in a hole the first thing to do is to stop digging."

Flanagan lasted barely two years as overall director, before resigning from a paid position to take on the lesser role of policy advisor. Even there he lasted only another six months. The leader's decision to stick with Rick Anderson despite his support for the "Yes" side on the Charlottetown Accord, and the party's chaotic 1992 leader-driven referendum campaign, while a success for Reform in the end, proved too much for both Harper and Flanagan. Harper withdrew from the executive, although he continued his work as a candidate in Calgary West and was eventually elected in 1993. Flanagan, meanwhile, returned to the university in 1993, having had a final rupture with the leader over his opposition to the proposed appointment of Rick Anderson. As Flanagan noted, "The party's roster of strategic advisers was temporarily wiped out ... and important operational staff became casualties too." In particular, for reasons that remain unclear, Manning also fired speech-writer George

Koch and communications manager Laurie Watson, a long-time employee, the day after the referendum vote.

This left Manning with Rick Anderson, the Montreal-born former federal Liberal and Ottawa manager of the giant Hill and Knowlton public-relations firm. It also left him with a problem, since Anderson was bitterly resented by many Reformers for two reasons. First, he was simply too slick and professional, the kind of political operator most of them despised. Worse still, he was an "Easterner" in a Western protest movement. The final straw for many was Anderson's support of the Charlottetown Accord, which inevitably became a matter of public knowledge. Nevertheless Manning persisted in his association with Anderson, who eventually became the campaign manager for the 1993 election campaign and has never looked back.

Manning revealed more than a little of his long-term thinking about the strategy of Reform in his comments defending his relationship with Anderson. "[He] represents the kind of person that we must eventually reconcile ourselves with," Manning would say, "if we are going to win Ontario." According to Flanagan, this was precisely his point when he objected to Anderson in the first place. He was concerned the party would "drift" from the right towards the centre, and end up focusing on Ontario to the detriment of Alberta and B.C. (Recent events have no doubt convinced Flanagan his concerns were justified.)

Meanwhile, Anderson's stated motive for joining the Reform team was not policy but his concern for "participatory democracy," a term he first encountered as a volunteer during the Trudeau years. (One of several brothers from a family long involved in Liberal politics, Anderson was among the least plugged-in of the bunch during the Trudeau years, due primarily to his youth and inexperience at the time. Rather than as a policy adviser, his main claim to fame was as an organizer, and specifically as the manager of third-place finisher Don Johnston's unsuccessful leadership bid in 1984.) Although many would argue Anderson's understanding of the term "participatory democracy" is defective if he truly believes there is a connection between the policies pursued by the Trudeau government in support of this concept and those articulated by Manning, it may well be that it was Manning's "common sense of the common people" populist approach that initially attracted Anderson to

Reform. Certainly it is the reason Anderson has repeatedly offered in public and in numerous private conversations.

Several federal Liberals nevertheless continue to believe Anderson's move was essentially one of convenience and opportunism, motivated by his lack of access and status within the federal Liberal Party under John Turner after the 1984 defeat. Others note pointedly that his alleged role in party affairs *before* the defeat has also been greatly exaggerated. In 1990 another new leader of the Liberal party, Jean Chrétien, replied, "Rick who?" when asked by reporters for his views on Anderson's "defection" from the Liberals and emerging role with the Reform Party.

Equally perplexing is the fact that Anderson, who evidently approves of the party's economic conservatism, has often aggressively disavowed the social and moral conservatism of many of its MPs and members, dismissing their views as the minority opinions of a small lunatic fringe within the party. When confronted with numerous examples during a panel discussion at Concordia University after the 1993 election, Anderson implied all of the quotes and individuals in question were either taken out of context or misunderstood. In the case of B.C. Reform MP Darrel Stinson, whom Anderson described as "obviously not one of our leading lights," the explanation was simply that every party has its share of bad apples. This perspective, while convenient in allowing Anderson to avoid responsibility for some of the less palatable Reform positions, flies in the face of persistent behaviour patterns on the part of some grassroots party members and, more disturbing still, of elected representatives of the Reform Party. Anderson may have chosen to discount the comments of these MPs, but Preston Manning soon discovered to his dismay that he was not also able to do so.

No Rednecks and Racists Allowed?

At a town-hall meeting in the riding of Okanagan–Shuswap, a large crowd listens patiently to the speeches of the candidates during the federal election in the fall of 1993. Several of the candidates make lengthy presentations about the platforms of their parties and their positions on the major issues of the day. The Reform candidate, Darrel

Stinson, stands up for only a few minutes of his alloted time, looking nervous and out of place. He tells the crowd everything they need to know is in the Reform "Blue Sheet." "Read it. If you have any questions, we'll be happy to answer them." Then he gives them the telephone number of his campaign office. Twice. During the question-and-answer period that follows, several people ask Stinson about his party's position on specific issues. "I haven't looked into that one myself but I know we have a position somewhere here in this," he says, holding up the "Blue Sheet." It falls to me, the Liberal candidate, to inform the audience of Reform's position, quoting from the sheet as a furious Stinson looks on.

Someone else in the audience, whom many suspect is an NDP supporter, asks Stinson about his previous experience in politics and elected office. Has he ever been elected to anything? Served on a school board or worked in the public sector? The response is uniformly negative, and Stinson begins to get annoyed. "No, I haven't had my nose to the trough before," says Stinson, as his campaign manager rolls her eyes. "I've worked with the Boy Scouts, though," he replies. In answer to another question about his background, he replies proudly that he has never taken unemployment insurance. "That's because you never had a job where you could qualify," one wag in the audience bellows.

The people in the front row are not amused. As usual at these meetings, they are Stinson supporters, carefully positioned to heckle the other candidates. The men with white hair and the women with blue rinses, they are surprisingly aggressive in a region noted for its civility and restraint, and they attack the Liberal and NDP candidates with a vengeance. Unaccustomed to public events, however, they fail to realize the rest of the audience cannot hear their comments. Most of the other candidates ignore them. As the candidate whom the protesters consider the greatest threat to their man, I sometimes decide to take them on. "Just a minute. Did everyone hear what this gentleman in the front row said? Would you care to repeat it so the whole room can hear, sir?" Faces purple with fury and hatred, the front row begins to take on frightening proportions. The possibility of cardiac arrest looms large. But the name-calling and racist comments cease, at least for the moment.

The questions to Stinson do not. He knows he is not doing well and, after having endured several of these events in the past few days, is becoming more uneasy and uncomfortable by the minute. His campaign manager appears to have given him firm directions for this event, after a disastrous outing a few days earlier in which, obviously unprepared, he spoke about crime and law enforcement at a televised event where the actual topic was the candidates' visions of the Okanagan in the year 2000. Stinson answers another question, this time on the health-care system, by saying "I don't read books like the professor here. I'll just do what you people tell me to." As the event comes to a close the candidates file out through a narrow hallway. One Reform supporter, a senior in a gold lamé bomber jacket and high heels, spits at me in passing while her friend says, "We don't need any high la-de-das here. Darrel will do us just fine."

Across British Columbia and Alberta similar scenes of overzealous Reform behaviour unfolded in many ridings. Although Okanagan–Shuswap may have been among the most extreme cases, the dumbing-down of politics in the 1993 election was a common phenomenon in Western Canada, as was the emergence of a large group of previously disaffected voters whose only interest was in expressing their negative and often prejudiced views. Yet Darrel Stinson went on to win the riding by a substantial majority, becoming a member of Preston Manning's first federal caucus.

Stinson, a self-described prospector and jack-of-all trades who drifted into the Okanagan from the coast some years earlier, was a virtual unknown in the riding until his involvement with the "No" side in the Charlottetown referendum campaign in 1992. It was largely on the strength of this effort — and the fact few believed Reform would do well in the next federal election — that Stinson was able to "capture" the Reform nomination more than a year before the writ was dropped. As a result many of the citizens of Okanagan–Shuswap, including many of those who voted for Stinson, felt their man would be a very small cog in the large wheel of federal politics. Certainly few of them expected Stinson to become a household name and the answer to a New Year's Day quiz in the *Globe and Mail* only a few short years later.

This was also the assessment of the Reform hierarchy. Rick Anderson's description of Stinson in early 1994 as "not one of our leading lights" was intended to be an understatement. Having embarrassed himself early on by suggesting in a local weekly column that Canada could use the provisions of the North American Free Trade Agreement (NAFTA) to save money by sending Canadian prisoners to Mexico, Stinson predictably disappeared from the political radar screen for some time. In three years he asked only a few questions in the House of Commons from his seat in the back, none of them memorable, and failed to make his mark as a minor deputy critic. Apart from another controversial column on the occasion of Remembrance Day in 1994 — when Stinson drew the ire of many ethnocultural groups with his attack on the Canadian government's decision to provide compensation for Japanese Canadians interned during the Second World War, simultaneously decrying the cost to the federal treasury and railing against the Japanese government's failure to provide redress for Canadian prisoners of war — the diminutive MP remained largely invisible.

Then, with only months to go before the 1997 election call, Stinson exploded one quiet day during a sitting of the House, storming across the floor of the Commons to challenge a Liberal MP to a fist fight while using a steady stream of provocative and decidedly unparliamentary language. For the next several days, to his leader's mortification, Darrel Stinson had the attention of the national media. The obscure MP no one had noticed before even appeared on *Newsworld* reporter Don Newman's program, and was shown repeatedly on *The National* marching across the floor with his fists up, asking the hapless Liberal MP if he had the "gonads" to take him on. (At barely more than five feet, overweight and out of shape, Stinson was hardly a menacing figure, but more of a caricature of an angry man.)

Darrel Stinson was evidently enjoying his three minutes of fame, but in the same three minutes all of Preston Manning's hopes for the rehabilitation of the Reform image went down the drain. Short of disowning Stinson, there was little he could do to dispel the lingering image of Reform as a redneck bunch. For better or worse, Manning and his caucus stuck by Stinson, blaming the Liberal member for having provoked him by calling him a racist.

Whether the incident had much impact on the national election results is impossible to determine. Reform was already in difficulty. At the end of the day the party ended up the Official Opposition by default, having lost support but holding on to enough seats to supplant the Bloc Québécois, which had collapsed in Quebec. Stinson, meanwhile, was re-elected, despite the predictions of the Eastern pundits that his sally forth across the floor of the Commons would end his career. Although his victory could certainly be attributed in part to the unbelievable gift he was handed when a former NDP MP hijacked the Liberal nomination process and attempted to run as a Liberal, it was also true that Stinson increased his share of the popular vote. Reformers in the riding proudly handed out T-shirts which read "I'm fed up and not going to take it any more," with pictures of Stinson front and centre. Evidently the whole experience did little to chasten Stinson, since he was at it again soon after the new Parliament was convened. In fact, it was barely under way when Stinson decided to take on none other than Conservative leader Jean Charest, marching towards him menacingly and calling him a "fat little, chubby little sucker."

The central-Canadian media naturally went wild. Stinson was everything Reform had been accused of and Manning had been busy denying for years. One column in the *Toronto Sun* of December 27, 1997, described Reformers as a "ribald collection of dung-kicking rednecks" and Stinson a "dim bulb clown with a short fuse." At the end of the year, columnist Jeffrey Simpson awarded Stinson one of his booby prizes, while the *Globe and Mail*'s parliamentary bureau placed Stinson in the "out" crowd, describing him as "the Parliament Hill Pugilist" and "the Commons Crasher."

Of course, Manning and the rest of the Reform team, including Rick Anderson, by now were going out of their way to demonstrate that Stinson was the exception, not the rule. Their task was a daunting one, however, since there was already so much evidence. Darrel Stinson may have been the most ludicrous example of Reform's ineptitude and ignorance, but he was neither the first nor the worst. And Preston Manning, for all his attempts to hand-pick his colleagues, would have to take much of the blame.

Manning had foreseen this problem as early as Vancouver in 1987, but had done little to discourage some of the individuals who would later cause him the most trouble. Instead, obsessed with his concern about the involvement of Western separatists, he had ignored the threat from the right's lunatic fringe and let any number of disaffected right-wing extremists attend, including many pro-life, anti-French, anti-immigration and victims' rights proponents. At the Winnipeg founding meeting only a few months later, delegates included Fred Debrecen, founder of the anti-French group One Nation, One Language. At the assembly in Saskatoon, inflammatory fringe author William Gairdner, a Reform favourite, was a keynote speaker.

The separatist dilemma, by contrast, was confronted head on in Winnipeg, when a motion was put forward to eliminate the separatist Western Canada Concept from among the groups Reform was planning to pay homage to in the preamble of its new constitution. Yet at the end of the day the new party and its new leader failed to take a stand. As the *Winnipeg Free Press* reported, not only was the motion defeated, but one delegate actually gave the reason. "Let's leave them in," he said. "We may need them later on."

By 1988 Manning apparently realized he had put a stop to the problem of Reform's lunatic-fringe image. Despite internal dissent, he refused to sign B.C. candidate Doug Collins's nomination papers because of his well-known views on race. Yet in 1991, having been warned in advance of more image problems, Manning and the party executive were inexplicably slow to take action until it was made public that Gordon LeGrand, the man seen across the country wiping his feet on the Quebec flag, had become active in the Reform association in Leeds–Grenville. A similar situation unfolded when it was learned four members of the neo-Nazi Heritage Front, including leader Wolfgang Droege, had become Reform members and even helped with crowd control at a major event in Toronto which Manning attended. In all cases the individuals in question were eventually expelled from the party, but the seeds of doubt about the Reform Party's true nature were germinating.

The problem of racism and prejudice resurfaced in 1993 during the election, and for a variety of reasons Manning was again less than forceful and prompt. He had little to say when Reformer Hugh Ramolla suggested "Hit her, Craig" in response to a question on domestic violence raised by NDP candidate Denise Giroux with his colleague Craig Chandler. It was only when Ramollan protested that his remarks had been in jest, as "everyone but Ms. Giroux and her femi-Nazis" should have known, that Manning finally took action and reprimanded Ramolla, who nevertheless remained a candidate. Similarly it was barely two weeks from the end of the campaign when Manning finally forced John Beck to resign. Beck, it will be recalled, was the Ontario Reform candidate who had told an audience at Osgoode Law School, "I feel the time has come for white anglo-saxons to get involved ... these people, coming from another country, one evil is as bad as another." As for Reform campaign manager John Tillman of Halifax, his expulsion from the party finally came after he had declared publicly, "Gone are the days of catering to radical women's groups, minority groups, etc. Gone are the days of protecting these and other parasites of society."

But while Beck and Tillman were history, many other Reform candidates were left to carry on, despite racist comments, and some of them became MPs. For example, the former Alberta Socred leader, Okanagan Centre MP Werner Schmidt, who found himself in difficulty after the election when it was learned his MP newsletter quoted from Adolf Hitler.

Of course, candidates might have been somewhat confused as to what was actually acceptable in the Reform Party, especially if they had been following closely the comments of their leader. Having explained that Reform "is a pro-immigration party," Preston Manning then noted that "it is a mistake to meet immigrants at the boat or plane and offer them a grant to preserve their culture." As for refugees, they "would not be entitled to all the provisions of the Charter just because they managed to get their foot on Canadian soil."

When the Reform caucus assembled in Ottawa in 1993 they were obviously labouring under a number of handicaps, the most obvious being the fact all but one of their MPs — Deborah Grey — was a newcomer. They were also quite unrepresentative of Canadian society as a whole and unfamiliar with many of the pressing policy issues of the day. Party executive Gordon Shaw had earlier told one reporter the ideal Reform candidate would be a clone of Preston Manning, and that is roughly what the party achieved. Like the Harris and Klein Conservatives, the Reform MPs were predominantly older, middle-class, white males. Only seven women and one debatable visible minority (MP Keith Martin of Esquimault–Juan de Fuca) were included in the fifty-two-member caucus.

Unlike their counterparts in the other parties, many of these new MPs also did not have much formal education, and even fewer had professional credentials. Half had not gone beyond high school. On the other hand, their religious commitments far exceeded those of legislators from other parties, with at least 40 per cent indicating they were connected with fundamentalist or evangelical religious groups and many of them claiming experience in formal or lay positions.

Despite their lack of political experience and atypical backgrounds, the Reformers came to Ottawa with a fixed set of ideas. Although it was soon obvious they were more intent on changing the system than recognizing there was much to learn, many observers were willing to give them time, and the benefit of the doubt. But Reform's performance over time did not improve. Many MPs continued to demonstrate a level of ignorance that amazed their parliamentary counterparts and a lack of tolerance that was strikingly out of synch with the values of mainstream Canadians. This fact was driven home daily in Question Period, where the newcomers in the Bloc Québécois regularly outperformed them, and in committees, where Bloc MPs were quick to master issues and learn the rules of the game, often using them to their advantage.

In the early days, Reform MPs such as Art Hanger and Herb Grubel were providing the press with more outrageous comments than they could handle. On Hanger's "tour" of Toronto as Justice critic he pointedly asked a storekeeper, "Do you notice that in Toronto there has been increased crime from certain groups, like Jamaicans?" Grubel, meanwhile, used a debate on the Yukon Indian land claim to express the view that Canadians "have been misguided when in the past we have given in to the demands of the native community to give them more physical goods, to allow them to live on their south sea island equivalent." As for the Reverend Mayfield, who later landed in personal difficulties after it was learned he had claimed extended sick leave from his church while running hard as a Reform candidate, his well-publicized contention that the flogging of Muslim women for failure to wear a veil was a practice similar to the use of dress codes in Canadian restaurants was not well received by most Canadians. Most Reformers, on the other hand, dismissed it as unimportant.

311

The Reformers' views on women also caused considerable controversy. MP Gary Breitkreuz declared, "We should try to keep our mothers in the home and that's where the whole Reform platform hangs together." Reform MP Paul Forseth cast doubt on the wisdom of that idea, however, when he announced in a debate in the House of Commons that "in domestic conflict more women than men are likely to resort to using a weapon against a spouse."

It was not just the Reform men who held these decidedly reactionary views either. Deborah Grey — the tough former teacher from Beaver River whom Preston Manning once referred to as "the Margaret Thatcher of the Prairies" — was well known for her views that affirmative action was a way for women to better themselves at the expense of men. When Herb Grubel made the astonishing statement that "having programs in support of single mothers causes mothers to be single and need support," his colleague Diane Ablonczy apparently agreed. She objected loudly to a proposal for child tax benefits for pregnant women, arguing that women would deliberately become pregnant to obtain the benefit. It was not long before comments such as these led the former chair of the National Action Committee on the Status of Women, Judy Rebick, to quip that "the Reform Party makes John Crosbie look like Gloria Steinem."

The issue of human-rights protection for homosexuals also caused enormous difficulties for Reform MPs, with Bob Ringma leading the way. Ringma, who was rapidly acquiring a reputation as someone who opened his mouth only to change feet, assured one interviewer that he would cheerfully relegate employees who were gay to the back of his store if customers found them offensive.

Although Manning finally stepped in to criticize Ringma, it was after much hesitation. Manning, after all, had once urged an audience to pray "to eradicate the moral bankruptcy of the nation, brought about by ... homosexuality and general moral laxity." He had also been forced to apologize for negative comments made about the possible role of homosexuals in the armed forces. It appeared that, for Manning, Ringma's sin had not been to think such thoughts, but to have uttered them publicly. Nor did Manning's half-hearted rebuke stop Ringma's colleagues Dave Chatters and Paul Forseth from agreeing with him.

Paul Forseth, meanwhile, had also been encouraged by some of his fellow MPs when he referred to affirmative-action and employment-equity legislation as a form of apartheid.

Although Preston Manning continued to insist Reform was "not another party of the strange and the extreme," he was also forced to explain away these and other incidents with the limp excuse that "every party has a few bad apples." Meanwhile, Reform MP Lee Morrison summed up the feeling of many other Reformers when he declared, "I have been called a redneck and it is a label I wear with considerable pride."

The Perils of Populism

The ink had not even dried on the returns from the 1993 election campaign when Preston Manning and his newly minted caucus also began to discover the perils of their populist platform. Partly through ignorance, and partly through cavalier disregard for some fundamental truths, Manning and his team had made a number of rash promises they would soon come to regret. Worse still, their electors and their members would not let them forget. Having set unreasonable expectations they were now trapped by their own words.

Among the very first of their problems was the realization that being an MP meant regular travel between Ottawa and the riding. While Darrel Stinson may have thought he would stay in his constituency office most of the time, going to Ottawa when the spirit moved him, few of his caucus colleagues had been *that* naïve. On the other hand, they appeared not to have considered the consequences of their various pledges to eschew what they considered "outrageous perks and privileges" of members. Had they given the matter much thought they would have realized, for example, that they would be required to travel farther than almost all other MPs, coming as they did from Western Canada. Not only that, but as dedicated populists most of them had pledged to spend at least each weekend in their riding.

The full horror of the situation began to dawn on some of them as their supporters, unable to grasp the typical demands on the time and energy of MPs, often expected them to make two or three round trips per week, and certainly to be present for some portion of every week. It was not long before they came to regret their careless criticism of the carefully planned parliamentary calendar system, which the Mulroney Conservatives had implemented expressly to accommodate their Western MPs, allowing them a full week each month in their riding. Certainly a number of them bitterly regretted having denounced MP travel in business class. They came to see that it was one thing for their constituents to travel in economy class on a two-hour jaunt to the coast or Winnipeg once or twice a year, and quite another to expect MPs to spend five or six hours in economy seats twice a week or more.

Travel was only the thin edge of the wedge. As their life in Ottawa began to take shape, many Reform MPs were quick to see the advantages of an on-site restaurant and other facilities, given their pressing schedules, long hours and the relative isolation of Parliament Hill.

More to the point, it was not long before several dejected apartment hunters came to the realization that their pay and expense allowances were far from generous in a situation where it was essential to maintain two residences. Staunch family men, few had expected to be away from their families for lengthy periods of time, yet they quickly saw they could not afford to bring them to Ottawa either.

Meanwhile, Preston Manning, intent on proving to voters that he was going to deliver on his promise of doing politics differently and representing a "new breed" of politician, was quick to engage in some carefully planned publicity stunts. He returned the keys of his government-authorized car to the chauffeur and slapped a For Sale sign on the windshield in a staged photo opportunity on Parliament Hill. He and many of his parliamentary members were also "sworn in" and took an "oath of allegiance" to their constituents in specially staged events in their respective ridings.

Not long after Parliament resumed, the issue of assisted suicides arose in parliamentary debate. Manning seized the opportunity to demonstrate the consultative nature of Reform. He organized a forum in Calgary paid for with Reform Party funds, and then used several forms of polling to determine the "will" of the "people." Of course a problem arose when it became clear the vast majority of his constituents, and those in neighbouring Reform ridings, were overwhelmingly in favour of legislation permitting such activity, while he and most of his caucus were adamantly opposed. It was his first real encounter with an unsettling reality.

Manning's religious belief that his powers of persuasion would be sufficient to convince all right-thinking individuals of the merits of his position had come into direct conflict with his political belief in the common sense of the common people. Luckily for Manning he was not obliged to resolve the issue in Parliament, but it is hardly surprising that no resources have since been dedicated to a similar campaign on other equally contentious issues in the ensuing years.

Manning was not so lucky on the matter of the party's secret financial assistance to him and his family, however. He quickly came to feel the wrath of the party as well as the ridicule of the media. Reform MPs had already agreed to take a reduction in salary and opt out of the parliamentary pension plan when it became known Manning and his wife were receiving the $43,000 expense allowance, for which no receipts were expected. Attempts to describe it as a normal practice among all parties fell on deaf Reform ears. If it was so normal a practice, why had the executive not discussed it with the membership? And why were no receipts required? More to the point, how could anyone spend $43,000 on suits and dry-cleaning?

Stephen Harper, by now the party's most prominent MP after the leader, dared to disagree with the arrangement as well. "In my opinion the position the council has adopted undercuts our ability to forcefully and credibly articulate the positions we've taken on some of these pay and perks issues," Harper told the national press. Another Calgary Reform MP, Jan Brown, agreed. "We'll be like sitting ducks there next week," she said. "This is just fodder for the government."

Manning quickly provided the executive with receipts, but the council moved equally promptly to publicly condemn Harper in a four-page memo which many believed Manning had either requested or written himself. The leader's public defence of the allowance was less decisive. "Our own media people and that are always telling us you've got to dress properly, you know, more different and better than if you were just on your own," he ventured, turning several shades of pink. Yet, despite the embarrassment, he apparently did not learn much from the episode, since it was only a few years later that he and his wife were back in the spotlight for having accepted the party's financial assistance for a vacation in Hawaii, with the justification that the leader had been absent on business travel for an extended period of time.

Attempts to change Manning's physical appearance and notoriously squeaky voice were another subject of considerable amusement for the mainstream media and press, and embarrassment for the leader and the party. From the ever-changing hairdos to the laser eye surgery, capped teeth and voice-modulation lessons, Preston Manning was increasingly being put in the hands of the image consultants he had so heartily despised at an earlier stage of his career when he urged the delegates in Vancouver in 1987 to ignore image and go for substance as they cast their ballot in Winnipeg.

There were a number of other cracks in the populist image along the way in the party's first term, but nothing to equal their spectacular difficulties shortly after their re-election in 1997. Who would have thought the issue of the official residence for the Leader of the Official Opposition would have posed such a challenge to the populism of Preston Manning and Reform? Stornoway was already known to Reformers as the "monstrosity" that Manning had earlier recommended selling and/or turning into a bingo hall. Yet the party membership that had ridiculed such "perks" as outrageous drains on the national coffers was forced to watch as their leader dithered for nearly a week and then finally announced he would indeed reside at Stornoway.

As Rick Anderson explained the decision, it was really the party's grassroots — four out of five members — that were pushing for Preston to take over the house, which had remained vacant during the previous four years when the Bloc had held the title of Official Opposition. Referring vaguely to the source of his numbers, Anderson continued: "Preston is genuinely reluctant to move there ... but there are a lot of party members and ordinary Canadians who say he really should be going in there because he's the leader of the Opposition." Ordinary Canadians may have been too busy debating the merits of Manning's accommodation to notice, but the media were quick to point out that, when no one was paying attention, Manning had already cheerfully accepted the same car and driver he had so publicly rejected just four years earlier.

The furore over Stornoway died down fairly quickly, however, in comparison with the eruption in London, Ontario, at the party's national convention in the summer of 1998.

Bad timing saw the convention open just as reports trickled in that Reform MPs had signed an agreement with the government on the infamous "gold-plated MPs' pension plan." Coming as it did hot on the heels of several Reform MPs defending an increase in their salaries and allowances — remembering the problems they encountered over accommodation in 1993, and acutely aware of the wicked ways of Ottawa which were wreaking havoc on Reform family values — this news was nothing less than a grenade lobbed into the convention hall. Try as he might, Reform MP Randy White was unable to convince delegates the Reform position was a principled one. "I hope people don't look at this and say 'Oh, those greedy Reformers'," White said, but this was the immediate response of many delegates who heard the news. In theory the deal was designed to provide some type of financial cushion for departing Reform MPs who had opted out of the plan; in reality it provided up to $100,000 in a severance package as a lump-sum payment. At the same time it also allowed MPs who had earlier opted out of the plan to opt back in, and several Reform MPs announced their intention of doing so, citing age and family responsibilities. Others refused to indicate their intentions publicly.

By the summer of 1998, as Preston Manning toured Asia and Europe on another "fact finding" mission paid for by the party, at a time when Reform MPs were still formally urged to refrain from travelling with parliamentary associations, there were many in the party and the caucus who began to question the leader's judgment, if not his ability to run the country. Revelations by the former American ambassador to Canada, James Blanchard, that Manning had actually called him during the 1995 referendum campaign to discuss possible scenarios in the event of a "Yes" vote led many Canadians to agree.

Rebels Within

Preston Manning was having major troubles with his caucus, and perhaps did not spend much time worrying about unfavourable coverage of his travels. The carefully orchestrated and near-absolute control of the party he had exercised for nearly ten years began to dissolve publicly in London in June, but his unsuccessful attempts to rein in his caucus were already widely known and ridiculed long before then. The mini-revolt of 1998 was only the most visible of the problems dividing the Reform caucus, problems which had been simmering for years.

The conflicts with Stephen Harper were not the only problems Manning encountered with the leading lights of his caucus. For many of his critics, these conflicts were further proof of Manning's inability to tolerate dissent and his need to be the only one in charge. Their views were reinforced when, in the end, it was his star MPs on the front benches and not the dullards and troublemakers who ended up leaving Manning and Reform by choosing not to run again.

The cases of Jan Brown and Jim Silye were typical. Among the most progressive and cosmopolitan of the Reform MPs, they also became known for their ability to shine in Question Period. Both were urban moderates and excellent communicators who developed positive relationships with the media and, in the case of Brown, a degree of national name recognition. Both were often unhappy with the "racist redneck" element in their caucus, and endured much criticism from other caucus members for their continuing attempts to broaden the base of Reform policies.

By early 1996, Brown, Silye and Stephen Harper were all reportedly reconsidering their future with the party. When Art Hanger announced he was going on a "fact-finding mission" to Singapore to explore the use of caning and other forms of corporal punishment in the penal system, most Canadians were astonished and amused. Brown and Silye were humiliated, and said so publicly. "I don't want to be campaigning for caning and whipping," said Silye, a millionaire Calgary businessman and former Stampeders star. Brown, another Calgary MP and a corporate consultant with two degrees, agreed with Silye and suggested Reform would lose mainstream voters if it did not shake its extremist image. For their comments the two were raked over the coals at a lengthy caucus meeting in which one MP after another took the floor to lambaste the two, accusing them of betrayal and warning that their comments could cost Reform the upcoming March by-election in Ontario. (Polls actually indicated Reform had little hope, and the results predictably returned a Liberal MP to Ottawa.)

Brown left the three-hour meeting "ashen-faced," escorted by Rick Anderson past the waiting media and saying nothing at the time. Silye stayed to speak with reporters but broke down midway through his *mea culpa*, in which he apologized to his colleagues for hurting their feelings. Later, however, Brown indicated she did not plan to apologize and refused to be a scapegoat for the party's evident difficulties in Etobicoke North. Instead she left Ottawa and spent several weeks at home in Calgary assessing what she termed "the fallout."

In the end this only delayed the inevitable. The split between the moderates and the rednecks was serious and apparently irreparable. Barely two months later, during debate on the government's proposed amendment to the Canadian Human Rights Act protecting homosexuals from discrimination, the Reform caucus erupted again. When B.C. MP Bob Ringma told reporters he would move gay or visible-minority employees to the back of the shop if they were costing him business, colleagues such as Dave Chatters, Leon Benoit and Myron Thompson agreed. In fact, Thompson went further, saying "If they were costing me business, I would remove them." Asked for her comments, Jan Brown replied, "I'm so saddened by this," while another moderate, Ian McClelland, suggested Ringma should apologize and promise not to say such things in the future.

Sensing the whole affair was getting completely out of control, Preston Manning decided to come down hard on the miscreants. His decision proved to be the final straw. Not only did he suspend Ringma and Chatters from the caucus for six weeks for their alleged deviation from party policy, but he dealt the same penalty to Brown for publicly criticizing her colleagues. Thompson and Benoit, meanwhile, were unaffected, as was MP Grant Hill, a doctor who said the bill "will produce and allow the promotion of an unhealthy lifestyle," a comment which drew immediate and public disapproval from another Reform MP and the only other doctor in the caucus, Keith Martin.

Shortly thereafter, Brown, Silye and Harper all announced they would not seek re-election, as did Ray Speaker, Hugh Hanrahan, and the lone Ontario MP, Ed Harper. Equally as telling as his comments about the racist redneck component of the caucus was Jim Silye's parting remark: "I have no interest in a future as an MP in a third party that is going nowhere and cannot change anything." Brown actually considered suing Manning for defamation of character after the leader circulated a letter explaining his decision in detail, but in the end decided to resign. (In the 1997 election she re-emerged to run against Manning in his own riding, reminding many voters of Nancy MacBeth's reappearance as a Liberal in Alberta against Ralph Klein.)

At the end of the day Reform lost nine MPs to attrition by the 1997 election, a huge number in such a small caucus. (Among them was the hapless Bob Ringma.) They also lost one of their very few women, MP Margaret Bridgman of Surrey North, who was challenged for the nomination by victims' rights activist Chuck Cadman, founder of CRY (Citizens, Responsibility and Youth), and lost. Despite attempts to paint this as a normal course of events, Reform was clearly suffering badly from its extremist image and found itself at 14 per cent in the polls with the election in sight. One political strategy to salvage their situation was to issue the platform for the next campaign well in advance. Another strategy was to deliberately recruit a number of bright young candidates from more mainstream backgrounds.

Perhaps recognizing he had been ultimately responsible for caucus problems, not only through lack of firm leadership, but also because he had signed the nomination papers of all of the candidates, Preston Manning took a more hands-on approach to recruiting for the 1997 campaign. He urged Reformers in all ridings to look carefully for the right candidate. Presumably Manning was expecting them to look for women, younger individuals and visible minorities. According to one of the party faifthful, however, the ideal candidate would be a "Preston Manning clone." The party, meanwhile, issued a hilarious and massive candidate declaration form which covered more possible situations than most voters could imagine.

The efforts bore little fruit. One candidate, Janice Lim in Ontario, indicated her support for Bob Ringma's comments although she herself was a woman and a visible minority. "I can't be a racist," Lim said, "because I come from a minority background myself," a comment which drew howls of outrage from members of the ethnic community and human rights activists. When the polls closed, the Reform caucus of sixty — eight more than in 1993 — contained only five professionals, and the number of women actually *declined*, from seven to four. Preston Manning not surprisingly concentrated on the four new visible-minority MPs: Rahim Jaffer of Edmonton, Deepak Obhrai of Calgary, Gurmant Singh Grewal of Surrey and Inky Mark of Dauphin–Swan River. However, Andrew Cardozo, past president of the Ethnocultural Council of Canada, cautioned that the presence of a few visible minorities was less important than their views.

Their views were soon put under scrutiny, and all of them were found to support an assimilationist approach to multicultural issues. Meanwhile, Reform MP Keith Martin was quick off the mark to criticize the party's electoral strategy, which had failed to produce any seats outside of Western Canada. For Martin, one of the primary reasons was the so-called attack ads on Quebec politicians, which many observers had described as racist. Arguing the real intent should have been to target all central-Canadian politicians who had mishandled the unity file, Martin said the ads were a mistake which the party must avoid in future if it hoped to become truly national in its appeal.

Obviously this was not the type of new beginning that Preston Manning had been hoping for, but there was more to come. Shortly after Parliament resumed, one of his veteran MPs, Jim Hart of Okanagan–Coquihalla, surprised almost all of his colleagues by calling for the legalization of marijuana and describing the RCMP's investigation into the medicinal uses of the drug as a "misguided use of resources." While this could hardly have been described as party policy, Hart was able to emerge unscathed by claiming that his constituents supported his position, the ultimate populist defence.

More revealing still was the debate which ensued on the proposed amendment to the constitution on the Quebec schools issue. So divisive was the issue in the Reform caucus that Preston Manning was forced to throw up his hands and announce there would be a free vote in order to avoid a highly embarrassing clash between his new constitutional critic,

Rahim Jaffer, and the party's official position, to say nothing of the clash between Jaffer and another new star MP, Jason Kenney, formerly of the Canadian Taxpayers' Federation. As the party's constitutional critic, Mr. Jaffer surprised everyone by standing up and supporting the amendment with detailed reasoning, and delivering much of his speech in French. Mr. Kenney soon followed, regrettably for Manning, arguing persuasively against the amendment.

Over the next twelve months a number of similar situations arose, until Whip Chuck Strahl began to routinely advise that the party's MPs would vote a particular way "unless otherwise instructed by their constituents." This avoided considerable controversy during votes, but it did not prevent some Reform MPs from speaking on both sides of an issue. Keith Martin, for example, indicated strong support for a suggestion by the Human Rights commissioner to include "social condition" as a grounds of discrimination in the Human Rights Act, despite the fact the party's official position was to eliminate all grounds and essentially gut the act. Meanwhile, his colleague Jim Abbott referred to the commissioner's suggestion as "the dumbest idea I've ever heard."

There were other clashes along the way, but nothing prepared the party or the leader for the explosion during the summer of 1998.

With the pension furore still uppermost in journalists' and party members' minds, Preston Manning made a tactical error by proceeding with a planned trip to Europe. During his absence the situation deteriorated rapidly. Under fire for their positions on the pension issue, several B.C. MPs began to fight back. Jim Hart, a moderate who had planned to opt back in to the pension plan, accused the party leadership of using "intimidating tactics" internally to prevent him from doing so, despite the fact Manning had said publicly each MP was free to make his or her own decision. Citing a loss of faith in Manning's leadership, he resigned as Justice critic and called for a "real" leadership review. "The current leader has taken the party as far as he can go," Hart said in a press release, while MP Ted White added that his constituents had told him "they've lost confidence that the leader can take us to the next level. I think that's correct."

Hart was joined in his criticism of Manning by at least four other Reform MPs, and the debate escalated. Others added oil to the flames by saying they were "reserving judgment." Six days later, threatened with expulsion, Hart resigned from the party to sit as an independent. Still other MPs, such as Dave Chatters of Alberta, began to speak publicly of resigning because they were frustrated by the public debacle unfolding so soon after their election. "I don't want to be part of the nitpicking and backstabbing that's going on," Chatters said. Confusing the issue even further, MP Keith Martin began to speak highly of Joe Clark and indicated his support for the United Alternative movement that Manning had advocated in his speech at the London convention. However, Martin refused to endorse Manning as the future leader of such a movement. Subsequently he also criticized the leader for demoting MP Bill Gilmour from the Environment critic's post because of his decision to opt into the pension plan. Meanwhile, Myron Thompson heatedly denounced the United Alternative option, declaring "I'm not letting go of Reform policies," just as Preston Manning was defending the decision to allow Parti Québécois member Rodrigue Biron to sit on the steering committee planning the United Alternative convention.

In the end, Manning came back from Europe, read the riot act to the caucus and brought in Cliff Fryers from Calgary to stamp out any further dissent. By the annual caucus retreat in Banff in August, matters appeared to have calmed down somewhat until Keith Martin and Rick Anderson engaged in a public shouting match over Martin's comments and the right of MPs to speak publicly. From there it was all downhill, with the event — originally planned as a strategy session before the return to the Commons in September — turning into a public relations disaster. Coverage of the dispute was followed in the nightly news by the revelations of law-and-order MP Jack Ramsay's sexual-assault charges and the pathetic image of Jim Hart asking to be readmitted to the party and the caucus.

After a humiliating period in limbo, which saw MPs shunning Hart, and their former colleague publicly grovelling and expressing his regret, the disgraced MP was finally taken back into the Reform fold. By now, the damage had been done. All Canadians could see what insiders had known for some time — the Reform caucus was deeply split between those radical social-conservative and largely rural MPs who wanted to stick to the party platform come hell or high water, and those moderate, primarily urban and economic conservative MPs who were only interested in sticking with the party if it moved towards the centre and had a reasonable chance of forming a government.

The Democratic Deficit

From the beginning the populist emphasis of Reform far exceeded anything Ralph Klein or Mike Harris imagined, especially in terms of their platform. Both Harris and Klein saw populism primarily as a communications mechanism to attract votes. Any attempts to "do politics differently" were mostly limited to establishing a more "consultative" policy process, at least superficially. In fact, in their impatience to implement the neo-conservative agenda and reduce the size of government, they were prepared to *subvert* the legislative process, usually by ignoring inconvenient procedures and regulations. However, having actually served in their respective legislatures before becoming their party's leaders, neither one contemplated actually changing parliamentary procedures in the way Manning and the Reformers did — presumably because they were aware of the reasons behind the rules. While no rational person would suggest rules and conventions should never be changed, it is only sensible to examine the reasons why procedures were put in place and then determine if they are still valid before deciding to dispense with them.

For Manning, by contrast, the desire to change the rules of the game was an objective in itself. It became the driving force behind many decisions, despite the fact neither he nor most of his MPs had any idea what the rules were, never mind why they had been established in the first place. Nor did Manning appear to have a good grasp of the way the various aspects of the legislative process were interconnected. As a systems analyst, he should have had a greater ability to appreciate the fact that changes could not be implemented in an *ad hoc* and haphazard fashion, since other elements of the system could be adversely affected. Yet, in January 1994, it seemed the Reformers were not prepared to give parliamentary rules and procedures a chance. Instead, it looked as if they were coming to Ottawa hell bent on changing them at the first opportunity, and asking questions later, if ever.

Part of the reason for this obsession, as Flanagan recounts, was the firm conviction that "the system" was responsible for many of the policy decisions affecting Western Canada that they so despised. This impression had been reinforced by Western Conservative MPs during the Mulroney years, as they were either unwilling or unable to defend the unpopular decisions of their government. It was also reinforced by the imperfect understanding of democracy that Manning and a number of his MPs appeared to suffer from, and their tendency to look south of the border for solutions to problems large and small. (Five years later, Reform actually enlisted an American senator from Oregon to advise them and help make their case for an elected Senate during the so-called senators-in-waiting election in Alberta in October 1998. Although Republican Gord Smith admitted to reporters he was "a little fuzzy" on the mechanics of the Canadian Senate, Manning continued to insist the Oregon example was an excellent one which should influence the prime minister to make a change.)

Whatever the motivation for their procedural concerns, the Reformers' arrival in Ottawa for the start of the new Parliament in January 1994 was marked by a number of comical and unsuccessful efforts to superficially change some elements of the system single-handedly. First, Manning announced he would not sit in the front row of the Reform section in the House of Commons, as other party leaders did. Then he informed the media there would be no one caucus "critic" for the various government portfolios, but rather teams of MPs assigned to broad policy sectors. He also left the first caucus meeting declaring Reform would not have a "Whip" but a "Caucus Facilitator."

Simple as these changes were, they were doomed to failure precisely because they ignored the underlying reasons for the way things were. Asking questions from the middle of the third row, Manning could hardly be seen or heard, and television coverage of his interventions was minimal. With no designated critic for the media to approach on a particular issue, journalists were often left with no Reform position at all to report on their nightly newscasts. At other times, they had three or four Reform positions to choose from, much to the leader's chagrin. With a "Facilitator" organizing their lives, caucus members felt free to ignore directives, and Reform was often left flat-footed with no speakers in the

House at key moments, and no MPs in committees. The setting-up of a fax line to accept questions from the public which the MPs planned to ask in the House during Question Period led to an overloaded line and a series of totally inappropriate questions on local and picayune matters, making Reform MPs look even more ridiculous. In addition, failing to understand that they were in Ottawa to represent *all* their constituents, they persisted in asking questions by identifying the sponsor, a procedure the Speaker gently attempted to wean them from over time, rather than simply ruling them out of order as he could more properly have done, according to the rules of the House.

Parliamentary committees became another immediate symbolic issue for Reform, and one which demonstrated only too graphically their lack of understanding of parliamentary democracy. These committees comprised backbench MPs from the various parties, represented proportionally on the basis of their standings in the House. The government side would therefore chair the committee and have more members than the Official Opposition — at the time, the Bloc — and the Opposition would in turn have more members than the third party (Reform) and others. Yet, despite their third-party status, Reform members immediately began to protest long and loud about the fact that they were not allowed to chair any committees. They also attempted to turn this into an issue of Western alienation, decrying the fact no "Westerners" were chairs of committees. When it was pointed out that several government MPs from Western Canada were in fact chairing and/or sitting on various parliamentary committees, however, Reform was obliged to drop this line of attack.

Nevertheless, the damage had been done. Many Westerners were left with the mistaken impression that the Liberal government had deliberately and quixotically excluded Reformers from important positions. Those who heard the Liberal message that it was a non-partisan decision, based on parliamentary rules of procedure, also heard the Reformers' retort that rules could always be changed, especially stuffy, old-fashioned rules of British colonialists and the Eastern Liberal establishment.

The irony of this whole debate was that most Reformers had little interest in parliamentary committees, and their attendance over time was poor. Only eleven Reformers attended the emergency session of the

Commons to end the national rail strike that was crippling the Western economy, and none attended the committee deliberations where the end of the Western grain subsidy was being discussed. Reformer Myron Thompson apparently spoke for many of his colleagues when he referred disdainfully to committees as a babysitting service for backbench MPs. Some members from other parties felt many Reformers were actually taking advantage of the furore to disguise their own lack of knowledge and ability to participate in the committee process, which often involved reading lengthy briefs and questioning expert witnesses.

Preston Manning stayed above that particular fray, but his own encounter with parliamentary conventions was fast approaching. With the tabling of the Liberals' first budget and Paul Martin's Budget Speech, Manning had his first real chance to show what he could do and what Reform thought about their vital campaign issue of the deficit and the debt. Yet, refusing to participate in the traditional Leaders' response debate that followed immediately on Martin's speech, Manning actually left Ottawa and went back to Alberta to "consult widely" before deciding what to say. When he came back two weeks later and announced he was ready to communicate the Reform position, no one was listening, least of all the national media, all of whom had long since moved on to another story.

Even more serious were Manning's initial comments which appeared to sanction an illegal tax revolt against the GST and to support the refusal of owners to register their firearms once legislation was introduced. Although he later "clarified" his comments, doubts remained and several of his backbenchers were less apologetic. The Reform leader was also unapologetic about a letter-writing campaign that his members engaged in to attempt to influence the Speaker of the House of Commons to declare them the Official Opposition. Reform's desire to replace the Bloc, despite the fact the Bloc had more MPs, was seen by most observers as an unflattering attempt at a power grab rather than a principled position. This perspective was reinforced as time passed and Reform tried one tactic after another to achieve their objective, which would coincidentally have resulted in greater financial and research assistance for the caucus and the leader.

In light of their repeated attempts to supplant the Bloc, one might have assumed that Reformers were busily engaged in the activities of the House, but this was simply not the case. Just as they avoided committees, many Reform MPs were difficult to find once Question Period had ended and the camera lights had been switched off. Manning's own attendance in the House was not impressive. Statistics compiled by the House of Commons' Table Research Branch indicated that Bloc leader Lucien Bouchard had actually spent more time in the Commons than Manning in 1994. And, in a move that most considered petty and rude, Manning also was deliberately absent from the swearing-in of the governor general, whom he accused of being a patronage appointment.

Then, in December 1995, after the narrow federalist win in the Quebec referendum and the government's decision to table a motion in the House of Commons concerning a veto for Quebec and the other regions of Canada, Manning called for the impeachment of the prime minister on the grounds of insanity, decrying his mishandling of the referendum campaign. This was not a slip of the tongue but a deliberate plan. Manning formally asked the Commons procedure committee to recommend a way for Parliament to petition the governor general for "the removal of a prime minister who fails to uphold the constitution ... or fails to protect the Canadian interest ..." He was obliged to take this unusual step to accomplish his bizarre objective since impeachment is an American procedure with no equivalent in the Canadian parliamentary system. (In an interesting twist, it later transpired that Manning himself had been in contact with the American ambassador to Canada to discuss various scenarios for foreign intervention should the referendum produce a "Yes" result, behaviour many Canadians considered far more objectionable.)

Not surprisingly, a number of constitutional and procedural experts were seriously concerned about the damage Manning and his party might be doing to Canadians' perceptions of the parliamentary system and the democratic process. University of Saskatchewan political scientist David Smith referred to Manning's "ignorance of the fundamental principles of Canadian parliamentary democracy" in a letter to the editor, stressing that it was "hard to conceive of so many constitutional misconceptions being harboured in one motion." Columnist Frances Russell of the *Winnipeg Free Press* decried his "republican set of direct democracy ideas alien to Canada's history and political culture" and declared on February 14 that Manning "keeps demonstrating that he grasps neither the rules nor the game."

Another of Reform's concerns was the concept of "direct democracy." Reform's belief in the "direct democracy" of referendums and recall was another American idea whose time had not come. At bottom, Preston Manning must have realized this was an issue on which he and his party could be burned. His own father, after all, had been the subject of the first and only recall attempt in Alberta under legislation Ernest Manning himself had supported, forcing the premier to change the legislation. As a result, the proposal which lone Reform MP Deborah Grey tabled in the Commons as a private member's bill after her 1988 by-election victory was a much-watered-down version of a party resolution, and one which would have been almost impossible to implement.

Many Westerners paid attention to the Reform hype on the subject, unaware of its incompatibility with the parliamentary system and seeing it, as Reform wanted them to, as a means of obtaining control of the same central Canadians whom they despised. Ironically, since then the concept of recall has had its most significant trial in the province of British Columbia, under an NDP government attempting to cast itself in populist mode. The results have served as a case study in why the concept is not helpful. Used primarily as a partisan tool by disappointed losers in the provincial election, it may soon come to be widely discredited. Like referendums, the recall has also proven time-consuming, costly and diffi-cult to invoke.

In the spring of 1998, having been in the Canadian Parliament for nearly five years, Preston Manning was still demonstrating a fundamen-tal lack of understanding of the rules of the game. As *Ottawa Citizen* deputy editor John Robson, a well-known right-wing Conservative, lamented in a column on "Manning's latest move," the Reform Party's bizarre attempt to declare unilaterally that a vote on a government motion concerning compensation for Hepatitis-C victims was not a vote of non-confidence in the government were a classic demonstration of their lack of understanding of responsible government. "If you want proof that Preston Manning is dangerously clueless about the function-ing of our parliamentary system," Mr. Robson warned, "look no further than his attempt today to assemble a majority vote in the Commons. Either Mr. Manning's understanding of Parliament is so defective that he doesn't grasp this point, or else he is lying," Robson fumed, concluding that, either way, he would not back Manning for prime minister. As the next chapter demonstrates, Robson's position was and is still supported by the vast majority of Canadians.

Reform in Action:
Lean, Mean
and Marginal

Reform is somewhat un-Canadian. It's about tidy numbers,
self-righteous sanctimoniousness and western grievances. It
cannot talk about the sea or about our reluctant fondness for
Quebec, about our sorrow at the way our aboriginal people
live, about the geographically diverse, bilingual, multicultural
mess of a great country we are.
— *Vancouver Sun*, April 8, 1994

What is striking about the Reform Party's social and economic
policies is the extent to which they are negative. They reveal a
party which does not want to form a government. It wants to
form an anti-government, a government reduced to as minimal
a role as the limits of political credibility will allow.
— Murray Dobbin, *Preston Manning and the Reform Party*

Our social conservatism is a combination
of Rambo and Mother Teresa.
— Preston Manning

In June 1997, the Reform Party became the first Western protest party in Canadian history to serve as the Official Opposition in Parliament. A major feat in itself, this remarkable accomplishment can be appreciated only in light of two additional facts. First, Reform acquired this status barely ten years after its formation. Second, the party succeeded where a number of other third parties, and most notably the NDP, had failed.

After its founding in 1987, Reform ran candidates for the first time in the 1988 federal election, but only in the West. For its efforts the party garnered 2 per cent of the popular vote and elected no one. In the next few years Reform made little progress. Two events provided sufficient motivation to keep the spirit alive, but failed to really advance the cause or enhance the party's basic credibility. The by-election victory of Deborah Grey in Beaver River put a lone Reform MP in the Commons, where she was seen as a curiosity and a one-term wonder, the typical result of by-election discontent. The election and subsequent appointment of Reformer Stan Waters as a senator from Alberta was seen in much the same vein. Waters died in 1991 without making much of a mark in Ottawa, while Grey's main contribution appeared to be in laying the groundwork for the future debate about the MPs' pension plan.

Brian Mulroney's decision to hold a referendum on the ill-fated Charlottetown Accord gave the fledgling party a national platform and an opportunity on which it was able to capitalize. Reform's popular support and name recognition increased dramatically during the referendum campaign. Although the party's numbers dropped again after the campaign concluded, this was largely due to the Conservative leadership race which saw Kim Campbell emerge the victor. As a result, the political capital they acquired through their stand on the constitutional issue, and the looming threat of the Bloc Québécois becoming the Official Opposition, provided them with a distinct advantage at election time. With Kim Campbell's self-destruction in the first weeks of the campaign, Reform and its leader used their newfound prominence to ride the huge tidal wave of public anger with the Mulroney government all the way to Ottawa. A classic protest vote, the 1993 election saw Reform elect fifty-two MPs — all but one from the West — to the national Parliament and forced the mainstream parties to acknowledge its existence.

Despite its impressive numbers, Reform continued to be viewed as an aberration by the mainstream parties throughout the next four years. Having taken only 18 per cent of the national popular vote, Reform was simply another regional protest party, not a new national party to be reckoned with. The common perception of Reform MPs was not positive either. They were widely seen as a raucous and undisciplined collection of radicals, rednecks and misfits who had been elected in anger, and whose time would quickly pass as the memory of the Mulroney government faded.

Political scientist Harold Clarke's analysis of the 1993 campaign confirmed the prevailing view of Reform as the beneficiary of the Conservatives' collapse. It demonstrated conclusively that Reform support was drawn overwhelmingly from alienated Conservatives, with some 80 per cent of the 1988 Conservative vote transferred to Reform in 1993. Another indication of Reform's limited credibility was its failure to elect more than one MP east of Manitoba. Although the party finished second in fifty-six ridings in Ontario, a point Preston Manning would often emphasize during the next four years, Tom Flanagan correctly noted that "many of these second-place showings were so far back as to be relatively meaningless." In fact, only one Reform candidate in Ontario came within 4,000 votes of the winner. More significant still, of the twenty-three Ontario ridings where they managed to take even half as many votes as the victor, the previous incumbent had been a Conservative.

The surviving two Conservative MPs in the Commons were still another grim and daily reminder of the fact that the demise of the Tories resulted in the wave of support for Reform, just as it had led to the creation of the Bloc Québécois. And so, while Reform had come from nowhere in a short period of time, many expected it to disappear as quickly, with the anticipated rehabilitation of the federal Conservatives following Mulroney's departure from the national stage.

Reform's electoral coup four years later cast considerable doubt on this assumption. With sixty Reform MPs in the House of Commons after the 1997 election, the party not only snatched the coveted mantle of Official Opposition from the "traitorous" Bloc Québécois, but served notice it was more than a flash in the pan.

Given its dismal performance in Ottawa over the previous four years,

Reform had surprised many political insiders simply by holding on to its seats in 1997, never mind adding a few more. Even more surprising was the fact that it accomplished this feat despite receiving a mere 19 per cent of the popular vote. In the end, it was the sharp decline in support for the Bloc Québécois that cemented Reform's position as the new Official Opposition. The Bloc's precipitous decline was hardly surprising though, since the party ran a disastrous campaign. Their obscure new leader, Gilles Duceppe, was no Lucien Bouchard. Possessing neither charisma nor eloquence, he not only failed to shine in the leaders' debates, but distinguished himself principally by getting lost with the party's tour bus and being photographed in a cheese factory wearing a ludicrous plastic cap. Unlike the 1993 campaign, many voters in Quebec expected the Bloc to have a detailed platform this time, and its inability to produce a comprehensive set of ideas on important policy matters sealed its fate.

Reformers were nevertheless entitled to take some of the credit for their astonishing come-from-behind results in the 1997 election. Barely sixteen months earlier, knowledgeable insiders from all parties were speaking meaningfully about the imminent demise of Reform. With the party's abysmal standing in the polls, hitting a low of 11 per cent just before the start of the campaign, most observers were not only predicting another Bloc stint as the Official Opposition, but writing Reform off entirely. The Liberals were firmly entrenched miles ahead of the rest of the pack, and even the Conservatives were ahead of Reform. The pundits concluded that a second Liberal majority government was a sure thing. If the Bloc did lose its status as the Opposition, it would only be due to the rejuvenation of the federal Conservatives under their impressive new leader, Jean Charest.

The pundits, of course, were wrong. With the 1997 election results, Reform demonstrated its staying power. It had twice come from nowhere, beating back serious challenges to its leadership and organization along the way and ending up as the Official Opposition a mere ten years after its formation.

The second striking aspect of Reform's unprecedented status as the Official Opposition was the fact that the party had succeeded where the NDP had failed, despite continuous efforts for more than fifty years.

Other protest parties had also tried to make waves in Ottawa, of course, but had fared much less well, rarely obtaining significant numbers of seats and fading quickly from the scene in disarray. The fate of the Progressives in the 1920s, for example, was a cautionary tale which constantly informed Preston Manning's drive to centralize control of the party apparatus and micro-manage its policies. The demise in 1979 of the erstwhile Social Credit contingent from Quebec — the Créditistes of Réal Caouette — demonstrated once again the unlikelihood that regional protest parties would succeed in the long run.

For the NDP, which had survived for nearly six decades and reconstituted itself out of the old Co-operative Commonwealth Federation (CCF) to avoid just such a fate, its decimation in the 1993 election was all the more surprising. Nearly wiped out along with the Tories, the party returned only a disappointing handful of MPs again in 1997. The presence of the upstart Reformers in the seats of the Official Opposition was a bitter pill for the surviving NDP MPs to swallow.

Ironically, Reform's victory was also a bittersweet one for Preston Manning. On the one hand, his members had been obsessed with the idea of replacing the Bloc and becoming the Official Opposition for much of the past four years. Now the prize was theirs. On the other hand, they had failed once again to make the slightest inroads past their Western base. Their share of the popular vote actually was static, and they had even lost their one seat in Ontario, despite having thrown most of their resources and the bulk of the leader's time into the campaign there. As Preston Manning faced the TV cameras on election night, he knew he had failed to make the breakthrough everyone had been expecting and he had been promising.

More to the point, he knew the party had come to a crossroads. It could either continue to express its radical right-wing views and remain in Opposition indefinitely — if it did not self-destruct — or it could attempt to move towards the centre and mainstream Canadian views, thereby risking the loss of its core supporters. The dilemma was a classic one any student of protest parties could have predicted, and one for which there were no good answers.

The measure of how far the party had already moved along this slippery slope of compromise could be seen in the evolution of its platform over the same ten-year period. From the straightforward and uncompromising language of the 1987 resolutions, to the obfuscating language Murray Dobbin has referred to as "deliberate ambiguity" in the 1993 "Blue Sheet" and the many caucus crises over the party's first four years in Parliament, the pattern of vacillation and accommodation is plainly visible. It reached a peak with the party's 1996 leadership crisis and the emergence of the "Fresh Start" platform for the 1997 election, a platform which, as Tom Flanagan and other hard-liners had feared, demonstrated the victory of the pragmatists over the ideologues.

The Mission

From day one, as leader of the Reform Party, Preston Manning announced his intention to "do politics differently." Manning's vision was certainly unlike anything Canadians had seen before. His purpose was almost evangelical. His mission was to convince voters from all of the mainstream parties that they should abandon not only the liberal consensus of the postwar era, but the Canadian consensus on national unity, based on tolerance and compromise.

As an ideologue, Manning had no use for either consensus or the building of coalitions. Politics, for him, was not the art of the possible but an opportunity to establish the one true way. Like his father before him, he persisted in believing that the sheer logic and validity of his arguments would eventually convince the voters, and that he would not need to compromise.

After ten years of Brian Mulroney's brokerage politics, in which virtually *all* positions were accommodated, seemingly without regard for the national interest or the public good, support for Manning's antithetical approach was perhaps only natural, at least on the constitutional front. Mulroney had not attempted the harder task of compromise, or the traditional federal role of defining the national interest and building consensus. Instead he had repeatedly given in and offered the provinces virtually everything they wanted. With the shameless brokering of interests and appeasement of Meech Lake and Charlottetown fresh in their memories, many Canadians were ready for a more hard-line position than they otherwise might have supported on the national-unity file.

Preston Manning is nothing if not an enigma, and his beliefs are a confusing mix of sophistication, naïveté and misinformation. There are several themes running through Manning's thinking and underpinning the party's policies, and it is almost impossible to predict which one will predominate at a given time. As Tom Flanagan has demonstrated in his brilliant analysis of Manning and Reform in the early years, these themes are used to "position" Reform to appeal to various interests. These multiple themes also explain Reform's sometimes contradictory policy positions and the leader's seemingly schizophrenic behaviour on occasion.

On the one hand, Manning is a committed doctrinaire ideologue. Like Mike Harris and Ralph Klein, he is an economic conservative. With his religious baggage and sense of mission, he also supports social- and moral-conservative positions that Harris and Klein avoid whenever possible, and is clearly the most radical of Canada's New Right politicians. These hard-line views, it should be noted, emerge most strongly when Manning is focusing on Reform's mission as the "Party of the Right," as he has generally done between elections.

Thus, Reform is more comparable to the American neo-conservatives than either the Klein or the Harris Conservatives. Its platform contains both the economic conservatism of Thatcher and Reagan, supporting the unfettered marketplace and the dismantling of government, and the social and moral conservatism of the Moral Majority, simultaneously calling for "law and order" policies of revenge and "family values" policies of homogeneity and conformity.

On the other hand, Reform is more fundamentally populist than the governments of Harris or Klein. The approach of the two provincial leaders is a classic example of what political scientist Margaret Canovan has termed "politicians' populism," which she defines as a "manipulative appeal to the people by politicians to integrate and legitimate political support." Preston Manning's populism, by contrast, is closer to the traditional protest populism described by academics such as David Laycock and John Richards as "plebiscitary" or "right-wing" populism, involving grassroots input to the party organization and policy determination.

Supporting Reform's populist philosophy, which Flanagan terms the "Party of the People" persona, are such guiding principles of the "Blue Sheet" as the well-known "We believe in the common sense of the common people," the phrase later adopted by Mike Harris for his own electoral purposes. But unlike the provincial neo-conservatives, Reform has a number of specific party policies supporting its principles — based on American models of direct democracy largely unsuitable to the Canadian parliamentary system — that would change the rules of the game and ensure that Reform MPs are merely representatives, not delegates, of their electors. There is also a great deal of emphasis on other accountability mechanisms for elected officials, as well as measures promoting the termination of so-called perks and privileges, and the elimination of patronage appointments.

How can these two positions — committed ideologue and grassroots populist — be reconciled? What could the party possibly stand for if every position were subject to approval or recall from the grassroots membership? If MPs were allowed to vote as they pleased on every matter, why bother to organize a political party and establish a right-wing platform?

Although Manning has obviously not resolved this conundrum intellectually, he has certainly learned to deal with it in tactical terms. When he dutifully consulted with his constitutents on the abortion issue, soon after going to Ottawa, he was horrified to discover that the vast majority favoured a pro-choice position, while he himself is an ardent pro-life proponent. The result was a prompt decision to conduct no more of those types of surveys, and to avoid discussing the issue in Parliament.

A similar pattern emerged when Manning discovered to his dismay that the grassroots members of his own party did not always share his views on key policy matters. When no amount of sermonizing from their pastoral leader would persuade some truly recalcitrant members to change their position, he was faced with another classic dilemma. In almost all cases, Manning resolved the conflict in favour of right-wing ideology over populist rhetoric. As a later examination of the party's growing pains demonstrates in detail, Manning has actually used populist language to justify top-down decisions on many occasions, referring piously to internal polls, task forces, straw votes and other dubious consultative methodology. When all else failed, he and his colleagues have also been prepared to take more direct action, expelling some dissidents and discrediting others, and generally manipulating the membership.

In short, although he has not had to face the challenge of governing, everything about Preston Manning's behaviour towards his own party membership over the past ten years suggests that, at the end of the day, his determination to impose a right-wing agenda would overcome his populist instincts and lead to an authoritarian regime easily equal to or surpassing that of Ralph Klein or Mike Harris. Support for this thesis comes from no less an authority on Preston Manning than *Alberta Report*'s Ted Byfield. A hard-line neo-conservative uninterested in populism except as it distracts from the real agenda, Byfield has often found himself in agreement with Tom Flanagan about the party's apparent drifting and indecision since going to Ottawa. Speaking of the inherent contradiction between neo-conservatism and true populism as Manning has articulated it, Byfield once said, "It always seems to me that he is advocating something [populism] that is absolutely incompatible with his own instincts. Nevertheless I think he is quite sincere in saying he believes in populism. And I think that will likely get him into trouble before he's finished, too, because it isn't his [first] instinct. Preston is an authoritarian of the first order, just as his father was."

As if this bizarre combination of conflicting themes were not sufficient, Preston Manning has consistently articulated at least two other themes for most of the party's history. "The West Wants In" theme, a phrase actually coined by Ted Byfield, was a significant element of this early Reform image. As Flanagan's so-called Party of Western Canada, Reform swept the West in 1993 on the wave of protest against the Conservative government of Brian Mulroney, a government many Westerners had expected to meet their concerns, given its large caucus from the region.

Yet this Western protest theme has also provided a quandary for Manning. First, there was the problem of the party's hard-right, blatantly anti-agriculture policies and commitment to eliminate government support for resource industries, positions which could logically have been expected to alienate farmers and rural voters. It is a tribute to Manning's powers of persuasion that he was able to convince them there was no real threat, something he was able to do by trotting out his strategy of "deliberate ambiguity." At the same time it should also be noted that Manning the pragmatist carefully ensured several platform planks *were* committed to the support and promotion of the energy and natural-resource sectors on which the party depended so heavily for funding.

A second difficulty with the Western protest theme was the issue of expansion, a problem Manning was forced to address head on at the Saskatoon assembly in 1991. To become a national party or actually take power inevitably required the party's expansion from its Western base. Here again Manning disregarded the problem of converging rather than parallel themes and overruled senior advisers, including Harper and Flanagan, who urged him to stick to the West. Having run candidates in Western Canada in 1988, Reform quickly moved to field candidates everywhere but Quebec in 1993, and campaigned heavily in Ontario. By 1997 the party was even running candidates in Quebec, while Preston Manning began taking French lessons and spent most of the campaign in Ontario.

The divisions within the party over the expansion issue have been, to put it mildly, significant. When the party's image has been threatened on this front, Manning has generally managed to salvage the situation by playing his next card, the theme Flanagan refers to as the "Party of English Canada." In this guise, Manning's well-defined and simplistic constitutional positions — and the mistakes Brian Mulroney and the Chrétien Liberals handed Manning — allowed him to solidify his support in opposition to "Quebec separatists."

Reform's attempt to utilize the "English Canada" theme during the 1997 election backfired, however, demonstrating the dilemma of its juggling act. In order to maintain the Western support it feared was slipping, the "Party of English Canada" theme was invoked through a series of negative television ads criticizing the Liberals and the prevalence of francophone Quebecers as leaders of the party and the country. While the ads may well have solidified some Western support, they did so at the expense of whatever backing the party may have had in central Canada, and especially Ontario, where Manning had been intent on making a breakthrough.

Riding a Wave of Anger

In the movie *The American President*, Democratic incumbent Andrew Shepherd (a thinly disguised Clinton clone played by superstar Michael

Douglas) sums up the platform of his Republican Moral Majority challenger, Senator Bob Rumson, a Gingrich understudy deftly portrayed by actor Richard Dreyfuss. In a few devastating lines the New Right's negative tone and appeal to voters' anger is laid bare. Referring to the many serious political problems facing his country, the President's character charges that his opponents on the far right "are not the least bit interested in solving them." Instead, he concludes, "They are interested in two things, and two things only. Making you afraid of them, and telling you who is to blame for them." This description of American neo-conservatives is one that could just as easily have been directed at the Reform Party and its platform by Jean Chrétien or Jean Charest, particularly in the early years. For many of the party faithful, the shoe still fits more than ten years later.

The Reform Party was founded in anger, as Philip Mayfield bluntly stated in his opening prayer at the Vancouver assembly in 1987. Its early members were angry, marginal citizens who were fed up and not prepared to remain silent any more. They were looking for a vehicle to express their pent-up hostilities — some with society, others with government or with central Canada — and they each found what they were looking for in Preston Manning's vision of a new protest party.

As we have seen, one of Manning's great strengths has been his ability to appeal simultaneously to a diverse number of concerns. His skill in evoking the various themes outlined above allowed him to consolidate the fledgling party's support. Putting concrete objectives for these various themes down on paper was a more difficult task, however. In the end it meant that Reform, too, was providing something for everyone. It also meant that Preston Manning was required to do some fancy footwork to present certain key policies in the ambiguous language at which he excelled.

The Winnipeg assembly in the fall of 1987 drafted the party's constitution and founding principles, but these were considerably expanded and even altered in Saskatoon in 1991, and again in Winnipeg in 1992. Taken together, these resolutions demonstrate quite plainly the diverse nature of the party's support. Some give a clear picture of a marginal group of social conservatives determined to find scapegoats for their problems. Others reflect the emphasis of the economic conservatives, such as Stephen Harper, on deficit reduction, deregulation and privatization, while still others meet the concerns of the populist members whose focus is on democratic process rather than issues.

It was predominantly this latter group of members who first became disenchanted and left the party in short order, after discovering the very real dichotomy between the theory of its grassroots populism and the reality of its top-down, authoritarian leadership. While resolutions might be fudged for years, the activities of the party executive were immediate and almost impossible to deny.

Conflict between certain Reform supporters and the party hierarchy began before the party had even launched its first real campaign, with the drafting and publication of the platform for the 1993 election, the "Blue Sheet." Although the platform still contained measures that mainstream Canadians would have described as radical by any definition, much effort was expended by the party executive in making certain the package was saleable. The worst excesses and most flagrant deviations from the pan-Canadian norm were excised. Similar effort was put into disguising the real intent of many of the party's planks, demonstrating yet again the "deliberate ambiguity" Dobbin accuses Manning of cultivating. As Edmonton consultant Fred Lennarson put it, "When Manning calls for a 'balanced' immigration policy, the racists hear 'We'll keep the Pakis and the niggers out.' Those hoping for something reasonable hear just that. 'Balanced' is a code word for true believers and a soothing reassurance to those who want reasonableness and moderation."

The platform, of course, had come not from the grassroots but from the executive's policy committee. As Ernest Manning made clear to his son many years before, it was the role of the executive to develop policies and the role of the members to go forth and proselytize. As a result, the preface to the "Blue Sheet," otherwise known as the "Statement of Principles and Policies," specifically noted that the document differed from earlier versions of resolutions. These changes, it stated reassuringly, "were made to ensure consistency with the Reform Party Election Platform."

No doubt Preston Manning's deliberate efforts to water down party resolutions, undertaken with the close cooperation of Stephen Harper, resulted from the unflattering reviews the party had been receiving in the Western media as well as the national press. From the *Edmonton*

Journal's editorial describing the party as "shrill and intolerant" to the *Calgary Herald*'s even more graphic description of Reform as "strident and repugnant," Western impressions of Reform were decidedly less favourable than those of the *Globe and Mail*, which merely referred to the party as "narrow-minded and disturbing." Nevertheless, it was readily apparent to Manning that he had little choice but to tone down the formal policy proposals — if not the rhetoric — if he were to have any hope of catching the wave when it finally arrived.

In addition to specific planks, the "Blue Sheet" contained no fewer than twenty-one "guiding principles," reminiscent of the U.S. Constitution's famous preamble, beginning "We hold these truths to be self-evident." Unfortunately the Reform principles were neither as inspiring nor as positive, and several were not self-evident. Although they included a number of obvious motherhood statements, such as "We believe in the rule of law," there were also a number of strikingly radical premises for a Canadian political party. Many of them epitomized the famous comment by Anatole France that individual liberty means little in a society where everyone — rich and poor alike — is equally free to sleep under bridges.

On the issue of the social safety net, for example, the role of government was nowhere to be found. Instead, Reformers supported a Darwinian vision of "every man for himself." The tenth principle in the "Blue Sheet" declared that Reformers "believe *Canadians* have a personal and collective responsibility to care and provide for the basic needs of people who are unable to care and provide for themselves." Lest there be any doubt, the section added as clarification, "We would actively encourage families, communities, non-governmental organizations and the private sector *to reassume their duties and responsibilities in social service areas*" (emphasis added).

Well-known Reform MPs would later reinforce the fears of moderates that this unassuming declaration of principle would have serious negative consequences for all of the programs of the welfare state if Reform ever seized the reins of power. "We believe that medicare is for the sick and not the poor," said Deborah Grey while extolling the virtues of user fees. Meanwhile, her colleague Paul Forseth explained that, for Reformers, "old age security is welfare for the aged." Yet when the party's position undermining medicare emerged as the party's Achilles' heel during the 1993 election, Preston Manning was quick to insist that universality "was implied" in the party's position of devolving responsibility to the provinces and eliminating national standards, despite the statement that "federal funding in support of such [health] insurance and services should be unconditional." To further confuse the issue, he also admitted that this position would undoubtedly lead to a two-tiered system of health care.

Reform's focus on the individual and personal responsibility could also be seen in the party's approach to issues of cultural diversity and in its policies relating to aboriginal peoples. Firmly opposed to multicultural-ism and "official" bilingualism, for example, the party declared it "supports the principle that individuals or groups are free to preserve their cultural heritage using their own resources." Likewise the "Blue Sheet" declared, "We reject comprehensive language legislation, whether in the nature of enforced bilingualism or unilingualism, regardless of the level of government" and instead "support a language policy based on freedom of speech." As for Native peoples, the party supported "enabling them to assume full responsibility for their well-being and ... the achievement of a state of self-reliance." Having deprived them of government support, the platform nevertheless felt obliged to state that "aboriginal individuals or groups are free to preserve their cultural heritage using their own economic resources."

Reform's guiding principle on economic matters was equally radical. The unfettered free market was the ultimate objective, with govern-ment's role either greatly reduced or eliminated. Like Ronald Reagan, Mike Harris and Ralph Klein, Reformers wholeheartedly subscribed to the notion that the primary purpose of economic activity was wealth creation. "We believe that the creation of wealth and productive jobs for Canadians is best achieved," the ninth principle declared, "through the operation of a broadly-based, free-enterprise economy in which private property, freedom of contract and the operation of the free markets are encouraged and respected."

In specific terms, this included support for the free-trade agreement and, despite its unpopularity, the GST — a position that Manning and Harper went out of their way at the Saskatoon assembly to ensure remained in the platform, despite heavy delegate pressure to eliminate the tax entirely. It also meant support for the inclusion of property rights in the Constitution, a long-time Manning concern, as well as the familiar neo-conservative obsession with union bashing. MP Herb Grubel managed to combine two of these issues at once when he declared that "a special target of all my interest ... is really unions. Free trade will put pressure on the elimination of these kinds of institutions, which I believe are unjust." Reflecting the importance of the party's support from the energy and resource sectors, the party's fourth principle put environmental concerns at the bottom of a long list of economic objectives when it stated a new appreciation of "our land" would include recognizing "the supreme importance of exploring, developing, renewing and conserving our natural resources."

One of the more amazing sections of the economic platform was the policy plank on agriculture. Despite strong initial opposition from farmers and other rural residents, the party's position was uncompromisingly consistent with its overall belief in unfettered free markets and the elimination of government intervention. As a result, the platform advocated "an agricultural policy based on market mechanisms with the objective of meeting the needs of consumers for safe, affordable and secure supplies of food ... This would mean a shift from a government-supported agricultural industry to an industry shaped by the free operation of comparative advantage between regions and commodities, free entry into all sectors of production and marketing, and free trade on a global basis." In practical terms, the sheet indicated this would mean the elimination of marketing boards, the Crow subsidy and the Feed Freight Assistance Program.

For the economic conservatives attracted to Reform, the platform's unequivocal emphasis on deficit reduction was the key. Polls had repeatedly demonstrated an overwhelming concern with the debt and deficit among moderate, middle-class voters in Western Canada, in sharp contrast to the priority given to unemployment and job creation by their central-Canadian counterparts. To some extent this Western emphasis on the debt was probably heightened by the fact the economies of Alberta and British Columbia had not been affected by the recession that had devastated Ontario. In fact, British Columbia was enjoying a lengthy period of economic growth, fuelled by its markets in the Asia–Pacific region and relatively stable prices for natural resources.

For many middle-class voters who were deserting the Conservatives in droves, Reform's commitment to eliminate the deficit, and to do so almost exclusively by imposing severe cuts in government spending, was really the only platform plank they cared about, although the specific proposals to introduce a Debt Retirement Plan, a flat tax and the privatization of almost all remaining Crown corporations were also attractive. In reality Reform's much-vaunted "Zero in Three" plan was seriously flawed, as its own proponents later admitted, but it captured considerable public attention at the time and served its purpose.

The other important component of Reform's economic plan was the elimination of the GST. Preston Manning had succeeded in ensuring the actual resolution only referred to the party's opposition to *increases* in the GST, and a "gradual staged elimination" of the unpopular tax *once the federal budget was balanced*, but this sleight of hand allowed individual candidates to claim the party was indeed planning to eliminate the hated tax, a fact many of them highlighted. In fact, the Reform position on the GST was less clear and less hard-line than that of the Liberals, who nevertheless ended up paying a political price for the contradiction between the clearly stated policy of their "Red Book" and the careless musings of their future deputy prime minister. Many observers argued that the Reform Party should have been extremely grateful for the diversion Sheila Copps and her by-election provided, so that no close scrutiny of their own ambivalent position on the tax ever occurred.

Discrepancies between Reform's rhetoric and reality were not limited to its economic policy. Despite Preston Manning's categorical claim that "the Reform Party of Canada is not a religious party," a significant portion of his membership obviously disagreed. So did Reform MP Myron Thompson, one of whose first acts on arriving in Ottawa was to defend "the founding principles and values this country was built on, and that was the Christian faith." Rejecting the concept of separation of church and state, many Reformers advocated the return of prayer and religious training in schools, the allocation of equal classroom time for the teaching of "creationism" along with "Darwinism" in science classes, and financial support for Charter schools. No doubt they were encouraged by another of Manning's comments, which left observers wondering about his real position. "Sure, I believe in the separation of Church and State too," he declared, "but I don't think that means the separation of religious values from political values."

The social- and moral-conservative elements of the party's platform were evident in the statement in the "Blue Sheet" that "we believe in freedom of conscience and religion, and the right of Canadians to advocate ... public policies which reflect their deeply held views." Among these views was the belief that "the importance of strengthening and protecting the family unit [is] essential to the well-being of individuals and society." The extent of religious influence on the platform was also apparent in a specific section on "Moral Decision-Making," which dealt with both abortion and capital punishment.

Reflecting the same approach as the fundamentalists in the American Moral Majority, Reform's law-and-order platform came down squarely on the side of Old Testament retribution and revenge. The "Blue Sheet" declared resoundingly that the party supported "a judicial system which places the punishment of crime and the protection of law-abiding citizens and their property ahead of all other objectives." Specific solutions promoted by the party predictably included tougher sentencing and parole provisions, the gutting of the rehabilitative objectives of the Young Offenders Act, and greatly enhanced support for the victims of crime.

What was missing from the Reform platform was almost as indicative as what was included. There were virtually no references to cultural policy or communications, women's issues or human rights, and no specific proposals for transportation, postsecondary education or many other significant policy sectors. In blatant contradistinction to the lengthy section on international trade, the party's entire foreign policy was outlined in a single vague paragraph. This was reinforced by the pro-American thrust of its final guiding principle — namely, that "Canadians should seek to maximize the benefits of our unique geographic and economic relationship with the United States."

For the populist element of the party, the "Blue Sheet" was accompanied by a separate document outlining procedural proposals for American-style "direct democracy." In a classic demonstration of the North American neo-conservative strategy of combining hard-right policies with populist appeal, the document's front page screamed in large letters, "So you don't trust politicians? Neither do we." Referring to the political system as "driven by party interest, special interest and self-interest," the document argued that "we have to do more than just change the players, we have to change the rules of the game." Among the platform proposals were the increased use of referenda, the introduction of a recall provision, and more free votes in the House of Commons.

Yet the actual provisions for each of these measures were once again severely watered down. The party supported "the principle" of recall, but provided no specific details. It "encouraged" the use of referenda, but only gave examples of where they might have been used in the past, such as on the free-trade agreement or the GST. Even more revealing was the party's proposal on freer votes in the House of Commons, carefully worded to refer only to the *Government* side. "MPs on the government side should be able to vote against legislation without fear of the defeat of government," the pamphlet trumpeted, even going so far as to offer the text of the statement that the prime minister could invoke to enable this measure to work. At no time did the campaign documents refer to the Reform Party's own official policy, as contained in a resolution put forward by the executive at the Saskatoon assembly and supported aggressively by Preston Manning.

The resolution, which emerged in response to a local constituency resolution calling for free votes by Reform MPs on all issues, was categorical in its support of the status quo. Calling the constituency resolution "naïve," the executive's counter-resolution instead concluded that "having had the full opportunity to express their views and vote freely in caucus, with such caucus votes always made public, Reform MPs shall vote with the Reform Party majority in the House." A caveat that MPs could differ "if instructed to abstain or vote otherwise by their constituents" was essentially window-dressing, since the party retained the right to determine what procedure should be used to make such determinations and when.

Although these and other examples of deliberate obfuscation could be found throughout the party's platform, there were few opportunities for citizens to verify Reform's plans during the 1993 election campaign. Copies of the "Blue Sheet" were not readily available in many areas, a fact often blamed by party organizers on a lack of resources. In some cases the prevalence of the Liberal party's more substantial counterpart, the "Red Book," was actually mocked by Reformers as an example of that party's profligacy and its reliance on the financial support of big business and the ubiquitous "special interests."

As the campaign progressed, Reform's platform became much less important in any event. Once polling results in the last two weeks of the campaign confirmed that the Liberals would not only form the government, but almost certainly achieve a majority, many Westerners put aside their plans to vote Liberal for strategic reasons. Since they had been doing so in order to ensure that a strong national government would be elected to deal with the "menace" of the Bloc Québécois, many then turned to Reform in an attempt to thwart the Bloc from becoming the Official Opposition. Meanwhile, the social-conservative vote was assured, secure in the knowledge that the code words of the platform were only window-dressing. Reform by now was building a substantial if unlikely coalition. But it was the large group of moderate, middle-class voters intent on throwing out the Conservatives and dealing with the debt and the deficit that made the difference for Reform. Their sweep of Alberta and British Columbia demonstrated that their unusual combination of themes could be sustained at least for the duration of an election campaign. The problems would follow once the first Reform caucus met in Ottawa in late 1993 and discovered they, too, reflected a broad range of different interests and concerns.

Like the membership of the party and the voters who had supported them, the caucus consisted of an improbable mix of True Believers and Pragmatic Protesters.

Strangers in the Promised Land

Despite the optimism of Reform's rookie MPs who went to Ottawa promising to make big changes to the system, the party's agenda was in trouble from the minute they arrived. First of all, the new MPs discovered that Opposition parties are not in control of the political agenda. Since the new Liberal government had its own agenda, clearly spelled out in the "Red Book," there was little Reformers could do to force the government to focus on their issues if it chose not to.

The shock waves of this discovery had barely rippled through the Reform caucus when they also discovered that no one in Ottawa — or in central Canada — took their agenda seriously. In fact, much of their platform, especially on social- and moral-conservative issues, was simply not on anyone's agenda, and their attempts to raise these issues in the House of Commons were met with stares of wonderment and terms of derision. Having observed the caucus in action after the 1993 election, columnist Peter Newman definitely did not mince his words when he complained that "Manning's Reform party has attracted some of the looniest fruitcakes ever to emerge from the political swamps."

Humorist Charles Gordon accused Reform of focusing on purely trivial, local and even non-political issues. "When you think about all the problems we face in Canada ..." Gordon wrote, "it is nice to know there is one party whose members are busy debating what Canadians should do about spanking." He went on to suggest that "there is something rather, well ... quaint, about a party that is divided on the issue of corporal punishment ... Other political parties do not divide on the issue because other political parties don't even think about it, one way or other." Describing many of Reform's policies as "so far outside the Canadian consensus" that most Canadians "don't even think about the issues," Gordon concluded that "Reform is not like other parties, because Reform thinks about things like that ... At last, an issue that you don't have to be an economist to understand."

Their economic agenda did not fare much better. Not only was no one prepared to contemplate the wholesale dismantling of government they proposed, but even their strong suit — their commitment to deficit reduction — was severely weakened by the completely unrealistic plan they had advanced during the election campaign. Preston Manning admitted as much in an interview in early January 1994, when he described the infamous "Zero in Three" proposal as "no longer feasible." This, of course, was an understatement, given the uproar over the figures the party used to defend its proposal during the campaign, figures which had apparently been taken from studies by the right-wing Vancouver think-tank, the Fraser Institute, but which were based on faulty assumptions, misapplied and/or misunderstood.

Manning attempted to salvage the situation by declaring that the problem was not the party's numbers, but the fact the deficit was larger than anticipated, so that more time would be needed or the cuts would be too severe. For someone whose original proposal included cutting $19 billion in spending by eliminating much of the federal government as it currently existed, gutting social programs and eliminating all forms of regional-development assistance as well as all "non-essential" programs such as multiculturalism, official bilingualism and foreign aid, this explanation seemed unlikely, to say the least. The speedy demise of Reform's deficit-reduction plan demonstrated very well the real difficulties of a party without experience in government and lacking knowledge of many aspects of the political process. The simplistic solutions which had seemed so appropriate in Salmon Arm or Moose Jaw during the campaign now appeared hopelessly inadequate.

The story of Reform's performance in the House of Commons over its first term was, first and foremost, the story of a party constantly struggling to *remake* its right-wing economic policies on the run, in response to the ever-shifting fiscal situation and the spectacular success of the Liberal government in appropriating the deficit-reduction issue for itself. Although public opinion had reluctantly come to accept the need for fiscal restraint, it was only too apparent Canadians trusted the Liberals, not Reform, to carry it out. With each successive Budget, Finance minister Paul Martin managed to reduce Reform's credibility on its foremost issue as he moved slowly but inexorably towards his goal of eliminating the deficit entirely. In the end, despite growing public support for the issue Reform had championed, the party gained none of the credit. Reform was reduced to criticism of the government's fiscal policy on the margins, initially deriding the pace of progress and, later, insisting on paying off the debt once the deficit was wrestled to the ground.

A second feature of Reform's record in the first four years was the relentless efforts of many true believers in the caucus to marshall public attention and support for the party's social-conservative policies on the family-values and law-and-order fronts. Here, ironically, it could be argued they achieved a measure of success completely out of proportion to popular support for the issues. Although they were originally ridiculed mercilessly by politicians in the mainstream parties and media, the effect of several years of lobbying on the issues and raising the profile of specific cases finally paid off. Despite considerable evidence to the contrary, they were eventually able to convince the government that the issues they were promoting were of concern to most Canadians, rather than a small minority. By achieving a degree of respectability and credibility for some of these issues, at least to the extent that they were examined by parliamentary committees, the party that opposed "special interests" so vehemently in theory had managed to advance the cause of a number of marginal single-issue groups to an extent previously unimaginable.

The third major area of Reform activity over the 1993–97 period was, of course, the Constitution, and here its impact was even more disproportional. As an allegedly national party sitting in the federal Parliament, its positions on the issues of Quebec, Canadian federalism and the Constitution were both unprecedented and hugely disruptive. This was particularly true during the 1995 referendum, although many other incidents over the four-year period contributed to the growing disbelief and disdain of mainstream parties for Reform's unconventional behaviour. As the 1997 election campaign demonstrated, the inevitable result of Reform's underlying theme as the "Party of English Canada" was American-style attack ads on Quebec politicians that offended the vast majority of Canadians.

Throughout the four years, Reform also suffered from sporadic eruptions of racism, extremism and completely unpredictable behaviour on the part of individual Reform MPs, some of whom never adapted to the parliamentary system or political realities. As we have seen, those who *did* adapt were not only in the minority, but frequently were the subject of criticism by their caucus colleagues. For some of the true believers, their more progressive comrades' positions were seen as "selling out" and succumbing to the Ottawa syndrome and mainstream politics.

The Slippery Slope

It is instructive to examine more closely the four main areas in which Reform attempted to influence policy. The party's early attempts to find its footing on the first, the economic front, were particularly revealing about its willingness to compromise *in order to succeed*. Once the "Zero in Three" plan was quietly shelved, it was more than two years before an alternative proposal emerged, but the 1995 Taxpayer's Budget was instantly criticized as being equally unrealistic. At its 1996 Vancouver assembly and in the "Fresh Start" platform that followed in October, Reform then switched its focus to an entirely new economic strategy to attract disgruntled middle-class voters — tax cuts. Simply put, the party that had emphasized the need to eliminate the deficit above all else in the 1993 election was now proposing in 1996 to introduce across-the-board *tax cuts*, and eventually a flat tax of 21–25 per cent which would also incorporate the elimination of the GST.

As political columnist Giles Gherson noted in an article in the *Ottawa Citizen* of October 18, 1996, the difference between the $11 billion in new spending cuts offered by Reform in its "Fresh Start" plan (including the *elimination* of federal welfare payments, sharply reduced equalization payments and Employment Insurance benefits) would be more than offset by the $13 billion in promised tax cuts (including income-tax cuts for families, capital-gains tax cuts for small-business people and entrepreneurs, and payroll-tax cuts). In fact, the difference would add $5 billion to the deficit! Gherson was not alone in concluding that Reform's sudden willingness to increase the deficit was directly related to the party's desire to move into Ontario. Manning's announcement of the "Fresh Start" platform for the 1997 election — a full year ahead of schedule — took place in London, Ontario, rather than Western Canada, leading more than one journalist to concur with Gherson that all of this was designed to benefit the "suburban-dwelling, insecure middle class" the party hoped to attract, and for whom the platform was also suddenly offering *increased* spending on health care and postsecondary education.

By 1998 Reform was calling for billions of dollars in government spending as it participated in the debate over what to do with the emerging federal surplus. Not only did the Reform proposal include more than $2 billion for increased spending on health care, but it earmarked an extra $1 billion for payments to Hepatitis-C victims. It also included nearly $7 billion in tax cuts over a three-year period, an obvious pitch to the same middle-class audience.

Perhaps because of the widespread perception that Reform's views were simply unimportant, little serious scrutiny of their position on a number of other economic-policy matters appeared to be carried out by the national media or the government. This often allowed various party spokespeople to contradict one another with impunity. At one point, for example, Reform speakers in a budget debate could be found simultaneously declaring they were opposed to all tax expenditures while arguing vociferously against any proposed reductions to the RRSP deduction for middle-class Canadians.

Even without scrutiny, Reform's credibility on economic matters was deteriorating rapidly, as the federal Liberals not only eliminated the deficit, but had the good fortune to preside over a period of low interest rates, decreasing inflation, and ultimately economic growth and job creation. Gherson's comparison of Preston Manning with Republican presidential candidate Bob Dole was particularly telling. "Like Bob Dole in the United States," Gherson wrote, "Manning is trying to shake [voter confidence in the Liberals] by portraying the Liberals as big-taxing, big-spending government technocrats who just don't get it." Yet with the Liberals having succeeded in four years where the Conservatives had failed in nearly ten years of trying, Manning's message, like Dole's, was falling on deaf ears.

The same could not be said of the social-conservative issues Reform was intent on raising in the Commons. Although few of their counterparts in the other parties agreed with them on these issues — or even believed they were issues that needed to be examined — the true believers in the Reform caucus soldiered on for years in this second policy area. On the law-and-order front, they raised everything from the need to severely limit the Young Offenders Act (with Myron Thompson advocating lowering the minimum age to ten) to a Victims' Bill of Rights, a referendum on capital punishment, American-style "three strikes and you're out" legislation, tougher parole provisions, and the repeal of section 745 of the Criminal Code, which provided for possible hearings for those serving life sentences. With Art Hanger's famous proposal to examine corporal punishment in Singapore, including the use of caning and paddling, Canadians dismissed much of Reform's early campaign as material from the lunatic fringe.

Yet as time went on, the relentless public repetition by Reform of individual case histories began to have an effect. The fear-mongering that was so evident in many of the MPs' questions on this issue began to resonate with a public that was being exposed to ever-increasing coverage of apparently random acts of violence. Unfortunately this was a classic case of a growing gap between reality and public perception, and Reform — despite having received copious information demonstrating the error of their views — persisted in exacerbating the public's misconceptions.

Everyone from Statistics Canada to professional experts such as B.C. criminologist Neil Boyd assured parliamentary committees that the incidence of most types of violent crimes was either holding at stable levels or declining. Even the right-wing Fraser Institute published a major study demonstrating that murder rates were down but that media coverage of homicides was rising dramatically. Still, Reformers chose to cater to public ignorance rather than play a constructive role in public education. In 1998, when the violent crime rate fell for the sixth year in a row and the homicide rate declined by 9 per cent, to its lowest level in thirty years, no fewer than three Reform MPs decided to table private members' bills calling for the return of the death penalty. Reform's position on justice issues was particularly misleading since, as domestic and international data had proven conclusively, the "get tough" policies and increased incarceration had no impact in reducing violence in society or preventing recidivism. Put another way, Reform's focus on increased retribution and revenge, rather than rehabilitation and crime prevention, was actually likely to make matters worse.

Having whipped up public fears, particularly in Western Canada, Reform then demonstrated once again its willingness to promote conflicting positions when it chose to make a *cause célèbre* out of the federal Liberals' gun-control legislation. While few observers would have denied that both the legislation and its implementation were flawed, the fact remained that a party presenting itself as the party of law and order was assuming a position that placed it in direct conflict with the Canadian chiefs of police and a variety of other groups it might have been expected to court.

As the *Globe and Mail* of May 12, 1994, correctly noted, Reform had only come to the "tough on crime" crusade late in life, having not really addressed the issue before the 1993 campaign. In fact, its real push only emerged after it appeared the Liberals had made a mockery of Reform's economic policy. "The Reform Party has now made law and order its signature tune," the editorial proclaimed. "It is clearly trying to portray itself as the party that cares about crime and the protection of society as a whole," the implication being that Liberals were not only "soft" on crime, but cared more about the rights of criminals than those of victims.

Preston Manning himself demonstrated the ulterior motive behind Reform's law-and-order campaign when he told a reporter that "crime is one of the hottest issues with the Canadian public right now." At the grassroots level, meanwhile, the radical extremists Manning's party had attracted were still active. One such group in the Vancouver South constituency passed a resolution which no doubt reflected the views of a large number of Reform members, calling for "no restrictions of any kind on civilian gun ownership and the right of citizens to arm for self-protec-tion." The problem for Manning, as usual, was that the views of his more extreme and alienated members simply were not reflective of the views of the vast majority of Canadians. As several surveys prior to the 1997 election demonstrated, Reform's opposition to gun control was well received only in Saskatchewan, and cost the party whatever potential support it might have attracted among mainstream Canadians and central-Canadian voters.

Growing Pains

In a moment of striking candour a young, enthusiastic Stephen Harper — serving at the time as Preston Manning's policy lieutenant — told a reporter covering a Reform convention, "It's amazing what you can get them [the members] to do once you convince them that it's the leader who is telling them." In the early days Harper was absolutely correct. As the Calgary executive's orchestration of the resolutions at the Saskatoon and Winnipeg conventions clearly demonstrated, Preston Manning and his small group of inner confidants were in total control of the new party.

Columnist John Dafoe reported this situation in graphic terms after the Saskatoon assembly, concluding, in an article for the *Globe and Mail* of April 13, 1991, "There was no doubt last weekend in Saskatoon about who was actually running the Reform party. Delegates were finely attuned to the wishes of their leader. At his urging they steered clear of policies that might have made the party appear more extreme. Many could be seen watching the leader for a sign — a nod or the twitch of an eyebrow — about how they should vote on issues of policy and strategy."

Disagreements did arise, but were dealt with quietly behind the scenes as much as possible. Later, when dissent began to surface publicly, a variety of pseudo-consultative tactics were employed to diffuse the various issues and achieve the desired result. As Dobbin has noted, the use of task forces was one of these tactics which Preston Manning picked up from his father and the Social Credit's approach to "direct democracy," just as Ralph Klein did. Similarly, the Party Policy Committee (PPC) was frequently employed by Manning to intimidate grassroots ideas, legitimate his own views and, as a last resort, to override the views of the membership.

On the question of forming provincial Reform parties, for example — something Preston Manning violently opposed — the leader himself appointed a task force of his closest advisers from the executive, a sort of inner circle of the governing "Calgary clique." The PPC task force was scheduled to hold ten meetings across the province. Manning attended the first, asking questions and sometimes guiding the discussion. At the end of the meeting, a vote on whether or not to form a provincial party resulted in a dead heat, despite the fact support for provincial expansion had been running at 60 per cent in the party just days before. Manning then stated publicly that, whatever happened, he had no intention of letting support for the new federal party be siphoned off to provincial wings, and he would refuse to support any such effort.

The "consultation" was a transparent farce. With the PPC having distributed questionnaires listing the points to be addressed at the meetings, as well as suggested responses, it could hardly have been a surprise to most Albertans when the remaining nine meetings all voted to reject provincial expansion as well. Certainly it came as no surprise to Peter McCormick, a political scientist who participated in the task force as an observer and reported that "the questionnaire was very skillfully done ... The task force drew up the questions but there's no doubt that Preston had most of the suggestions and they just went along with what he said."

Over the next several years Manning would utilize several other so-called consultative techniques to support his views, most of which had little or no scientific justification. In Reform newsletters, for example, the

"Referendum Column" was ostensibly a forum to allow the grassroots to air their views on a number of important policy matters. In reality, members never knew who had participated or how many, or even who decided what questions to ask in the first place. Often the "results" provided by the newsletter, and the leader afterwards, referred only vaguely to "the majority," or a large number, without indicating how many participants were involved or what the actual percentages for and against had been. On other occasions, such as the famous GST policy reversal, percentages were deliberately quoted to support the leader's position, although they were essentially meaningless because of the small numbers involved. With less than 1 per cent of eligible members voting on the issue, the 60 per cent who supported Manning's proposal on the GST hardly justified the leader's repeated description of the results as overwhelmingly in favour. Yet throughout his leadership Manning has frequently referred to the results of such straw votes to legitimate his objectives.

A practical problem with the consultative approach came to light in 1993 when it was learned that workers at Reform headquarters had been unable to process all of the responses to the party's various questionnaires. Instead, they had been looking at only a small sample and shredding the rest. In an article on the revelations by *Globe and Mail* reporter Miro Cernetig, in March 1993, Reform official Gordon Shaw first defended the practice and indicated that about one-third of most questionnaires were actually read. Then other party insiders reported that in at least one instance only 100 or 200 of more than 40,000 responses were actually examined. In the end, officials announced the practice had been discontinued to avoid antagonizing members.

Preston Manning, meanwhile, often intervened in the supposedly grassroots policy process more directly, distributing open letters or writing commentaries on various consituency resolutions. Dobbin cites the case of several proposed amendments to the party's constitution in 1991, many of which were intended by constituency associations to curb the excessive and already resented powers of the Calgary head office. Manning actually wrote a "Leader's Comments" on the proposed amendments, "suggesting" that resolutions which could not meet the test of his criteria should not be approved. "I believe members and delegates should ask serious questions about the following proposals," he wrote, and then cast his net even further with the phrase "or any other proposals like them." Perhaps because most of the members had little experience with other political parties, few of them found this intervention unusual; certainly it was the type of direct interference by the leadership that no other mainstream party members would have tolerated. In any event it worked — only one of the resolutions Manning opposed was passed without serious amendments, and most were defeated outright.

As the policy process moved towards the platform, surviving consituency resolutions that contradicted the thinking of the leadership came in for direct criticism by the PPC. The so-called Exposure Draft, or penultimate version of the platform document, juxtaposed the offending constituency resolutions with those proposed by the PPC. While the PPC resolutions contained lengthy explanations under the heading "Rationale," the constituency resolutions were presented without comment, except for the note that they had no rationale. Others were described derisively as "naïve," "politically unacceptable" or "highly impractical." Not surprisingly, only a handful made it past the PPC, and even fewer went forward to the platform.

Even more disturbing was the leadership's tendency to marginalize dissenting members, not just their policy proposals. Many former members reported vicious rumour campaigns apparently started by the head office, in which they were variously described as difficult people, extremists, or mavericks deliberately disobeying party directives. Chief among these victims was Richard Chambers, the former president of the party's Saskatoon–Humboldt constituency association.

Although Chambers was not the first local party official to cross paths with Virgil Anderson and Harry Meyers, two influential members of the Calgary executive, he was likely the most determined and experienced. Unfortunately for the executive, they had underestimated the situation and their man. Chambers, a university political-science student at the time, was not only knowledgeable and articulate, but methodical and well organized. He acquired a pile of documents from head office over the course of his dispute with them over the date of a candidate-selection meeting, and each document was more intimidating and outrageously out of proportion to the issue than the last. He also kept careful records of meetings and phone conversations, and saved receipts for documents forwarded to the Calgary office. When accusations that he and his executive were being deliberately disobedient and had failed to follow proper procedures first surfaced, Chambers took the executive on. He insisted on hearings as guaranteed in the party's constitution, and eventually forced his accusers to retract certain accusations in the face of irrefutable evidence to the contrary. On at least two occasions, the full council voted in his favour, rejecting the sanctions proposed by Harry Meyers.

Chambers did not win in the end. Votes of the council were overturned, and Preston Manning himself intervened, calling Chambers and repeating several accusations made by Anderson and Meyers. According to Chambers, who forwarded his concerns to the Reform caucus in a memo dated April 15, 1996, Manning indicated he would not visit the riding during an election if the association persisted with its plans, nor was it certain the riding would receive party funds for the campaign. Last but hardly least, "Mr. Manning also suggested that if elected as a Member of Parliament our candidate would not receive any caucus appointments because his constituency did not follow the nomination guidelines."

Disgusted with the behaviour of the party executive and the leader's complicity, Chambers not only left the party, but stated his concerns publicly and repeatedly. His charges of hypocrisy and authoritarian behaviour had considerable and damaging effect on the party's image, a result the Calgary clique apparently had not anticipated. One Chambers article, published later that year in the *Saskatoon Star–Phoenix* and widely distributed, made a number of accusations which were never directly contradicted. Instead, a number of Reform supporters responded to the piece by criticizing the author and accusing him of various forms of marginal and extremist behaviour, including pro-Nazi sympathies, a charge he not only heatedly denied, but for which he received considerable support from non-Reform acquaintances.

Among Chambers's comments was the devastating critique that "silence reigns supreme in the party, as everyone realizes that any criticism of Manning or the party structure will result in mobilization of the entire party apparatus against the individual making such an observation." A bitter Chambers concluded that Manning's ability to appoint friends and sympathizers to virtually all of the paid party positions as well as control the executive meant there was little hope for commited populists to reform Reform. "The Reform movement has been hijacked by a one-man band and his cult following of religious cranks and political opportunists," Chambers wrote, thereby ensuring that several former colleagues and associates in the party would now be afraid to appear with him in public.

As national coverage of his experience increased, Chambers also began to receive letters from individuals across the country who had had similar experiences. Some were still party members. One wrote, "You will understand why I cannot sign this letter." Another explained that he had been through a very similar experience, "including the intimidation and threats and the isolation or shunning, as well as the Friendly Fire scenario ... We appealed the decision of the council and they held a kangaroo court in Calgary." The letter's author concluded, "From what I have read, your candidate is finished, you are finished and quite likely your executive will be toast as well. "

It was rapidly becoming apparent that winning fifty-two seats in 1993 not only had failed to solve the problem of maintaining control, but had made it worse. Quite possibly because Manning, the caucus and the party executive believed they had much more to gain in the next election, and much more to lose, their grasp on the reins tightened and their problems with dissidents — anyone who did not toe the party line at all times — increased. By 1996 these problems were becoming the source of almost daily news stories in some parts of the country. From the mass excommunication of members in several Winnipeg ridings to the near-total reorganization of Reform's Ontario executive, the Calgary clique demonstrated a willingness to sacrifice individual members and suffer short-term pain for what they undoubtedly believed would be long-term gains in terms of discipline and control.

The Ontario situation was most instructive, since it indicated that Chambers's experiences were indeed part of a much larger pattern. According to several insiders, the changes proposed by head office in early 1995 to tighten their control over the activities of Ontario constituencies were expected to be unpopular. In fact, it was anticipated that up to twenty-five riding presidents would resign — a "casualty figure" the party found acceptable and possibly desirable, so that it could install its own choices. In yet another memo from the national executive's Harry Meyers, dated January 21, 1995, the pretext for head-office intervention in Ontario's organization was the need to examine problems of "fracturing," caused by "significant differences in philosophies." Moreover, this intervention was allegedly undertaken "at the request of Ontario councillors," who remained nameless. The results were quite specific, however. "Wayne Hutchinson has resigned as Executive Councillor and Darlene Florence has requested a reassignment by the end of January," the memo explained reassuringly. "In addition, the position of Assistant Manager has been vacated by Gordon Johnson," it added almost as an afterthought, before giving the reason. "In order to allow the party to move forward ... these changes should allow the Ontario President's Forum to proceed without being absorbed by the past difficulties associated with fracturing ..." Put much more simply by a disgruntled former vice-president, "They were out to get certain people, and they did."

Not surprisingly the changes proved counter-productive. Predictably the internal wrangling did serious damage to Reform's public image. Many members quit, and most of them did not go quietly. Several moved to other parties to fight back. Others went public with stories of authoritarian behaviour and "Gestapo" tactics. When Maurice Brown, one of three elected Ontario representatives on the national executive, was also forced to resign, he quit the party and promptly moved over to run the campaign of a Conservative candidate in eastern Ontario in the 1997 election. According to Brown, "Under no stretch of the imagination is [Reform] a grassroots party. It's a top-down party. It's control-oriented. It's deadly afraid of power moving to Ontario."

His views were shared by many others, including Charles Conn, a Reform candidate in 1993 who told reporters in the spring of 1997 that "they are preaching one thing and practising another." Although he had not yet decided to rip up his membership card, Conn indicated he would not run again and was seriously considering voting Conservative in the upcoming election. A fellow Reformer, who spoke on condition of anonymity because "if they find out you say things like this, you're dead, finished, gone," stressed that his major concern was the tactic of vilifying dissidents. "We're a democracy aren't we? ... Yet anytime they don't like what someone is doing, they would refer to them as dissidents ... Then rumours would be started about them. They would be taken off committees. Whisper campaigns would begin. Money missing from the accounts. All that sort of stuff."

These comments were all the more instructive as they came at a time when Preston Manning himself was under attack for accepting the infamous unreceipted personal expense allowance of $43,000 a year from the party executive, a deal which had just recently been revealed. Since the reports were true, the executive not only defended the practice vigorously, but attempted to shift the focus to culprits within the party. Describing the reports and interest in the allowance as "another one of those damned smear campaigns," the inimitable Harry Meyers threatened to seek out and punish whoever gave the media the information. His reaction was echoed by Deborah Grey, who declared in a menacing tone, "There is someone who wants to get information out, and we have all our horses in line to find out who it was."

Manning himself seemed largely oblivious to the controversy. Demonstrating a characteristic lack of political judgment, he first attempted to shrug it off and then belatedly offered receipts for his expenses to the executive. Despite the furore, however, he did not offer to relinquish the party-sponsored perk that was being paid for with grassroots membership fees and donations. According to no less an expert than former policy adviser Tom Flanagan, the executive's behaviour was entirely predictable, and in keeping with what he termed Reform's "culture of concealment," in which information was communicated only on a "need to know" basis. His article for the *Globe and Mail* of September 26, 1996, also described the Calgary executive as one hell-bent on imposing unanimity by intimidating any dissidents, despite Reform's external image of folksy populism. The irony of this was immediately evident to anyone who had read Manning's 1992 treatise on the New Canada, in which he warned that "the perversion of populism, or the disintegration of a populist party ... occurs from within rather than without."

Despite these revelations, most Canadians were unprepared for Manning's personal decision to use intimidation tactics against the same two provincial premiers who shared his neo-conservative vision — Ralph Klein and Mike Harris. Having fought and won the battle to keep eager

Reform grassroots members from forming provincial Reform parties several years earlier, Preston Manning amazed more than a few political observers with his strong-arm tactics in early 1996. Apparently upset by the by-election loss of Reform in Toronto (a solidly Liberal riding which Reform should never have expected to win), Manning decided to focus Reform discontent on two Conservative MPPs who had campaigned for the federal Conservative candidate, even though Reformers sat on their executives. "All Reformers have to know for sure who their allies and opponents are," Harry Meyers explained, when it was learned Manning supported "using intimidation to force Tory members of provincial legislatures to stay neutral" in the next federal election, by threatening to have Reformers run against them provincially if they did not. In the case of Alberta, this strategy meant Reform would be "pitting candidates against Premier Ralph Klein, who endorses Tory leader Jean Charest, while Reform-supporting MLAs such as Stockwell Day and Jon Havelock would not be opposed in the next provincial election."

This startling position was widely criticized by Reformers as well as most Canadians. By mid-1996 a number of discontented Reformers were planning to stage various protests at the Vancouver assembly in June. On May 17 an unsigned letter by the "Oshawa Group"— claiming to represent 87 past or current Reform riding executives and 1,200 members in Ontario — appeared in the *Toronto Sun* calling for the resignation of Preston Manning before the next election. Dismissed by MP Deborah Grey as a total fabrication almost immediately, it was followed within days by the announcement that a former Reform candidate from Saskatchewan, Andrew Jackson, planned to challenge Manning for the leadership at the convention. This surprising news appeared on June 8. By June 10, Jackson had been stripped of his status as a delegate to the convention by an emergency vote of his riding association's executive. Not only would he not be allowed to challenge the leader, but he would not be permitted to attend the convention.

By September, the entire ten-member executive of Scarborough East resigned in fury after a year-long battle with party organizers. The president, Andrew Flint, had been one of the first party members in Ontario and someone Tom Flanagan had earlier referred to as one of the party's "white knights." His departure marked another crisis for the party in a province where they badly wanted to win more seats in the next federal election. Flint, who also ripped up his membership card and left the party, claimed the association had been the victim of "scurrilous allegations" and "racist epithets." He also accused the party of becoming "like a cult" in its pursuit of power and control of its membership. "The only communication that Manning wants to have with the membership is to elicit funds or get more members," Flint fumed, perhaps not realizing that this description of Reform's communications is one that many members of mainstream parties would recognize. The problem, for Manning and Reform, was that they had promised to be a populist, grassroots movement and do things differently. Now, as many of their disillusioned supporters were discovering, the party was reverting to mainstream behaviour in order to succeed.

Nor did the executive's belief in the need for top-down management of the party abate after its 1993 success at the polls. Not content with controlling the membership and its organization, the Calgary head office quickly acquired a reputation for jousting with its elected MPs as well, a habit that continued throughout most of the party's first term in Ottawa.

Here again, the conflict between populism and the neo-conservative agenda was inevitable, just as Tom Flanagan had predicted. From its treatment of star Reformers such as Stephen Harper to Jim Silye and Jan Brown, the Calgary executive continued to give the impression it believed it was in absolute charge of the Reform agenda, while the MPs in Ottawa were merely keeping seats warm in the House of Commons.

Although the elected and volunteer wings of political parties frequently experience some conflict, the problem was magnified in Reform's case by the zealous nature of the membership and their lack of understanding of the policy process in a parliamentary system. Just as Preston Manning had failed to understand the system when he disappeared from Ottawa for nearly two weeks to consult on the Budget, returning to empty seats and no interest in Reform's tardy announcement of its position, so, too, many Reformers in the Calgary executive and elsewhere simply did not understand the need for quick decisions by the caucus on a whole range of policy matters the "Blue Sheet" had never even considered.

In the end it took an intervention from the only experienced legislator in the group — Ray Speaker — to avoid what might otherwise have become a knock-down, drag-out battle between MPs and the party executive. In July 1994, MPs demanded a special midsummer retreat at which their criticism of the leader and the executive's "high-handed" treatment of MPs, including criticism of individual members and policy statements made by the leader without any consultation, could be aired privately.

Emerging from the meetings, Speaker told reporters, "The caucus has matured enough and learned enough about the process that they can run their own show." He indicated there would be a new system in which caucus would have the final say on policy matters, after working in "partnership" with the leader's office and individual MPs. "In the Reform Party, it is very important that all of these decisions are finalized by the caucus group," Speaker explained. Apparently believing things were different in other parties, he continued, "The caucus consists of 52 members who represent people out there and constituents must have an input into what our priorities are." Echoing Speaker's remarks was Stephen Harper, who said, "It's been a good two days for the caucus. We've got to where we need to be."

Rick Anderson appeared to be equally conciliatory about the executive's role. "Although I think that rationally the Council understands the day-to-day focus is on the caucus," Anderson said, "there is sometimes an emotional and instinctive reaction against that." This, of course, was an understatement. Harper was seriously mistaken about the caucus having achieved a measure of independence, as he would later learn to his dismay, prompting him to leave politics entirely. Beneath the conciliatory language the real attitude of head office was succinctly summed up by a senior council member interviewed at the same time, who adamantly insisted the council, not the caucus, was "the keeper of the policy flame." The role of caucus was merely to "demonstrate Reform's agenda in the Commons." Or, as the then party president, Cliff Fryers, declared, "Preston Manning is all-powerful in the party, not because he exercises an iron hand but because he's a true visionary and our spiritual leader — a far bigger leader than most."

As the Reform Party headed towards its mid-term assembly in Vancouver in June 1996, mired at 14 per cent in the polls, the larger-than-life leader was in real trouble with the grassroots membership. Some were upset over his apparent softening on hard-right issues they supported, such as the Bob Ringma affair and the turban issue in the RCMP, and some were frustrated by the lack of progress made in setting the agenda in Ottawa. The conference in Vancouver was described by many pundits as a "make or break" affair for both Manning and the party.

The Fresh Start

Despite attempts to control the delegate-selection process for the Vancouver assembly, the disagreement between the hard-line social conservatives and other Reform members was patently obvious at the four-day meeting. On the one hand, Vancouver constituency president Jim Bray told reporters that Manning's attempt to "clear out these nean- derthals and malcontents" would eventually leave the party "stronger in the long run." On the other hand, Reformers from Dave Chatters's Athabaska riding complained, "What happened to the good old grass- roots party where the MPs are supposed to represent our views?" Firmly supporting their man in the wake of his suspension by Manning, the delegates declared that the leader "will pay dearly for this mistake because you will definitely lose the support of the majority of the people that have put a lot of sweat into this organization." Wenda Kyle, a constituency president from Victoria, went further. "Sometimes people who found parties don't have the holding power," she said. "People are questioning whether he [Manning] is the right man."

Manning's major address to the assembly recognized there were a number of problems, both organizational and conceptual, with the way Reform had performed since the 1993 election. In fact, his speech began with the statement "The Reform Party is at a crossroads." Next he reinforced the commitment he and his father had made twenty years earlier to form a new social-conservative party that would replace the old mainstream parties. Making clear his determination to expand the party's base and become a national alternative to the Liberals, Manning stressed that voters would not accept Reform as this alternative "until we can satisfy them that we have our act together on these fundamen- tal questions." To do this, he declared, would require self-discipline, from the membership and the caucus. "Openness cannot be unlimited," he declared, and "free expression as a price and benefit of membership of the party must be circumscribed ..."

Determined to demonstrate that Reform was not a party of "kooks, racists and bigots," organizers had gone out of their way to recruit delegates who showed a different side of Reform to the world, orchestrating positive interventions just as the Republicans had done for Bob Dole's nomination convention. Some Reformers even borrowed Dole's "Mainstream, not extreme" slogan. As one report in the *Ottawa Citizen* of June 10 noted, "The event was clearly stage-managed to present the party as more inclusive and mainstream. A string of delegates representing minorities, Quebec, young people and women stood to give Reform glowing testimonials."

Nevertheless, many opposing views were being expressed by individuals grumbling in the corridors, and not everyone was convinced by Manning's appeal. When Bryan Thomas — the so-called whiz kid and advertising guru picked by the executive to fashion the next election campaign, having successfully run the 1995 campaign of Mike Harris in Ontario — suggested including a visibly gay male among the many individuals on the cover of the party's platform document, to demonstrate the party was not prejudiced, the silence was deafening. The leader later told reporters that idea would definitely be rejected.

Among those the leader and other delegates had failed to impress was a seventeen-year-old Victoria delegate, Ken Glowinski, who actually told reporters he was planning to leave the party. "I'm a moderate," Glowinski explained. "I thought Preston Manning could move the party to the centre. But now I realize this is impossible. The tone of the convention was still incredibly extreme ... There's an anti-gay, anti-moderate tone throughout. It's ignorance I guess. I'm pretty dispirited by it all." The youth delegate's views were reinforced by the commentaries of several journalists covering the event, including Jane O'Hara of the *Vancouver Province*, who concluded, "You usually have to pay good money in a museum to watch such an unseemly display of dinosaurs."

The party was also "swimming upstream" on policy matters, to use Manning's own terminology. Despite the focus of most Canadians on issues relating to job creation and the social safety net, Reformers spent most of their time at the convention discussing law-and-order issues, a flat-tax system and a new set of policies to handle "the Quebec question." In almost all cases, the solutions proposed and accepted by the assembly delegates could only have been described, yet again, as negative. Reformers agreed to abolish the GST, the Official Languages Act, special status for Quebec, the Young Offenders Act and all forms of parole (for all offenders, regardless of the crime). They also called for national referendums on capital punishment, any future tax hikes, and all proposed constitutional amendments. As a concession to their new image as moderates, they withdrew a proposal to outlaw the Bloc Québécois and remove the party's MPs from Parliament, along with several others relating to gay rights and the issue of spousal benefits.

At the end of the day Manning easily survived the mandatory leadership-review vote, receiving the support of 86 per cent of delegates. Although this was down from the 93 per cent he had received two years earlier, it was seen as a strong mandate for the changes he was proposing, and the "Fresh Start" the party was going to make heading into the home stretch for the next election.

As Manning said himself, the theme of a "fresh start" was intended to have two meanings: a fresh start for Canada as it approached the twenty-first century, and a fresh start for his party and caucus, who had admittedly made mistakes in their early days in Ottawa.

To demonstrate they were still the party committed to doing politics differently, Reform shortly afterwards released the entire text of its platform for the upcoming election, nearly a year ahead of schedule. In a widely trumpeted public-relations event in London, Ontario, Preston Manning unveiled the party's Fresh Start document before an adoring crowd of white-haired seniors.

The party's platform was a self-described "six-point plan" to "build a better future together." It included economic policies designed to greatly decrease the size of government, cutting overall spending by a staggering $15 billion. It also promised to lower personal income taxes by more than $2,000 per year for the "average family," and move towards a flat tax, a measure which critics argued would benefit the rich and hurt the middle class and low-income earners. In addition, the document indicated a large number of government departments — such as Indian Affairs and Transport Canada — were to be "very significantly reduced in scope"— and most Crown corporations, including the CBC, Via Rail and Canada Post, were to be privatized.

Most important, however, was the overall emphasis on tax reduction as the best way to utilize the so-called deficit dividend that would result from balancing the budget by March 1999. Strikingly similar to the *Contract with America*'s emphasis on tax cuts and family values, this approach represented a dramatic about-face from Reform's insistence over the previous three years on deficit reduction at all costs, and it led to a number of critical assessments of their plan almost immediately. To their horror, one of the first critics of their "Fresh Start" was none other than Ralph Klein, who publicly took issue with the emphasis on tax cuts. "Before any federal politician talks about tax cuts," Klein thundered, "they should get the budget balanced and start paying down the debt."

More in keeping with its past positions, the Reform platform on the social-policy front was predictably unforgiving. Under the rubric of "personal security," for example, the Reform platform pledged to enact a Victims' Bill of Rights, eliminate both the Young Offenders Act and parole for violent offenders, repeal the Liberals' gun-registration legislation, hold a binding referendum on capital punishment, and introduce "Three Strikes" legislation for repeat offenders.

In a section which pledged to "repair" the social safety net, the platform further proposed to essentially privatize the Canada Pension Plan, turning it into a costly and enforced form of RRSP which would not cover either disability insurance or other measures currently provided by the government plan. Reform's "Fresh Start" also pledged to greatly reduce the scope and coverage of Employment Insurance. Although there was a promise to increase spending for health care and education, it was clearly stated these increases would come from the "savings" accrued from cuts in other areas of government spending, such as welfare and regional equalization programs.

Preston Manning had high hopes for the "Fresh Start" plan. No doubt he hoped to capitalize on his head start for the next election in the same way that Mike Harris had done with his "Common Sense Revolution" platform, but the public was simply not buying the radical neo-conservative message, especially in Ontario. As polls repeatedly demonstrated over the next several months, most Canadians wanted to use the deficit dividend to reinvest in the social safety net, and very few were prepared to reduce the role of government to the extent Reform was contemplating. As for the social-conservative message on law and order and family values, it fell on largely deaf ears.

Reform's position going into the 1997 election looked bleak indeed. Stuck at 11 per cent in the polls, it looked as if the party was lacking not only credible leadership, but a credible platform. With the Liberals at more than 50 per cent in the polls, the only real question in many observers' minds was how large the second Liberal majority would be. For Reformers, the real question was whether they would survive, and whether Preston Manning would be able to find another wave.

Realpolitik and the Watershed Election

A funny thing happened on the way to election day in 1997. Both the Liberals and the Conservatives miscalculated badly, throwing Reform a lifeline, while the federal NDP simply never got out of the starting gate. The election that was supposed to be a Liberal cakewalk became a closely contested race in which many pundits believed another week of campaigning could easily have cost the Liberals their majority. As it was the Liberals barely managed to hang on, salvaging a four-seat lead over the Opposition parties by the skin of their teeth, with Reform the prime beneficiary of the debacle.

The campaign started off badly and deteriorated rapidly. The Liberals' election strategists were determined to call the election before the four-year point in the government's mandate, despite overwhelming expert advice to the contrary. As a result the party found itself in trouble in the court of public opinion before it dropped the starter's flag. Comparisons with the Peterson Liberals in Ontario were almost inevitable, and so began the long list of miscues and unanticipated events which in the end nearly made the Ontario scenario a self-fulfilling prophecy. The prime minister's actual announcement of the election call added fuel to the fire. As he left Rideau Hall after handing in the government's resignation, Jean Chrétien appeared totally unprepared to answer reporters' questions about the reason for the timing of the election, despite months of internal debate and planning.

Fate intervened soon after in the form of the catastrophic Manitoba floods. Although the chief electoral officer personally visited the flood area and announced that the election could and should proceed as planned, many Manitobans were outraged with the decision and blamed it on the government. Their outrage had already been provoked, however, when the prime minister briefly visited one of the many flashpoints the previous week and was photographed throwing a bag of sand on a dyke before hurriedly leaving. It was Manitoba Liberal MPs who were left holding the bag. Some, such as Winnipeg's Reg Alcock, found themselves spending the rest of the campaign living down the image of unconcern by pouring their efforts into relief work and ignoring partisan politics, an approach that earned Alcock a second term. Others were not so lucky.

In Saskatchewan, meanwhile, voters were more than a little miffed with the amendments to the federal Election Act which had recently been implemented in order to coordinate the timing of the election across the country. For Saskatchewan voters, the fact no one in official Ottawa had taken into consideration their year-round use of daylight saving time was simply one more example of "the East's" lack of concern for Western Canada, a fault they once again attributed to the governing Liberals. But this slight was nothing compared with the major concern of Saskatchewan voters. The single most important issue dominating the election debate in that province was the federal government's much-criticized gun-control legislation. In fact, Saskatchewan was repeatedly found by pollsters to be the only province in the country where a majority of citizens opposed the legislation. Although several reasons were offered by analysts, the most likely seemed to be the predominantly rural nature of the population since, by contrast, both Alberta and British Columbia — with their large urban centres — were firmly supportive of the bill.

Although the Liberals realistically had little hope of a major breakthrough in the West, their strategists persisted in predicting significant gains in British Columbia, a province where their reputation had suffered badly and repeatedly in the past few years. The mishandling of the Mifflin Plan announcing the government's strategy for the salmon fishery had been a setback. The disastrous about-face on the constitutional-amendment proposal after the 1995 referendum — in which B.C. was originally included as part of a Western region rather than being given status as a separate Pacific region — was even more serious. With the Liberal government's subsequent decision to respond to Reform's misinformed bullying on the so-called faint hope clause, section 745 of the Criminal Code, the Liberals lost whatever credibility they had left. Having given in to the radical right's demands for changes to the section, rather than standing by the legislation and explaining the flaws in Reform's position, the Liberals had achieved a lose–lose situation. Not only had the bill been modified, confounding its original intent, but the changes were inevitably seen as insufficient. Worse still, the decision to make minor changes was perceived as an admission that Reform had been right all along. Reformers, not Liberals, received the credit for the modifications, as they did for the changes to the constitutional-amending formula.

During the 1997 campaign, the Reform Party took full advantage of these strategic errors. Their American-style personal attack ads in British Columbia on the section 745 issue — accusing individual Liberals such as cabinet minister David Anderson of supporting parole for serial killer Clifford Olson — were a case in point, as were their fear-mongering tactics on the gun-control issue in Saskatchewan. At the end of the day, the Liberals failed to make inroads in B.C. and lost all but three of their seats in Alberta and Saskatchewan.

The Reformers would not likely have received as much support as they eventually did had it not also been for the failure of the Conservatives and the NDP to make any type of comeback in Western Canada. Although this was predicted by most knowledgeable observers, Liberal strategists compounded the problem by failing to recognize the complete absence of Conservative support west of Ontario. They devoted considerable funds to campaign ads attacking the Tories in Western Canada while ignoring Reform, a blunder that several defeated Liberal MPs were quick to blame in the election post-mortem.

The Conservatives, meanwhile, gave up whatever chance of an electoral comeback they might have had in Ontario by pursuing a far more right-wing agenda than they would normally have done. This miscalculation apparently was due to the victory within the campaign team of the aggressive new group of young Blue Tories and actual Harris Tories, who had been at loggerheads with the veteran, more progressive Charest wing of the party for some time. Charest, evidently outnumbered, out of funds and in need of the Harris provincial election machine, had unwisely succumbed. In the end, the Conservatives' modest revival ironically occurred in Atlantic Canada, not Ontario, due to the Liberals' cuts to the social safety net and the unwillingness of most voters to make a dramatic switch to the NDP. Luckily for Jean Charest, the majority of his candidates in Atlantic Canada had ignored the official party platform with its Harris overtones, and espoused the traditional Red Tory policies that had elected Conservatives in the region in the past. Nevertheless the failure of the Conservatives to make a major breakthrough left Charest with a small band of MPs in the House of Commons, and the humiliating status of fifth party.

As the results rolled in on election night, it became increasingly obvious the Liberals had nearly snatched defeat from the jaws of victory. They maintained a slim four-seat margin and were able to claim victory only by pointing out that this was the first back-to-back Liberal majority government since Mackenzie King's. With many a stunned and glassy look among the Liberal troops at the traditional party later that night in downtown Ottawa, it began to dawn on party insiders that the "ragtag collection of racists, kooks and rednecks" pretending to be a political party was now about to take its place across the aisle from the government as Her Majesty's Loyal Opposition.

Kinder, Gentler Reform?

One of the first questions many observers asked themselves the day after the 1997 election was whether success would spoil Reform. Would it be a kinder, gentler Reform Party that Canadians would see as it adjusted to its new status? And would the trappings of official Ottawa capture Reformers as they had many other protest movements, making them think twice about their radical policies and become more receptive to the Canadian norms of compromise and moderation?

At first glance it appeared the answer was a resounding "No!" Preston Manning assured listeners that Reform had no intention of moderating its views or becoming more conciliatory. Quite the contrary, he assured supporters, Reform would hold the government's feet to the flame more stubbornly than ever. While their performance in the House of Commons when the new Parliament convened seemed to confirm the fact that the majority of the party's elected MPs were not moderates, it also confirmed the fact that they had not mastered the art of parliamentary debate. Nor did they succeed in keeping public attention on the government's "misguided" policies. Instead, Reformers quickly reverted to form and engaged in the infamous "Flag Flap" debate with the Bloc almost immediately.

Another setback for the party — and a more serious one — was its admission that its emphasis on debt reduction in the 1997 platform had been an abysmal failure. Instead, like Mike Harris in Ontario, Preston Manning soon decided that tax cuts, rather than debt reduction, were an essential element of the neo-conservative appeal to the middle class.

Meanwhile, Manning's opportunistic call for a review of judicial appointments to the Supreme Court, after a series of unpopular Court decisions attracted public attention, sparked a heated debate on the subject of judicial activism, but did little to enhance the party's image. Like the earlier attempt by Jon Havelock in Alberta, Manning's comments produced a furious reply from the judges themselves. This included a lengthy lecture from Chief Justice Antonio Lamer on the importance of judicial independence, and speculation on his part as to whether the Court might need to explain its decisions in more detail in the future, given the low level of public knowledge of the complex issues involved and what Lamer termed "inadequate reporting of decisions."

By the summer of 1998, Preston Manning and everyone else knew Reform had hit the wall in terms of the party's growth potential. Any further expansion could only come, Manning believed, from a concerted effort to attract Conservative voters to join with Reform in an attempt to defeat the Liberals. And so, at the Reform Convention in London, Ontario, in May, Preston Manning did the unthinkable. He admitted defeat by calling for a conference on a United Alternative, designed to bring together "Blue" Tories and Reformers for the winning combination. In making this call, Manning acknowledged that his own leadership would be laid on the line, as would the fate of the original Reformers, all of whom would risk being swamped by waves of Conservatives flocking to join the "Unite the Right" movement.

9

Ignorant Gladiators
and Phony Populists

War Is Peace
Freedom Is Slavery
Ignorance Is Strength
— George Orwell, *1984*

My first thought was, "I wonder what I'll do tomorrow?,"
because that sounds pretty easy. [But] the more you get into it
the more you find that these issues are very complex ...
— Ontario cabinet minister Al Leach

You know, the party takes a stand on these things for the election and it's sincere, but sometimes when you get down here
you find out there's a reason why things are done a certain way
— Reform MP Chuck Strahl

May 1998. A hot afternoon in London, Ontario. Delegates to the
Reform national convention have been debating proposed amendments
to their party's constitution for hours. The TV cameras focus on the
closed curtains at the front of the hall, but nothing happens. Plenary

chair Chuck Strahl, the party's parliamentary Whip, is having no luck whipping the delegates into line. He needs their consent to alter the original agenda and stage a "Ceremonial Welcome" for Preston Manning, his wife, Sandra, and several other founding members of the party, all of whom are already gathered behind the curtains and waiting to walk on. He doesn't get it.

The delegates refuse to go along, evidently unconcerned about providing interesting coverage for the nationally televised event. Instead, they insist on finishing their deliberations and having a recorded vote, a process which takes another full hour. Manning and the others are left to cool their heels backstage while the television audience is left to hear more deathless prose on the subject of party organization. "Isn't democracy fun?" a beleaguered Strahl muses, trying with limited success to make light of the latest contretemps befalling his party in what was to have been its finest hour.

As the *Globe and Mail's* parliamentary correspondent, Ed Greenspon, characterized the event, grassroots discontent was the "soupe du jour" at the party's gathering. The amendments being debated most hotly were ones originating with the party hierarchy, calling for reduced provincial membership on the executive — a move that most of the grassroots rejected as an unvarnished power grab by Manning and his closest advisers. Never had the split between the grassroots membership and the party elites, including the caucus, been greater or more obvious. The revelation only two days earlier that an agreement had been reached between Reform and the Liberal government on the MPs' pension plan did nothing to soften the mood of the delegates or the MPs. House Leader Randy White, who negotiated the deal for Reform, responded to one reporter's questions about his personal plans for the pension by snapping, "That's private and none of your concern."

This was an amazing statement from one of the leading lights in a party that built its reputation — and its electoral base — on its populist image. It added a jarring note to the proceedings, contrasting badly with the leader's earlier assurance that Reform was a truly democratic party whose policies came from the grassroots up. "You can't climb a tree from the top down," Manning declared. Apparently determined to ensure his message was understood, or simply unable to stop himself, he went on to offer several more homilies worthy of Garrison Keillor. "You can't build a house by starting with the roof," he opined, before switching metaphors yet again and concluding, "You can't organize an expedition to Mount Everest with a summit conference at the top."

By now the audience, most of whom were unlikely to consider a trip outside of North America, never mind to the Himalayas, appeared more confused than reassured. Why was the leader harping on the obvious? The confusion turned to anxious looks and open disagreement as Manning got down to the real agenda, which had nothing to do with the grassroots and everything to do with his own ambition. Undeterred by the looks, he forged ahead with bold new talk of a "United Alternative." He proposed the party open itself up to members of the Conservative party and other like-minded individuals in order to take power. As a concession to the doubters, he also assured delegates he would not alter the party's positions "one iota" to attract the hordes of new recruits he was anticipating. How these two positions were to be reconciled remained unclear.

Although the delegates eventually endorsed Manning's plan to test the waters on the "United Alternative," many were heard to mumble loudly about their misgivings. Typical delegate Ted Chapman of Wild Rose, Alberta, summed up the true feelings of many who reluctantly went along with the idea when he said, "Let's just be ourselves. We're Reformers. That's it." Their resistance was all the more striking since the delegates had essentially been hand-picked by the executive, as Reform MPs Jim Hart and Ted White made clear only two months later when they attacked the leader *in absentia*.

The populist symbolism continued at the convention as Manning's wife, Sandra, offered thanks to all the volunteers in the party, handing out awards to various grassroots members for their hard work. "Where are you, Leroy? Will Leroy Brown please stand up?" she gushed at one point. The viewers' ability to take the event seriously was further compromised by suggestions from the party's chief advertising official, Bryan Thomas, for new ways to raise badly needed funds. Pointing to declining revenues and membership, Thomas actually suggested combining the sale of party memberships with Amway products, subscriptions to *Alberta Report* and discounts at various hotels.

The delegates, for their part, seemed to find these proposals perfectly reasonable. A sea of white faces with grey-haired men, fewer women and the occasional youth delegate, they looked more like a congregation at a revival meeting than delegates to the annual convention of a political party. Of course, this was understandable, since many of them actually had strong ties with fundamentalist religious groups. So much so that they insisted on referring to their national convention as a Reform "assembly" in deference to their evangelical roots.

The highlight of the otherwise boring convention for many television viewers came at the opening session, when Reform MP Deborah Grey roared into the convention centre astride a $23,000 Honda motorcycle. For the delegates, however, the highlight of the event was neither Grey's flashy entrance nor the leader's dry and lengthy discourse on unifying the right. It was the barn-burning address delivered by their keynote speaker, Alberta treasurer Stockwell Day, who confirmed his reputation as a hard-line fundamentalist.

Reform's 1998 convention was a microcosm of all that is typical and unsettling about the neo-conservative movement in Canada. It showcased the extreme right-wing views of the membership and the party's superficially populist approach. It reinforced the perception that the radical right is the domain of white middle-aged men and seniors. It underlined the strong religious influence on many of their policies. It also highlighted the lack of knowledge and limited experience of the membership — their ignorance of policy issues and the parliamentary process, and their determination not to let inconvenient facts get in the way of their opinions.

Even some Reform MPs appeared frustrated by their inability to explain the nuances of complex policy issues to the membership without being attacked as elitist, or as selling out and straying from the party's hard line. At the same time the heated debate over the proposed changes to the make-up of the party's executive — changes which several members were quick to point out had not even gone through the appropriate channels before being put to the delegates at the convention as amendments — clearly confirmed the reality of a top-down, authoritarian style of leadership, despite Manning's opening remarks.

The London meeting also brought into the open another interesting phenomenon — namely, the many links among the various elements of the neo-conservative movement in Canada today. Although few delegates seemed surprised, many casual observers of Canadian politics were more than a little perplexed to see Stockwell Day, a provincial Conservative, delivering the keynote address to federal Reformers.

Yet the public had no real excuse for being taken by surprise. Stockwell Day's speech was one of the more public displays of the ties binding Canada's neo-cons, but it was hardly the first. In fact, the love-in at the Reform convention was only one of the many examples of the close relationship among Canadian neo-conservatives. As previous chapters have shown, their links with one another — and with their counterparts in the United States and elsewhere — are extensive and important. They were evident soon after Reform's 1993 election sweep in Western Canada, when Preston Manning was interviewed in Washington paying homage to Newt Gingrich. They surfaced again the following year, when Mike Harris visited Gingrich's protégé, Republican governor Christine Whitman of New Jersey, for pointers on his "Common Sense" election campaign. Since his victory in 1995 it has become more obvious with every premiers' conference that Harris and Alberta's Ralph Klein have formed a mutual-admiration society. In November 1997, fresh from an election win that elevated his party to the rank of Official Opposition, Preston Manning even made a pilgrimage to London to visit the Baroness Thatcher, now sitting with the elites in the House of Lords.

When former B.C. premier Bill Vander Zalm, a long-time Socred, jumped on the bandwagon in early 1998, the true extent of the cross-partisan connections was plainly visible, even for those Canadians who previously paid little attention to the radical right. For many it was a startling development, suggesting the neo-conservative agenda was more deeply entrenched — at least in Western Canada — than had been previously recognized. With "the Zalm" as president of the B.C. Reform Party, some Alberta Conservatives actually began speaking openly about the desirability of a Reform victory in the next provincial election. As for the federal Conservatives, the potential for a strong provincial showing by Reform was an ominous development for a party that was pinning its hopes for a national revival on the West.

Perhaps one of the most dramatic symbols of the close ties among Canadian neo-conservatives was Stockwell Day's subsequent announcement in the fall of 1998 that he and some other "well-known" Conservatives had agreed to work closely with Preston Manning's designated Reform point men to organize a "United Alternative" convention. Day's definition of the term "well-known" was debatable. Apart from former Mulroney adviser Peter White (a close friend of newspaper baron Conrad Black's), the list of those lined up to play along with Reform's unconventional plan contained almost no federal Tories and few traditional Conservatives of note. Instead, it was a Who's Who of the new right-wing Tory elite from Alberta and Ontario. Ralph Klein's close friend and former adviser, Rod Love, and Ontario Conservative cabinet minister Tony Clement, one of Mike Harris's former "whiz kids," figured prominently among the organizers.

Veteran Conservative strategist Dalton Camp was not alone in his scathing criticism of the venture, but he was among the most direct. In a column in the *Toronto Star* he even went so far as to say, "There could be a worse catastrophe than another Liberal government"— the very thing members of the "United Alternative" group had expressly stated they were out to prevent. Camp argued that the participation of Conservatives in the unity plan would be such a catastrophe. "The sellout of a national party in order to improve the fortunes of Preston Manning would be a Canadian calamity and a rebuke to history," he thundered. He also decried the group's argument that Reform principles must be preserved, declaring "most Tories have principles too." For Camp, the whole unification idea was not only self-serving, but ludicrous, particularly since the conservatism of Stockwell Day "is viewed by most Tories as embedded in the lunatic fringe."

To almost no one's surprise, neither Joe Clark nor Hugh Segal nor any other well-known Tory veterans were prepared to participate in the event. They made their views crystal clear during the federal leadership campaign, leaving the only pro-Reform candidate, Manitoba minister Brian Pallister, in the dust. Pallister's rejection by the party membership proved once again how negatively the Harris and Klein Conservatives are perceived by their own traditional namesakes. Indeed, Canada's neo-conservatives are more heartily detested by progressive Conservatives than by members of the other mainstream parties, precisely because they constitute a personal as well as political affront.

One federal party organizer involved in the leadership race fumed that Harris and Klein "are not really Conservatives at all." By using the party label, he argued, "they have attracted voters who would never have supported the Reform party. People thought they were voting for the same mainstream political party they supported in the past ... and instead they have elected Reform governments in sheep's clothing."

Ralph Klein's subsequent decision to be a keynote speaker at the "Unite the Right" event did nothing to enhance his popularity with traditional Conservatives, nor did his comment that the federal Tories were on "life support." The federal party had not yet concluded its leadership struggle with the coronation of former prime minister Joe Clark when the pressure from the Far Right began. In an open letter to Clark in the *Calgary Herald* on September 29, 1998, Rod Love told the former prime minister he would need to reconsider his categorical refusal to participate and "adapt or perish." Former Reform MP Stephen Harper echoed Love's views in an opinion piece for Conrad Black's new *National Post* on October 28. Pointing out that Clark and Segal — traditional Red Tories — took more than 70 per cent of the vote in the first round of the leadership (suggesting most Conservatives agreed with the progressive Red Tory approach), Harper perversely argued Clark would need to rethink his refusal to participate in Reform's initiative because, "with Ralph Klein's decision to support the UA the current trickle [of Blue Tories to the UA] could become a torrent."

Harper also went on to describe a Reform/Conservative alliance as the only "real hope" of defeating the Liberal party for a generation. This view was reiterated by Ontario Solicitor General Bob Runciman, one of the most right-wing members of Mike Harris's cabinet. In an interview with the *Ottawa Citizen* on October 28, Runciman told reporters he was "distressed" by Clark's "refusal to recognize the need to join Conservative forces if the Liberals are ever to be defeated." As for Runciman's boss, Mike Harris, the premier "repeated his moral support for the idea of forging a single conservative alternative" but indicated he was "too busy" to get involved himself. His equivocal statement was nevertheless taken by many to mean that he was giving his ministers *carte blanche* to participate, and Runciman himself indicated he expected several of his colleagues to follow his lead.

In the end, the February 1999 meeting resolved nothing. It attracted more than 1,200 delegates, who listened to speeches by Ralph Klein and Preston Manning before voting to form a new federal political party. With Tory Joe Clark conspicuously absent, and Preston Manning declaring he would be a candidate for the leadership of the new party, should federal Reformers approve the merger, it appeared that the "fight for the right" had just begun.

Dangerous Liaisons

The alliances among Canada's neo-conservatives are unusual in several ways. To begin with, they breach the convention of strong partisan distinctions that has been prevalent in Canadian politics. With three major parties representing the three basic political philosophies, Canadians have long been accustomed to having a meaningful choice. Unlike the Americans with their two-party brokerage politics, Canadians have also expected their political parties to take different stands on issues and stick with them. The parliamentary system itself has also encouraged an adversarial approach to politics along party lines. Meanwhile, the concept of coalitions has been rejected out of hand, except in emergencies such as the war effort. NDP leader Ed Broadbent was reminded of this when he mused about the possibility of a Liberal–NDP alliance to defeat the Mulroney Conservatives during the 1988 election campaign and saw his party's support plummet. The Ontario NDP learned the same hard lesson when they were co-opted by David Peterson after the 1985 provincial election dealt him a minority government.

As North Dakota senator and Canadian–U.S. relations expert David Nething observed in 1987, traditionally "Canadian politics is 'hardball' all the way. There does not appear to be any blurring of political differences, unlike in our country ..." Canadians also have expected their politicians to stick with one political party. Examples of individual politicians switching allegiance and still receiving the support of their constituents are few and far between. Instead, the field is strewn with the prostrate bodies of formerly popular legislators unable to carry their supporters with them to the enemy camp. In this context the spectacle of Conservative and Social Credit politicians consorting with Reformers is one that appears to fly in the face of tradition. This pattern may also help to explain the preference of the neo-conservatives for taking over existing parties and, conversely, the much greater difficulty of the newly created Reform Party in attracting votes nationally.

Nething also was struck by the fact that regional concerns have traditionally been the one factor important enough to overcome these strong partisan attachments. Reporting on his years as head of the American delegation for the Canada–U.S.A. Legislative Project, the senator noted, "Canadian legislators inevitably put forward and vigorously defend their views on the basis of the geographic region they represent." Indeed. Who could fail to recall the rancorous debates between Liberal premier Ross Thatcher in Saskatchewan and his party's counterparts running the show in Ottawa? Or the support Conservatives Bill Davis of Ontario and Richard Hatfield of New Brunswick gave to a federal Liberal constitutional initiative because they felt it benefited their provinces' large linguistic minorities? Who can forget the battles between Ontario and Alberta over energy prices and environmental and transportation issues when both had Conservative governments? Or the long-standing tendency of the Ontario government to support the federal administration regardless of the political party in power, believing the interests of Canada's largest province were synonymous with those of the central government?

Seen in this light, the new reality of the premiers of Ontario and Alberta presenting a united front against Ottawa, and provincial Conservatives consorting with an upstart federal fringe party instead of their own federal counterparts, is standing the country's conventional political wisdom on its head. As in Britain and the United States, the promotion of neo-conservative values in Canada has clearly resulted in a reconfiguration of the broader political scene and made for some very strange bedfellows.

Critics of alliances among Canada's neo-conservatives are wise to preach caution. The new politicians of the Far Right — regardless of party name or regional base — promote values foreign to the traditional Canadian political culture. As in Britain and the United States, they break the long-standing liberal consensus about the role of the state and the importance of social integration. They are single-minded and committed to dismantling the infrastructure of the state and withdrawing government entirely from the marketplace. As legislators, they criticize, undermine and ignore fundamental tenets of parliamentary democracy, the rule of law and the Canadian Constitution. Whether it is Preston Manning decrying House of Commons procedures or the composition of parliamentary committees, Stockwell Day rejecting the separation of church and state, or Ralph Klein's Justice minister, Jon Havelock, advocating a hands-on approach to the judiciary and dismissing use of the Charter's notwithstanding clause as a minor detail, Canada's neo-conservatives are universally impatient and authoritarian. Simply put, the very politicians who revel in denouncing the "undemocratic" practices of mainstream political parties have proven time and time again they are the ones who do not understand the term.

They also share a fascination with all things American. This, too, breaks with tradition, since most Canadians have traditionally rejected American political practices as a matter of course, jealously guarding their national self-image as different from and superior to that of the United States. In *The Big Picture*, their 1990 analysis of Canadian political culture, former Conservative pollster Allan Gregg and journalist Michael Posner wrote, "What made Canadians distinct was that we weren't Americans — and we were proud of it." From the comments of the current premier of Ontario, who has praised policies in New Jersey and Michigan while describing the neighbouring province of Quebec as "our major trading partner," to those of the Leader of the Official Opposition, who has urged the federal government to adopt American-style procedures for confirming appointments, recalling legislators and impeaching the prime minister, the neo-conservatives often appear to have more in common with their Republican counterparts in the United States than with their fellow Canadians.

Ideology was certainly the starting point in uniting Canada's far-right crusaders in common cause. The neo-conservatives' words and actions are almost identical because they are grounded in a common political philosophy. Regardless of party labels, the underlying values and beliefs of these apostles of the radical right are the same — so much so that many of their public speeches are virtually interchangeable. Few Canadians realize it was Preston Manning's 1991 statement "We believe in the common sense of the common people" that Mike Harris picked up and used so successfully in his "Common Sense Revolution" of 1995. Or that it was Newt Gingrich in the Republicans' 1994 *Contract with America* who first identified the tax cut/family values themes used by the Reform Party in their 1996 pre-election platform, declaring "After forty years of putting government first, [we] will put families first ... Our plan is designed to deliver relief to taxpayers from the heavy burden of government, by letting families keep more of their hard-earned dollars to pursue their own individual goals ..." Whether they came to their views late in their political career, like Ralph Klein, or held these radical opinions from the beginning, like Manning and Harris, there is little doubt they are all true believers.

Important as these shared views are, however, they would not normally have been sufficient to transcend the great divides of partisan politics and geography. As earlier chapters have shown, the neo-cons have much more in common than their zealous commitment to right-wing ideology. First and foremost, they are self-proclaimed populists, deriving their political support from carefully cultivated anti-establishment rhetoric. Canadian neo-conservatives at all levels have adopted an exaggerated, folksy egalitarianism to promote their agenda — one that otherwise would have been viewed by many voters as unacceptably elitist. Whether they are busy defending the West against Ottawa and Bay Street, or small-town Ontario against Queen's Park, the New Right in Canada are all masters at portraying themselves as the little guy battling the establishment Goliath. And they recognize this quality in each other. Mike Harris and Ralph Klein are soul mates, having little in common with predecessors like Lougheed or Davis, or some of their more traditional current counterparts, such as lawyer Pat Binns of P.E.I. and Gary Filmon in Manitoba.

Even after coming to power, these self-styled populists have continued to cultivate their image as political outsiders, following the example set by Newt Gingrich. And with good reason. Few political veterans would have believed that a congressman with sixteen years in Washington under his belt could lead the Republicans to their 1994 landslide by portraying them as the new broom that would sweep the Capital clean. More than six years after their arrival in Ottawa, most Reform MPs continue to talk about "professional politicians" and "mainstream parties" as if they were a breed apart. Despite their status as the Official Opposition, they refuse to admit they are now part of the political establishment. This denial is understandable, since their worst fear is losing many of their original supporters by appearing to sell out to the elites. Having accepted everything from the leader's official residence at Stornoway to the MPs' pension plans they once castigated so passionately, the danger is clear and present. It is also of their own making, as the stormy Reform caucus retreat in Banff in September 1998 demonstrated.

Mike Harris and Ralph Klein have faced an even greater challenge to their anti-establishment credentials. Unlike Preston Manning, they have actually formed a government. Nevertheless, they have persevered manfully to overcome this handicap, managing with considerable success to portray themselves as some sort of temporary caretakers, intent on dismantling the very machinery of government they control. As his current term enters the home stretch, Harris has already begun to prepare the groundwork for the next election. He has spoken often in recent interviews about the need for another term of office to "finish the job" of "cleaning up the mess" and eliminating big government once and for all, just as Ralph Klein did in Alberta before his landslide re-election in 1997. Like Ronald Reagan, both men are still presenting themselves as citizen activists reluctantly doing their political duty. To this end they frequently stress their desire to leave politics as soon as their work is done, returning happily to the real world.

The New Face of the New Right

What makes the neo-conservative politicians so different? It is not just their willingness to form alliances across party lines, to ignore certain basic principles of parliamentary democracy, or to project a populist image. Many of them also lack the traditional skills and training common to Canadian politicians. Regrettably, their limited range of background and life experience makes them less sensitive to differences and less tolerant of other points of view.

The New Right's lack of diversity is startling. Canada's neo-conservatives are a walking advertisement for Grey Power, and many of the politicians of the radical right are older than their counterparts in mainstream political parties. While Canadian legislators have been getting younger

387

with every election for the past two decades, these right-wing newcomers have reversed the trend, with many of them entering the political arena much later in life. As well, while the other parties reflect the realities of a culturally diverse society, and one in which more and more women are participating in political life every day, the neo-conservatives are still overwhelmingly represented by white males in suits.

Canadian neo-conservatives may not have a "Whites Only" sign posted over the doorways of their caucus rooms, but they might as well. Despite their growing sensitivity to criticism which they would earlier have ignored, and some half-hearted efforts to remedy the situation by recruiting more minority members, there have been few takers. Reform's transparent efforts to describe itself as more culturally diverse than its mainstream opponents have fallen on disbelieving ears. Token evidence of cultural diversity — Reform MP Rahim Jaffer or Ontario Conservative cabinet minister Dave Tsubouchi, for example — cannot disguise the fact that their party's exclusionary policies are simply not attractive to most members of minority groups.

The reason is patently obvious, as one critic pointed out in response to Mike Harris's call in October 1998 for ridings to recruit more women and visible-minority candidates for his party in the next election. Even if one were to accept the argument that few adherents of the Far Right are actually racists, their anti-immigration, anti-multiculturalism and anti-aboriginal policies are bound to have a chilling effect on members of ethnocultural communities. As federal Conservative candidate Hugh Segal said when announcing he was withdrawing from the leadership race, "We have to build a coalition that has a place for ... minorities and women and young people. It has to be a coalition that includes people of colour and new Canadians, and it has to be a coalition in which people who aren't well off feel comfortable. And I want to be as clear as I can. Any coalition centred around Preston Manning cannot meet any of these goals."

A similar gulf exists between the New Right and other political parties on the issue of gender. The New Right is definitely a boys' club. Although politics in Canada has traditionally been a male preserve, the participation of women at all levels had been increasing, albeit slowly, during the past two decades. This record, although not overly impressive in comparison with the progress made by women in some other Western democracies, seems much more laudatory in hindsight. In 1995 the Harris cabinet contained only two women, a number which has not increased despite two cabinet shuffles. The Klein government has a similar male bias, with only three female cabinet ministers out of nineteen, despite the fact that women make up nearly one-third of his caucus.

As for the Reform Party, the pictures of male-dominated party gatherings tell the tale. At the elected level, the number of women in the Official Opposition's caucus actually declined, from 7 in 1993 to 4 in 1997. Indeed, with the notable exception of the highly visible Deborah Gray and the deferential Diane Ablonczy (whose role has been to implement the Leader's instructions to the letter, not to provide counsel), women have played a minor — almost invisible — role as Reform MPs and Opposition critics. As former MP Jan Brown concluded, there was a place for women in the Reform caucus and it was at the back of the bus. They were to be seen in Question Period and not heard offering advice in caucus. The revelations of Sandra Manning's quaint advice to the spouses of new Reform MPs only served to underline this notion of women Reformers as second-class members.

There are also a number of less obvious but equally significant differences between the neo-conservatives and their traditional counterparts. Although rural communities are in decline and the vast majority of the population lives in urban areas, the New Right's political elites come from predominantly rural roots. Thatcher and Reagan counted on rural support for their majorities, as Newt Gingrich did in 1994. Just as rural Alberta delivered key votes for Ralph Klein and rural Ontario came through for Mike Harris, so Reform has scored its strongest victories in the rural areas of Alberta and B.C. Vancouver and Edmonton, by contrast, remain largely out of its grasp, as does the urban heartland of Canada. Given this background, of course, the issues raised by neo-conservative legislators are often ones that fail to resonate with urban populations, or with their more traditional urban-based liberal politicians. Not surprisingly, many observers have commented that neo-conservatism in some respects can be seen as a form of "rural revenge" on city dwellers.

In an increasingly secular society, another fundamental difference is the fact that neo-conservatives are also likely to be members of fundamentalist religious groups. Unlike traditional legislators, who come from main-stream religious backgrounds (Anglican and Catholic being the most common), the neo-conservatives have a striking number of members belonging to evangelical and other fundamentalist sects. The American phenomenon of the Moral Majority is only the most visible and best organized of these groups which, in Canada, are located predominantly in the West, and are closely linked with the populist protest tradition of Alberta and the B.C. Bible Belt. With most Canadians having accepted the separation of church and state long ago, the image of Reformers insisting on time for prayer in the House of Commons and Alberta's attorney general putting his religious beliefs on the public agenda are both unusual and unsettling. Preston Manning's own religious back-ground has played a major role in the development of his political views as well as the positions of the Reform Party. For Ralph Klein and Mike Harris, neither of whom are moral conservatives themselves, the pres-ence of such a large contingent of the religious right within their caucuses has been both inconvenient and occasionally problematic, as the gay-rights issue in Alberta demonstrated. In short, although the neo-conservatives frequently claim to represent the "silent majority," they themselves appear to be in the minority.

A comparison with elected members in other political parties, and with previous generations of Canadian legislators, reveals other equally disturb-ing trends. The typical neo-conservative politician is less well-educated and less likely to have professional credentials or managerial experience. At a time when the vast majority of Canada's federal legislators possess at least one postsecondary degree, for example, more than two-thirds of Reformers have only a high-school education. Unlike most legislators, whose profes-sional qualifications have been *increasing* along with their educational levels over the past several decades, neo-conservative politicians are more likely to be small business people or tradespeople. Canada is not a nation of shop-keepers, but our Far Right certainly is.

The low level of educational attainment of the neo-conservatives has proven especially problematic. One result of this decrease in formal train-ing among the New Right legislators is that they are placed in a difficult position when evaluating the recommendations of their own bureau-crats, or the testimony of expert witnesses before legislative committees.

Ralph Klein recognized this drawback himself early on in his career in provincial politics. Asked by reporters what he thought his biggest challenge in Edmonton would be, he immediately referred to his lack of formal training and replied quite candidly, "Certainly, my lack of business experience, my inability to properly read financial statements." Others, such as B.C. Reform leader Bill Vander Zalm, have seemed less aware of their limitations. Actively attacking the Nisga'a land claim agreement despite his admittedly scanty knowledge of the details, the former premier blamed "too much Indian drumming as one reason why non-native politicians sometimes get befuddled in their dealings with native leaders," according to a *Globe and Mail* report on November 30, 1998.

Another apparent consequence of the neo-cons' lack of formal education has been a disturbing tendency on the part of many to encourage a negative attitude towards professionalism. This *anti-intellectualism* on occasion borders on the fanatical. Speeches by some of Klein's and Harris's ministers, to say nothing of Reform MPs, regularly dismiss the findings of "ivory-tower academics," "so-called experts" and "government bureaucrats." Political scientists David Taras and Allan Tupper conclude that such an approach "represents the triumph of the world of street smarts and hard knocks over the world of books and abstractions." Sheryl McInnes of Alberta's Common Front has suggested the practical consequences of this attitude are that "people think they don't need to be educated to know what's going on. We see this in the government's idea that nurses don't need a degree, that they only need six weeks in a hospital ward ..."

There are similar consequences to the neo-conservatives' overwhelming background in small business. Who could be surprised by their tendency to believe that running a government is like running a business? Or wonder why they are so receptive to arguments against unions, with whom they have little or no experience, and hostile to programs such as affirmative action, about which their only experience as a small business is likely to be both anecdotal and negative?

The Politics of Anger and Resentment

Given the zeal with which they pursue their new career, a surprising number of New Right politicians also have little or no previous involvement in political activities, including membership in a political party. In addition, they are less likely than their mainstream counterparts to have run for or held office in *any* other type of organization before entering politics. Some admit they rarely voted before their decision to enter the political arena. In short, they are "outsiders" whose previous attachment to the political process was marginal at best.

What made them change their minds? Unlike Canada's mainstream politicians, a large majority of Canada's neo-conservatives were motivated to enter the political arena by a single issue. For many economic conservatives, it was one of the unpopular initiatives of the Mulroney government that proved to be the straw that broke the camel's back. The failure of the federal Conservatives to reduce the deficit after two terms in office, and their appalling record on patronage and corruption after having created the issue during the 1988 election, were key factors in mobilizing many of the disaffected. For many in Western Canada, the Charlottetown Accord was the final blow. For others, especially Albertans, it was the introduction of the GST that rankled most.

For social and moral conservatives, by contrast, the one big issue prompting them to enter the fray was resentment over the rapid pace of social change and the increasingly lax attitudes of society, which they believed were destroying the traditional family and the community. Prominent among their concerns were specific cases related to affirmative action, gay rights, pornography, abortion, welfare and victims' rights issues.

These individuals had previously been non-partisan as well as non-political. So were their original efforts to stem the tide of permissiveness. Since the objective was to bring about change quickly, mainstream parties were the logical targets. The anti-abortion movement, for example, began by indiscriminately hijacking Liberal and Conservative nominations in safe ridings. They did not distinguish between parties, but between winners and losers. Local activists targeted whichever party was likely to win in a given riding. Their efforts were often successful, but they failed to achieve their real objective, and eventually concluded that another strategy was necessary.

The defeat of star Liberal candidate Patrick Johnson of Toronto in 1988 by a pro-life coalition supporting Tom Wappel was a classic example of this failed strategy. Wappel, who went on to win the riding for the

Liberals and then contested the party leadership in 1990, was unable to make any impact as an individual MP, even though he was on the Government side. Viewed as an illegitimate interloper by long-time Liberals, he was deliberately left to languish on the backbenches after the party regained power in 1993, proving conclusively to the pro-life movement that its strategy of attempting to work within existing parties was futile. Having decided to take another tack, they joined the neo-conservative movement and became among its most aggressive supporters.

With the Liberals' subsequent mishandling of both the gun-control legislation and the Alberta-based campaign to repeal section 745 of the Criminal Code (the so-called faint hope clause, which provided those serving life sentences with the possibility of applying for parole, although it was rarely granted), even more of these moral conservatives joined the Reform bandwagon and/or voted for their provincial Tory counterparts. Across Western Canada the combination of fear and fury raised by Reform's disinformation campaigns, and Liberal incompetence on the gun-control and parole files, soon had devastating consequences for the governing party. In the 1997 election, gun control was virtually the only important issue on the agenda in ridings across Saskatchewan. Opponents succeeded in ousting all but one of the sitting Liberal MPs. In British Columbia, meanwhile, the vigorous anti-745 campaign turned particularly nasty, and was one of the determining factors in the failure of the Liberals to make any headway in that province.

It is important to note that these reasons for citizens becoming politically active are not typical. Traditionally, Canadian legislators at both the provincial and the federal level have cited quite different motives for entering politics. While "the desire to make a difference" is the most common reason cited, it is difficult to separate from other responses such as "to serve my country" and "to give something back" to the community or society. They rarely have a specific agenda item, and they rarely indicate a desire to replace someone else, or reverse a particular policy decision, as an important factor in their decision. Put simply, the most typical responses of elected representatives about their reasons for becoming involved in politics and running for public office are positive, not negative.

Not surprisingly, many of the New Right's leadership and their supporters have close links with single-issue interest groups. In several cases the leadership of single-issue groups have not only supported neo-conservative parties, but joined them as gladiators themselves. The complex version of musical chairs played by Reform MPs, the National Citizens' Coalition and the Canadian Taxpayers' Federation is just one example of this intimate and ongoing relationship, as the next chapter demonstrates in detail. The close connection of the moral conservatives with special-interest groups such as the pro-life and anti–gun control organizations is equally revealing, the election of prominent victims' rights spokespersons under the Reform and Harris banners being only one visible symbol of these symbiotic relationships. In the end, the distinction between interest groups and political parties appears to have been blurred by the neo-conservatives, ironically the very politicians who argue so vehemently against any government policies or programs to benefit "special interests."

One could easily ask whether the backgrounds of politicians make any difference. The neo-conservatives automatically dismiss such concerns as hopelessly elitist. What really matters, they argue, is how politicians do their job.

This view is partly true but, as usual with the radical right, overly simplistic. With Western democracies facing critical challenges from economic globalization, environmental degradation, international migration and cultural tribalism, the ability to handle complex issues is arguably more critical now than ever before. Yet the neo-conservatives are deliberately replacing competence with intuition, and experience with amateur enthusiasm. In the United States, George Bush and William Buckley have been upstaged by the likes of Rush Limbaugh, Pat Buchanan and, until recently, Newt Gingrich. In Canada, the premiers of two of Canada's most important provinces have only a high-school diploma. Some of their ministers, and several Reform MPs, have even less formal education. Ignorance, as George Orwell's hapless hero Winston Smith discovered, does not equal strength. Politicians operating from a base of ignorance are at a distinct disadvantage, and so are the citizens they represent.

This raises the question of how the neo-conservative newcomers managed to be chosen as candidates, never mind win elections. In the not-too-distant past, few of them would have considered running for public office, and fewer still would have been successful. As we have seen, their surprising success has resulted partly from Canadians' widespread desire to reject the "establishment" in difficult times. It has also been the inevitable consequence of the marked decline in respect for elected representatives. Personal attacks, vitriolic press coverage and intrusive demands on the privacy and personal finances of politicians have driven many outstanding potential candidates from the field, leaving it wide open for the less qualified and the uninformed to occupy.

Ignorant Gladiators

American political scientist Lester Milbrath began to address the issue of who participates in politics, and why, in the late 1960s, when voter participation in that country began to decline dramatically. Worried about the effect this lack of participation in the political process might have on government policies, he began to examine the levels of citizen activity elsewhere. He divided these activities into three broad categories — a hierarchy of participation, moving from the least to the most involved. Then he measured political behaviour in other Western democracies in terms of these categories. His study revealed a similar pattern of citizen participation in all healthy democracies.

For example, Milbrath found that only a small percentage of the population — whom he termed the *apathetic* — were totally uninvolved in the political process. The vast majority of citizens were engaged in the political culture, at least to the extent that they voted and discussed political issues with friends and acquaintances. They became more involved on a particular issue if it affected them, and occasionally communicated with their elected representatives through petitions or letter-writing campaigns. This large segment of the population was described by Milbrath as *spectators*. Finally, he found that only a small group of individuals were normally very active in the political process — by joining a political party, holding office in the party or raising funds and working on election campaigns or, ultimately, running for public office.

These findings were not surprising since politics is, by its very nature, elitist. Only a tiny fraction of citizens normally has the time, inclination or ability to become engaged in the political arena on a full-time basis. Milbrath called these individuals — who essentially constitute the political elite of a country — *gladiators.*

For the most part, he found that individuals in the "apathetic" category were true outsiders, only marginally integrated economically or socially as well. For many, their alienation stemmed from a lack of education and/or employment. An added barrier often was posed by social, physical or mental problems. In the United States, race predictably played an important role in determining the composition of the apathetic group. Large numbers of black Americans, believing themselves powerless to change the system, rejected the electoral process as an instrument of white domination, just as Ronald Reagan's advisers hoped.

In contrast to apathetic citizens, both "spectators" and "gladiators" were generally well educated and successful. Although money played a role in determining the level of their participation — with the upper middle class and the wealthy more likely to participate intensively than the average middle-class individual — the factors which ultimately determined whether a citizen would remain in the spectator category or become a gladiator appeared to be individual interests, family influence and, most important, occupation, with professionals much more likely to become gladiators than those involved in business or the sciences. Since Milbrath's ground-breaking study, other political scientists have built on his initial analysis. In Canada, for example, Mishler, Kornberg and others have all examined the levels of participation of citizens and speculated on reasons for Canadian participation patterns.

For obvious reasons it is seen as desirable for democracies to have a large number of spectators, and very few apathetic citizens. Ideally, spectators would be well educated and well informed, in order for them to make wise political choices. No society has an ideal situation, but one in which a large number of citizens opted out of the system and failed to participate, or where the majority of spectators were uninformed, would likely encounter serious difficulties in maintaining a healthy level of citizen participation.

The best-case scenario would clearly be one in which there were highly qualified gladiators. While the ignorance of the apathetic is a social concern, it poses no political problem since they do not influence decision making. *Ignorant gladiators*, on the other hand, would constitute a political worst-case scenario.

Using these terms Canada has traditionally been described as a nation of spectators. Although the range of spectator activities has been rather low — being limited, for the most part, to voting — the percentage of spectators has always been fairly high. At roughly 75 per cent, the numbers of Canadians who regularly voted in federal elections, for example, far exceeded the American figures and those of several European democracies. By contrast, the apathetic were a small percentage of the population.

At the same time, the high levels of literacy and near-universal public communications systems meant that Canadian spectators were reasonably well informed. Even more important, our gladiators on the whole were very well prepared for public office. In a country with a high standard of living, universal access to education and a large middle class, these findings were, quite frankly, to be expected, but were nevertheless reassuring.

Recently, however, a number of disturbing trends have begun to emerge. The percentage of apathetic citizens is believed to have increased. Some have argued the level of awareness and participation rate of Canadian spectators are declining. For some Canadians, the emphasis has shifted away from political parties to single-issue interest groups, a phenomenon with significant consequences for participation in the political process. Most important is the decline in the qualifications of our gladiators. In the past ten years, with the emergence of Canadian neo-conservative politicians, the profile of our political elites has undergone an unexpected transformation. From a norm of well-educated and prepared professionals, there has been a striking increase in the number of outsiders with little formal training or other relevant preparation to take over the reins of power.

No one suggests there is only one career path or appropriate set of credentials for those who plan to run for public office. Life experience, as much as education, *could* give individuals the ability to manage change, accommodate different points of view, and accurately reflect the mainstream values and beliefs of the culture they represent. Unfortunately, few of the individuals attracted to the neo-conservative ideology have demonstrated these qualities. The greater the neo-conservative leadership's emphasis on moral and social conservatism, the more likely the supporters will be uncompromising in their views.

Once elected, an MP's ignorance of the issues and the political process could perhaps still be overcome with hard work and an open mind. Unfortunately an open mind is also something very few neo-conservatives appear to possess, as Jan Brown and Jim Silye learned to their dismay. The problem is made worse by the neo-conservatives' failure to recognize their own shortcomings. Indeed, as previous chapters have shown, their very ignorance of "the system" is seen by many of the New Right politicians as a virtue, not a failing. Those who suggest that a problem exists are accused of being elitists or, worse still, members of the "old guard" or the "tired old mainstream parties."

Many of the New Right's politicians are self-made men and proud of it. Unfortunately, they often assume their success in other endeavours will guarantee their success in politics. This is simply not the case, since entrepreneurial skills are rarely suited to the political process. It is certainly possible to succeed in business with few formal qualifications. Natural intelligence, a charming personality and shrewd people skills can overcome much in the private sector, as the rise of Matthew Barrett from bank teller to president of one of Canada's largest banks demonstrates. John Snobelen's grade-eleven education was no barrier to his becoming a millionaire running a waste-disposal business. But, just as a lack of appropriate formal training would prevent both of these men from becoming doctors, lawyers or other professionals — a situation few would question — their ignorance of parliamentary government and the policy process also puts them at a disadvantage in running a government and making important decisions on complex policy matters. This is not elitism, but reality.

The leadership of the New Right has been quick to portray their lack of preparation for public office as a positive quality. Their lack of exposure to the issues or the processes they are about to confront, they argue, will put them in a much better position to make the necessary changes. They will not be "captured" by the system, which they already know intuitively is flawed and in need of substantial reform. It was this very thinking that led Mike Harris to make such inappropriate cabinet appointments. Or, as Reform leader Preston Manning said when questioned by reporters about the glaring lack of qualifications and experience of his caucus in 1993, "Experience in what? Making a jackass of yourself in Question Period?"

Unfortunately the consequences of this limited world view have been serious and sweeping. One Darrel Stinson or Al Palladini in the legislature may not be a problem, but a cabinet or caucus full of such politicians is another matter. Despite his supporter's claim that "Darrel will do us just fine," the facts suggest otherwise. The dumbing-down of politics in Canada has had profound implications for national and provincial policy making, intergovernmental relations, and even the quality of constituency representation.

The anti-intellectualism of so many of the New Right's membership and supporters has been amply demonstrated elsewhere, but bears repeating, since the implications for politics are so significant. When even someone like Diane Ablonczy, a Reform MP with a university degree and professional training, says she relies more on the impressions of her constituents than on the scientific findings of experts or data from Statistics Canada, the policy-making process is in serious difficulty. If credentials and expertise are rejected by the New Right as the basis for decision making and replaced with "common sense," rational arguments will be powerless to oppose their agenda.

The importance of their rigidity cannot be overestimated. It is this narrowness that leads them to propose simplistic solutions at a time when political issues are becoming more and more complex. Once they are in power, this inclination to disregard expert advice in favour of anecdotal evidence, coupled with their authoritarian approach, leads them to single-mindedly pursue their solutions even in the face of overwhelming evidence that these approaches will not work. Worse still, they often generalize from single events to develop sweepingly broad policies. As they are unable to think strategically, their solutions are invariably short-term and *ad hoc*, frequently leading to unanticipated consequences. The pattern of decision making by the Klein and Harris governments, as demonstrated in previous chapters, has been overwhelmingly one of "act in haste, repent at leisure," whether they are changing their formulae to close schools, cap property taxes or alter the rules for welfare benefits.

Equally unsettling is their obvious lack of understanding of many essential democratic principles. Many of the New Right's gladiators appear to believe a government's primary purpose is to satisfy the concerns of those who elected it, not some vague concept such as "the public good" or "the national interest." Policies are put forward in response to problems which their "client groups" have raised. In short, their agenda is determined in large measure by others. Although they describe this reactive approach as "open," "consultative" and "democratic," their consultation process does not include those who oppose them. This is why Mike Harris feels free to disregard the welfare of Toronto in favour of the 905-area-code suburbs that elected him; why Ralph Klein caters to Calgary, the oil patch and rural Alberta at the expense of Edmonton and the professional class; and why Preston Manning believes he can attack Quebec with impunity.

At the individual level, meanwhile, the New Right's populist view of elected MPs and MLAs as representatives rather than delegates has had profound implications for the relationship between citizens and legislators, and indirectly for the operation of the parliamentary system.

Of course, the existence of uninformed politicians is not new. There have always been isolated examples in virtually every political party, but they were generally few and far between. In the past these individuals remained on the backbenches, out of sight and far from power. Some proved to be excellent constituency representatives, content to deal with the demands of their riding and mastering issues of importance to their constituents. While their lack of formal training and experience may have meant they could not participate as fully in policy debates as could some of their colleagues, it did not prevent them from sharing mainstream values and beliefs.

All of this changed with the conscious decision of Conservative leader Brian Mulroney to actively recruit candidates from the Western protest movement and the Quebec separatist camp for his 1984 election campaign. The size of his election victory only heightened a political problem that would have inevitably surfaced at some point during his mandate. Not only were the views and beliefs of these new Tory MPs at odds with the more traditional Conservative veterans in the caucus, but their knowledge of the political system and the issues of the day was minimal. This led, among other things, to a constant search for ways to occupy the far-right Western contingent. From his early, ill-fated efforts to placate the newly emerging "family values" caucus with legislation on prostitution, pornography and abortion, to his later attempts to keep them in line through patronage and fiscal conservatism, Mulroney was always personally uncomfortable with the demands of his Western radicals. Yet from a political point of view he knew he must keep them under control, and could never afford to ignore them for long.

With the collapse of the Tories, the Western radical right was able to exert much greater influence within the new Reform Party which rose from the ashes. Ignorant gladiators of the New Right have not only become increasingly numerous, but they have taken control of the agenda in traditional political parties in two provinces as well as forming new ones at both the federal and the provincial level.

Yet this sea change in who chooses to run for public office has received remarkably little attention, despite the fact that it has far-reaching consequences for the public-policy agenda. Ignorance of the issues, and a naïve pursuit of a populist, anti-intellectual approach to governance, are not only disruptive, but dangerous. These new politicians have created issues where none existed, and seriously misled the public on issues of real importance. Quite apart from the damage caused by their political agenda, they have also damaged voters' faith in the democratic process. At the same time, their repeated attacks on the integrity of individual politicians and bureaucrats have produced a situation in which few individuals of note are willing to consider seeking public office, contributing to a further decline in the qualifications of legislators.

Many supporters of the New Right are basically disaffected. Their attachment to the political process has been minimal because their views were not reflected by any of the mainstream political parties. In hard times, when they were most likely to be receptive to the neo-conservative message, they were also attracted by the negative "attack ad" mentality of the politicians selling that message. Catering to voters' worst instincts at a time when they are most vulnerable, Canadian neo-conservatives, like their counterparts elsewhere, have not been above using inflammatory and misleading rhetoric.

As political scientists Trevor Harrison and Gordon Laxer describe so well in the Alberta context, Ralph Klein's government has called on the renowned generosity of Albertans, "convincing [them] that there is a major crisis, that everyone must sacrifice for the 'war effort'." Regrettably,

"Klein's message also appeals to the mean-spirited side ... In keeping with the lurch towards American right-wing politics, the focus is on the 'enemy within'. In a perversion of traditional populist rhetoric, public servants, welfare recipients, even university students and pensioners are now branded 'special interests'. It is their selfish demands, so the government claims, that have now produced the enormous crisis of provincial debt and deficits." With very few changes, of course, this analysis could easily applied to the Ontario of Mike Harris, where unions are the latest "enemy within," or to the New Canada of Preston Manning.

At the same time, it is difficult to ignore the fact that many neo-conservative concerns have struck a chord with a significant minority of the general public. As earlier chapters demonstrated, much of the neo-cons' success has been due to their ability to identify the crucial "hot buttons" in their respective electorates — something liberals in the traditional parties failed to do — and exploit them to great advantage. As a result, the implementation of their agenda has polarized their societies and provoked widespread alienation. The earlier amusement and disdain of their critics have turned to outrage and disbelief. This was not what most voters expected from the "good old boys" they elected, whose anti-elitism appealed to an electorate tired of arrogance and cronyism. For many, the way in which the neo-conservatives have handled the reins of power has been a greater shock to the system than their lack of preparation, or even the radical agenda they are promoting.

Authoritarian Populism

Had it not been for this lack of tolerance and compassion it might have been easy to dismiss our own "ignorant gladiators" of the New Right as mere buffoons enjoying their ten seconds of fame before fading from view. Certainly this was the attitude taken by many mainstream politicians and much of the media elite before, and even for some time after, their electoral successes. Columnist John Ibbitson's admission that few well-known Ontario journalists were taking Mike Harris seriously during the 1995 election campaign could easily have been echoed by most members of the parliamentary press gallery — and the governing Liberals — in their attitude towards the Reform Party before and immediately after the 1993 election. Although the Reformers finished a surprisingly strong third and sent fifty-two MPs to Ottawa, few "important" journalists took them seriously for the first two years. For many Parliament Hill veterans, the most common question in those early days was "Who *are* these yokels and who voted for them?"

Had they remained on the margins of the political process, Canada's neo-conservatives no doubt would have continued to provoke only mild amusement or disdain from their critics. After all, Al Palladini's ludicrous notion that all Ontario drivers are equipped with cell phones only became important when he became the Minister of Transport. Art Hanger's obsession with caning and other forms of corporal punishment only became an issue when, as the Reform Justice critic, he proposed to travel to Singapore to officially "investigate" the matter, thereby casting doubt on Canada's image abroad as an enlightened society.

But the fact is that the ignorant gladiators are no longer on the outside looking in. Instead, through a combination of good timing and deliberate manipulation by others, they have been surprisingly successful in moving to the centre ring, if not the centre of the political spectrum. They have achieved a degree of legitimacy and, in some cases, political power, unimaginable even a decade ago. And they have, like Margaret Thatcher, been prepared to exercise their power to the limit, and beyond, in order to implement their neo-conservative agenda.

Force of will alone would not have accomplished their purpose. Given their lack of experience and expertise, New Right politicians in Canada have been extremely fortunate in obtaining assistance to first promote and then implement their agenda. Their surprising rise from humble beginnings to their current status in such a relatively short period of time is understandable only if it is put in the context of the very substantial assistance they have received from the corporate elites and single-issue interest groups whose causes they promote. As the next chapter demonstrates, the assistance provided by many of these individuals — both directly and through other organizations — has been nothing short of invaluable in advancing the neo-conservative cause and bestowing a crucial air of legitimacy on their agenda.

10

For Whose Benefit?

We identify with the current worldwide movement to ... break
the tyranny of modern "Family Compacts" of bureaucrats,
politicians and special interests that exercise a tyranny of a
minority over democratic majorities.
— Preston Manning, *The New Canada*

We always hear from the vocal special interest groups who
argue for increased government spending. But what about the
silent majority?
— Moira Wright, Canadian Taxpayers' Federation

If you would prefer Reform legislation to what you have now,
get off your butt and work to elect a Reform government.
Wishing only works for the fairies at the bottom of your garden.
— Dave Tomlinson, National Firearms Association

What do Stan Waters, Ralph Klein, Mike Harris, Preston Manning,
Conrad Black, the Fraser Institute's Michael Walker and journalists
Barbara Amiel and Diane Francis have in common? That is, *in addition*
to their neo-conservative ideology? The answer, as any astute observer of
Canadian politics on the far right would know immediately, is that they
are all recipients of the National Citizens' Coalition's highest accolade,
the Colin M. Brown Freedom Award.

Most Canadians are unaware of this fact, since they have little or no detailed knowledge of the National Citizens' Coalition (NCC), let alone its founder, Colin Brown. In fact, until roughly ten years ago, very few Canadians had even heard of this obscure right-wing organization and the people behind it. Brown himself is described in the awards literature as having waged "a ceaseless battle against big government and big unions," but it was a battle with little public recognition.

Like the Mannings, the original supporters of the NCC were men out of step with the times, but determined to make a difference and unconcerned about their lack of public support. And, like the Reform Party whose career path it has so closely mirrored, the NCC has recently achieved a measure of success and respectability unimaginable before the advent of the Mulroney government in Ottawa.

Nor is the NCC the only marginal organization whose reputation and credibility have taken a surprising turn for the better in the past decade. From the Canadian Taxpayers' Federation to the Fraser Institute, the National Firearms Association and R.E.A.L. Women, any number of groups once thought to be marginal players have become significant actors in the Canadian policy process, their views listened to with respect and deference by not only the federal Reform Party, but also its more successful provincial cousins, the Harris and Klein governments.

Everyone who has ever worked in a large organization knows the value of outside opinion in helping to sell a project or an idea to management. If someone else thinks it would be a good idea, the plan immediately takes on heightened credibility. The greater the number of independent consultants who can be cited in support of a project, the more likely it is to receive the management seal of approval, even if those outside consultants are merely repeating what the in-house experts have been saying for some time.

The same phenomenon has been at work in the case of Canada's neo-conservative political parties and the interest groups and think-tanks that share their views. Forming a mutual-admiration society has resulted in huge advantages for both. For the political parties, the supportive statements of the leadership of these groups and the reports of the think-tanks have lent an air of non-partisan credibility to the neo-cons' positions. At the same time, marginal special-interest groups and research bodies have been handed a ready-made platform for the wide-spread circulation of their views. The result is that groups which previously functioned on the fringe, with no hope of a national audience, are now able to communicate their views through the media prism of the Official Opposition in Ottawa and the governments of two of Canada's most important provinces.

In a pluralist democracy, the interaction of stakeholder groups and political parties is normally neither surprising nor distressing. Political parties are intended to aggregate the concerns of a wide range of citizen groups. Yet not all citizens can easily express their views in modern democracies, usually due to a lack of funding and personnel. In the 1970s, intent on enhancing the participation of as many citizens as possible, liberal governments encouraged the creation of specific groups to represent those citizens whose voice was not being heard. From ethno-cultural and linguistic minorities to women, people with disabilities, consumers and the elderly, efforts were made to level the political playing field by providing assistance to those whose lack of funds and organization had left them mute in the face of strong, well-funded business and industry lobbies.

The problem with the neo-conservatives is that they have made a career out of attacking these traditional liberal interest groups as unacceptable "special" interests, accusing them of representing a tyrannical minority of Canadians and unduly influencing the mainstream political parties. Since most of these liberal groups have spent the past twenty years criticizing political parties of all stripes — as both the Trudeau government and the Rae government in Ontario could attest — the irony of the Far Right's attacks is striking. At the same time, the neo-cons themselves have established close links with marginal far-right groups, whom they do *not* see as special interests, but rather as representatives of what the Republicans term the "silent majority." Reinforcing one another's arguments has given many of these groups and politicians a legitimacy they could hardly have dared to hope for previously, and provided a veneer of credibility for the claims of Canadian neo-conservatives that they represent a sizeable proportion of the population.

It goes without saying this could not have been accomplished without access to considerable financial resources. In fact, money is one thing most of these groups were never lacking. Nor were they lacking connections. The relationship between Canada's neo-conservative politicians and the leadership of the various right-wing special interests is often more direct, personal and pervasive than the relationships the neo-conservatives allege exist between mainstream political parties and the liberal groups, as the cases of the National Citizens' Coalition and the Canadian Taxpayers' Federation demonstrate.

Lobby Groups Lend a Hand

In 1967 an angry millionaire who made his fortune selling life insurance decided he had had enough of government intervention in his life. He needed no help from the government in looking after himself, and neither should anyone else. "The less a government does, the more the man in the street has to do. And he enjoys doing it," Colin M. Brown used to say. And so, when the "socialists" in Ottawa proposed a national medicare plan, Brown decided to vent his spleen. He took out full-page ads in papers across the country, saying "So, how would you like your open heart surgery done by a civil servant?!" His ad even threatened that "people will die" if the new system was put in place and doctors became salaried employees of the state.

The ads were viewed with approval by Colin Brown's old friend Ernest Manning. Manning had long been in agreement with Brown on a wide range of issues, and suggested Brown should do something more concrete about his views since they were obviously so strongly held. By the early 1970s Brown had severed all connections with the federal Conservatives, whom he — like Manning — considered to be blatant socialists just like the Liberals, so he had no partisan commitment and time on his hands.

By 1975 Brown had decided to take Manning up on his suggestion. He formally established the National Citizens' Coalition with $100,000 seed money and a board of directors that included future Reform senator Stan Waters and Ernest Manning. Allegedly a grassroots movement of disgruntled citizens, the group certainly took on some of the outward forms of populism. But, as several of its critics soon observed, it operated more in the fashion of a private club and increasingly promoted a right-wing business agenda along with some elements of the social-conservative viewpoint.

In its activities the group followed Brown's early example, focusing on single issues, using national ads and encouraging letter-writing campaigns to Ottawa. One of the NCC's early efforts was a scurrilous anti-immigration campaign that focused on the Vietnamese refugees arriving in the late 1970s. Brown himself led the charge, attempting to distinguish between this "invasion" of Asian boat people and the somehow more felicitous arrival of Hungarians fleeing communism in 1957. His explanation left little doubt as to his racist views. "I think the Hungarians have made marvellous citizens," Brown declared, "but the bloodlines run the same way. We all come from Europe so they fit in. You wouldn't know if the people next door to you are Hungarian or not. They don't all go and gather in a ghetto."

With the Clark government having agreed to accept up to 50,000 of these displaced persons, the NCC ads predicted an eventual influx of more than 750,000 immigrants since each of the refugees was allowed to sponsor relatives. These numbers were not only hypothetical but wildly misleading. Rather than the 15 additional relatives per refugee the NCC predicted, the final number amounted to 40,000, or fewer than 1 sponsored relative per refugee. More to the point, however, was the total lack of attention the vast majority of citizens paid to the NCC ads, as Canadians from one end of the country to the other opened their homes and their hearts to the refugees.

Partly because of this unsuccessful experience and also because of its business-oriented membership, the NCC then devoted most of its efforts over the next few years to issues related to its economic-conservative agenda rather than to the social and moral conservatism that was so obviously out of step with mainstream Canadian thinking. In short order the organization attacked the progressive taxation plans of the MacEachen Budget of 1981, the controversial National Energy Program (NEP) and the revisions to the Canada Health Act proposed by Health minister Monique Bégin in 1984. Its actions undoubtedly contributed to the withdrawal of the MacEachen Budget, and its campaign against the NEP was so successful that a Calgary millionaire reportedly offered to bankroll a Western branch office for the NCC in that city. Only the group's attack on medicare could have been described as a dismal failure.

As the NCC was hardly alone in its opposition to the taxation plans or the NEP, the impact of its role in those policy processes is difficult to evaluate. This was definitely not the case with the NCC's vigorous opposition to federal legislation designed to limit spending during election campaigns by third parties — that is, by any groups or organizations other than the political parties contesting the election. In this instance, the NCC not only led the charge, but essentially fought the battle single-handedly, and could claim that the results were the direct consequence of its opposition.

Initially the issue was of little interest outside of Ottawa. Nor was it a contentious political issue in Parliament. All of the parties in the House of Commons had agreed to the legislation, which seemed to politicians of all political stripes to be a rational way of ensuring elections remained as level a playing field as possible. Electoral legislation already imposed limits on the total spending of political parties during a campaign for the same reason, and this additional measure was simply intended to ensure that no outside financial support would upset the balance. With the American model of out-of-control spending by business interests seriously undermining the democratic legitimacy of the electoral process south of the border — epitomized by the Political Action Committees against which Newt Gingrich would soon be railing — Canadian legislators felt this was a reasonable precaution, even though no obvious examples of such spending had arisen as yet in Canada.

The NCC saw things differently. Instead of a measure designed to preserve the democratic process, Colin Brown and his cohorts saw Bill C-169 as a threat to freedom of speech and to the right of Canadian businessmen to spend their money as they chose. According to journalist Murray Dobbin in his seminal work on this issue in *The Myth of the Good Corporate Citizen*, the backers of the NCC spent some $200,000 to defend that right in a challenge that was carefully filed with the Alberta Supreme Court. Their victory in 1984 led directly to the debacle of the 1988 "free trade" election, in which business interests spent $3.6 million on ads in their drive to ensure the victory of the Mulroney Conservatives and the free-trade agreement.

This amount essentially doubled the Conservatives' advertising budget without affecting in any way their spending limits. As the study director for the Lortie Commission on Electoral Reform, Jane Hiebert, reported a year later, the "independent expenditures in the 1988 election undermined the principles of fairness and equity." Moreover, they had a demonstrable effect. Hiebert's research team established that in the last week of the campaign alone, the "pro-FTA advertisements resulted in a net 5.5% change in voter intentions," primarily by convincing pro-FTA Liberal voters to switch their votes to the Conservatives for that reason alone.

The NCC's 1984 court victory gave it the kind of prominence that it had been looking for. Until then it had still been seen as "an unimportant right-wing fringe group, paid little attention by most politicians, the media and even shunned by other right-wing lobby groups." Now it was able to attract mainstream media attention as a defender of free speech, despite the inaccuracy of that label. This success was quickly followed by the group's second big break. According to Toronto writer Nick Fillmore, that break "came with the landslide victory of the Mulroney government. The politics of the federal government suddenly moved sharply in the direction of the NCC [and] the coalition knew it could mobilize right-wing opinion in the country to eventually push the government even further ... In addition, as many as fifty Tory backbenchers were longtime NCC supporters." Almost immediately after the Conservatives' victory, the NCC also moved to set up a Canadian Opportunities Society, modelled on the American Conservative Opportunities Society, of which Newt Gingrich was one of the more prominent members. The stated purpose of the Canadian society was to organize the fifty Tory MPs to promote various social- and moral-conservative causes within the Mulroney caucus.

In the next ten years, the NCC expanded its activities to oppose not only government activities of which it disapproved, but also those of social-action groups and labour unions. One of its most expensive (and unsuccessful) ventures was its attempt to use the case of an individual teacher, Merv Levigne of Ontario, to overturn the traditional union practice of allocating a portion of union dues for social-action purposes. The lobby group's lawyers argued this was a violation of civil liberties unless the unions first obtained each contributor's explicit consent. Although the case was lost on appeal and the cost to the NCC was reputed to be nearly $1 million, it did not give up its assault on the unions.

By 1995 the NCC had taken another tack and established a new project, "Canadians Against Forced Unionism," with the goal of promoting American-style "right-to-work" legislation in each province. The director of this project, Rob Anders — who would later be elected as a Reform MP in the 1997 election — indicated that Alberta would be the first target. Anders's message was simple and simplistic. With great enthusiasm he announced, "The time has come to free Alberta's workers." Ralph Klein was reportedly attracted to the idea, but eventually rejected the NCC's proposal, concluding it was unnecessary because Alberta's level of unionization was already among the lowest in the country and declining rapidly.

The NCC had also been busy earlier in Alberta, spending over $50,000 on a single ad campaign to defeat Conservative incumbent Jim Hawkes in the 1993 election. The ads made a mockery of the group's claim that it did not lobby politicians directly, and led to a number of pointed questions about the sources of its income, particularly as Hawkes had been a central Conservative player in the original passage of Bill C-169. The group was even less circumspect in British Columbia, where it ran ads stating simply "Don't vote for Glen Clark's NDP" during the 1996 election. When Clark's government was returned to power — largely due to the political incompetence of the Campbell Liberals, who persisted in trying to outflank the provincial Reform Party on the far right rather than presenting a centre–left alternative to the NDP — the NCC announced it would pay for the absurd legal challenge of a Kelowna businessman, David Stockwell, to overturn the results by arguing that NDP politicians had "lied" in their campaign promises.

Meanwhile in Ontario the NCC had been extremely active against the NDP government of Bob Rae. One of its projects, Ontarians for Responsible Government (ORG), was expressly created to bring about the Rae government's downfall. Starting earlier with billboard advertisements that read "So how do you like socialism so far?" the NCC's anti-government campaign was in full swing by 1995. ORG reportedly spent some $560,000 in Ontario's election year to achieve its objective. After it succeeded, it switched its tactics to supporting the Harris government. According to Dobbin, ORG spent considerable sums of money on advertisements to counter the union-led campaigns against the Harris government in the early days, and particularly to respond to the Days of Action campaign.

The overall thrust of the NCC's views is clearly reflected in the group's motto "More Freedom Through Less Government." Over the past ten years the areas of government on which the group has concentrated its attacks include MPs' pensions, pay equity (a violation of civil rights) and minimum-wage legislation, cuts to government spending, "cleaning up" social programs and eliminating universality, and Senate reform. It has also published an annual "report" on tax measures it dislikes, called *Tales from the Tax Trough*. On the other side of the neo-conservative ledger, the group has promoted compulsory balanced-budget legislation, deregulation of environmental and labour standards, and the creation of private hospitals.

Ironically, despite its desire to eliminate much of the role of government as we now know it, the NCC has always favoured a strong government defence role. During the late 1970s representatives of the group actually went to Washington to counter peace initiatives of the Canadian government and individual citizens, apologizing for them and placing ads indicating Canadians understood the "debt" they owed to Americans in protecting the "free world." They also held meetings with several American right-wing groups including the pro–Star Wars Heritage Foundation.

David Somerville, the man Colin Brown picked to run the NCC for what ended up being the next twenty years, provides further evidence of the radical right-wing views the organization supports. A former journalist with the *Toronto Sun*, Somerville had an earlier claim to fame as the author of a book on then prime minister Pierre Trudeau, *Trudeau Revealed*, in which the popular Liberal leader was described as a Machiavellian plotter intent on turning Canada into a one-party socialist state.

Somerville once called the NCC a "red meat for breakfast" type of organization, combative and determined. Those who know him well have described him as both tenacious and arrogant, convinced of the

412

merits of his own point of view and intolerant of others. On universality of social programs, for example, Somerville is adamant. "It's not a sacred trust, it's a sacred cow," he declared angrily when he learned of Brian Mulroney's election commitment to the social safety net, although he need hardly have worried. Canadians soon learned the tenuous value of all such Mulroney promises. "We have to do away with it sooner or later," he declared, and in the end it was sooner. (An address to the Colin M. Brown memorial dinner in 1994 by Reform MP Stephen Harper listed as the first accomplishment of the group over the previous five years the fact that "universality has been severely reduced: it is virtually dead as a concept in most areas of public policy.") When Somerville himself received the Brown award on his departure in 1988, he cited the demise of universality as a major victory.

In 1994 Somerville was asked to address the Ontario Conservatives' platform committee, the group of whiz kids Mike Harris had assembled for his "Common Sense Revolution." According to a report on his presentation in the NCC's June 1994 *Consensus,* Somerville urged Harris to "come out strongly in favour of privatization, contracting-out, repeal of pro–labour union laws and immediate action to eliminate the deficit," measures which all found their way into the CSR platform.

Somerville's connections with the Reform Party were even more direct. He attended virtually all of their assemblies during his term of office as an "observer." At the founding convention of Reform in 1987, he told reporters, "If NCC supporters notice a remarkable similarity between the political agendas of the Reform Party of Canada and the NCC, it may be because an estimated one third of the delegates are NCC supporters." Although he continued to argue the NCC was beholden to no other organization, he nevertheless declared enthusiastically after Preston Manning's speech in 1991 at the Saskatoon convention that "it was conceivable to think of him, for the first time, as Prime Minister Manning." Not surprisingly, an NCC poll released that summer also indicated more than 60 per cent of NCC members outside of Quebec planned to vote Reform.

While these connections between the lobby group and the political neo-conservatives are reasonably transparent, the financial backing for the NCC is not. In fact, its real supporters are far removed from the populist image it attempts to present when advancing its agenda.

Revenge of the Corporate Welfare Bums?

Many of the NCC's fiercest critics have pointed out the incongruity of an organization which attacks others for supposedly undemocratic practices while organizing itself along similar lines. Claiming a membership of some 40,000–45,000 individuals, it has consistently refused to release any list of names. Even more striking is the fact that it is neither a citizen-based grassroots organization nor a coalition of any traditional kind. Its constitution actually distinguishes between "voting" and "public" members; as so-called public members, ordinary citizens are not entitled to vote, attend meetings or even be informed of meetings. Instead they merely receive copies of the NCC newsletter, *The Bulldog*. Voting members, by contrast, are entitled not only to attend meetings, but also to select the four members of the board of directors. Only two voting members are required for a quorum, and only three directors are necessary to conduct NCC business, leading more than one sceptic to conclude that "the whole organization could be run out of David Somerville's closet."

Nor has the secretive lobby group ever explained its sources of funding, despite its obvious affluence. In fact, it vigorously opposed proposed amendments to the Election Act that would have required the publication of the names of all contributors donating more than $250 to third-party organizations such as itself. Registered as a non-profit organization, the NCC has always made much of the fact that "we neither seek nor accept government handouts."

The duplicity of this claim is obvious to those familiar with the income tax system. There is more than a little irony associated with the fact that the lobby group's contributors can take advantage of a tax provision without being accused of dining at the tax trough. While the NCC is not a charitable organization whose contributions are tax-receiptable, its contributors — mostly businesses and large corporations — *can* deduct their payments as a business expense instead. This point was made emphatically by the widely regarded Canadian tax lawyer Arthur Drache in an article for the *Financial Post* of June 25, 1995. "Businesses are much more able to make their views heard with tax-deductible dollars than are individuals," Drache argued, allowing lobby groups such as the

NCC "to operate on handsome budgets" far beyond the wildest dreams of most charitable organizations.

The organization's budget in 1997 was nearly $3 million. Although it refuses to divulge its sources, some assumptions can be made about its funding from its list of directors and those attending various events, including the award dinners at which the recipients are provided with a cash prize of $10,000. In that context, Canadian Labour Congress president Dennis McDermott's accusation that the NCC is merely "a front for some of the wealthiest and most powerful corporations and individuals in the country" appears to be well founded. Frequently listed "Patrons of Freedom"— who pay for advertising and support specific events such as the dinners — have included Edward Bronfman and Thomas Bata, Magna International, the John Deere Foundation, Massey Ferguson, Rogers Cable, the Upper Lakes Shipping Corporation, Brascan, the Power Corporation, Royal Trust, the Bank of Montreal, Canadian Pacific and Bell Canada, to name just a random few. Fillmore's detailed analysis of advisory-board members revealed ties to "thirty-nine major corporations ... eight major insurance companies, seven advertising agencies and more than fifty lesser corporations."

The NCC was founded in 1975, the same year as the Business Council on National Issues (BCNI), a somewhat more mainstream organization set up by Chairman Alfred Powis of Noranda because he believed that "the private sector is increasingly subject to uninformed but strident and highly publicized attacks which seem to have a pervasive impact on government policies." Simply put, many of the corporate elite in Canada were anxious about the perceived centre–left leaning tendencies of the Trudeau government and incensed over the "corporate welfare bums" label that the NDP's David Lewis had applied to them so successfully in the last federal election. Their response, the BCNI, was a straightforward business lobby organization designed to counter what some in the corporate sector believed to be the undue influence of social-action groups on economic and fiscal policies of the government. Its one-time spokesperson, Tom D'Aquino, is a former federal bureaucrat familiar with the workings of government, whose recently reported claims to have directly influenced economic policy during the Mulroney years have been the subject of considerable controversy, derision and speculation.

For those with even more right-wing tendencies among the corporate elite, however, this exclusively economic focus and transparent agenda were not sufficient. The result was the NCC, a more broadly focused organization whose alleged populist support made it a less obvious target of anti-business criticism.

A few years later, the same tactic was used to create another agent for the corporate elite, the Canadian Taxpayers' Federation. According to the CTF's mission statement, its threefold purpose is to "act as a watchdog on government spending, promote responsible fiscal and democratic reforms and mobilize taxpayers to exercise their democratic responsibilities." Although this may sound reasonably innocuous in theory, the actual activities of the CTF have been anything but passive. Originally formed as a protest group in Saskatchewan in 1990 to combat Brian Mulroney's despised GST, by 1998 the original Resolution One Association had become the CTF and allegedly grown from 2,000 to some 85,000 members. It also had offices in the four Western provinces and Ontario, and a national office in Ottawa.

The connection with the business elite in this second so-called grassroots citizens' movement is both as strong and as obscure as in the NCC. The CTF's own documents go out of their way to insist that it is "not a lobby group." Nor is it a special interest. "Our role is to address government policy on the basis of efficiency and cost," the documents declare. "What we are is a *common* interest group working for the benefit of all taxpayers." Obviously it has not occurred to CTF members that taxpayers themselves might constitute a special interest. According to Andrew Hilton of *The Lobby Monitor*, the CTF avoids referring to itself as a lobby group specifically because it fears that this "delegitimizes their desired status as a grassroots movement."

The similarities with the NCC in terms of organization, decision making and memberships are striking. Like the NCC, the CTF in reality is neither a grassroots movement nor a democratically run organization. One critic has actually described it as "more of a pyramid sales group than a bottom-up grassroots movement," and an examination of CTF recruiting tactics explains why.

Incredibly, the entire operation of the CTF depends on the recruitment of new members by some sixty-five salespeople operating on commissions. Each salesperson can earn up to 50 per cent of new membership fees and 30 per cent of renewal memberships. In 1991 the Consumers' Association of Canada issued a warning about the CTF, noting that approximately 59.5 per cent of membership fees went to the CTF sales force, field managers and "consultant" Kevin Avram, the Saskatchewan businessman who first organized the Resolution One Association out of which the CTF grew.

With memberships running at $55 per individual or $107 per business, the earnings of individual sales staff are not likely to be phenomenal, but the fact remains that prospective members are not advised of the commissions. In an article for *This Magazine* in July 1995 by Scott Piatkowski, Jason Kenney, then president of the CTF, said the commission "is not necessarily disclosed. It's answered if asked, but there is no requirement to tell potential supporters." The group's Member Development manager, Tom Charette, concurred and explained that "we can't afford to pay them a salary, so we need to compensate them for their work somehow." He also argued that "salary or commission, the real point is what our supporters receive in return for their financial support." This plea of poverty is interesting, since other accounts indicate the CTF annual budget is $4.5 million and the group employs a total staff of one hundred.

What members receive is not particularly impressive — six issues of *The Taxpayer* and, if they have access to a fax line, weekly printouts of the federation update, *Tax Talk*, which is also distributed to more than five hundred media outlets. Occasionally they are asked for their opinions through the use of general questionnaires, or encouraged to fill out and mail coupons to politicians. Like the members of the NCC, the CTF's business members are able to write off their contributions as a business expense. Jason Kenney's response to criticism of this situation was typical. "I don't accept that a tax expenditure is the same as a subsidy," he told Piatkowski. "To do so would be to accept that the government has a legitimate right to every dollar that's out there," he added as an apparent *non sequitur*. Like the NCC's, the CTF's members never attend general meetings or vote on any activities of the organization either. Instead the self-appointed executive makes all decisions in secret.

Its initial activities were carefully chosen to cultivate the populist image, however, and it has never lost sight of that objective. Having

417

established its reputation by holding rallies across the country to "axe the tax" in its early days, its promotion of such grassroots activities has not abated — the message has simply been updated. Before the 1995 Budget was brought down in March, for example, the CTF sponsored no fewer than eighteen protest rallies across the country whose theme was "No New Taxes." These rallies were also deliberately coordinated with others sponsored by the Reform Party and the National Citizens' Coalition for maximum effect.

The federation leadership has always forcefully denied the existence of any additional motives beyond those stated in its mandate. Yet any casual observer of the CTF's literature cannot fail to note the group's neo-conservative approach to the role of government in general. As well-known tax expert Neil Brooks has stated, the CTF's "anti-tax rhetoric disguises a view that government should play a minimal role." This opinion of the federation is shared by David Perry of the Canadian Tax Foundation, who notes that much of the group's anti-tax sentiment is based on ignorance of the actual situation in Canada and elsewhere, "a perception of reality rather than reality ... If we look at the U.S. — which is still at 1980 tax rates — it does appear that we have an onerous burden. But, compared to other industrialized countries, particularly in western Europe, Canada's total tax burden is near the middle of the pack."

Many other tax experts and traditional liberals have also pointed out that the benefits received from government in exchange for taxes have to be taken into account as well, particularly in the case of Canada–U.S. comparisons. It is generally accepted that such a comparison of tax rates and levels of benefits demonstrates that most Canadians and Americans "come out even." Kenney's response to this, however, is instructive. "We only look at taxes, not benefits," he told Piatkowski, leading Brooks and many other critics to conclude that the CTF agenda is simply lower taxes, not fairer taxes.

Despite their equally vigorous assertion that it has no other political agenda, the long list of other activities on which the CTF engages governments in battle betrays that claim. *The Taxpayer* routinely calls for balanced-budget legislation; privatization and deregulation of government programs and services; and the elimination of "wasteful" government spending on programs such as job training, multiculturalism and official bilingualism. It has even called for the approval of extra billing by doctors. Moreover, the CTF emphatically argues the "debt crisis" which it is now promoting *faute de mieux* — in light of the success which the federal Liberal government and many provinces have had in eliminating their deficits — must be addressed through even more cuts to government spending rather than increased taxes or other measures.

According to Kenney, "with the exception of special interest groups who feed voraciously at the public trough, public opinion is unanimous" that there can be no more increases in taxes, period.

Among the groups that the CTF over time has identified as special interests are the Canadian AIDS Society, human-rights and literacy groups, and the National Anti-Poverty Association. By contrast the Canadian Manufacturers' Association or the Canadian Federation of Independent Business are, to paraphrase the CTF's own words, *common* interest groups that defend the rights of all businesses.

This one-sided view of the world is also applied to the CTF's inter-pretation of political activities. Once again its official documents stress that no officials of its group are allowed to have any partisan affiliations, and the organization itself is strictly non-partisan. Yet in reality its past and current presidents have close links with the federal Reform and Conservative parties. Public-service union president Darryl Bean has called the CTF "a front for the Reform Party," and it is not difficult to understand the source of his accusations. Preston Manning has often been asked to address the group's anti-tax rallies. At one such event in Pickering, Ontario, in 1995, media accounts routinely reported some 3,500 Reform Party supporters in attendance, and Manning received a standing ovation.

Even closer to home is the large number of similarities between the Reform Party platform on direct democracy initiatives and those of the CTF. Declaring itself interested in promoting "democratic reforms," the CTF has called for almost everything contained in the "Blue Sheet," including referendums, recall, a triple-E Senate and the elimination of MPs' pensions and perks. (It will be remembered that Jason Kenney got his start with the Alberta branch of the CTF when he successfully confronted Premier Ralph Klein on the legislators' pensions there in

1992, prompting Klein to scrap the pension plan entirely.)

Other interesting connections can easily be found as well. CTF board member Norm Baker has also been a highly visible member of the NCC. (In fact, it was Baker who organized the NCC's speaking event in Regina with one of Margaret Thatcher's most prominent financial advisers, Madsen Pirie.) Another board member, Andy Crooks, ran unsuccessfully for a Reform nomination in a Calgary riding in 1992, and Jason Kenney became a Reform MP in 1997.

As we have seen, these connections were part of a larger picture of interaction between the various right-wing lobby groups and the neo-conservative politicians. While former Reform MP Stephen Harper was taking the helm at the NCC in 1997, Rob Anders of the NCC and Jason Kenney of the CTF both took their place in the Reform caucus after the 1997 election. Anders and Kenney, meanwhile, continued to be members of the Fraser Institute, where former intern Ezra Levant cut his teeth on neo-conservative dogma before making the same trek to the nation's capital to become Preston Manning's chief policy adviser. It is to the role of this suddenly influential institute and other right-wing think-tanks in promoting Canada's neo-conservative values that we now turn.

Right-Thinking Research

The Fraser Institute is another formerly obscure group whose rise to prominence coincided nicely with the advent of Canada's neo-conservative politicians, and it has been front and centre in the far right's fight to rethink Canadians' political values and beliefs.

It is no coincidence the Fraser Institute first saw the light of day as the NDP government of Dave Barrett was beginning to make an impact at the legislature in Victoria, and just as the Trudeau Liberals were beginning to cause anxiety attacks on Bay Street. Among the corporate backers was the indefatigable Alfred Powis of Noranda, who believed the creation of a lobby group such as the NCC was not enough. According to Dobbin, Powis felt "what was also needed was a think-tank that would re-establish the dominance of free enterprise ideas, the values of the market, and property rights." The mission statement of the institute is almost identical in tone and content. Its self-declared purpose is to "redirect public attention to the role markets can play in providing for the economic and social well-being of Canadians."

Certainly that it is exactly what Michael Walker set out to do. The Fraser Institute was established in Vancouver in 1974 by Walker — a former employee of the federal Finance Department who had experienced a right-wing conversion on the road to British Columbia — with $200,000 in seed money from his friends Jack Clyne and Pat Boyle of MacMillan Bloedel, and the support of a number of other corporate backers.

Walker's pitch was that the "problems" British Columbia's corporate elite were experiencing were not unique. In fact, he informed them there were similar difficulties for business throughout the liberal-democratic world, where the Keynesian economic and social consensus had become so well entrenched. He argued what was needed was an "international" institute to bring a new degree of respectability to the views of the fledgling institute, promoting the economic conservativism of Margaret Thatcher's hero, Friedrich Hayek, and Ronald Reagan's inspiration, Milton Friedman, a personal friend of Walker's.

As a result, the institute was set up in the same fashion as several other right-wing groups in Britain and the United States, employing a core group of researchers and also engaging like-minded neo-conservative academics from other countries to conduct specific studies. To further heighten the international and academic cachet of its work, a second board was set up and given prominence in institute literature, deliberately overshadowing the real power and corporate funds behind the organization. While the board of trustees represents a Who's Who of the business elite in Canada, it is almost never referred to; instead, the board of advisers has successfully been established as the academic window dressing. With a mandate "to oversee the research and editorial activities of the institute," this second, publicly visible board consists of a carefully selected "panel of scholars from Canada, the United States and Europe."

There can be little doubt as to the ideological leanings of these scholars. Among the Canadian academics, for example, is Herb Grubel, a former Reform MP. American neo-conservative William F. Buckley, whose brother-in-law is former Social Credit bagman Austin Thorne in British Columbia, has been a frequent speaker at institute events, as has

Milton Friedman himself. Other board members include Sir Alan Waters, a former personal economic adviser to Margaret Thatcher, and Anthony Fisher, founder of the British Institute of Economic Affairs, on which the Fraser Institute was in part modelled. Other role models for the Fraser included the extremist American Enterprise Institute and the Institute for Religion and Democracy.

Observing these developments in more detail, one critic of the Fraser's work has referred to the institute as one of a series of "Friedmanite franchises." Others have pointed to the continuing influence of American neo-conservatives through their generous funding of Fraser initiatives. The research and training leading to the institute's Freedom Index, for example, was bankrolled by the American Liberty Fund, a body with a $115-million budget. The American Lilly Endowment provided the institute's largest single grant, at $3.5 million. Paul Havemann's in-depth research on the institute's operations have led him to conclude that "the funding sources and methods of the Fraser Institute reveal its close integration into the U.S. network of specialized, affluent entities whose goal is to dismantle New Deal liberalism, to overcome an 'excess of democracy'... and to promote a Social Darwinism ..."

Walker himself bristles at the thought of being described as right-wing, claiming that a left–right continuum is meaningless and should be replaced by a more appropriate phrase, such as "free-marketeering" ideology. Nevertheless, as late as 1987 Walker was espousing views that have been described by one commentator as "technicolour weirdness"of a seriously social-conservative variety. Dismissing the utility of poverty indicators used by Statistics Canada, for example, Walker argued that "in some cases poverty ... is simply a reflection of the fact that the sufferers were dealt an unlucky intellectual or physical allocation from the roulette wheel of genetic inheritance."

The institute's relentless pursuit of free-marketeering has also demonstrated a distinctly anti-democratic component. Milton Friedman's startling intervention at the 1986 institute-sponsored "Freedom, Democracy and Welfare" Forum — protesting the statement that "democracy is an ultimate value" — led to a fascinating series of exchanges. Friedman declared, "You can't say that majority voting is a basic right ... That's a proposition I object to very strenuously." The institute's senior economist, Walter Block, agreed: "Why does it follow that we should have an equal right to vote in the political process?"

Friedman followed up his thoughts in a *Fraser Forum* article which concluded, "One of the things that troubles me very much is that I believe a relatively free economy is a necessary condition for a democratic society. But I also believe there is evidence that a democratic society, once established, destroys a free economy." Not content to stop there, he suggested that it was the pursuit of wealth that was the ultimate social value, while the pursuit of social justice would lead to total ruin.

Block's views on the role of unions were equally instructive. "Unions are just institutions that engage in prohibition of entry into labour markets," he stated, and often are no better than organized "bands of criminals." At the 1986 seminar, Block's thinking took an even more radical turn to the right, criticizing the whole "human rights trend" and explaining that when strong individuals are able to "meet harsh conditions with resolve and strength of character [this] carries over until the third or fourth generation. But eventually later generations get weaker. They become involved in pornography and rights for homosexuals and things like that."

Walker summed up the findings of the seminar as "majority rule of itself has no particular virtues." He did not change this view over time. Several years later he referred to the "tyranny of the majority" and the need to restrain the powers of Parliament, when testifying before a House of Commons Finance Committee. Like his friend Milton Friedman, he has also referred on many occasions to the dangers of an "excess of democracy."

Not surprisingly, the ideas of Walker and the institute originally were dismissed as rantings from the far-right fringe. As journalist Clive Thompson put it, "In the Just Society seventies the Institute's hard core necoconservative and libertarian stances — blaming unions for unemployment in an early book, for example — were mocked, and journalists and politicians alike dismissed them as a group of economic cranks."

No one is mocking Michael Walker now. Today the institute has a full-time staff of twenty-two and a budget of $2.35 million. Its 1996 annual report describes it as Canada's "largest, privately-funded public policy research organization." It has published more than two hundred books and literally thousands of articles over the past two decades, and sponsored any number of national and international conferences on specific topics. Its magazine, *Fraser Forum*, is distributed to some 1,300 subscribers, as well as a number of targeted individuals such as parliamentarians and provincial legislators. Its visibility has grown to the point where it may well be perceived by many as the pre-eminent right-wing think-tank in the country, totally overshadowing the far more academically credible and, by comparison, moderate work of the C.D. Howe Institute.

One of the ways in which it has achieved this remarkable growth in prestige and name-recognition is through Walker's brilliant use of the media. As an allegedly non-partisan think-tank with academic credentials and no visible ties to business, the institute has aggressively courted the media from the beginning, offering the results of its studies for public consumption as a public service. Although there was little interest in the early years on the part of the mainstream media, the Byfields — Ted and his son Link — were, of course, more than willing to publish articles on the institute and its work. With the advent of the Mulroney government and the growth of more neo-conservative political thought south of the border, the credibility of the institute began to grow along with its penetration of mainstream media, many of whom apparently mistakenly believed it was connected with Simon Fraser University. For others, its primary utility was that of a "Western" source of information — however dubious — to balance the prevailing views from central Canada.

A number of critics have focused on the institute's astonishing relationship with Canada's media, and in particular with Conrad Black's Southam chain as well as with the Byfields' *Alberta Report* and *Western Report*. With Black's representative, David Radler of Hollinger, and Black's wife, Barbara Amiel, having served on the board of trustees of the Fraser Institute, the importance of the media to the institute's credibility was evidently obvious to Walker from the beginning and he has always emphasized the institute's media strategy.

Clearly it has paid off. The institute's 1996 annual report claimed 3,108 references were made to its work in the media that year, up almost 51 per cent from the previous year. One analysis by Clive Thompson claims there were 200 references to the Fraser Institute in the *Globe and Mail* alone over the previous two years. He also notes a brief guest editorial stint at the *Globe* by Owen Lippert, a senior analyst at the Fraser, and the presence of two more Fraser associates — William Watson and John Robson — on the editorial board of the revamped *Ottawa Citizen* after its takeover by Conrad Black. Meanwhile, the institute's seminar series received more than 105 hours of coverage on cable television in 1996 alone.

As Thompson also notes, much of the Fraser Institute's phenomenal success at drawing attention to its work has been the result of an aggressive self-promotion campaign. News conferences and press releases are the order of the day. Authors are actively promoted and readily available for interviews. Faxed summaries of all reports are delivered regularly to some 450 radio stations across the country, as well as pre-packaged editorials for the broadcast and print media. Dobbin also stresses the importance of the institute's contacts with "talk radio" stations, a medium largely ignored by mainstream reporting and centre–left organizations, but one which has proven highly effective for the right-wing think-tank, whose name recognition is now among the highest of any in the country.

Several media-savvy gimmicks have also proved hugely successfully at promoting the institute's agenda, such as the concept of "Tax Freedom Day" and the "Debt Clock." One critic notes that "the institute's media job has been so successful that some of its ideas are no longer associated with the Fraser thinkers — they're just ideas. Tax Freedom Day, a concept they invented in 1977, is now so commonplace that many people don't know it came from the institute." While this may prove disquieting for its originators, the pervasiveness of this and other right-wing concepts the institute has flogged is an ominous indication of their success in changing "the ideological fabric" of Canada.

Over the years the institute has aggressively challenged what it sees to be a number of liberal establishment icons, from the Poverty Index of Statistics Canada to the Human Rights and Quality of Living Indices of the United Nations. One *Fraser Forum* article entitled "Canadian Poverty Rate Greatly Exaggerated" has been so widely distributed and frequently recycled it is included in most mainstream debate on the issue. Meanwhile, the institute's own "Economic Freedom Index" is designed to counter other liberal-democratic measurements of a "successful" society, focusing instead on business practices, government regulation and state intervention. According to the designers of the index, this is necessary to counter "value-laden rating systems which indicate that democracy is the best way to advance economic freedom." As one commentator pointed out, this has led to a situation in which Singapore, with its public floggings and state-run terrorism, is classified by the Fraser's free-marketeering scale as a freer society than social-democratic Sweden.

A sampling of topics from recent articles and seminars provides an excellent overview of the hard right turn the Fraser Institute is intent on imposing on Canada's political culture. They cover the gamut from "Canada's Failing Education System Needs Charter Schools" and "Regulatory Overkill" to "The Case of B.C. Hydro: A Blueprint for Privatization" and "Why the Flat Tax Is a Good Idea." On a more local and regional basis, they have also produced reports attacking marketing boards, rent controls and land banks, and supporting the concept of user fees for local services. A full week before the Mackay Report on bank mergers was released in the fall of 1998, the Fraser Institute's own report on bank mergers was released to widespread national coverage. The *Ottawa Citizen* through to the *Calgary Herald* and the *Vancouver Province* carried the story headlined "Study Says Consumers Will Save Through Bank Mergers," while two of the study's authors appeared on CBC Radio's *As It Happens* and Vancouver's *Bill Good Show*. Although in the end the Liberal government decided to reject the proposed mergers, few observers doubted that Paul Martin's lengthy period of deliberation — and the hastily mounted counter-campaign by consumers' groups and others opposed to the banks' plans — were at least partly the result of pressure applied by the institute's propaganda campaign.

In addition to its assiduous attention to the media, the Institute has also made a point of targeting young Canadians, and particularly those likely to make an impact on the future of the economy. It produces a newletter, *The Canadian Student Review*, and distributes some 20,000 copies on university campuses across the country. It also sponsors essay-writing contests with topics such as "Free Market Solutions to Environmental Problems." Potentially far more significant are the six seminars the institute runs annually for a total of 1,000 students at a fee of $200 per student. It also spends substantially more money on additional "leadership seminars" for a much smaller, select group of students. Although no information about partisan attachments is solicited as a condition of attendance, one informal poll at a recent seminar suggested more than a third of participants had ties with the Reform Party and/or the provincial Conservative parties of Mike Harris and Ralph Klein.

Despite his denial of partisan connections, Walker has attended several Reform events and has a number of Reform supporters on the board of trustees, to say nothing of the roles played by Ezra Levant and Herb Grubel. It was Fraser Institute figures that Reform used, to its regret, when preparing the "Zero in Three" proposal for its 1993 platform. And it was Fraser Institute data that twenty-two of the fifty-two Reform MPs in the House of Commons regularly referred to in speeches during their first term of office. In an interview for *Equity Magazine* in November 1995, Walker himself happily recounted details of a northern fishing holiday with Ontario's premier Mike Harris and former Republican president George Bush. He also noted that Harris attended an institute seminar on taxation the day after he was elected premier.

Yet the institute not only remains officially non-partisan, but has been awarded the enviable status of a charitable organization. This classification, which many have criticized and questioned over the years, has allowed the institute to benefit from very substantial contributions for which other such bodies simply would not be eligible. In the view of Ken Georgetti, head of the B.C. Federation of Labour, "The Fraser Institute is a parasite abusing its charitable tax status." Georgetti cites the example of another group with the broad purpose of nuclear disarmament whose application for such status was rejected because it was considered "too political." Georgetti's chagrin is visible. "If that's political then what's the Fraser Institute? They push an agenda from behind a veil of neutrality, but they're not!" Walker's response is simple. "Economics is not political," he replies, suggesting that several different political parties have adopted their agenda.

Disturbing as these facts may be, they would undoubtedly be less significant if it were not for the fact that much of what the Fraser Institute produces is of highly questionable accuracy, in terms of both methodology and bias. Many outside analyses have concluded that the institute's National Media Archives (NMA), for example, is seriously affected by the neo-conservative slant of its producers. An extensive study of NMA publications over a two-year period by journalist Kathleen Cross found that "while purporting to promote objectivity and expose a lack of balance in journalism, the NMA itself manifests a consistent pattern of innuendo, decontextualized results and selective interpretation."

Many Fraser studies include anecdotal evidence, uncontrolled surveys and inappropriate data — for example, the use of exclusively American statistics in an article on the impact of government regulations on industry, yet with recomendations for the Canadian context. As head of one important section of the federal Liberal government's National Forum on Health Care, former Ontario NDP leader Stephen Lewis was repeatedly confronted by Fraser Institute material on waiting lists for health-care treatment, which purported to support the concept of private versus public health care. Yet on further examination it transpired the information had been compiled informally through random interviews with sympathetic individuals, and was described by one panel member as "methodological garbage."

As Murray Dobbin points out, the sheer volume of Fraser Institute activities makes it difficult to assess the academic validity of much of its work. However, one study by an international group of lawyers and economists who examined materials presented at a Fraser seminar in 1996 on labour legislation provides an informative indication. In an article entitled "Bad Work: A Review of Papers from a Fraser Institute Conference on Right-to-Work Laws," the authors "documented a multitude of errors" that appeared to be the result of "a determined anti-union political agenda." Examples of these errors included a speaker who claimed legislation violated the Charter of Rights and Freedoms when the courts had recently ruled it did not, and another who referred to legislation that had been repealed ten years earlier. Simply put, "the Institute repeatedly demonstrates a willlingness to make claims that are unsubstantiated or even contradicted by available data."

Despite having achieved a level of prominence and legitimacy few would have dreamed of even fifteen years ago, the recent successes of the Fraser Institute have not made its executive director cautious. On the contrary, as all Canadians now know to his chagrin, Michael Walker has even bigger plans for the country's richest right-wing institute. The wildly ambitious five-year plan he had presented in November 1996 at an annual meeting —"Towards the New Millennium" — not only made its way into the hands of *Edmonton Journal* columnist Linda Goyette, but into a scathing column which revealed the strategy and agenda of the institute only too clearly.

Apart from some obvious objectives such as increasing the circulation of the *Fraser Forum* and the number of university students who attend seminars, the document focused on two major points: first, increasing its corporate funding by more than 100 per cent, to achieve an annual budget of nearly $5 million, and second, to "expand our penetration into the national media." Almost everything else about the plan flowed from these two ideas. Instead of concentrating on books, which are more difficult to promote, more expensive and certainly more academically challenging, the institute should, in Walker's view, concentrate increasingly on short "Critical Issues" newsletters. Instead of merely focusing on talk radio and alternative media, the institute should attempt to move up to the big leagues and "receive more coverage in the *Economist*, the *Wall Street Journal* and *Business Week*." Similarly the *Fraser Forum* should move from a monthly journal to a weekly magazine and increase its circulation from 1,500 to 20,000 by publishing non-academic articles by such icons of the American right as P.J. O'Rourke, thereby "including more humour in the articles to attract and retain regular readers." There is even a proposal for the institute to prepare a regular column for overworked, downsized newspaper editors to adopt in its entirety, preferably beginning with the issue of privatization of medicare. Ever alert to the need for allies, the document also proposed "developing a database of journalists who respond to our material and catalogue the extent to which particular journalists cover our releases."

Not surprisingly, Michael Walker was extremely unhappy about the release of his plan, since, as Clive Thompson points out, "a media manipulation strategy works best if no one knows you have one." Nor did many members of the fourth estate appreciate Walker's description of their trade as "second-hand dealers in ideas."

Farther Right

The Fraser Institute's dominance of the media at present has tended to obscure not only the methodological problems of its research, but also the very real existence of other, even more radical so-called think-tanks with even less claim to academic credibility.

A second and far more obscure radical-right think-tank is one very few Canadians have ever heard of, the Northern Foundation. Its own literature describes it as being in the vanguard of creative thinking on social and moral conservatism, and its membership list confirms this self-ascribed role. By comparison, the views of the Northen Foundation sponsors make even the Fraser Institute appear to be a reasonable mainstream organization.

Not surprisingly, given what we have already learned, the founders of the Northern group were also motivated to take action partly as a result of their profound discontent with the Mulroney government. According to its promotional material, the foundation was established in 1988 "by individuals who were concerned and angered by the continuing deterioration of their country." In the view of the founders, "common sense had been drowned out while unprincipled politicians, arrogant bureaucrats and leftist media elites did all the talking — and thinking — on behalf of everybody. There was no party or movement to fight for the needs and aspirations of the majority of Canadians who were small "c" conservatives ..."

Among the founding members of the group were representatives of R.E.A.L. women, the Association for the Preservation of English (APEC), as well as right-wing authors William Gairdner and Peter Brimelow, and Link Byfield, son of Ted Byfield and publisher of *Alberta Report*. Another founding member was Stephen Harper. Interestingly, Harper was subsequently asked to leave the group because his views were considered to be not sufficiently far right. Harper, meanwhile, has since referred derogatively to the group as "quasi-fascists."

The nature of the organization's concerns can easily be seen by examining a brief list of recent speakers at foundation gatherings. They include Dr. Walter Block of the Fraser Institute, Ron Leitch, the founder of APEC, and Gwen Landolt, the first president of R.E.A.L. Women. They also include the leaders of the Christian Heritage Party, the Canadian

Christian Anti-Communist Crusade, the founder of Renaissance Canada, and Paul Fromm, a former member of the neo-fascist Western Guard, as well as the right-wing columnist Lubor Zink.

The foundation produces a quarterly newsletter, *The Northern Voice*, which "regularly provides space for these same individuals, their views and their organizations." Although several members of the foundation have close ties to Reform and/or the Klein Conservatives, University of Alberta political scientist Trevor Harrison believes the Northern Foundation is not really a front for the Reform Party, or any other political neo-conservatives, so much as it is an umbrella organization for extremist single-issue interest groups. It is "a vehicle for bringing together several disparate right-wing groups and otherwise disseminating an extreme conservative ideology."

This is not to suggest that such single-issue groups have not been of considerable benefit to neo-conservative politicians at both the federal and provincial levels. In fact, as the discussion below demonstrates, they have not only worked closely with Canada's right-wing politicians to bring about specific changes to legislation and government policies, but they have done so with great success, despite the fact they continue to represent a small minority viewpoint.

Nouveau Special Interests

The failure of neo-conservative politicians to acknowledge their close links with special interest groups is a continuing irony. Yet, because of their implicit belief in the silent majority, they appear genuinely convinced that groups representing women, the homeless, people with disabilities or the environment are *special* interests while victims' rights groups, the gun-control lobby and the pro-life movement are not.

In part, this contradiction is probably explained by the fact that the first category of social-action groups has been encouraged and supported by government, politically and financially, while the groups represented by the neo-conservatives have not. The right-wing use of the term "special" therefore implies financial and legal assistance, either through sustaining grants or legislation such as employment equity and affirmative action.

Of course, the underlying problem is the failure on the part of the neo-conservatives to recognize that support for these groups arose precisely because they were disadvantaged — that society was not providing a level playing field for them. This is a problem for the Far Right, in large measure because they do not recognize the legitimate distinction between "equal" and "equitable." Whether in the case of Ralph Klein's handling of the gay-rights issue, Mike Harris's repeal of affirmative-action legislation, or the Reform Party's insistence on provincial equality in constitutional discussions and its rejection of a whole range of federal programs, including the promotion of multiculturalism and minority language rights, the issue is the same for the Far Right. Instead of seeing governmental action as righting a wrong or promoting fairness and equity, the neo-conservatives interpret the situation as one of special treatment and unfair advantage.

The virulence with which some of the new breed of reactionary interest groups have pursued their agenda is well documented, but their close linkages to politicians of the New Right — while obvious in the United States — are much less well known and visible in Canada.

Perhaps nowhere are these linkages more significant than with respect to the gun lobby. Unlike the NCC and the CTF, whose third-party spending benefits right-wing political parties but only indirectly, the National Firearms Association is neither concerned about maintaining a fiction of impartiality nor registered as a charitable organization. As a result, it not only *can*, but *does* engage directly in political activities with impunity. As NFA director John Bauer wrote in a newletter for the Manitoba chapter, the Reform Party "has chosen to listen to us" and agreed to repeal unpopular Liberal legislation, allowing the NFA "to participate in drafting alternative legislation."

As a result the NFA launched a fundraising campaign, "Give a Loonie to Save a Gun," in which every gun owner was urged to send the Reform Party headquarters in Calgary a dollar for every gun they possessed. An optimisitic Bauer proudly predicted that this could amount to $21 million in the Reform Party's war chest for the 1997 election campaign, but actual results were never published. Meanwhile, during the 1995 by-elections the national president of the NFA, Dave Tomlinson, campaigned directly for Reform. According to one report, both money and personnel were committed by the NFA to the campaign in the

Labrador by-election. Tomlinson's contribution included a flyer indicating the Reform Party was the only one to "protect the gun community." In addition, Tomlinson wrote, "the Reform Party now recognizes us as a powerful political bloc and is wooing us for support."

As *Ottawa Citizen* columnist Ken MacQueen noted at the time, no one else was giving the NFA the same recognition that Reform was. Barely 1 per cent of Canadians identified gun control as an important policy priority in a year-end poll by Angus Reid. (Capital punishment, meanwhile, did not even rate a mention, despite the intense efforts of many Reformers to raise the issue in the Commons at every possible opportunity.) "Security," MacQueen surmised, "for most Canadians does not come from owning a gun, but from knowing your neighbour doesn't." As for the political consequences of the Reform/NFA lobby, MacQueen correctly noted that Reform's fundraising activities had been dismally unsuccessful since the 1993 election, especially with the corporate sector. This, in turn, "made Reform, as the firearms association knows, more dependent on its generosity ... [and] it is not shy about throwing around its weight."

The NFA soon prepared and sold a document entitled "Party Time," a so-called guide for political action on the part of gun owners. The objective, according to the introduction, was "to form a majority in every political party in Canada." While this was clearly an unrealistic goal, the guide also offered more practical advice which, in the case of the Reform Party, was very likely achievable. "It's actually easy," the piece enthused, suggesting that there was no need for a nationally organized campaign. Instead, "local gun clubs can take control of local MPs."

Another logical consequence of the NFA's approach was a plan to defeat anti–gun lobby MPs, and this, of course, is precisely what transpired in Saskatchewan in the 1997 election. "Operation Elimination," the NFA's campaign to "take out" Liberal MPs in 1997, was particularly successful in that province, where the population's overwhelmingly rural base evidently overcame other concerns and made it the only province where a majority of citizens opposed the legislation.

It is instructive to note that the citizens of Alberta, with two large urban centres, did not share the concerns of the population in Saskatchewan, and the issue of gun control was a minor issue during the 1997 election.

Neverthless, it was the government of Ralph Klein which first made good on an earlier threat to "opt out" of the financing and administration of the gun-registry system, leaving it to the federal government.

The tone and tenor of the NFA's opposition to the legislation have had other significant consequences. Few of the bill's supporters would argue the legislation is perfect — in fact, a number of problems were identified early on and lengthy consultations took place, while its implementation was delayed, to correct them — but the hyperbole and religious zeal of the gun lobby have drowned out legitimate concerns. One consequence has been that many gun owners and their sympathizers have completely unfounded concerns about the intent of the legislation, concerns raised by the NFA using the same anti-government language employed by their counterparts in the United States. Many have referred to the "right to bear arms," a provision of the U.S. Constitution not found in Canada. There has also been a disturbing increase in the use of rhetoric previously heard only from extremist American "survivalists" who view the U.S. government and the United Nations as a common enemy.

In a rally on Parliament Hill in late September 1998, shortly before the registration provision of the bill came into force, an estimated 20,000 protesters listened to organizer Al Dorans and thirty additional speakers, including Reform leader Preston Manning. Dorans and other speakers argued the bill was the "thin edge of the wedge" which would ultimately lead to the state confiscating all citizen-owned weapons. "This is the home-invasion bill," Dorans alleged. "It allows police to search your home without a warrant on the grounds of sheer suspicion ... This is also the theft of private property without compensation. If they can steal your firearms they can steal your pensions." In another huge leap of logic Dorans continued: "They can say we went to the Kyoto Conference and we don't want oil and gas going into the water or the air so all two-stroke engines are hereby eliminated ... The same can be said for lawnmowers, snowmobiles or all-terrain vehicles. Guns are just the tip of the iceberg."

As we have seen, the NFA is not the only special-interest group that has closely aligned itself with the Reform Party and the neo-conservative movement, but it is among the most effective in having captured the justice agenda of the parties in question. Another frequently visible supporter of the Far Right in Canada, and especially of the Reform Party, has been the reactionary organization devoted to "family values," R.E.A.L. Women. Many representatives and officials of this organization have participated in the Reform Party since its inception. According to R.E.A.L. Women vice-president Judy Anderson, the organization's support for the party is based on mutual self-interest. "We're both against equal pay for work of equal value, we're against so much government intervention into family and private life, which is what the radical feminists want ... The Reform Party seems to support many of the philosophical ideas that we have."

Over the course of its first two terms in office, the Reform Party's opposition to affirmative-action and pay-equity legislation, and its support for "fathers' rights" activists in controversial hearings on revisions to divorce and alimony legislation, reinforced the R.E.A.L. Women's assertion that they shared the same views on social- and moral-conservative issues. Most recently, these views have extended to the issue of gay rights, which the organization believes to be another unacceptable assault on family values. While other Canadians were expressing shock at the statements of Reformers such as Dave Chatters and Bob Ringma, supporters of R.E.A.L. Women felt their views were finally receiving proper recognition within the political system.

Their founder, Gwen Landolt, speaking to a national meeting of the organization in Kelowna in 1997, described the "gay rights activists' challenge" as even more serious than that of the radical feminists, who she believes have been driven back. (With the imminent collapse of the National Action Committee on the Status of Women, this argument, at least, could well be proven correct.) According to Landolt, the group's plans to launch a counter-attack in Ontario, seeking intervenor status in a legal case involving same-sex benefits, was essential to the survival of the family unit. "If we don't get involved," she declared, "this could mean the end of the game for the family and traditional values." Ms. Landolt and other supporters of R.E.A.L. Women were undeterred by polling results demonstrating that the vast majority of Canadians were unconcerned about the issue and generally supportive of the protection of homosexual rights.

Other single-issue groups with close links to the Far Right are those sponsoring "victims' rights" concerns, such as Victims of Violence,

435

Mothers Against Drunk Driving (MADD), and Citizens Against Violence Everywhere Advocating Its Termination (CAVEAT). While some of these groups have been formed on the basis of personal experience, others have apparently resulted from heightened public fears encouraged by extensive media coverage of isolated but sensational events such as the Paul Bernardo and Clifford Olson cases. Gary Rosenfeldt, president of the Victims of Violence group, is the father of one of Olson's victims, while the daughter of Priscilla de Villiers of CAVEAT was the victim of a widely reported murder in Ontario. Chuck Cadman, another parent of a young murder victim, moved on from running a victims' rights group to successfully challenge incumbent Reform MP Margaret Bridgman in Surrey North in 1997, winning the subsequent election and becoming a staunch victims' rights advocate within the bosom of the Reform caucus in Ottawa. An earlier chapter noted the extraordinary mention of Priscilla de Villiers and her CAVEAT group in the Speech from the Throne of the Harris government. Solicitor General Bob Runciman repeatedly called on Ottawa to amend or repeal the Young Offenders Act and introduce more severe sentencing provisions. Meanwhile, the Klein government was an enthusiastic supporter of the Alberta-based campaign to repeal the so-called faint hope clause, largely as a result of pressure from an intensive public-relations campaign in Calgary centred on the potential parole of an individual convicted of killing a young Calgary girl many years earlier. Headlines splashed across the front pages of the *Calgary Herald* and the *Calgary Sun* urged readers to fill out forms for a letter-writing campaign and send a message to the justice minister in Ottawa.

The federal Liberals have responded to this intense pressure from a small minority in a variety of ways that have pleased virtually no one. Having amended the Young Offenders Act, altered parole provisions including section 745 of the Criminal Code, and introduced legislation to establish a national resource centre for crime victims, their measures have consistently been described as too little, too late by the neo-conservatives. At the same time they have enraged liberal progressives, including almost all experts on rehabilitation and juvenile offenders, several of whom have described the new measures as "unnecessary", "regressive" and "counterproductive." Although Liberal Justice minister Anne McLellan has continued to oppose another measure proposed by such groups — a Victims' Bill of Rights — because departmental officials have advised that it would infringe on provincial jurisdiction, she has indicated support for the concept of a national ombudsman for crime victims. Another active group in the fight for victims' rights, MADD Canada, has not only called on the federal government to establish such a Bill of Rights, but has proposed specific measures to lower the legal limit for drinking and driving (from 0.08 to 0.05 per cent) and give police wider powers for stopping motorists and administering breathalyser tests.

Many of these proposals lack scientific evidence to support the claims of these groups that their solutions would be effective. A variety of legal experts, by contrast, have suggested that the existing provisions are sufficient to enable law enforcement officers to perform their duties; the real problem, they feel, is the unrealistic expectations of some groups as to what can be accomplished. There is also a tendency to ignore jurisdictional issues, and statistics demonstrating that Canadians do not support most of the extreme measures proposed. Reform MP Ian McClelland argued that, despite the contrary evidence of polls, "Canadians are sick and tired of this molly-coddling of criminals at the expense of law-abiding citizens through this cappuccino liberalism." In April 1998, the national MADD president, Susan MacAskill, declared optimistically, "Our objective is to stop impaired driving ..."

Perhaps the most revealing aspect of Ms. MacAskill's statements was her recognition that much of the problem in terms of "victims' rights" stems from a high degree of citizen ignorance about the legal process and, by extension, the political process. "Citizens of this country have no experience of the criminal justice system and they do not know what their rights are, what they are entitled to know, who to go to," Ms. MacAskill lamented. "We feel there has to be a system in place where someone has the responsibility to ensure that their rights are recognized."

As we have seen, this high level of citizen ignorance and apathy has been an important factor in the success of neo-conservative politicians in the 1990s, exploited by them for their own ends. Regrettably, their success has also been possible because they were filling a void left by the failure of liberal philosophy to redefine itself to successive generations, and the reluctance of liberal politicians to defend liberal values.

Return to Reason: Rebuilding the Civil Society

> Liberalism is, I think, resurgent. One reason is that more and more people are becoming so painfully aware of the alternative.
>
> — J.K. Galbraith

In a meeting in downtown Toronto, school board officials fend off attacks from furious parents who blame them for the looming school closures the board has announced. The officials explain the many problems with the government's new funding formula. There is simply not enough money to keep 130 schools open. Students will have to be bused, and programs will have to be cancelled. There is nothing they can do. They have already cut as much as they can from their administrative budget, and the government's own rules say they cannot raise money by selling property to make up for the shortfall. One parent sums up the feelings of many when she exclaims, "I'm sick of hearing who's to blame. You're both responsible, and it's my kids who will suffer. No one is putting the children first."

Her comments reflect the attitude of many Ontario voters. As the negative effects of the government's policies become more visible, it appears the Harris Conservatives have pulled off a remarkable public-relations feat. Through a combination of relentless self-promotion — including unprecedented expenditures of taxpayers' funds on shameless propaganda

— and weak political opposition, Mike Harris and his team have largely avoided taking responsibility for the consequences of their "slash and burn" agenda. Instead, they have managed to convince a substantial number of voters that the "fat cats," the "lazy, overpaid bureaucrats" and "the special interests" are responsible for almost all of the problems.

The argument is simple but, to a surprising extent, effective. Blame bureaucratic inefficiency and new computers, not the cuts to the public service that have left the few remaining staff vainly attempting to process claims as fast as when there were three times as many workers. Long waits for family support cheques? Line-ups for drivers' licences? Delays in processing title searches? Same answer. Nothing to do with the "Common Sense Revolution" of the Tories. Property taxes soaring, municipal services falling apart? Not Mike Harris's fault. It's up to those spendthrift local politicians to handle your tax money more carefully. It's out of the provincial government's hands now. You don't like what the local politicians are doing? Throw them out of office!

Across the country, in Ralph Klein's Alberta, the story is the same. The divide-and-conquer tactics of the government have continued to prevent organized, coherent opposition to the Klein Revolution. Many Albertans are unhappy with the decreased level of service provided by the few remaining government programs, but, like some residents of Ontario, they are either unable or unwilling to make direct connections between the government's policies and their personal situation. Of course, there are exceptions to this scenario, primarily in the delivery of health care. This is an area where the vast majority of citizens are perfectly clear about the impact of government spending cuts. Health care has been the Achilles' heel of both provincial administrations, just as it has forced federal Reformers to rethink their previous support for a privatized health-care system.

The fact remains that the Klein government has been re-elected for a second term. The Reform Party is now the Official Opposition in the federal Parliament, despite receiving only 19 per cent of the popular vote, and Mike Harris, who won a large majority in the legislature with less than a majority of votes, due to the vagaries of a multiparty system, is entering another election campaign with the support of a significant proportion of the population, despite their serious reservations about his government's authoritarian style as well as some of his more radical policies.

One of the inescapable conclusions of this examination of the New Right's success in Canada is that it results not only from their astute adaptation of neo-conservatism to the Canadian context, but to accidents of timing and, in no small measure, to the failure of others.

Hijacking the System

How did Ralph Klein and Mike Harris get so far so fast? The similarities are striking. Despite the disadvantage of being outsiders in their own political parties, both men managed to seize the leadership of established, mainstream party organizations with a long history of forming a government. Even more remarkable is the fact that they did so despite considerable opposition from their party's traditional elites. In a sense, Klein and Harris hijacked their own parties, something they could do only because their parties were temporarily in trouble, out of power and out of favour with the voters. Lacking the perks of power, many of their parties' elites opted out. Uninterested in who would lead the party in opposition, and facing what seemed certain to be a considerable period of time in the political wilderness, the keepers of the flame let it flicker and die.

The apathy of the party elites helped the very outsiders they opposed. Worse still, only when it was far too late to prevent a "hostile takeover" did traditional Ontario and Alberta Tories realize that the direct-vote system they had decided to put in place to attract popular and media attention was in fact a recipe for disaster, neutralizing their influence with the membership and opening up the process to unproven newcomers. The irony of the federal Tories making the same mistake years later, and almost losing the party leadership to someone who — however capable or attractive his position on the issues — was clearly not a Conservative, should give other party elites considerable pause.

There is also an element of self-fulfilling prophecy in the role played by the fledgling Reform Party. By their own admission, the Reform threat influenced both Harris and Klein to take their respective parties even further to the right, to avoid the possibility of Reformers establishing provincial beachheads. In this context the fact that Preston Manning was obliged to create an entirely new federal party is a key

440

factor in why he and Reform are going nowhere. Starting from scratch is always a more difficult proposition than taking over an existing operation and performing a makeover. Voter loyalty, while declining, is still a factor in Canadian politics, and Reform has been unable to overcome that dilemma, among others, in its efforts to break out of Western Canada, where the tradition of protest parties was born and voters are more comfortable with changing allegiance.

The importance of the rural vote also cannot be overlooked. Some observers have even described this as a form of "rural revenge." Rural voters have long felt their priorities are lost in the overwhelming emphasis of all parties on the country's urban majorities. Most rural residents are unaware that, despite the democratic imperative of equal representation — the well-known concept of "one person, one vote" — Canada has a lengthy tradition of according rural voters a disproportionate voice through the adoption of an electoral formula that permits flexible riding size. The trade-off between the limits on the geographic size of ridings and the number of voters per riding has meant that voters in Three Hills, Alberta, or Vernon, B.C., already receive more bang for their buck than the voters of downtown Montreal or North York. In recent years, however, this effort to moderate the effects of population imbalances has backfired. Partly through clever appeals on the part of the neo-conservatives, and partly through blatant gerrymandering of the system, rural voters in Alberta have managed to overshadow the urban majority in Edmonton, just as rural and suburban Ontario voters have overwhelmed the huge majority of citizens in Toronto and other major urban centres. The phenomenon is even more evident in Western Canada in federal elections. Preston Manning and Reform have been shut out of nearly all the major urban centres, from Vancouver to Edmonton and Winnipeg, with the notable exception of Calgary, yet they have taken all but a handful of Western seats in two elections.

There is more to the neo-conservatives' success than simply their ability to take advantage of flaws and weaknesses in the political system. Even more important has been their relentless drive to undermine the liberal consensus, and it is here that they have been effective largely through the failure of liberals to defend their values and beliefs, or to articulate a compelling alternative vision.

Sins of Omission

Canada's neo-conservatives have relied heavily on their ability to manipulate a disgruntled and fearful middle class. The brilliance of their strategy, as former Ontario premier Bob Rae has noted, has been their ability "to convince the working majority that their fate lies with the wealthy and not with the vulnerable." Overturning the liberal ethic of community and collective responsibility, they have persuaded the middle class that they can survive only by saving themselves and throwing in their lot with the best interests of corporate Canada and the global business elites.

This argument, in turn, has only been successful because of the widespread and mistaken presumption of much of the middle class — in other Western liberal democracies as well as Canada — that they have been responsible for their own success. As Canadian economist John Kenneth Galbraith has described in painful detail in *The Culture of Contentment*, successive generations of middle-class voters have become too removed from the origins of the liberal consensus. Smug in their accomplishments and sublimely unaware that their success has been possible only due to state-sponsored education, health-care and labour programs from which they, of all citizens, have benefited the most, they have lost their attachment to the social contract and the welfare state, a development which liberal politicians failed to recognize and correct in time.

Instead, with each generation more removed from the perils of the free market than the last, they prospered sufficiently to create their own reality, building suburban and exurban communities with private education, private medical care and, as American society in particular deteriorated, private security forces. When globalization took its toll, many of the middle class sank into poverty and lost faith in the system, while those who survived not only prospered, but continued to believe it was due to their own foresight and ability. Either way, the state became less important in their lives.

This trend has led more recently to the creation of a smaller and more technically oriented upper middle class. The growing gap between techno-elites and techno-serfs has been described by noted economist and former Secretary of Labor Robert Reich as potentially even more dangerous to liberal democracy, since these upper-middle-class professionals are increasingly able to cross national borders at will, selling their expertise to the highest bidder. The result has been what Reich calls "the secession" of upper-middle-class America: literally, the demise of these citizens' attachment to their native country and their transformation into an international technocratic elite with no allegiances except to the capitalist class.

In Canada, with its more advanced commitment to the welfare state, the result has also been the willingness of the suburban middle class to allow the deterioration of the social safety net — from which they no longer perceive themselves to benefit — in order to maintain their standard of living.

All of these developments, of course, were only possible because of the abject failure of the liberal political elites to recognize the very real threat of the New Right and respond to it appropriately. Convinced that the liberal values and beliefs they had struggled to establish were now firmly entrenched for all time, they first ridiculed and then dismissed early neo-conservative efforts to modify or discredit them. As Canadian writer Michael Ignatieff warned in a speech delivered in early 1998 at the University of Toronto, "Nothing has done the electoral and moral credibility of liberalism more harm than the failure to take this attack seriously."

Just as liberal politicians failed to address the issues in a timely fashion, so a number of liberal interest groups failed to recognize the degree to which some of their pursuits were not enthusiastically supported by a significant minority of the population. Seemingly oblivious to this lack of firm support, they spent less time on promotional work with the public as time passed, preferring to focus their energies on their proactive agenda, criticizing and making increasing demands on the very liberal politicians who had encouraged their participation in the political process. Perhaps equally important was their failure to rein in the more extreme advocates among them. Much of the discontent on which the neo-conservatives have cleverly capitalized can be directly attributed to the extremist nature of a small minority of women's rights, environmental or human rights activists, whose strident demands regrettably produced an equal but opposite reaction.

Astute as Canada's neo-conservatives have been, however, they have also been greatly aided by another factor which demonstrates the frailty of liberal democracy in the late twentieth century, particularly in Canada. Voter apathy, and voter ignorance, are phenomena that have boosted the fortunes of all three of Canada's leading New Right politicians immeasurably. Like Ronald Reagan, Canada's neo-conservatives were aware of the fact they could seize power on the basis of a minority coalition of voters. The failure of some citizens to vote, and the failure of others to understand the consequences of the New Right's political agenda, played into the hands of those politicians counting on the "deliberate ambiguity" of their message to attract sufficient voters. For Preston Manning, this minority coalition meant becoming the federal Official Opposition solely on the strength of his Western rural support. For Klein and Harris, it meant riding to victory on the coat-tails of rural ridings and their provincial fundamentalist, social-conservative minorities. For all three it meant appealing to a disgruntled and fearful middle class, ignorant of the long-term consequences of the right-wing game plan.

In short, the success of the neo-conservative agenda in Canada must be attributed in part to the failure of liberal politicians, the media and the educational system to perform the vital function of political education. As Jon Pammett and Jean-Luc Pepin noted in their symposium on this subject more than a decade ago, the widespread absence of civic classes in the public school system, the failure of most politicians to recognize the importance of their role as educators, and the increasingly superficial coverage of political issues accorded by an unequipped media — emphasizing entertainment over information — have all contributed to this disturbing state of affairs.

Deconstructing Canada

There can be little doubt that Ralph Klein, Canada's original neo-conservative, has gone farthest with the right-wing agenda. He was able to make such progress not only because he was the first, but because Alberta's political culture was already much further to the right. Nevertheless, it is also important to keep in mind that the province's level of government intervention and services at the start of the Klein era was much higher than in Ontario prior to the 1995 election. As we have seen, cuts could be made by Klein in Alberta without imposing the same level of pain and sacrifice as in Ontario. Even after more severe measures had been introduced to take the province further right, the level of provincial support for some services continued to be close to the Canadian average.

Mike Harris, by contrast, has been obliged to work within the context of a different political culture, and with considerably less popular support. His initial cuts drove Ontario's level of government services far below the national average, particularly in areas such as education where the province had already maintained below-average levels of support for years. In addition, the wild discrepancy between the cost of living in Toronto and the rest of the province meant that across-the-board spending reductions produced a disproportionate effect in the province's major urban centre.

Nevertheless, the events of the past several years have demonstrated that Harris likely will never be in a position to impose certain elements of the Klein Revolution on the citizens of Ontario, short of imposing martial law. His government's about-face on the privatization of the LCBO and Ontario Hydro, and its obvious confusion on the social housing and education files, have provided ample evidence that the Tories' re-election concerns are sufficient to overcome neo-conservative principles.

Both Harris and Klein have also been fortunate in their timing, taking over ailing economies and then benefiting from favourable economic conditions, which have allowed them to deliver on their major promises to the middle class regarding taxation and deficit reduction. At the same time, their willingness to make pragmatic decisions on social- and moral-conservative issues, unlike Preston Manning and Reform, has been a significant factor in their continued success. Indeed, a major reason why Reform has no political future is the party's continued insistence on the American brand of moral conservatism, which is so completely alien to the Canadian political culture.

Obviously Klein and Harris have made major changes in their provinces. If their parties win another term of office, these changes will be difficult, if not impossible, to reverse, a fact many critics of the Far Right have noted with increasing distress. Once privatized, for example, the infrastructure that took liberal politicians several generations to construct will be unaffordable for any future government. Adding to this dilemma is the fact that the tax cuts Harris and Klein have implemented will be difficult for future governments to reverse, even if the intent were simply to return to some semblance of pre–neo-conservative levels.

Yet the viewpoint of most Canadians has not changed dramatically since 1992, as several polls in late 1998 demonstrated conclusively. Despite the claims of Harris and Klein that they have a majority mandate for their assault on the welfare state, fully 71 per cent of respondents to the fifteenth annual *Maclean's*–CBC poll indicated they were concerned about a growing gap between rich and poor, and 50 per cent strongly believed government should intervene directly to correct the situation and bridge the gap. These findings suggest neo-conservatism in Canada is having a disproportionate impact, since it now controls two of most important provinces as well as the Official Opposition. Ironically, with the federal government's current policy of maintaining intergovernmental peace at all costs, the neo-conservatives may have the potential to become a bigger threat to Canada's political culture than the Bloc Québécois, the vast majority of whose members, while arguing for separation, continue to share classic liberal values.

At a time when almost all of Europe has returned to liberal centre–left governments and the United States to the Democrats, the irony of Canada's last-minute foray into neo-conservatism is even more marked. Luckily, the implementation of the Far Right's agenda has been limited to the provincial level, and the damage so far has been contained. Canadians have not suffered the massive upheavals that rocked Britain and the United States, a consolation more easily appreciated after examining the heavy price both countries continue to pay for their right-wing experiment in terms of their deeply divided societies.

To avoid a similar fate, Canada's liberal politicians and activists must redouble their efforts, not simply to discredit the neo-conservative agenda, but to demonstrate the ongoing merit of liberal values and a civil society. As Robert Reich's merciless analysis of Bill Clinton's "Jerry Springer presidency" demonstrated, the lack of a viable liberal policy agenda and a coherent, consistent message left a policy vacuum which the Republican right was able to fill with scandal-mongering, character debates and an appeal to the past. Similarly, the reluctance of most Democrats to defend liberalism, and the positive role of the state, left voters with few leadership alternatives. These conclusions suggest that Canada's liberals must take immediate action on a number of fronts, both domestic and international, if they are to avoid the worst of the neo-conservative excesses.

Above all, there is a need for a concerted communications strategy to demonstrate the continued relevance of liberal values and the importance of the welfare state, and to adopt concrete policies which bolster and update the programs that make up the social safety net. This is particularly important in order to avoid further disruptions brought about by globalization — disruptions which have been instrumental in causing widespread political discontent in the first place. With much of Europe forging ahead with policies designed to promote social cohesion, North America, and Canada in particular, cannot afford to ignore the importance of Galbraith's aptly named "humane agenda" for social peace.

Nor can liberal politicians ignore all aspects of the populist agenda promoted by many in the New Right. Where their proposals for so-called direct-democracy mechanisms are unworkable or inappropriate, the reasons for their rejection must be carefully explained. Meanwhile, the underlying public concern about the perceived lack of responsiveness and transparency in the political system, which the populists have recognized and capitalized on, must be addressed in concrete fashion. At the federal level, the Chrétien Liberals' early attempts to do this through the commitments in their 1993 "Red Book" were exemplary. Their subsequent failure to follow through on several of those commitments, epitomized by their reluctant and outdated handling of the code-of-ethics issue, implies a lack of understanding of the underlying problem. With several new and emerging issues of good governance looming large — including such areas as electronic privacy, whistle-blowing legislation and the merit principle — liberal governments must once again take the initiative, demonstrating leadership as an employer as well as a regulator.

As for the perennial problem of western alienation, only a concerted effort on the part of the federal government will convince westerners that their long-term interests lie with the national interest, and not the regional shortsightedness promoted by the right. It may also be that the time has come for serious consideration of proposals to rebalance and heighten the legitimacy of the political system. Can Western alienation be addressed solely through an aggressive educational and promotional effort on the part of the federal government, or will alterations to the electoral system — such as the oft-discussed move to proportional representation — and other institutional changes such as Senate reform be necessary elements of renewed social cohesion and national unity? Equally pressing, will mainstream political parties be able to reassert their vital role as aggregators of public interest and renew voter attachment?

These and other domestic measures must be accompanied by complementary initiatives at the international level. The importance of liberal-democratic governments taking the initiative and reasserting their authority over multinational corporations and the international business agenda cannot be overemphasized. If citizens are to regain their confidence in the role of the state, the state must be seen as capable of addressing crucial problems originating outside its borders. In the era of globalization, this can be accomplished only through joint efforts, with liberal democracies making common cause through international bodies and regulatory frameworks. Such bodies already exist for many aspects of economic and fiscal policy, but have been under-utilized; nothing prevents others from being set up to deal with complementary social- and cultural-policy issues if the political will exists. The record of bodies such as the NAFTA Commission for Environmental Cooperation, for example, demonstrates both the potential of this approach and the current reluctance of liberal politicians to pursue it aggressively.

As Canadian author John Ralston Saul indicated at a colloquium in Ottawa in February 1998 on international trade agreements and related issues, a forum jointly sponsored by Canadian and European parliamentarians, the central problem of governmental inaction appears to be psychological. Having adopted the neo-conservative mindset about the inevitability of globalization, most liberal politicians seem convinced that their options are limited to the parameters of the neo-conservative paradigm. Yet many opponents of neo-conservatism have provided thought-provoking options for governments prepared to think "outside the box" and reject the right-wing paradigm. Nobel Prize–winning economist James Tobin's plan for a tax on the electronic transfer of funds, and other innovative options such as the proposed Blue Sky tax on international travel to fund environmental efforts, are only two of the more widely debated. In fact, globalization could arguably be perceived as providing an opportunity for liberal politicians to expand the liberal consensus, rather than abandoning it.

By contrast, the continued failure of liberal politicians to take the threat of neo-conservatism seriously — not only in terms of political power, but in light of its potential to disrupt the political culture of the country — could result in a lengthy period of social unrest and the deterioration of the key values of compassion and tolerance that have distinguished Canadian society in the twentieth century. The choice, as Vaclav Havel said, is theirs.

Notes

Chapter 1

page 8 "unwavering commitment" and "deep feeling" Hugo Young and Anne Sloman, *The Thatcher Phenomenon* (London: BBC, 1986), 17, 21.

page 8 "a certain impatience" Peter Riddell, *The Thatcher Government* (Oxford: Basil Blackwell, 1985), 7.

page 10 "very much an intruder" Riddell, 21.

page 10 "overthrow of tyrant king" As quoted in Young and Sloman, 33.

page 11 "Economics [are] the method" Kenneth Minogue and Michael Biddis, *Thatcherism* (London: Macmillan, 1987), 27.

page 13 "catch the plum" David Butler and Dennis Kavanaugh, *The British General Election of 1979* (New York: St. Martin's Press, 1997), 340.

page 13 "Margaret is a crusader" Young and Sloman, 105.

page 13 "she has nonetheless flouted" Peter Hennessy, *Cabinet* (Oxford: Basil Blackwell, 1986), 122.

page 13 "her total contempt" Martin Holmes, *The First Thatcher Government* (Boulder, Colorado: Westview Press, 1985), 208, and *The Financial Times,* January 11, 1986.

page 13 "all other views" Young and Sloman, 55.

page 17 "She wins arguments" Young and Sloman, 136.

page 18 "had never expected to see the day" Holmes, 79.

page 20 "This represresentation of Reagan" Joel Kreiger, *Reagan, Thatcher and the Politics of Decline* (Cambridge: Polity Press, 1986),156.

page 22 "driven almost to distraction" Ferguson and Rogers, eds., *The Hidden Election* (New York: Pantheon, 1981), 13.

page 22 "collective nervous breakdown" Ferguson and Rogers, 4.

page 22, 23 "I don't want everyone to vote" Godfrey Hodgson, *The World Turned Upside Right* (New York: Houghton Mifflin, 1996), 249.

page 23 "female voter" Zillah Eisenstein, *Feminism and Sexuality: Crisis in Liberal America* (New York: Monthly Review Press, 1984), 29.

page 25 "pushed through the greatest" John Palmer, ed., *Perspectives on the Reagan Years* (Washington, DC: Urban Institutes Press, 1986), 127, 341.

pages 25–26 "the combination of delayed and cancelled flights" B. Harrison and B. Bluestone, *The Great U-Turn* (New York: Basic Books, 1990), 160.

page 26 Kevin Phillips, *The Emerging Republican Majority* (New York: Arlington House, 1969), 99.

page 26 "What I want to see" Hodgson, 261.

page 27 "the new suburbs" Kevin Phillips, *The Politics of Rich and Poor: Wealth and the American Electorate in the Reagan Aftermath* (New York: Harper Collins, 1991), 197.

page 27 "overall a disproportionate" *The Politics of Rich and Poor*, 202.

page 27 "the most racist" Robert Leachmen, *Greed Is Not Enough: Reaganomics*

(New York: Pantheon, 1982), 8–9.

page 27 "unashamedly seeks" Hayward Burns, "Racial Equality: The Action is not Affirmative," *The Nation* 239, no. 9 (September 29, 1984): 264–8.

page 29 "knows so little" Hodgson, 246–7.

page 30 "errors of judgement" Krieger, 169,183.

page 31 "sold us down the river" Hodgson, 250.

page 31 "spends too much time" Alan Crawford, *Thunder on the Right: The New Right and the Politics of Resentment* (New York: Pantheon, 1980), 176.

page 37 "What has given the New Right" Rosalind Petchesky, "Anti-abortion, Anti-feminism and the Rise of the New Right," *Feminist Studies* 7, no. 2 (summer 1981): 207.

page 38 "You have coalition" *Business Week*, July 10, 1995, 48, and *Time*, December 18, 1995, 21.

page 38 "keep his head down" *Newsweek*, December 11, 1995, 40.

page 39 "the Democrats [were reduced]" *Congressional Quarterly*, January 6, 1996, 22.

page 40 "There's a whole world" Editorial, *Globe and Mail*, August 15, 1996, A16.

page 42 "acid-tongued, overweight suit-and-tie conservative" Hugo Gurdon, *The Daily Telegraph*, reprinted in the *Ottawa Citizen*, April 12, 1998, A10.

page 45 revolution versus evolution theory See the works of Luis Hartz, Ken McRae and Gad Horowitz, for example.

Chapter 2

page 54 "I wasn't looking" David G. Wood, *The Lougheed Legacy* (Toronto: Key Porter, 1985), 13.

page 60 "a triumph of style" A. Hustak, *Peter Lougheed* (Toronto: McClelland and Stewart, 1979), 138.

page 60 "a significant staff" Hustak, 140.

page 62 "Albertans did not talk" Mark Lisac, *The Klein Revolution* (Edmonton: NeWest Press, 1995), 39.

page 66 source of leaks was Klein in ventilation shaft Lisac, 62.

page 67 "It finally got to the point" Frank Dabbs, *Ralph Klein: A Maverick Life* (Vancouver: Greystone Books, 1995).

page 69 "the perfect Munchkin mayor" Ron Wood, "The City," *Calgary Magazine*.

page 69 "fit in well with Klein's evolving conservatism" *Ralph Klein: A Maverick Life*, 50.

page 70 once he was found by a reporter *Ralph Klein: A Maverick Life*, 52.

page 70 "eastern bums and creeps" *Calgary Herald*, January 7, 1982.

page 71 Quotations by Crosbie et al. *Alberta Report*, January 25, 1982, 10.

page 73 "massaged public opinion" *Ralph Klein: A Maverick Life*, 57.

page 73 "the Sunnyside flip flop" *Ralph Klein: A Maverick Life*, 57.

page 74 "the amount of money" Lisac, 24.

page 77 Bob Blair episode *Ralph Klein: A Maverick Life*, 88.

page 79 "Ralph was off" Lisac, 39.

page 79 "the cure was to restore" Lisac, 92.

page 80 "with an open vote" Lisac, 93.

page 81 "bringing them back to the grassroots" David Stewart, "Klein's Makeover of the Alberta Conservatives," in *The Trojan Horse: Alberta and the Future of Canada*, eds. Trevor Harrison and Gordon Laxer (Montreal: Black Rose Books, 1995), 40.

page 82 "Klein kneecapped anyone" Lisac, 73.

page 83 "I've waited all my political life" Lisac, 81.

page 85 "Yes, sir. You just watch" Lisac, 84.

page 85 "red-faced, spluttering and barely coherent" *Saturday Night*, May 1994, 50.

page 86 "No ifs, no ands" *Ralph Klein: A Maverick Life*, 109.

page 88 "like Wayne without Shuster" *Calgary Herald*, December 9, 1997, A24.

page 89 "Why can't everyone" *Ralph Klein: A Maverick Life*, 54.

page 91 paragraph on Kowalski vs. the Klein Gang Drawn from *Ralph Klein: A Maverick Life*, chapter 15.

page 99 "That is certainly something we have to consider" *Calgary Herald*, January 12, 1993, A1.

page 100 reporting procedures of the police *Edmonton Journal*, March 8, 1994, A6.

page 101 "minority identified as one" *Edmonton Journal*, April 22, 1994, A1.

page 103 "it appalled me!" *Alberta Report*, April 6, 1998, 10-11.

Chapter 3

page 107 "rally around the community, the farm and the province" *Globe and Mail*, February 18, 1995, D2.

page 107 "Albertans don't cooperate" Joanne Helmer, "Redefining Normal: Life in the New Alberta," in *The Trojan Horse: Alberta and the Future of Canada*, eds. Trevor Harrison and Gordon Laxer (Montreal: Black Rose Books, 1995), 72.

page 110 "like a mortgage" Gillian Stewart, "Klein the Chameleon," in *The Trojan Horse*, 32.

page 112 "know what it's like to hurt" Mark Lisac, *The Klein Revolution* (Edmonton: NeWest Press, 1995), 235.

page 114 "we've moved past it to another agenda" "Klein of the Times," *Saturday Night*, May 1994, 52.

page 115 "the restructuring ... a full list" Helmer, "Redefining Normal: Life in the New Alberta," in *The Trojan Horse*, 74.

page 118 "hire extra teachers" *Edmonton Journal,* February 13, 1998.

page 119 "going through the roof" Kevin Taft, *Shredding the Public Interest* (Edmonton: University of Alberta Press, 1997), 25.

page 120 "lowest level of provincial services in the country" M. McMillan, *Leading the Way or Missing the Mark?: The Klein Government's Fiscal Plan* (Edmonton: Western Centre for Economic Research, 1996), 14.

page 120 "look for it elsewhere" Lisac, 152.

page 122 "no alternative but to cut services and increase taxes" Budget speech, Alberta Treasury, March 1984.

page 122 "That's the stupid way" *Calgary Herald,* September 1, 1993.

page 124 "so there was no need to discuss it" Lisac, 122.

page 127 "large new areas of privatized services" Gordon Laxer, "The Privatization of Public Life," in *The Trojan Horse,* 105.

pages 127–128 "are not named in the Act" L. Adkin, "Democratic Resistance to Folksy Fascism," *Canadian Dimension* (April–May 1995): 32.

page 128 "can still happen and is happening" *Calgary Herald,* March 23, 1995, B7.

page 130 "We'll have a cabinet meeting," etc. All quotes from *Maclean's,* September 7, 1998, 34–36.

page 137 "it was a giant step" *Globe and Mail,* April 10, 1998.

page 139 "as well as Ralph Klein has" Steward, "Klein the Chameleon," in *The Trojan Horse,* 32.

page 140 "the nonsense of the Liberal Opposition" *Calgary Herald,* March 15, 1998.

page 140 "opportunity for debate from all parties" L. Blakeman, "The Death of Democracy," *Oliver Community League News* (winter 1997).

page 141 "too difficult for seniors and the public to read" Kevin Taft, *Shredding the Public Interest,* 38.

page 142 "determined to usurp judicial independence" *Calgary Herald,* March 16, 1998.

page 142 "I'm also not going to blink" Legislative Assembly of Alberta, Hansard, October 21, 1993.

page 143 "at the pleasure of the legislature" Lisac, 142.

page 145 "right down to the judiciary" Alberta Report, September 16, 1996, 9.

Chapter 4

page 148 "You have to credit" *Toronto Star,* June 6, 1998, C5.

page 148 "I would think that" *Toronto Star,* June 8, 1998, A7.

page 148 "That's how we grew up" *Toronto Star,* June 8, 1998, A7.

page 151 "you have to understand" Bob Rae, *From Protest to Power* (Toronto: Viking, 1996), 221.

page 152 "*La methode Harris*" *Le Devoir,* October 30, 1997, 46.

page 153 "The only thing" John Ibbitson, *Promised Land* (Scarborough, Ontario: Prentice Hall, 1997), 8.

page 155 "found himself on the ideological fringe" Ibbitson, 16.

page 155 "attempted to say" Legislative Assembly of Ontario, Hansard, November 5, 1985, 1396–1400.

page 157 "I'm more sensitive" As quoted in Ibbitson, 9.

page 157 "I think times are tough" *Toronto Star*, April 2, 1996.

page 157 "minimum wage jobs" *Toronto Star*, May 1, 1996.

page 158 "If they can't compete" *Toronto Star*, July 17, 1996.

pages 158–159 "Uh, probably ... hockey book" *Ottawa Citizen*, April 25, 1997.

page 159 "I don't control the police" *Canadian Dimension*, May/June 1996.

page 161 "would today most likely still be railing" Ibbitson, 27.

page 161 "self-reinforcing, centre-left consensus" T. Long, "What the Conservative Win in Ontario Means for All of Canada," *Fraser Forum*, November 1995, 8.

page 163 "The grown-ups basically left" Ibbitson, 37.

page 163 "In the final months" Ibbitson, 42.

page 165 "wasn't ready" *Toronto Star*, June 9, 1990, B1.

page 166 "Mike's not about revolution" Ibbitson, 64.

page 166 Harris trip to New Jersey *Toronto Star*, February 18, 1996, A1.

page 167 "I didn't check" *Toronto Star*, May 10, 1994.

page 167 minimize the importance of the American influence See P. Woolstencroft, "Reclaiming the Pink Palace," in *The Government and Politics of Ontario*, 5th ed., ed. Graham White (Toronto: University of Toronto Press, 1997), 388.

page 167 Michigan's environmental standards Leslie Coventry thesis citation in Sid Noel, ed., *Revolution at Queen's Park* (Toronto: Lorimer, 1997), 17.

page 168 "eliminate barriers to growth" Mark Mullins, *Common Sense Revolution*, 1994, 2.

page 169 "was regularly queried" Ibbitson, 104.

page 170 "They would also ... convey" Ibbitson, 102.

page 170 "a one-person Blitzkrieg" Guy Crittendon, "Inside the Harris Kremlin," *Globe and Mail*, November 1, 1997, D9.

page 170 at least as great Ian Urquart, *Toronto Star*, August 29, 1998, B1.

page 171 "The direction of this administration" *Toronto Star*, August 30, 1997.

page 171 "Inside the Harris Kremlin" Crittendon.

page 174 "Right now, all we basically have is a bridge" *Ottawa Citizen*, April 17, 1996.

page 175 "didn't want his Transportation minister" Ibbitson, 108.

page 176 "Mike, this is Al" Ibbitson, 108.

page 177 "The government has hired" *Globe and Mail*, October 11, 1997.

page 178 "Culture is not a frills ministry" *Toronto Star*, May 5, 1996.

page 179 "It's rough" *Toronto Sun*, July 6, 1995.

page 180 "best salesman" *Globe and Mail*, October 11, 1997.

page 180 "I think it's great" *Globe and Mail*, July 13, 1998, A5.

page 182 "not just an act of courage" *Toronto Star*, September 12, 1995.

page 182 "I've been a trustee" *Ottawa Sun*, April 29, 1996, 12.

page 183 "Completely lost" Legislative Assembly of Ontario, Hansard, December 12, 1995.

page 183 "They didn't research it" *Toronto Star*, June 2, 1996, A16.

page 185 "only a court order" *Globe and Mail*, April 28, 1998, A3.

Chapter 5

page 189 "operative norms"—"managerial efficiency" See Sid Noel, "The Ontario Political Culture: An Interpretation," in *The Government and Politics of Ontario*, 5th ed., ed. Graham White (Toronto: University of Toronto Press, 1997), 49–70.

page 190 "is best described as a 'red tory' province" John Wilson, "Ontario's Political Culture at the End of the Century," in *Revolution at Queen's Park*, ed. Sid Noel (Toronto: Lorimer, 1997), 58.

page 190 "pragmatic balancing" Claire Hoy, *Bill Davis* (Toronto: Methuen, 1985), 217.

page 191 "a partnership between" Sid Noel, "The Ontario Political Culture: An Interpretation," in *The Government and Politics of Ontario*, 60.

page 191 "We've had a minimum" Hoy, 217.

page 191 "the boss never talks" Hoy, 216.

page 191 "can't abide the far right" Hoy, 220.

page 192 "That might get you defeated" Hoy, 217.

page 193 "the NDP is discredited" *Globe and Mail*, April 29, 1995, A1.

pages 193–194 Judd interview *Toronto Star*, "Harris hit by hard core of voter distrust," April 30, 1995, A6.

page 194 "modern masterpiece" John Ibbitson, *Promised Land* (Scarborough, Ontario: Prentice Hall, 1997), vii–viii.

page 195 "we're not coming back" Ibbitson, 73.

page 196 "the single most important factor" Dungan, Murphy and Wilson, "Sources of the Recession in Canada and Ontario," Institute of Policy Analysis, University of Toronto, 1993, i.

page 197 for nearly fifty years Peter McCormick, "Provincial Party Systems 1945–1993," in *Canadian Parties in Transition*, eds. B. Tanguay and A. Gagnon (Toronto: Nelson, 1996), 363.

page 201 Ontario voters wanted a tax cut "Voters find [Harris's] tax promises unbelievable," *Toronto Star*, April 30, 1995, A6.

page 202 "take a meat cleaver" Thomas Walkom, "The Harris Government: Restoration or Revolution?" in *The Government and Politics of Ontario*, 407.

page 203 "problems that did not exist" Thomas Walkom, "The Harris Government: Restoration or Revolution?" in *The Government and Politics of Ontario*, 407.

page 206 "volatility of party support" Geoffrey Hale, "Changing Patterns of Party Support in Ontario," in *Revolution at Queen's Park*, 105–125.

pages 209–210 "the manner in which the bill's advocates conducted debate" Brian Tanguay, "Not in Ontario: From the Social Contract to the Common Sense Revolution," in *Revolution at Queen's Park*, 28.

page 210 "The numbers became a proxy" "The Inevitable Backlash," *Toronto Star*, November 19, 1995, F4.

Chapter 6

page 212 "assumed office but" David Cameron and Graham White, "Cycling Into Saigon: The Tories Take Power in Ontario," paper delivered to the Canadian Political Science Association, June 1996, 21.

page 214 "there are barricades" *Ottawa Citizen*, May 1, 1998, A10.

page 214 "in the health field" Thomas Walkom, "The Harris Government: Restoration or Revolution?" in Graham White, ed., *The Government and Politics of Ontario*, 5th ed. (Toronto: University of Toronto Press, 1997), 414.

page 215 "Harris has taken a real relish" *Toronto Star*, June 6, 1998, C1.

page 221 "We have a long wait" John Ibbitson, *Promised Land* (Scarborough, Ontario: Prentice Hall, 1997), 143.

page 222 "at breakneck speed" *Toronto Star*, June 13, 1998, E2.

page 223 "vexing political problems" David Cameron and Graham White, "Cycling into Saigon," 21.

page 227 "We are seeing here" Legislative Assembly of Ontario, Hansard, March 18, 1996.

page 229 "The forests are basically going to be transferred" *Globe and Mail*, April 12, 1996, A4.

page 230 "it's quite obvious" *Globe and Mail*, April 12, 1996, A4.

pages 230–231 "Mr. Davis had a sense" Legislative Assembly of Ontario, Hansard, June 29, 1996, 1630.

page 231 "cold-hearted face" *Globe and Mail*, Friday, April 12, 1996, A14.

page 231 "you have to understand" *London Free Press*, January 22, 1997, A1.

pages 232–233 "the Harris government" Sid Noel, "Ontario's Tory Revolution," in *Revolution at Queen's Park*, ed. Sid Noel (Toronto: Lorimer, 1997) 3.

page 233 "wrong in principle" Ibbitson, 260.

page 235 "cut expenses" *Globe and Mail*, January 21, 1997, A5.

page 235 "Mr. Premier" *Toronto Sun*, December 13, 1997.

page 236 "Mel is Mel" *Toronto Sun*, December 13, 1997.

page 237 "the size of the pot" *Globe and Mail*, May 2, 1997, A5.

page 237 "Those who are proceeding" *Ottawa Citizen*, June 9, 1998, A6.

page 238 "Where did you get the right" *Toronto Star*, December 19, 1996.

page 238 "like talking to a crazy person" Ibbitson, 265.

page 244 "We had been picked up" *Globe and Mail*, November 22, 1997, A8.

pages 244–245 "in the past" *Globe and Mail*, November 22, 1998, A8.

page 246 "their style of governing" *Ottawa Citizen*, December 9, 1997, A3.

page 247 "will suffer [the consequences]" John Wilson, "Ontario's Political Culture at the End of the Century," in *Revolution at Queen's Park*, 71.

page 249 "rising tide" *Globe and Mail*, June 6, 1998, A27.

pages 249–250 "a huge sense of frustration" *Globe and Mail*, November 28, 1997, A5A.

page 250 "total lack of credibility" *Toronto Star*, July 11, 1997, A12.

page 250 "if the limits become inconvenient" *Globe and Mail*, February 14, 1998, A2.

page 251 "has a blind spot" *Toronto Star*, May 1, 1998, A3.

page 252 "has turned its back" *Globe and Mail*, June 17, 1998, A5.

page 253 "the spending figure" *Globe and Mail*, June 22, 1998, A5.

page 256 "Quite frankly" *Ottawa Citizen*, April 12, 1996.

page 257 "We now have a bottom line" *Ottawa Citizen*, February 3, 1998, A5.

page 257 "the government's new rules" *Ottawa Citizen*, April 24, 1998, A2.

page 259 "restitution initiatives tried elsewhere" *Toronto Star*, June 10, 1996, A17.

page 264 "it's the old saw" *Ottawa Citizen*, April 18, 1996, A3.

page 267 "there may be one or two" *Ottawa Citizen*, June 9, 1998, A6.

page 268 Wal-Mart clause *Toronto Star*, June 15, 1998, A16.

page 271 "The council is larger" *Ottawa Citizen*, April 27, 1998, A8.

page 271 "stacking the deck" *Toronto Star*, June 13, 1998, E5.

page 272 "the limitations here" *Ottawa Citizen*, June 25, 1998, A8.

page 273 Lundholm letter *Globe and Mail*, June 13, 1998, D7.

pages 273–274 Miller letter *Toronto Star*, June 12, 1998, A24.

page 277 almost the reverse Rand Dyck, *Provincial Politics in Canada* (Scarborough, Ontario: Prentice Hall, 1996), 5.

page 278 "need a bogeyman to run against" *Toronto Star*, October 24, 1998, B1.

page 279 "between private and public" Thomas Walkom, "The Harris Government: Restoration or Revolution?" in *The Government and Politics of Ontario*, 416.

Chapter 7

page 284 "oil and gas industry" Murray Dobbin, *Preston Manning and the Reform Party* (Toronto: James Lorimer, 1991), 34.

page 288 "Preston understood he would have to be more circumspect" Frank

Dabbs, *Preston Manning: The Roots of Reform* (Vancouver: Greystone, 1997), 86.

page 289 "The guy always turned out to be Preston Manning" As quoted in *Preston Manning and the Reform Party*, 66.

page 289 "marginal to the Canadian political process" *Preston Manning and the Reform Party*, 66.

page 290 "I'll forget how" *Preston Manning: The Roots of Reform*, 86.

page 291 "tightening immigration policies" D. Harrington, "Who Are the Separatists?" in *Western Separatism*, G. Stevenson and L. Pratt, eds. (Edmonton: Hurtig, 1981), 25.

page 295 "In other words, nominate Preston" *Western Report*, June 8, 1998, 8.

page 295 "it was a leader picking a party" Quoted in *Preston Manning and the Reform Party*, 120.

page 296 "bunch of right-wing Christian fanatics" *Alberta Report*, November 9, 1987, 15.

page 297 "rarely involved in organizations with formal structures" *Preston Manning and the Reform Party*, 213.

page 299 "the party's hardest-driving administrator" Thomas Flanagan, "Behold Preston Agonistes," *Globe and Mail*, June 1998, A23.

page 299 "to implement that vision" *Ottawa Citizen*, May 26, 1998.

page 302 "Manning's deepest interest ... the first thing to do is to stop digging" Thomas Flanagan, *Waiting for the Wave: The Reform Party and Preston Manning* (Toronto: Stoddart, 1995), 77–78.

page 303 "if we are going to win Ontario" Flanagan, 87.

page 309 "Hit her, Craig" Flanagan, 153.

page 310 "I feel the time has come" Flanagan, 152.

page 310 "Gone are the days" Trevor Harrison, *Of Passionate Intensity* (Toronto: University of Toronto Press, 1997), 311.

page 311 "certain groups, like Jamaicans" *Toronto Star*, March 14, 1994.

page 312 "south sea island equivalent" House of Commons, Hansard, June 9, 1994, 5071.

page 313 "urged an audience to pray" *Toronto Star*, June 17, 1997, A20.

Chapter 8

page 333 "many of these second-place showings" Thomas Flanagan, *Waiting for the Wave: The Reform Party and Preston Manning* (Toronto: Stoddart, 1995), 154.

page 337 "manipulative appeal to the people" As quoted in Trevor Harrison, *Of Passionate Intensity* (Toronto: University of Toronto Press, 1997). For more details see M. Canovan, *Populism* (New York: Harcourt Brace, 1981).

page 342 "When Manning calls for a 'balanced' immigration policy" As quoted in Murray Dobbin, *Preston Manning and the Reform Party*

(Toronto: James Lorimer, 1991), 120.

page 350 "some of the looniest fruitcakes" Peter Newman, *Maclean's*, April 22, 1996, 42.

page 350 "There is something rather, well, quaint, about that" Charles Gordon, *Ottawa Citizen*, March 8, 1996.

page 357 "went along with what he said" As quoted in *Preston Manning and the Reform Party*, 126.

page 363 "Money missing from the accounts" *Toronto Star*, April 11, 1997, A28.

page 367 "a lot of sweat into this organization" *Alberta Report*, May 20, 1996.

page 370 "they should get the budget balanced and start paying down the debt" *Edmonton Journal*, October 19, 1996.

Chapter 9

page 377 "soupe du jour" *Globe and Mail*, May 29, 1998, A3.

page 378 "Let's just be ourselves" *Globe and Mail*, May 29, 1998, A3.

page 378 "Will Leroy Brown please stand up?" As cited by Mordecai Richler in "Reform is contained, but anger might not be," *Ottawa Citizen*, June 28, 1998.

page 381 "viewed by most Tories as embedded in the lunatic fringe" "Tories Should be Wary of True Blue Reformers," *Toronto Star*, 1998.

page 384 "Canadian legislators inevitably put forward" David Nething, "The Role of State and Provincial Legislators," in Robert J. Fleming, *Canadian Legislatures: 1987/88*, 39 (Ottawa: Ampersand, 1988), 39.

page 391 "my inability to properly read financial statements" As quoted in Mark Lisac, *The Klein Revolution* (Edmonton: NeWest Press, 1995), 152.

page 391 "over the world of books and abstractions" David Taras and Allan Tupper, "Politics and Deficits: Alberta's Challenge to the Canadian Political Agenda," in Douglas M. Brown and Janet Hiebert, eds., *Canada: The State of the Federation* (Kingston, Ontario: Institute of Intergovernmental Relations, Queen's University Press, 1994), 61–83.

page 391 "six weeks in a hospital ward" Joanne Helmer, "Redefining Normal: Life in the New Alberta," in *The Trojan Horse: Alberta and the Future of Canada*, Trevor Harrison and Gordon Laxer, eds. (Montreal: Black Rose Books, 1995), 75.

pages 401–402 "crisis of provincial debt and deficits" Harrison and Laxer, "Introduction," *The Trojan Horse*, 6.

Chapter 10

page 408 "They don't all go and gather in a ghetto" N. Fillmore, "The Right Stuff," *This Magazine*, July 1986, 11.

page 413 "one third of the delegates" *Consensus*, June 1987.

page 413 "as Prime Minister Manning" *Consensus*, April 1991.

page 417 the group employs a total staff of one hundred Guy Marsden, *Canadian Dimension*, September 1995.

page 418 "total tax burden is near the middle of the pack" As quoted in Scott Piatkowski, "Tax Scam," *This Magazine*, July 1995.

page 422 "to promote a social Darwinism" Paul Havemann, "Marketing the New Establishment Ideology in Canada," *Crime and Social Justice*, no. 26 (1986): 15.

page 423 "a group of economic cranks" Clive Thompson, "Ever Wonder What Think Tanks Think About?" *Catholic New Times*, September 7, 1997, 10–11.

page 425 "the Institute's media job has been so successful" Clive Thompson, *Catholic New Times*, 10–11.

page 426 made a point of targeting young Canadians Charles Gordon, "The Fraser Institute Wants Your Children," *Ottawa Citizen*, October 25, 1998.

page 427 fishing holiday with premier Mike Harris Jeff Keller, "Does Michael Walker Have the Right Stuff?" *Equity Magazine* 13, no. 9 (November 1995): 28–31.

page 428 "while purporting to promote objectivity" Kathleen Cross, "Off Balance: How the Fraser Institute Slants Its News," *Canadian Forum*, October 1997.

page 428 "contradicted by available data" As quoted in Murray Dobbin, *The Myth of the Good Corporate Citizen* (Toronto: Stoddart, 1998), 196.

page 431 "a vehicle for bringing together" Trevor Harrison, *Of Passionate Intensity* (Toronto: University of Toronto Press, 1997), 122.

page 434 "Guns are just the tip of the iceberg" *Ottawa Citizen*, September 21, 1998, A3.

Conclusion

page 443 "Nothing has done ... more harm" *Toronto Star*, January 9, 1998, A7.

Select Bibliography

Books

Braid, Don, and Sydney Sharpe. *Storming Babylon: Preston Manning and the Rise of the Reform Party.* Toronto: Key Porter, 1992.

Clarke, Tony. *Silent Coup.* Ottawa: Canadian Centre for Policy Alternatives, 1997.

Conservative Central Office. *The Right Approach: A Statement of Conservative Aims.* London: October 1976.

Cooper, Barry. *The Klein Achievement.* Toronto: University of Toronto Press, 1996.

Crawford, Alan. *Thunder on the Right: The New Right and the Politics of Resentment.* New York: Pantheon, 1980.

Dabbs, Frank. *Preston Manning: The Roots of Reform.* Vancouver: Greystone, 1997.

Dabbs, Frank. *Ralph Klein: A Maverick Life.* Vancouver: Greystone Books, 1995.

Dobbin, Murray. *The Myth of the Good Corporate Citizen.* Toronto: Stoddart, 1998.

Dobbin, Murray. *Preston Manning and the Reform Party.* Toronto: James Lorimer, 1991.

Flanagan, Thomas. *Waiting for the Wave: The Reform Party and Preston Manning.* Toronto: Stoddart, 1995.

Fleming, Robert J. *Canadian Legislatures: 1987/88.* Ottawa: Ampersand, 1988.

Galbraith, John Kenneth. *The Culture of Contentment.* New York: Houghton Mifflin, 1992.

Galbraith, John Kenneth. *The Good Society.* New York: Houghton Mifflin, 1996.

Gardiner, George. *Margaret Thatcher: From Childhood to Leadership.* London: William Kimber, 1975.

Gingrich, Newt. *Lessons Learned the Hard Way.* New York: HarperCollins, 1998.

Harrison, B., and B. Bluestone. *The Great U-Turn*. New York: Basic Books, 1990.

Harrison, Trevor, and Gordon Laxer, eds. *The Trojan Horse: Alberta and the Future of Canada*. Montreal: Black Rose Books, 1995.

Harrison, Trevor. *Of Passionate Intensity*. Toronto: University of Toronto Press, 1997.

Hodgson, Godfrey. *The World Turned Rightside Up*. New York: Houghton Mifflin, 1996.

Hoy, Claire. *Bill Davis*. Toronto: Methuen, 1985.

Hustak, Alan. *Peter Lougheed: A Biography*. Toronto: McClelland & Stewart, 1979.

Ibbitson, John. *Promised Land*. Scarborough, Ontario: Prentice Hall, 1997.

Krieger, Joel. *Reagan, Thatcher and the Politics of Decline*. Cambridge: Polity, 1986.

Lasch, Christopher. *The Revolt of the Elites*. New York: W.W. Norton, 1995.

Leruez, Jacques, ed. *Le Thatcherisme: Doctrine et action*. Paris, CNRS, 1985.

Lipset, Seymour. *Continental Divide: The Values and Institutions of the United States and Canada*. New York: Routledge, 1990.

Lisac, Mark. *The Klein Revolution*. Edmonton.: NeWest Press, 1995.

Macpherson, C.B. *Democracy in Alberta: Social Credit and the Party System*. Toronto: University of Toronto Press, 1977.

Manning, Preston. *The New Canada*. Toronto: Macmillan, 1992.

Minogue, Kenneth, and Michael Biddis. *Thatcherism*. London: Macmillan, 1987.

Mishler, William. *Political Participation in Canada*. Toronto: Macmillan, 1979.

Morris, Ruth. *Listen Ontaro!* Oakville: Mosaic Press, 1997.

Nikiforuk, Andrew. *Running on Empty: Alberta After the Boom*. Alberta: NeWest Press, 1987, 91–101. See chapter 12, in particular.

Noel, Sid, ed. *Revolution at Queen's Park*. Toronto: Lorimer, 1997.

Pammett, Jon, and Jean-Luc Pepin. *Political Education in Canada*. Ottawa: IRPP, 1988.

Phillips, Kevin. *The Emerging Republican Majority*. New York: Arlington House, 1969.

Phillips, Kevin. *The Politics of Rich and Poor*. New York: HarperCollins, 1991.

Rae, Bob. *From Protest to Power*. Toronto: Viking, 1996.

Rahall, Monier M. *Banksters and Prairie Boys*. Edmonton: Monopoly, 1997.

Reich, Robert. *The Resurgent Liberal*. New York: Random House, 1989.

Republican National Committee. *Contract with America*. New York: Random House, 1994.

Riddell, Peter. *The Thatcher Government*. Oxford: Basil Blackwell, 1985.

Saul, John Ralston. *The Unconscious Civilization*. Concord, Ontario: Anansi Press, 1995.

Stevenson, G., and L. Pratt. eds. *Western Separatism*. Edmonton: Hurtig, 1981.

Taft, Kevin. *Shredding the Public Interest*. Edmonton: University of Alberta Press, 1997.

Tupper, Allen, and Roger Gibbins. *Government and Politics in Alberta*. Edmonton: University of Alberta Press, 1992.

White, Graham. ed. *The Government and Politics of Ontario*. 5th ed. Toronto: University of Toronto Press, 1997.

Wood, David G. *The Lougheed Legacy*. Toronto: Key Porter, 1985.

Young, Hugo, and Anne Sloman. *The Thatcher Phenomenon*. London: BBC, 1986.

Articles

"A Warning Shot from Peter Lougheed: We Have to Help Those Who Can't Look After Themselves." *Maclean's*, August 21, 1995, 32.

"From Red Tories to Ralph's Tories: Alberta's PCs Celebrate 25 Years in Power." *Western Report*, September 16, 1996, 10–11.

"Redneck Ralph." *Alberta Report*, January 25, 1982, 10–13.

Archer, Keith, and F. Ellis. "Opinion Structure of Reform Party Activists." *CJPS* 27, no. 2 (June 1994): 227–308.

Harrison, Trevor and Harvey Krahn. "Populism and the Rise of the Reform Party in Alberta." *CRSA* 32, no. 2 (May 1995): 127–50.

Laycock, David. "Reforming Canadian Democracy? Institutions and Ideology in the Reform Party Project." *CJPS* 27, no. 2 (June 1994): 213–247.

Miller, Robert. "An Interview with Peter Lougheed." *Parliamentary Government* (1989): 3–6.

Index

A

B